FIRE
IN THE SKY

MICHAEL MOLKENTIN

FIRE
IN THE SKY

The Australian Flying Corps in the First World War

ALLEN&UNWIN

Cover photographs: Two Bristol Fighters of No. 1 Australian Flying Corps in Palestine in 1918, Australian War Memorial Negative Number B02209; Airmen and mechanics of No. 3 Squadron Australian Flying Corps with an RE8 at Villers-Bocage in July 1918, courtesy of Les Parsons and the Crawford family.

This edition published in 2012

First published in 2010

Copyright © Michael Molkentin 2010

All rights reserved. No part of this book may be reproduced or transmitted in any form or by any means, electronic or mechanical, including photocopying, recording or by any information storage and retrieval system, without prior permission in writing from the publisher. The Australian *Copyright Act 1968* (the Act) allows a maximum of one chapter or 10 per cent of this book, whichever is the greater, to be photocopied by any educational institution for its educational purposes provided that the educational institution (or body that administers it) has given a remuneration notice to Copyright Agency Limited (CAL) under the Act.

Allen & Unwin
83 Alexander Street
Crows Nest NSW 2065
Australia
Phone: (61 2) 8425 0100
Fax: (61 2) 9906 2218
Email: info@allenandunwin.com
Web: www.allenandunwin.com

Cataloguing-in-Publication details are available
from the National Library of Australia
www.librariesaustralia.nla.gov.au

ISBN 978 1 74331 269 8

Internal design by Lisa White
Maps by Mapgraphics
Set in 11/16 pt Minion by Post Pre-press Group, Australia
Printed and bound in Australia by the SOS Print + Media Group

10 9 8 7 6 5 4 3

MIX
Paper from responsible sources
FSC® C011217

The paper in this book is FSC® certified.
FSC® promotes environmentally responsible, socially beneficial and economically viable management of the world's forests.

CONTENTS

Maps	vii
Foreword	ix
Text notes	xi
Prologue: 5 September 1918, Douai sector, France	xiii
1 'This portentous omen' The birth of military aviation in Australia	1
2 'A merry life while it lasts' Life and death in the Australian Flying Corps	25
3 'This God-forsaken country' Egypt and Sinai, 1916	54
4 'An intense rivalry in the air' War above the trenches, Gaza, January to August 1917	78
5 'A regular God damn aviator' No. 1 Squadron's coming of age	106
6 'An extraordinary fighting force' Battle for the skies, summer 1918	130
7 'Nine miles of dead' The Battle of Megiddo, September and October 1918	152
8 'Survival of the luckiest' Training in Britain, 1917–18	177

FIRE IN THE SKY

9 'A red kangaroo on the cowling'
    The Australian Flying Corps on the Western Front, 1917   195

10 'Absolute hell let loose'
    The German spring offensives, 1918   222

11 'The nearest thing to a holiday is a wet day'
    From German offensive to British counter-offensive, April to July 1918   249

12 'Down where the war is being won'
    The British offensive, July and August 1918   277

13 'Good sport to the man in the air'
    Fighting to the finish, September to November 1918   302

14 'It will surprise most people to find that the Australians did so much flying'
    Legacy of the Australian Flying Corps   330

Notes   341

Note on sources and further reading   373

Acknowledgements   379

Bibliography   383

Index   396

MAPS

Map 1:	Mesopotamia	14
Map 2:	Egypt–Sinai, 1916	60
Map 3:	Palestine, 1917–18	118
Map 4:	The Western Front, 1917–18	196

MAPS

FOREWORD

In the years leading up to the First World War, aviation was in its infancy. It was a novelty practised by gentlemen enthusiasts who, despite their zeal, had difficulty convincing governments and militaries of the usefulness of aircrafts to national defence.

Australia was among a very small number of nations outside of Europe in 'making a start' with military flying before the war. In the two years preceding the conflict, the government of the day showed great foresight by investigating the implications that 'flying machines' (as they were then quaintly known) might have on the nation's defence. The Central Flying School was established in the sheep paddocks of Point Cook, Victoria, in the months leading up to the war. Its first four student pilots began their training as the nations of Europe mobilised.

From these humble beginnings, the Australian Flying Corps came to field eight and a half squadrons overseas during the war. Over 500 Australian airmen served in the units, flying in Mesopotamia, Palestine, Britain and on the Western Front between 1915 and 1918. By the Armistice, they had distinguished themselves in the full gamut of operations demanded of the flying services: reconnaissance, bombing, artillery observation, ground attack, offensive patrolling and even battlefield resupply from the air. Two officers came home having commanded wings; nine had led squadrons. There were 57 Australian aces. One Australian received a Victoria Cross and 40 had received the Distinguished Flying Cross. Two, in fact, received this award three times, being among just four British and dominion pilots to do so during the war.

These highly experienced individuals had, for the most part, gone to war as amateurs with no impulse to make a career out of flying. They came home to form the nucleus of the Royal Australian Air Force (established in 1921) and to develop Australia's civil aviation industry. Names like Richard Williams, George Jones, Henry Wrigley, Ross Smith, Lawrence Wackett and Hudson Fysh are pillars in the history of Australian aviation. The fact that they had their beginnings in the timber and fabric 'flying machines' of the Australian Flying Corps is less well known. The professionalism, courage, esprit de corps and values displayed by AFC aircrew and support personnel laid the foundations for the successes experienced by the RAAF in global air campaigns and humanitarian support operations in the past nine decades.

Since the publication of the AFC's official history in 1923, the story of these men has received scant attention. With *Fire in the Sky*, Michael Molkentin addresses this oversight. It is an important book; an engaging and eminently readable story populated by ordinary Australians who found themselves in the extraordinary circumstances of history's first air war. His work is thoroughly well-informed, drawing on the records of British and Australian archives as well as collections held privately by families. From the recesses of the past, Mr Molkentin has salvaged the voices of many of these remarkable men. He has, with this book, re-established an important and fascinating chapter of our nation's history.

Mark Binskin, AM
Air Marshal
Chief of Air Force

TEXT NOTES

I've used the term 'Turkish' rather than 'Ottoman' throughout the text for clarity, despite the latter being the more historically correct term. My chosen spelling of place names (especially in Palestine and Flanders) sometimes doesn't reflect modern conventions, but matches the contemporary spellings, as used by Australia's official historians.

I have attempted to avoid acronyms and abbreviations. The only regularly used exceptions are AIF (Australian Imperial Force), AFC (Australian Flying Corps), BEF (British Expeditionary Force—the British Army on the Western Front), RFC (Royal Flying Corps—the British Army's flying arm before 1 April 1918) and RAF (Royal Air Force—the amalgamated British army and naval air arms, post 1 April 1918). Occasionally, the acronym 'HA' appears in quoted excerpts from pilots' combat reports—it stands for 'hostile aircraft'.

In the past, there has been substantial confusion over the correct nomenclature for the Australian squadrons. Prior to January 1918, the four Australian squadrons on active service had RFC numbers. The first Australian squadron formed was, for example, known as 'No. 67 (Australian) Squadron'. In January 1918, Australian squadrons officially adopted a number within the AFC's structure, with No. 67 (Australian) Squadron thus becoming No. 1 Squadron Australian Flying Corps. The corresponding British and Australian designations are as follows:

No. 67 (Australian) Squadron	No. 1 Squadron Australian Flying Corps
No. 68 (Australian) Squadron	No. 2 Squadron Australian Flying Corps
No. 69 (Australian) Squadron	No. 3 Squadron Australian Flying Corps
No. 71 (Australian) Squadron	No. 4 Squadron Australian Flying Corps

For simplicity, I follow the official historian's lead and refer to the Australian squadrons throughout the text by their Australian numbers.

Speed and distance measurements have been converted to metric values, except where they are part of quotations. Height remains in feet throughout the text, as it does in modern aviation vernacular.

PROLOGUE
5 September 1918, Douai sector, France

Five Sopwith Camel biplanes break through the wispy cloud as the late afternoon sun settles on the horizon. In the open cockpit of each, dressed from head to toe in fur-lined leather and enclosed in a maze of timber, wire and fabric, perches a young Australian pilot. They have travelled halfway around the world to fight the Germans in the skies above northern France.

Leading the V-shaped formation is 23-year-old Norm Trescowthick. Two years earlier, he had been making boots in Melbourne. Now his seven months of active service flying and six enemy 'victories' have made him a veteran fighter pilot.

Following close behind Trescowthick are Max Eddie and Duncan Carter, aged 24 and 25 respectively. Although veterans of the trenches, they are relative newcomers to the air war, having arrived at the squadron only six weeks ago. Close behind and slightly above them is Alex Lockley. At just twenty years old, he—like Trescowthick—has experience in these skies beyond his tender age—seven months and two 'kills' to his credit. Above and behind Lockley, at the formation's tail, is one of the squadron's 'old hands', Len Taplin. An electrical engineer from Parramatta, Taplin had enlisted in the Australian Imperial Force three years before, at the age of nineteen. In mid-1917, after nine months in the trenches, he volunteered for the flying corps. By his 23rd birthday, he had fought in the skies above both Palestine and the Western Front, shot down a dozen enemy aircraft and earned a Distinguished Flying Cross. His squadron mates considered him an exceptionally daring and aggressive pilot.

These young men were all born in the decade before the world's first powered aircraft had even flown. They grew up in an era where motor vehicles were a novelty, and as curious teenagers they had watched as aviation first came to Australia; initially in the form of balloons and gliders, and later as powered boxkites capable of flying several hundred metres, but only in the calmest conditions. And here they are, hurtling along at almost 200 kilometres an hour, 11 000 feet above the French countryside, at the controls of a Sopwith Camel.

Three and a half kilometres below raged the war most commonly experienced by men between 1914 and 1918 and most often remembered by Australians today. It was the war of artillery, gas, barbed wire and machine guns that had continued ceaselessly for four years along a 700 kilometre line, the infamous Western Front. To the five pilots crouching low in their cockpits to avoid the chilling slipstream and the stench of burnt castor oil, though, it appeared only as a long irregular smudge that stretched off and became lost on the northern and the southern horizons. From up here it seemed benign, silent and still, undeserving of its terrible reputation. Only pilots like Len Taplin, who had once languished down there with the diggers, could ever appreciate the vast gulf—both physical and mental—that separated the battles being fought on the ground and those in the sky.

The flight's leader, Norm Trescowthick, scanned the dark blue void around him for the British squadron they were scheduled to rendezvous with before crossing into enemy skies. Safety in numbers was the game at this late stage of the war. The day of the 'lone eagle', the celebrity fighter 'ace' who prowled the skies alone looking for a duel with a worthy opponent, had long passed. Any notions that this war in the air was somehow honourable or chivalrous had gone the way of thousands of pilots on both sides—that is, hurtling towards the ground in flames without a parachute. Such was the reality that underpinned the supposed glamour of being a fighter pilot in 1918.

Trescowthick saw no sign of the British squadrons. No matter. Buoyed by the recent successes the Australians had enjoyed against German pilots in this sector, he led the four other 'Camels' up to 14 000 feet and turned north. The lack of oxygen and biting cold at that height could lull a pilot into drowsiness. But, at the back of the formation, Taplin was on edge.

PROLOGUE

For the last ten weeks, he had been patrolling these skies and hard experience had taught him that German 'circuses' of dozens of Fokkers prowled high above their own side of the line, waiting to pounce on smaller enemy formations.

At a hand signal from Trescowthick, the Australians loosened formation. Taplin edged his Camel 1000 feet higher into a covering position above and behind the others. As the formation headed north, the town of Douai emerged from the patchwork fields far below. These pilots were very familiar with towns just like it on their own side of the line. When not up here, they were down there: shopping, hunting, playing football and drinking in the local bars. Afternoons whiled away in towns like Douai represented one half of their extraordinary double life. It was another world entirely down there—one completely at odds with the deadly business of patrolling.

In an instant, the sky was full of aircraft. Poised above the others, Taplin watched as 30 German fighters descended upon them from high above. At the front of the 'V', Trescowthick saw they were about to be cut off and gave the hand signal to dive for home. He pushed his stick forward and the Camel plunged, sweeping underneath the enemy formation. Casting a glance over his shoulder, Trescowthick was dismayed to see that his four pilots hadn't followed. They were surrounded, the sky about them alive with movement. Brightly painted Fokkers zoomed and tumbled in all directions. Streams of tracer bullets stitched smoke trails across the dark blue. As he swept through the clouds to safety, Trescowthick glimpsed Lockley haul his plane's nose up and fire into the underside of a Fokker. It tumbled away out of control.

From above the dogfight, Taplin picked out the enemy leader and dived. The German pilot pulled up and they went head to head. A burst from Taplin's double Vickers machine guns and the red and white Fokker was spinning down, smoking. Before he could do anything else, though, another enemy pilot was underneath him in the perfect killing position. Bullets punched through the cockpit floor, showering Taplin with splinters of wood. A bullet caught his hand, breaking the wrist and leaving his leather gauntlet torn and bloody. His Camel immediately stalled, and half rolled right on to the tail of his attacker. 'Poetic justice,' thought Taplin as, struggling with his left hand only, he levelled out and thumbed the firing buttons on top of the control column. The machine guns before his face clattered and flashed and the offending Fokker arched over and hurtled earthwards. At that moment, Lockley's Camel tumbled past, following it to the ground. Craning his neck around, Taplin saw the sky smeared with the smoke of Eddie and Carter's machines, also making their long plunge to earth.

Alone and surrounded, he was quickly overwhelmed by the enemy circus's onslaught. Tracer bullets swished past him from every direction as he worked the stick and rudders furiously, snapping off bursts at anything that flashed through his gun sight. An explosive bullet smashed the crank handle on his machine gun and sent a metal splinter through his nose. Taplin spent the following moments dazed. Sky and earth gyrated around him as his aircraft went into an uncontrolled spinning dive.

With just a thousand feet to spare, he regained consciousness and control. Two Fokkers had followed him down and were closing in for the kill. Struggling with one hand, he turned to meet them head on. With a single gun, he managed a lucky shot that sent one careering into a row of poplar trees below. The other broke off. Miraculously, Taplin had survived an attack by some 30 enemy aircraft.

With his engine just about done, the battered and bleeding Australian pilot made for the lines. For several minutes, the Camel spluttered and lurched westward. Nearing the front, German soldiers raised rifles to him. Finally, that brown smudge—nothing like its benign appearance from several thousand feet—emerged in full detail. With just a few hundred metres to go, Taplin's Camel was hit again. The engine coughed, seized and the biplane plunged headlong into a trench. There was a cacophony of splintering timber and Len Taplin's world went black.

The names of Len Taplin's three flying companions, Max Eddie, Duncan Carter and Alex Lockley, appear on the Roll of Honour at the Australian War Memorial in Canberra. Here, in a tranquil courtyard, two vast bronze panelled walls record the names of more than 102 000 Australians who have died in military service since 1885. The entire western wall is almost completely dominated by those killed in the nation's most destructive war—the 'Great' or '1914–18' War, as it was known to the generation that endured it.

PROLOGUE

Visitors who wander along this wall pass the names of 61 348 men and women killed on active service with the Australian Imperial Force (AIF)—the nation's volunteer military force for overseas service during the war. They are arranged in order of unit type: the artillery, light horse and infantry coming first and occupying the greatest number of panels; these are followed by the less well-known units: the signallers, tunnellers, engineers, cyclists, dentists, postal workers and even veterinarians. Finally, on the very last two panels are 205 names listed under 'Flying Corps'. These men, along with 3500 others who served in the Australian Flying Corps, represent Australia's contribution to the war that raged above the trenches. They and their experiences dwell outside the popular mythology of Anzac, largely unfamiliar to most Australians today.

Air warfare did not exist when the First World War began. The major armies of Europe only began experimenting with 'flying machines' (mechanical novelties, less than a decade old themselves) in the few years before it. Outside Europe, Australia was one of very few nations to make a start in military aviation before 1914. In August, the month war began, Australia's first military flying school opened at Point Cook in Victoria with just two instructors and four pupils. Throughout the war, Australia would be the only British Empire dominion to raise and field its own national military air arm.

The importance of aircraft was almost immediately evident above the battlefields of Europe, and within a year of its beginning the AFC had part of a squadron on active service in Mesopotamia (modern-day Iraq). Further commitments came in 1916 when a complete Australian squadron deployed for action in Egypt. In the following year, another three formed and trained in Britain to prepare for service in the war's main theatre, the Western Front. The AFC also established four training squadrons in Britain in 1917 to provide the front-line units with replacement airmen and mechanics.

This book tells the story of these forgotten few of Australia's involvement in the First World War. Although a numerically small group, making up just over 1 per cent of all Australians who served overseas, they distinguished themselves in every theatre they fought in, and well and truly matched the celebrated achievements of Australian infantry and light horsemen.

The pilots—the select few who are at the heart of this story—experienced a war completely unlike that of their comrades in the trenches. After negotiating a highly competitive selection process, inundated by others eager to get out of the trenches, they faced a crude and dangerous training program that killed more Australian airmen during the war than the enemy did. At the front, on aerodromes behind the line, sharp bursts of extreme danger punctuated a comparatively comfortable and even leisurely war. The result was a strange, tense existence, which proved extraordinarily strenuous for those who experienced it.

Then, of course, there were the far more numerous ground crew—fitters, riggers, armourers, vulcanisers, instrument repairers, and so on. Their battlefield was in the aerodrome's hangars and workshops. Their fight was a perpetual one, against the primitive engines, airframes and guns that carried the pilots across the lines each day. They were masters of improvisation—often technically brilliant men hand-picked to work with equipment that was daily pushed to its limits. Their story is told here too—they wrote prodigiously about their work, and in doing so inadvertently preserved for us a sense of day-to-day life on a service aerodrome and the unique culture that evolved there within the squadrons' tightly knit communities.

This book tries to allow both groups of men to speak for themselves, through their letters, diaries, memoirs and reminiscences. The records they left behind are immense and cover a broad range of experiences, giving us insight not just into combat, but also their social and cultural backgrounds, training, leisure, leave, their relationships with each other and their families, and finally their homecoming to a nation that idolised its 'flying men'.

In addition to the 3720 men who served in the AFC during the First World War, another few hundred Australians joined the British Royal Flying Corps (RFC) and Royal Naval Air Service (RNAS). Their story is just as significant, but beyond the scope of this book, and will need to await the attention of another historian.

Most American and British books about the First Air War are of the 'aces and aeroplanes' variety. They tend to fixate on a few celebrity fighter pilots and their aircraft. I have avoided this approach, not simply because it has been well and truly done, but because these preoccupations are not reflected in the writings of the AFC's airmen and mechanics. Australian pilots rarely dwelt on the intricacies of the aircraft they flew. They judged and evaluated them, of course, and often remembered them with either fondness or acrimony, but didn't tend to discuss them in terms of horsepower, rate of climb, compression levels, paint schemes, and so on. It was even more unusual for Australian pilots to make much of 'victory tallies' and 'aces'. In fact, in the dozens of private records written by AFC personnel during the war that I consulted for this book, I did not find the expression 'ace' once. This term, readily used by aero-historians today, was not applied in British and Australian squadrons at all during the war, and only came into vogue after it. As one AFC pilot explained to an interviewer in the late 1960s: 'The term Ace was unknown to us then, and indeed would have seemed at the time vulgar.'

This isn't to say Australia's more successful fighter pilots don't feature in this book—some of them are major characters in the story. But the criteria for their inclusion has far more to do with their contribution as leaders in their squadrons and the records they left behind than the number of Germans they shot down. For the most part, though, the men who populate the following pages are ordinary Australians who found themselves involved in an extraordinary and totally unprecedented experience of war.[1]

1

'THIS PORTENTOUS OMEN'

The birth of military aviation in Australia

Australian Flying Corps officers and cadets watch a Bristol Boxkite flying at Point Cook, c. March 1916. *AWM DAAV00005*

> Australia with her happy-go-lucky don't-care-a-hang-as-long-as-the-Melbourne-Cup-is-run style is totally disregarding this portentous omen.
>
> —Charles Lindsay-Campbell, The Aerial League of Australia, 1910

'The threshold of the air age': Military aviation comes to Australia, 1909–14

On Saturday, 19 March 1910, the people of Melbourne woke to astonishing news in their morning newspaper. In a bare paddock, 30 kilometres north of the city, the Hungarian-American escapologist Harry Houdini had become the first man to make a powered flight over Australian soil. After a month of failed attempts, Houdini had managed to get off the ground in his Voisin biplane three times during the previous morning. On his third and longest flight, the 'bird man'—as the press had dubbed him—stayed aloft for three and a half minutes, completing a 3-kilometre circuit at about 100 feet. 'Freedom and exhilaration, that's what it is,' explained an elated Houdini. 'I know what it is to fly now in real earnest.'[1]

Houdini's accomplishment came at a time when Australia's military leaders were already considering the potential 'flying machines' might have in national defence. The successful crossing of the English Channel by air the previous July, by French engineer Louis Blériot, suggested to militaries and governments around the globe that traditional defence strategy was on the verge of a radical and permanent shift. A conference at Sydney's United Service Institution four months after Houdini's flight, for example, featured a paper titled 'The Air Age and its Military Significance'. In it, one of the army's intelligence officers argued that the military was on 'the threshold of the Air Age', and it was only natural to ask, 'To what defensive purpose can it be put?' He predicted that aircraft, coupled with the day's other technological wonder—wireless radio—would 'revolutionise modern war tactics', first by removing the element of surprise and second, by 'bringing about perfection in the power to strike from a distance'.[2]

For the time being, though, the Australian government made no formal commitments to military aviation. Australian defence matters were bound up in the concept of 'imperial defence'—a broad strategy for the empire based on close consultation and cooperation with Britain and the other dominions, none of which was making a start in military aviation beyond experimentation at this stage either. Nevertheless, there were voices in Australia pushing for action. The Aerial League of Australia, a lobby group of enthusiastic amateurs whose 'prime object was to awaken national interest in Aviation for defence purposes', pressured the Australian government in the months following Houdini's flight to invest in a military aviation school.[3]

The League held public meetings to fire up public concern over Australia's defence arrangements and wrote letters to newspapers, criticising what it saw as government negligence. On 8 October 1910, for example, the League's secretary, Charles Lindsay-Campbell, claimed in the *Brisbane Courier* that 'the principal Powers have now their representatives at all the established English and Continental aviation schools ... thus preparing themselves for any possible crisis'. In his judgement: 'Australia with her happy-go-lucky don't-care-a-hang-as-long-as-the-Melbourne-Cup-is-run style is totally disregarding this portentous omen.' The government, he argued, should immediately select two dozen Australians and send them to the overseas schools. He concluded by exhorting readers to take up this cause by pressuring their local MPs, lest 'you yourself are traitor to your country'.

A few months later, on 9 January 1911, Lindsay-Campbell submitted a proposal for the establishment of a 'Commonwealth Aviation School and Corps' to the Minister of Defence, George Pearce. He proposed that the new school train civilians for service in a military aviation corps. It should, he argued, be established in his native Queensland ('owing to climatic conditions'), and would require three aircraft, a controller, a pilot-instructor and a pair of mechanics. Campbell predicted the corps would expand to have a school in every state within twelve months. He, along with fellow aviator Gaston Cugnet (who had trained in France under the famous pioneer Blériot), would undertake the dual role of pilot instructor and controller.[4]

A week later, the Military Board (responsible for the administration of Australia's military) met to discuss the proposal. It acknowledged 'a considerable amount of agitation ... outside the forces for the formation of an Aviation Corps', but remained sceptical of zealous, civilian enthusiasts like Campbell and Cugnet who were seen to be acting from an 'interested' position. The board discussed the progress of military flying in Britain, noting that despite exhaustive tests, the British War Office (responsible for the British Army's administration) had not yet decided to form a flying corps. In line with the government's commitment to imperial defence, the board concluded that it should 'as far as possible adopt the pattern of equipment in use by the British Army'. Pearce, who was scheduled to visit Britain in May for a conference on imperial defence, would gauge progress there before making any decisions. In the meantime, the Military Board sent a telegram to the Australian High Commission in London: 'Newspapers here agitating formation aviation corps can War Office give advice [?]'[5]

The High Commissioner's office replied at the end of the month, emphasising the crude state of military aviation in Britain that was not realised by the civilian 'agitators' in Australia. At this stage, he explained, 'there is nothing definite to report, because it has not yet been practically proved to what extent Aviation has, or will, become a factor in the equipment of the Army'. The British had done nothing further than detail a few officers to undertake experiments at Salisbury Plain. In addition, while there had been some promising steps forward, there was 'a formidable list of failures and disasters', and hence the army was proceeding with caution.[6] Besides, Britain was at this time strategically geared towards expanding its navy, the service that had won and then guarded the empire for over 200 years. Resources thus were scarce for experiments in unreliable and unproven technology that was barely a decade old.

Pearce attended the Imperial Conference in London during May and June 1911. Although aviation didn't feature on the agenda, in his memoirs he pointed to two specific instances, which confirmed in his mind that Australia needed to make a start in military flying. The first was an apparently secret briefing given to all dominion ministers, warning that war with Germany was likely within the next four years. The second was a visit to Brooklands aerodrome just outside of London, where the British Army was experimenting with aircraft. He later wrote: 'What I saw that day and the talks I had with the flying men convinced me of the wisdom of having a flying school in the Defence Department.'[7]

Pearce returned to Australia, and in December 1911 advertised for two expert mechanics and aviators, and tenders for instructional flying machines, in *The Commonwealth of Australia Gazette* as well as two of Britain's aviation magazines, *Flight* and *The Aeroplane*. The High Commissioner's office in London received 50 applications and consulted with the British War Office during May and June 1912 to select suitable candidates and machines. As these first steps towards an Australian Flying Corps took place, the British established the Royal Flying Corps (RFC). Other dominions also expressed interest in forming their own flying arms, but other than Australia, none did. Nor would they during the coming war. (Canada, it should be said, did form two squadrons just before the end of the war, but neither saw active service.)

On 2 July 1912, on the British War Office's recommendation, the Australian Department of Defence ordered two Bristol BE biplanes and two Deperdussin monoplanes at a total cost of £2600—about the value of a terrace of houses in suburban Sydney at the time. A few days later, it settled on two instructors, Henry Petre (pronounced 'Peter') and Harry Busteed. An Australian working as a test pilot for the Bristol Company, Busteed initially accepted but then changed his mind when he realised that he could earn substantially more than the Australian government's comparatively meagre offer of £400 by staying in Europe. In October, the Defence Department selected another Australian, Eric Harrison, as his replacement.

Both Petre and Harrison were ideal candidates to instruct Australia's first military pilots. Henry Petre, a 27-year-old English lawyer, had been caught up in the excitement of Blériot's flight across the English Channel in July 1909. That year, he left his firm and borrowed £250 to begin an aircraft design company with his brother. It took them six months, but they built a crude monoplane that Petre crashed on its first flight. The company went broke shortly afterwards. Borrowing additional money, Petre took formal lessons and qualified for his Royal Aero Club Certificate (the day's internationally recognised pilot's licence) in September 1911. Afterwards, he found work designing and testing for a number of aviation firms, including Deperdussin. Significantly, he was an expert in this company's monoplane, of which the Australian government had just purchased two.

The other instructor, Eric Harrison, shared Petre's persistent dedication to aviation but little else. An Australian, he had worked for one of Melbourne's largest mechanical firms before emmigrating to England in 1911 to learn to fly. After qualifying for his certificate (the third Australian to do so), he secured a position as a pilot and instructor with the British and Colonial Aeroplane Company. For nine months, he worked all around Europe—including at Bristol's school in Germany, where he tutored pilots in the German military. He reasoned that while the Australian government's

£400 salary was 'not a great deal better than I am doing now', he would 'sooner be at home'.[8]

Meanwhile, again on the British War Office's advice, the Military Board purchased an additional training aircraft (bringing the total to five) that would be more suited to 'elementary instruction'.[9] It was one of the Bristol Company's earlier 'boxkite' designs and was a popular training machine in Britain. The Defence Department had to apply for more funding, and it was close to the end of 1912 before the additional order could be placed.

With instructors and machines on the way, the Military Board agreed on 20 September 1912 to a proposal for the formation of a flying school and corps. It was decided that the school would be situated in Canberra, near the new Royal Military College at Duntroon. Pilot cadets should be young, single and fit. The board also absolved the government from paying compensation to cadets involved in accidents.[10]

Petre arrived in Australia in January 1913 to organise the school. He visited Canberra at the end of the month, but found it unsuitable because of its hilly terrain and distance from the coast. Petre also later told Richard Williams, a cadet on the first school's course, that he was 'not going to be isolated in the bush'.[11] He consequently inspected several sites around Melbourne, and in June proposed a 295-hectare site at Point Cook, 20 kilometres west of Melbourne, which the government purchased for £12 880.

'A ragtime show': The Central Flying School, Point Cook

Harrison and Petre's work in establishing the Central Flying School during the first half of 1914 confirmed that they were ideal for the job. Both skilled administrators as well as pilots, they hired staff, supervised the construction of roads and accommodation at the site, designed temporary canvas hangars and oversaw the repair of the school's aircraft, which unfortunately had been damaged in transit from Britain.

At the end of July 1914, the school advertised for its first four students. The newspapers announced that it sought four men from either the permanent or citizen (part-time) military forces to learn 'the art of flying'—that is, cross-country navigation, aerial observation and photography, meteorology and aviation theory. Applicants, according to *The Argus* of 31 July 1914, should be:

Aged between 20 and 26. Not of higher rank than captain. With not less than two years commissioned service. Under 14 stone [88kg] in weight. Unmarried. Certified by a medical officer as physically qualified. He must, moreover, be a good map-reader and field sketcher and must possess a fair knowledge of internal combustion engines.

As applications for the school flooded in, a crisis unfolded in the Balkans that, through a tangle of European politics and imperial obligations, held vital significance for Australia. A Serbian nationalist had assassinated the heir to the Austrian throne, the Archduke Franz Ferdinand, on 28 June 1914. This presented the Austrian government with a long-sought excuse to invade and annex Serbia. Acting on their own strategic interests in the Balkans, the Russians began a pre-emptive mobilisation against Austria and her ally, Germany, on 31 July. Germany responded by mobilising against Russia and her ally, France, the following day. When German armies crossed into neutral Belgium on their way to Paris, Britain declared war on Germany. Australia's involvement was a foregone conclusion. Simply put, as Prime Minister Joseph Cook told the people of Horsham in Victoria: 'when the Empire is at war, so is Australia at war'.

Against the background of this unfolding catastrophe, the school selected its first pupils. On Saturday, 15 August, 24-year-old Richard Williams, a lieutenant in the Army's Administration and Instruction Corps, was in his element. An ambitious man intent on making a career out of soldiering, Williams was working at Army District and Brigade Headquarters to recruit and organise volunteers for the recently announced Australian Imperial Force. He was, nearly literally, being buried in paperwork as thousands of Australian men rushed to enlist. A letter of acceptance into the Central Flying School arrived that Saturday afternoon with orders to report at Werribee Station for flight training on Monday.

At Werribee, Williams met the three other pupils. Unlike him, they were part-time soldiers. The most senior in rank and age was 26-year-old Tom White. A metalworker for his family's small business in Melbourne, White was, according to his biographer, 'pugnacious and impatient for success, with a disdain for authority and a suspicion of elites born of his humble background, small business family and limited education'.[12] The ambition that he shared with Williams, and the background that he did not, would bring the two into personal conflict several times in the future. The other two pupils were lieutenants. Twenty-three-year-old George Merz was a recent medical graduate of the University of Melbourne, where he served in the University Rifles. He was noted for his 'intellectual brilliance and professional dedication', but in contrast to Williams and White demonstrated 'an appealing modesty'.[13] The fourth student, David Manwell, was 24 years old, a commissioning agent from Queenscliff who served in the light horse, and almost certainly would have embarked for service at Gallipoli had he not been accepted into the flying school's inaugural course.

Williams was suitably impressed when Harrison met them at the station in, of all things, a motorcar. 'This was the first army motor vehicle I had seen,' he later recalled, adding, 'the usual Army transport was horse drawn'. Any notion that the flying corps was a cut above the rest of the army quickly vanished, though, as they arrived amidst the sprawling sheep paddocks of Point Cook. 'There,' as Williams later recalled, 'we found an establishment which had no military air about it at all.' An old tin shed and some 'lean tos' just behind the beach housed stores and a diesel generator. At the other end of the property, among a plantation of pine and gum trees, a ramshackle collection of tents served as accommodation and messes for the pupils, instructors and a handful of ground staff. The kitchen was a shipping case and the nearest water supply was 6.5 kilometres away. Nearby, some larger canvas tents housed the school's two BE2a biplanes and Deperdussin monoplanes. The principal training machine—the Bristol Boxkite—was stored in the only permanent structure onsite: a rusty, old farm shed. 'As a permanent officer, I rather thought, "This is a ragtime show,"' recalled Williams. 'Just a ... grazing paddock, long grass and that was it.'[14]

According to the Flight School's log book, Merz had the first flight the day after their arrival. Harrison took him up in the Boxkite, and flew around the aerodrome at 100 feet. They landed after five minutes. The others got a turn the following morning.

The Boxkite was in some respects an ideal training machine. It had a biplane design, although not in the classic First World War sense. It had neither a fuselage nor a cockpit; the tail was attached to the wings by a long timber boom. The instructor sat in the centre of the lower wing, with the engine and propeller behind, facing backwards. The pupil sat close behind the instructor with a leg on each side of him so he could reach forward and handle the control stick. To learn about the rudders, he watched the instructor's feet on the rudder bar. After a few flights like this, instructor and pupil switched positions.

With the exception of a barometer, the Boxkite lacked instruments. Its 40 horsepower engine didn't have a throttle either—just an 'on–off' switch. White recalled: 'The senses took the place of the instruments. One's eyes and ears did duty as engine counters; the rush of the air in the face told whether the climb or glide was at the right angle.'[15] Nevertheless, the Boxkite was remarkably safe to fly. Its 14 metre wingspan and light weight meant that when it stalled, it didn't dive; instead, in Williams' words, it 'fell rather like a falling leaf.'[16]

The pupils learned to fly within the aerodrome's boundaries at between 50 and 200 feet.[17] Aside from taking off and landing, the only manoeuvre they learned was the shallow turn. With a top speed of 60 kilometres per hour, the lumbering Boxkite was incapable of sharp banks or anything approaching the type of aerobatics that would be standard training in 1917 and 1918.

Williams went solo after about a fortnight, with two hours and 45 minutes of dual instruction under his belt. He took off, climbed to 50 feet without turning and landed straight ahead.[18] White took his first solo after only an hour and 55 minutes' instruction. Trying to outdo the others by landing close to the hangar, he misjudged his speed and piled the aircraft up on top of it. 'Over-confidence,' was White's excuse; his only injury was a bruised ego.

At this point, the ardent young students became frustrated with shortcomings in the school's program. After going solo, their instruction practically stopped. Pupils received no further instruction unless they sought it—'something a confident young man seldom does,' Williams admitted.[19] The breadth of instruction also fell short of the pupils' expectations. Having no compasses or cameras prevented instruction in navigation, cross-country flying and aerial photography. Theoretical instruction on the ground was limited too. The pupils learned the basics of internal combustion engines and aeroplane rigging by volunteering in the workshops.

Then there was the school's limited equipment. Damage to the Boxkite held up training for days at a stretch while it was repaired. There were four accidents during the course (with White and Manwell each crashing twice), and each time flying stopped for several days. This, combined with the Boxkite's requirement for perfectly still conditions—usually fleetingly at dawn and dusk—meant instruction lacked continuity. 'We were lucky,' recalled Williams, 'if we flew on two or three consecutive days and during the course there were periods of 5, 8, 6 and 16 days when there was no flying.'[20] The pupils found the long stretches of idleness in between flights exasperating. Williams found it especially difficult 'kicking his heels' while the rest of the AIF prepared to embark for their 'great adventure' overseas.[21]

Bored with the Boxkite, after a few weeks the pupils began nagging Petre and Harrison to let them fly the much faster and more manoeuvrable BE2a—a machine that, although soon antiquated, was at this time playing an important role in Britain's early battles against the advancing Germans in France. Harrison thought they weren't experienced enough—'not until you can take the Boxkite to 1500 feet and do an engine-off landing,' he told them. White, in his typically brash manner, put his hand up first. 'We talked it over and thought it could be done,' he wrote. 'So I had a shot at it.' He took it up to altitude, switched off his engine and began the descent. Things went well until, at 400 feet, he got into an out-of-control spiral. 'The front elevator and port wing tip hitting the earth with a crash, shaking off the tanks and the engine, and catapulting me, followed by the seat, clear of the plane.'[22] White was fortunate to emerge with nothing worse than some bumps and scrapes, and another bruise on his ego. For the time being, the BE2a remained, tantalisingly, in its canvas hangar.

In late October, the pupils sat a theoretical examination on basic aviation theory and aeronautical engineering. Practical flying examinations followed during the first week of November. They had to fly a series of figure of eights and then glide to land in a circle, 40 metres across. All students passed, although White failed on his first attempt, making Williams the Central Flying School's first graduate pilot.[23] It was a fitting accolade for the man who would, eight years later, become the Royal Australian Air Force's founding chief. Yet his instructors wouldn't have picked it at the time. Petre regarded Williams as 'consistent though not brilliant'. In fact, according to

Petre, Merz—who graduated with distinction—was the only decent pilot among them at the end of the course. He considered that White was 'an unreliable flyer, lacking in judgement' and Manwell a pilot of 'such incompetence and want of judgement that it is a little doubtful whether he would make a good flying officer'.[24]

Perhaps for this reason, the Military Board extended the course for two weeks following the graduation. The newly qualified pilots again turned their thoughts to the BE2a. Williams took up Harrison's challenge and successfully got the Boxkite up to 1500 feet and landed safely with his engine switched off. Harrison, who Williams thought was guarding his career prospects by limiting what he taught the pupils, still refused him permission to fly the BE2a. Harrison went off to Sydney and, according to Williams, ordered one of the mechanics to do all he could to prevent the students from flying the BE2a. On the course's second-last day, though, Petre relented. After a quick demonstration, Williams and Merz took it in turns to take the BE2a up. Williams spent 35 minutes in the air over Werribee and Sunshine, getting up to 3750 feet. It was, he thought, 'a wonderful experience' and, with its greater speed and an altimeter, speed gauge and compass, 'much easier to fly than the Boxkite'.[25] Williams touched down safely and ran out of petrol moments later. The BE2a stopped dead out on the paddock and the broad silence of Point Cook settled on him.

Thus ended Australia's first military aviation training course. It was an anticlimax for the nation's first four graduate pilots. There were neither Australian squadrons for them to serve in at this time, nor plans to establish any. They returned to their old units, it appearing to White there was 'little chance of our seeing active-service flying'.[26]

'A state of turmoil': The Mesopotamian Half Flight

While Australia's first four aviation pupils were learning to fly at Point Cook between August and November 1914, a series of battles were raging in Europe that would shape the conflict to come. In August, German armies crossed through neutral Belgium, intending to encircle Paris and knock France out of the war within six weeks. The tiny British Expeditionary Force (BEF) and a French army mounted a well-executed fighting withdrawal to the River Marne, just north of Paris, where they unleashed a strong counter-attack.

The Germans retreated to high ground and began to dig trenches. These formed the genesis of the 'Western Front'—a 700-kilometre long line of fortifications that would remain unbroken for the next four years.

To the surprise of some, 'flying machines' demonstrated their usefulness from the outset. During the chaotic retreat towards Paris, British and French commanders relied on airmen's reports when all other communications failed. The Germans used reconnaissance aircraft too, removing the element of surprise—and hence the prospect of a sweeping, decisive victory—from the battlefield. Other possibilities for aircraft also emerged during these dramatic first weeks of the war. A British corps commander, Douglas Haig—who later commanded the BEF and has often been incorrectly maligned for his supposed lack of foresight—appreciated how pilots could direct artillery fire against enemy targets obscured behind terrain.[27] Although unarmed themselves, aircraft also appeared to have offensive potential. Pilots improvised by taking pistols, rifles and grenades—even bricks—aloft. One British observer shot an enemy pilot with a rifle after firing 100 rounds at him. The enemy machine crashed, becoming the RFC's first aerial victory and marking the beginning of aerial combat.[28] By the end of 1914, as the reality of stalemate—and a long, technology-dominated war—settled in, flying corps on both sides of the line started to grow rapidly.

The deadlock in Europe prompted Britain's government to look elsewhere for victory in 1915. It perceived Germany's ally Turkey, whose vast but deteriorating empire stretched from the Balkans across the Middle East to the Persian Gulf, as a chink in the enemy coalition. In Australia, the best-known 'sideshow' campaign against Turkey occurred on the Gallipoli peninsula between April and December 1915. It is almost unknown to Australians today, however, that while Gallipoli raged another equally ferocious series of battles took place at the other end of the Turkish Empire, in Mesopotamia. There, in what today is known as Iraq, Australia sent its first airmen into combat.

On 8 February 1915, the Australian government received an unexpected telegram from the Viceroy of India. It requested Australian pilots, mechanics, aircraft and equipment for a campaign in the Turkish-held Tigris Valley.[29] The Australian government promptly replied with an offer of four pilots, 'about' twenty mechanics, two motor vehicles and tools. It dubbed the force a 'half flight', on account of it being about half the strength of a standard RFC flight—at this time, four aircraft with airmen and mechanics to operate them.

The available pilots in Australia at the time included the four new graduates, their instructors and an additional man, William Treloar, a 24-year-old motor mechanic from Melbourne who had learned to fly in England before the war. From this pool, the Department of Defence selected Henry Petre to command, with George Merz (dux of the first course), Tom White and Treloar. Richard Williams, who was supervising AIF training at Broadmeadows, helped White select mechanics from army volunteers with relevant trade skills. Patternmakers, boat-builders and carpenters were chosen as aircraft riggers, while Williams sought motor mechanics, fitters and blacksmiths to be aircraft engine mechanics.[30] They selected 41 volunteers who received a fortnight's crash course in aircraft maintenance before embarking for Bombay on 20 April 1915.

From Bombay, Half Flight travelled to Basra, 75 kilometres downstream from where the Tigris and Euphrates rivers meet and flow to the sea (see Map 1). There, in the cradle of civilisation, they met two British airmen from the Indian Army (Captains Broke-Smith and Reilly) and an Australian in the New Zealand Army, William Burn, attached as an aerial observer. Things at Basra were, in one mechanic's words, 'in a state of turmoil'.[31] Aside from a few spare parts and a pair of lorries, there was none of the equipment or facilities promised Half Flight. The men established a makeshift aerodrome in a small Arab cemetery—the only dry ground they could find.[32] 'The city and its environs,' explained White, 'are so intersected by canals which irrigate the date plantations that the country in the flood season appears to consist of a number of palm covered islands.'[33] Half Flight received three aircraft, two-seater Maurice Farman biplanes donated by the Rajah of Gwailor. One was in bad shape following service in Egypt and, with their air-cooled engines, the planes were totally unsuited to the stifling climate. As the Turks had no aircraft in the theatre, however, they had the potential to be of some use to British operations.

Half Flight was attached to the Indian Expeditionary Force D, a mixed British and Indian formation consisting of two infantry divisions and a cavalry brigade. The mandate of its commander, General Sir John Nixon,

MAP 1 Mesopotamia

was to secure the region's oil deposits from the Turks and uncooperative Arab tribes. Rather than establish a strong defensive position in the Basra region, he envisaged a bold advance along the Euphrates and Tigris towards Baghdad. Half Flight had only four days to establish its depot at Basra before Nixon began his push up the Tigris River on 31 May. For the rest of the campaign, most of Half Flight's personnel and equipment would remain at Basra while small detachments operated up-river from forward aerodromes.

The British commenced the campaign with an attack on Kurna on 31 May. Petre and Burn (as observer) flew the unit's first sorties by reconnoitring enemy positions at the town. Their intelligence helped the British win a stunning victory, capturing the town and 2000 of its garrison by the day's end. White and Reilly flew upstream the following day and found enemy troops crammed on to paddle-steamers making a hasty retreat. Their aircraft was unarmed, but White improvised by throwing a few small bombs among the enemy transports. He missed, but frightened one captain into running aground. The commander of 6th Indian Division, General Sir

Charles Townshend, sailed into Amara on 2 June. Two days later, Petre and Burn were reporting 'no sign of enemy' 50 kilometres further upstream.[34]

To keep up with the advance, Half Flight's forward detachment moved up-river to Amara almost as soon as it was clear of enemy soldiers. Following the pilots up the river on steamers was the small army of mechanics, riggers, batmen, labourers, cooks and staff that made up the overwhelming bulk of Half Flight. They were a motley collection, 'as diverse and unique as was humanely possible,' opined White. Alongside riggers from Carlton and mechanics from Manchester were Muslim, Hindu and Christian Indians, 'a Persian or two and Arabs using tools of trade such as Noah used'.[35] To grease the wheels of this veritable island Babel, all the airmen received commissions in the Royal Flying Corps and temporary appointments to the Indian Army. The Australians were, however, glad to keep their distinctly national uniforms and shoulder badges.

Upstream, the climate became diabolical. During the day, it hovered at 40°C in the shade and mosquitoes inundated the camp. In a letter to his parents, White described writing on a table 'absolutely covered with hundreds of mosquitoes ... the noise they make when flying around was just like the wind whistling loudly'.[36] Despite doses of quinine every second day, many men fell sick. Petre, in a report to the General Staff in Melbourne, highlighted the operational difficulties of working upstream. As well as finding it virtually impossible to get parts and supplies, the mechanics could only manage 'short bursts' of work in the heat. Despite constant maintenance, the air-cooled engines simply couldn't cope in the conditions. To reinforce the point, he described flying at 5000 feet wearing 'a khaki drill jacket and a thin cotton shirt only without feeling at all cold'. Nevertheless, as Petre also explained, Half Flight had made a 'truly amazing' difference in the campaign: 'From the first day that aeroplanes have been employed the Turkish forces have retreated continuously.'[37]

Being further upstream also placed the airmen and mechanics in a wilderness populated by Arabs and Bedouins of questionable allegiance. White considered 'conquered territory in the rear of the most advanced fighting troops ... practically a no-man's land roamed over by ruthless and merciless Arabs'.[38] The men at the forward aerodromes were anxious. At Amara, they built a mud wall, 2.5 metres high, around the camp and posted sentries

FIRE IN THE SKY

at night. One of the Australian mechanics also ran a barbed wire fence, connected to an electric magneto, around the perimeter.[39]

With the lower Tigris clear of enemy, General Nixon switched his attention to the Euphrates. At the beginning of July, Half Flight began reconnoitring the river with two newly arrived Caudron G III aircraft. Despite being more powerful than the Farmans, their engines were even more vulnerable to the hot conditions. White dismissed them as 'mere toys more suitable for a flying school than for active service'.[40] Nevertheless, Petre, Burn, Reilly and Treloar managed valuable mapping and communications work for the Euphrates force as it worked its way up-river. On 24 July, after a pitched battle in dreadful swampland conditions, Nasiriyeh fell to British troops, thus fulfilling Nixon's objective of securing the oilfields.

During its return journey to the Basra depot, Half Flight paid a high price for its success. The two Caudrons were halfway home when Reilly's engine failed. He made an emergency landing near Abu Salibiq, while Merz and Burn flew on in the other machine. Impressed with recent British victories, the local Arabs treated Reilly kindly. Within a few hours, his engine was running again and after spending the night at Abu Salibiq he made it back to Basra. Merz and Burn were not so fortunate. They didn't show up at Basra and when Petre located their abandoned machine from the air, 40 kilometres from Abu Salibiq, things didn't look promising. The crew members were nowhere to be seen, and the aircraft had been hacked to pieces.[41]

Petre organised search parties and put the Expeditionary Force's political officers on the case. The evidence they gathered was circumstantial and at times contradictory, but the reports of two alleged eyewitnesses claimed that armed Arabs had attacked Merz and Burn when they landed with engine trouble. The airmen, armed only with revolvers, fled into the marshlands and fought a running battle with their assailants. After 8 kilometres, one of them was wounded and the Arabs overpowered and killed them both. There was no trace of their bodies, although some evidence pointed to a tribe that occupied the village of Gurmatali.[42] Tom White led a company of Indian troops to the village in search of the 'human jackals' responsible.[43] They found none of the dead men's possessions, but noted how all of the young, able-bodied males fled into the jungle just prior to their arrival. In spiteful retribution, White's party burned some of the Arab villagers' homes.

George Merz was the AFC's first airman to be killed in action. His death was a blow to the squadron, especially his best mate Tom White. White remembered how Merz, 'a brilliant medico and best of good fellows, had worked hard the night before his last flight with suffering wounded in a sweltering, understaffed hospital at Nasiriyeh'.[44] His and Burn's bodies never turned up. Today, they are commemorated on the Commonwealth War Graves Commission memorial in Basra, a town occupied once again by British troops following the 2003 invasion of Iraq.

'The Mecca of our little army': The push for Baghdad, August 1915–April 1916

With the fall of Nasiriyeh, Nixon had achieved his original campaign goal of securing local British oil interests. The Turks were now well clear of Basra, having established themselves along the Tigris before Baghdad—the so-called 'second capital' of the Turkish Empire.[45] Nixon thereafter set his eyes upon this prize that sat astride the Tigris, a further 160 kilometres upstream from his advanced posts at Amara, hoping to offset the disaster unfolding at the other end of the Turkish Empire on the Gallipoli Peninsula. In charge of the Tigris campaign would be Major General Charles Townshend.

For six weeks, Half Flight prepared to support the Indian Expeditionary Force's next advance along the Tigris. The men and machines were almost worked into the ground by Townshend's relentless demands for reconnaissance and small bombing raids—usually against recalcitrant Arabs—and the notorious *shamal*, a seasonal northwesterly wind that blows up to 65 kilometres per hour. Canvas hangars collapsed time and again and the machines struggled to fly against it. The mechanics also laboured to finish converting the barges to carry the unit upstream. Work days ran from 6.00 a.m. until 10.00 p.m.[46]

Morale had a momentary shot in the arm when the members of No. 30 Squadron RFC arrived as reinforcements on 24 August. With them came four new aircraft, all Martinsyde biplanes. Petre was bitterly disappointed on his first test flight to find that they took 23 minutes to climb to 5000 feet and could only achieve 80 kilometres per hour—marginally faster than the *shamal*.

In the first week of September, nine mechanics from Half Flight moved north to establish a forward aerodrome at Ali Gharbi. The airmen flew from there to support Major General Townshend's force as it pushed along the Tigris to Sanniyat. On 16 September, Treloar and his British observer Basil Atkins received orders to conduct an important reconnaissance ahead of the forward British forces to pinpoint the location of the enemy's main line:

> We were just over their front line on its left flank. There we find redoubts, trenches and information enough to keep Atkins sketching and writing at his fastest rate. A little puff of smoke over to our left quickly followed by others shows us plainly that we have succeeded in our mission and that the Turk has betrayed himself by using his artillery on us.

Over the enemy trenches, their engine failed. Treloar glided towards the only dry ground nearby, skimming over an irrigation ditch crammed with enemy soldiers. The Caudron touched down in a 'perfect hail of rifle fire':

> The bullets were whizzing past our heads, going through the bracing wires. We jumped out of the machine quickly and placed our hands up but as the firing continued we took what cover we could eventually daring to try and run ... but before going many paces we were surrounded by some Turkish irregulars who started to loot us at once, tearing off most of our clothes and equipment.[47]

Just as the two men thought they might share the fate of Merz and Burn, a Turkish officer turned up and took them into custody. They would spend three long years languishing in Turkish prisons before seeing Australia again.

With Treloar's accident, the squadron had only two aircraft left to support Townshend's assault on Kut on 27 September. Nevertheless, the pilots kept British headquarters informed of the enemy's positions, as well as those of the Indian cavalry, as they outran their telephone lines. By nightfall, the Turks were in full retreat and in the following days the airmen dropped some newly arrived 20 lb bombs on to the fleeing enemy transports. Part of the squadron moved upstream to Kut on 30 September, and then further on to Aziziyeh, 'a mere cluster of mud houses about ... fifty miles below Bagdhad' on 6 October.[48] From there, the airmen reconnoitred the Tigris's upper reaches, discovering the enemy had retreated to a main defensive position at Ctesiphon while maintaining large outposts along the river. The nearest, Kutaniyeh, containing some 2000 Turks, was just 8 kilometres from their aerodrome.

White and his British observer, Yeats-Brown, were photographing Ctesiphon early one morning in October when their engine began to cough and splutter:

> Commencing a glide to the flank of the position, I passed a chit to Y-B, explaining why, with some purple phrases concerning engines in general. Then, with full throttle and diving steeply for a few hundred feet, on the off chance of the fault remedying itself, much to our relief it picked up its revolutions again, and I was able to pass him a 'Praise be to Allah' bulletin.

Minutes later, though, the engine failed again. With a trailing wind, White was able to glide just past Zeur and touch down in country dotted with enemy camps:

> As the engine was still running feebly, I decided not to attempt repairs so close to the enemy, but to taxi till the engine stopped. The wind having given us a good start, Y-B stood up in the observer's seat armed with a rifle, on the alert for pursuers, and to keep a look out for bad ground.

With intermittent bursts of power from the engine, the aircraft 'rolled and bumped' along the rough ground, 'at a rate that would not have disgraced many a motor car,' thought White. They trundled past Kutaniyeh and its 2000-strong garrison, who were apparently left too dumbstruck by the sight to pursue them. After they made it on to an old road, the engine suddenly roared back to life and they took off, flying the last few kilometres to Aziziyeh. They had taxied some 24 kilometres through enemy territory, a journey White proudly claimed was a 'a taxi-ing record'.[49]

Buoyed by intelligence reports that the enemy had no reserves in Baghdad, Nixon disregarded advice from the British government and planned an assault on Ctesiphon.[50] The airmen assisted the planning stage by taking photographs and correcting the army's hopelessly inaccurate maps. As with all things in this campaign, improvisation was the rule. Lacking proper aerial photography equipment, the pilots used their own ordinary reflex cameras through a hole cut in the cockpit floor. Petre mounted a garden rake to his cockpit and, with the help of specially spaced pegs, used triangulation to accurately plot enemy positions on a map.

The daily reconnaissance trip over the enemy lines during the month prior to Townshend's big offensive was risky, strenuous business, as White recalled:

> Flying the sluggish Farman from point to point over the enemy defences on a gusty day, mapping the position with the garden rake device held to the forehead and supporting a map board on the knees on which bearing and calculations were written, while guns 4000 feet below dotted the atmosphere with shrapnel bursts, was an experience that kept mind and body alert and quickly dissipated any early morning lethargy.[51]

Townshend intended to attack the enemy's main force at Ctesiphon frontally and with a flanking movement, to cut off its retreat. To guard his force from interference from Baghdad or beyond, he endeavoured to disrupt the enemy's communications prior to zero hour. Townshend's headquarters asked the squadron to destroy enemy telegraph lines prior to the move against Ctesiphon. White and Yeats-Brown volunteered for the job—reasoning their engine was running well and they were both unmarried. After much discussion, it was decided that they should land outside Baghdad and blow up the telegraph poles with guncotton charges.

Their prospects for success seemed reasonable, as Baghdad apparently contained few troops; however, those of making it home were substantially less. At a range of almost 100 kilometres, the target was beyond the Farman's range. With a few extra cans of fuel, they might just make the return journey—although not if the wind didn't cooperate. To top it off, the job was set for Friday, 13 November. Although no one said it at the time, it all amounted to something of a suicide mission.

White and Yeats-Brown took off early, their machine lumbering under the weight of extra fuel and oil cans. They climbed above the dawn fog and followed the Tigris north. Skirting around the Turkish positions at Seleucia, Baghdad 'suddenly loomed through the mists in the East'. To White, it was 'the Mecca of our little army' that 'appeared like some wonderful city of enchantment' after the squalor of Azizeyeh. White's imagination, reared on the likes of *The Arabian Nights,* ran wild:

> Seen from the air on this early November morn, with the sun gleaming off the gold cupolas and minarets of the mosques of Khazimain, with date plantations fringing the silver waters of the Tigris into hazy infinity, the historic city of the Caliphs appeared indescribably beautiful and fantastic as a dream city.[52]

A disconcerting realisation that the British intelligence was flawed cut the moment short. Baghdad was, in fact, full of enemy troops. And the telegraph line didn't run across the desert as expected, but rather along one of the main roads heading out of town. White contemplated heading back to alert Townshend of the enemy reinforcements, but decided it was more important to destroy the wires.

He selected a spot, 13 kilometres out of Baghdad, where the telegraph lines strayed away from the road a little. Spiralling down, he cut the engine and was only a few feet off the ground when a sudden gust of wind from behind thrust them forward. The Farman touched down too fast and collided with a telegraph pole, leaving one of the wings badly damaged.

Yeats-Brown leapt from the cockpit and shimmied up the nearest pole with his guncotton and detonators. 'Then,' as White recalled, 'the ground seemed literally to spawn Arabs.' He shot one with his rifle, causing the others to take cover in a canal. Seizing the opportunity, White refilled the petrol tanks and inspected the broken wing, as 'bullets zipped past uncomfortably close, kicked up dust beneath, or whizzed through the machine'.

In an instant, Yeats-Brown was at his side and with an ear-splitting crash the telegraph pole exploded in a cloud of dust. The firing then intensified as the Turkish cavalry arrived and began firing at them from the other side. Despite the hopelessness of their situation, Yeats-Brown planted another explosive while White tried to fire up the engine. Miraculously it started, but before they could move the second telegraph line came down and its wires fouled the propeller. 'Only then,' claimed White, 'did I realise our utter helplessness.'

A throng of Arab fighters quickly surrounded and seized the airmen. One bashed White with a club, splitting his forehead open. Another took to Yeats-Brown with a hammer and pulled off his flying jacket. Just when it seemed that they would be killed on the spot, two Turkish officers turned up and began dragging them away. Enraged, the Arabs argued with the officers. What followed was the most intense few minutes of the two airmen's lives. White described how more and more Arabs gathered around and 'each new arrival would put his rifle to our heads and was only dissuaded from blowing out our brains after much persuasion from the Turks'. After what seemed like hours, the two Turks managed to get White and Yeats-Brown into a military outpost. After a nerve-racking ride into Baghdad, pursued by armed Arabs all the way, they became prisoners of the Turks—or, as White later dubbed his memoir, *Guests of the Unspeakable*.[53]

White and Yeats-Brown's failure to return meant General Nixon remained unaware of the Turkish reinforcements as he planned to attack Ctesiphon. Ironically, he also banned further flights over the city, thus denying himself the opportunity to learn about the Turkish reinforcements.[54]

Major-General Townshend's over-stretched and exhausted 6th Division attacked Ctesiphon on 22 November 1915. The British managed to capture the first two enemy lines but were held there by unexpectedly strong reinforcements. A powerful Turkish counter-attack over the following two days revealed to Townshend what White and Yeats-Brown had discovered at Baghdad—that contrary to British intelligence, the Turks had reserves to protect Ctesiphon that far outnumbered 6th Division. Within 48 hours, the British had suffered 4500 casualties, or about of third of their number, and were in full retreat towards Kut. Half Flight's only original member, Petre, reported on the pursuit and dropped a few 100 lb bombs on Turkish troops, but otherwise could contribute little to stem the enemy's pursuit. On 3 December, some 11 600 of Townshend's troops arrived in Kut, where they were promptly cut off and surrounded.

Petre and a few of the mechanics got away in the nick of time, but most of their equipment, riverboats and ground crew were trapped. Petre and some British reinforcements from the Royal Naval Air Service established themselves at Ali Gharbi, and over the next few months air-dropped supplies to the besieged garrison. They delivered food, medical supplies, money, spare parts and even a 30 kilogram millstone to grind corn. In all, Petre and the British pilots managed to deliver 8.5 tonnes of supplies. It was not enough, though. On 29 April 1916, the emaciated British garrison surrendered to the Turks. Just 2000 of the 13 000 would survive three years in captivity. Only two of the nine Australian Half Flight members survived.

The fall of Kut effectively ended the AFC's first campaign. Petre came down with typhoid in May 1916 and went to India to recover. Afterwards, he returned to his native England and flew with a British squadron in France.[55] Petre survived the war, returned to his law practice and died in 1962.

Four pilots and 58 ground crew served in Australia's first overseas air campaign.[56] They experienced the formative days of aerial warfare, a time when the army's expectations of airmen far outstripped what their equipment was capable of doing. Obscured by Gallipoli, as so many important milestones of our military history are, their work is today almost unknown to Australians. Yet Half Flight's resourcefulness, tenacity and operational effectiveness are well and truly worthy of a place in the Anzac narrative.

'Applications came from all over Australia': The formation of No. 1 Squadron Australian Flying Corps

While the members of Half Flight sweltered on the Tigris, the Central Flying School at Point Cook ran three more courses. By the end of 1915, 24 more pilots had graduated. Lawrence Wackett, a student on the school's third course in late 1915 found that it had flourished under Eric Harrison's leadership. In stark contrast to the 'ragtime show' that Williams had described a year before, Wackett reported a 'good engineering workshop, well equipped with machine tools' and 'four cottages for the married staff, quarters for mechanics'. He slept not under canvas, but in 'a very comfortable officers mess with individual rooms for about a dozen officers' and did advanced training on the BE2a.

At the end of 1915, these 24 qualified pilots enabled the Australian government to accept a British invitation to form a complete Australian squadron. 'Such units,' the British Secretary of State explained, 'would take their place in the general organisation of the RFC but will be given distinguishing designations.' The British would supply the higher command, organisation and equipment. The Australians only needed to send pilots and a ground crew.[57]

During November and December 1915, Eric Harrison organised the squadron. It would be officially known as No. 67 (Australian) Squadron, Royal Flying Corps, although colloquially (and in January 1918, officially) it was No. 1 Squadron AFC. Harrison recalled Richard Williams from his work with the army at Broadmeadows training camp to command C Flight. As the unit's most experienced pilot (with 35 hours on his log book), and a veteran administrator, he helped Harrison select and train ground staff. 'We had a free hand,' he recalled, 'in selecting men at the recruiting centres and depots and applications came from all over Australia so soon as it was known that a squadron was being formed.'[58] Still, as he and Harrison found, filling some of the squadron's more specialist roles proved difficult. The navy had snapped up the few wireless operators in the country, so they had to train volunteers in Morse code from scratch.[59] Getting aircraft riggers was difficult too, as the only similar vocational skill was held by sailors who knew how to splice lines.

Central Flying School couldn't cope with the demands, and hence No. 1 Squadron's ground crew received almost no training. A few got to swing the Boxkite or BE2a's propeller, but that was about it. The pilots weren't much better off. The men assigned to Williams' Flight had done about fourteen hours each at Point Cook. As he recalled: 'None of us had seen a machine gun more modern or lighter than a water cooled Vickers . . . nor had we seen a camera or wireless set designed for use in aircraft.'[60]

In light of this, the British Secretary of State advised the Australian government to send the squadron to Egypt where it could receive equipment and further training sooner than it would be able to in Britain's overstretched flying schools. Armed with rifle and bayonet, with neither aircraft nor the skills to operate them, the men of No. 1 Squadron were about to take their place at the sharp end of the most technologically sophisticated war the world had ever seen.

2

'A MERRY LIFE WHILE IT LASTS'
Life and death in the Australian Flying Corps

Pilots Fred Haig and Eustace Headlam of No. 1 Squadron relax between patrols, early 1918. *Vyner collection*

> They get the feeling that they may be here today gone tomorrow with the result ... that they might as well have a merry life while it lasts.
>
> —Captain John Harris, No. 1 Squadron, Australian Flying Corps

'A kind of family teamwork': The aerodrome

The 195 men and 28 officers of No. 1 Squadron were the start of a corps that would expand exponentially over the next three years. By the war's end, the Australian Flying Corps would contain 3720 men spread across eight squadrons.[1] In late 1916 and early 1917, three more units—Nos 2, 3 and 4 respectively—would follow No. 1 Squadron overseas, although their ultimate destination was the Western Front. In 1917, the AFC also established four training units (Nos 5, 6, 7 and 8) in Britain. All Australian squadrons operated within the structure of Britain's much larger air service, the Royal Flying Corps, but retained their national identity and remained under Australian administration.

The majority of the AFC held the rank of 'Air Mechanic'. They worked long hours in the squadron hangars and workshops and seldom faced mortal danger. Only a minority of the AFC—563 in total—actually flew.[2] They were nearly always commissioned officers, although practically none had flown prior to 1914. Some enlisted in the AFC and attended flying schools in Australia but the vast majority fought in the infantry, artillery or light horse before doing a training course in England and joining a squadron. Two of the Australian squadrons (Nos 2 and 4) flew single-seat scouts (what later generations would dub 'fighters'), and hence only employed pilots. The other two squadrons (Nos 1 and 3) were bombing and reconnaissance units that flew two-seaters, and hence used both pilots and observers.

In any case, be they pilots, observers or air mechanics, the AFC offered a select few Australian men a remarkably different experience of war from that faced by their counterparts in the trenches.

The AFC's primary unit was the squadron. It was a uniquely composed fighting force, in which only a minimal portion of its members did the fighting (all officers) while the majority (enlisted men and non-commissioned officers) undertook highly specialised support roles. Although the exact figures varied in different theatres and at different stages of the war, a two-seater unit with eighteen aircraft would usually have eighteen pilots, a dozen or so observers and 218 ground crew.

At the front, the squadron's 250 or so members lived and worked on a service aerodrome. Typically situated between 10 and 20 kilometres behind the front line, at its most basic it was an improvised affair consisting of canvas tents pitched on the edge of a suitably flat grass paddock the size of a couple of football fields. Some were large enough to accommodate several squadrons at once while others hosted just one. Squadrons moved aerodromes frequently, at the behest of offensives, enemy activity and changes in the front line's position. No. 2 Squadron's experience was typical: it operated from a dozen different aerodromes during its seventeen months on the Western Front. Its longest stint at one—Reclinghem—was twelve weeks while during the chaotic days of the German offensive in early April 1918, it occupied Bertangles for just 48 hours before moving on.

The basic unit everyone on the aerodrome identified with was the 'flight'. Australian squadrons, like British ones, consisted of four flights. Headquarters Flight took care of the command, administration, discipline and the unit's internal economy. The flying and fighting was done by three other flights, designated 'A', 'B' and 'C'. Each contained between six and eight aircraft, as many pilots and enough ground crew (fitters, riggers and armourers) to maintain them. Although specific arrangements varied, the classic set-up involved each flight operating out of a single, large canvas hangar. According to No. 4 Squadron's commanding officer, Wilfred McCloughry, each flight was:

> commanded by a Captain (Flight Commander) who is responsible to the Squadron Commander [usually a Major] for the condition and serviceability of his machines, and to the training of Pilots in his Flight. The Flight consists of about thirty-two men, including—One Flight Sergeant (Chief Mechanic), Two Sergeant Mechanics (one fitter and one rigger) and Four Corporals (two fitters and two riggers). These NCOs are so distributed that a fitter and rigger is entirely in charge and responsible for each machine, the NCOs supervising generally, and each having to overlook a certain number of machines.[3]

Observer Les Sutherland described this arrangement as 'a kind of family teamwork' in which each member—flyer, fitter, rigger and armourer—'must all work together to get the best out of the bus'.[4]

Behind the hangars were the squadron's workshops, technical store, armoury and transport depot. These usually included a main tent (the assembly shop), surrounded by a number of mobile workshops mounted on lorries. Each carried its own 'lathes, drills, grinders, generators and tool chests' and was able to 'cope with any job the squadron may require ... keep our engines running, supply us with electric light, and care for all our transport'. Part of the workshop was devoted to instruments and usually employed ex-civilian watchmakers to maintain the squadron's 'watches, air-speed indicators, rev-counters, altimeters, camera mechanisms and bomb-sights'. An equipment store carried thousands of spare parts—'everything,' Sutherland recalled, 'from a Leyland lorry to a tin of bully-beef'—and a Wireless Telegraphy section maintained squadron communications with the outside world.[5]

Often located opposite the hangars and workshops, on the other side of the landing field, were the living quarters. Two things usually dictated the style and comfort of dwellings: the age of the aerodrome and a squadron member's rank. At Baizeux, No. 2 Squadron's aerodrome was an older establishment, occupying part of a farm. The officers shared the farmhouse with a French family, with Dick Howard describing his room as 'quite comfortable' with its 'carpet, a fireplace, a little outhouse for washing, draped with red [muslin] and a few photos on the wall'.[6] Private Vern Knuckey and the rest of the squadron's men meanwhile slept in the barns and stables, 30 men to a loft, sharing with hordes of rats and lice. Yet Knuckey and his fellows were dry, warm and 'very thankful'—most recognised that they had previously had it much worse in the trenches.[7]

At newer aerodromes, accommodation for all ranks was Spartan in comparison. The two Australian scout squadrons—Nos 2 and 4—were the first to use Reclinghem aerodrome in July 1918. It was an empty paddock on a hilltop with no fixed structures, meaning that men and officers alike had to make do with tents. Lieutenant Alex Lockley claimed that, camped under the trees of an orchard at the aerodrome's edge, they were nonetheless 'very comfortable'[8]—although, as his mate Thomas Edols found, the canvas roof 'leaked most gloriously' in bad weather: 'It is so nice to wake up in the night with an ear full of water.'[9]

Accommodation, like most aspects of the service aerodrome, had an improvised air about it. In officers' rooms, upturned crates served as tables and candles flickered on top of bottles. Warmth might radiate from a coal brazier purloined from an abandoned French home while the pilots reclined, smoking, on wicker camp stretchers they had purchased at their own expense in the nearest town. Coloured drapes, a few photographs and perhaps a cat snoozing by the brazier dressed the whole scene up with a homely air. But it was a delicate façade. Pilots lived from their suitcases and kept things ready to move, as transfer, injury and death gave squadrons a perpetually changing roster. Arriving at his squadron in France, Edgar Percival had the unsettling experience of learning that he was the fourth officer to occupy a particular bunk in a week—the others had all been shot down, he learned, from his somewhat insensitive batman who grumbled at the prospect of getting yet another new pilot settled.[10]

The officers, non-commissioned officers and men all dined in separate messes. Their comfort, culinary quality and amenities likewise varied greatly—although, as with the sleeping arrangements, rank usually was the decisive factor.

'From all walks of life': The Australian airman

Arthur 'Harry' Cobby, the AFC's highest-scoring pilot, said of his fellow airmen: 'We came from all walks of life—farmer, bank clerk, college graduate, and one or two university people with degrees. One was a dentist, another was an engineer, and another was a doctor.' Of course, this group hardly represents 'all walks of life', but rather illustrates the exclusive background of Australia's first combat aviators.

The average Australian pilot or observer from the First World War was from society's middle or upper classes. Roughly half came from specialised industrial backgrounds such as engineering, mechanics or electrical work.[11] Those who were engineers before the war (about a quarter) came from a very narrow social niche; just 1 per cent of the working male population did this kind of work in Australia in 1911.[12] If the AFC aviator wasn't from industry, he was almost certainly what we would today call a 'white-collar worker'—a student, clerk or public servant.

As a group, Australian airmen were more thoroughly educated than their counterparts in the infantry. At least half had attended private schools, and as many as two-thirds had some kind of tertiary education.[13] Although there is no evidence that a private or tertiary education was a specific prerequisite for flying service, recruiters were instructed that 'the moral effects' of a flying applicant's civilian life were of the 'highest importance' in assessing his suitability as a pilot. According to *Medical Requirements for the Australian Flying Corps, 1918*, 'The youth who has developed courage, self-reliance, alertness, and a sense of obligation to "play the game"' was ideal. In comparison, 'the less-fortunate youth whose circumstances have tended towards a monotonous, unadventurous, or unsocial life' was unsuitable.[14]

Another factor that set the Australian airman apart was his youth. The vast majority were under 24 years old, with the average age dropping as the war progressed from 25 in 1916 to 21 in 1918. From the earliest days of the war, British military doctors supposed that flying was a young man's game. Subsequent experience confirmed this, and in August 1917 the AFC's age limit for pilots and observers was 30, with a strong preference 'for those under 23'.[15] For the rest of the AIF, the age limit was 45 years. Older men like Vern Knuckey, a 30-year-old driver in No. 3 Squadron, could only hope to get into flying school by lowering their age—a strange reversal of the situation in the rest of the AIF, where numerous men lied to make themselves old enough to enlist. When the scrupulous Knuckey put his real age on his application, his commanding officer told him he was 'too honest' and to 'hold out no hope' of getting into a cockpit.[16]

Needless to say, competition to get out of the trenches and into the AFC was stiff. Lawrence Smith, a 21-year-old light horse veteran of Gallipoli and the Sinai, volunteered for the AFC in 1917. He didn't have Knuckey's scruples when it came to stretching the facts a bit to fit the bill.

> At last I went in and I went through the act and the major said to me 'How old are you Smith?'
>
> 'I'm nineteen sir.'
>
> 'Oh. Can you ride a horse?'
>
> 'Of course I can ride a horse—I was in the light horse.'
>
> He said, 'What school did you go to, Smith?'
>
> Well of course, I did jam it on a bit. I said, 'Well I went to a very good school in England sir, and then of course, when I came here to Australia I went to the Sydney Grammar School.'
>
> 'Ah,' he said, 'excellent. By the way, what does your father do?'

'Oh, my father is a retired sea captain'. Oh, It sounded beautiful.

So we all returned to our units and in about three weeks or so I got a dispatch saying that I had been accepted and I was to report to No. 1 Squadron forthwith.[17]

'You would never think that the Great War was on at all': The Australian airman on the ground

'This is the finest place in the world,' Edmund Cornish wrote to his mother shortly after arriving at No. 2 Squadron's aerodrome at Reclinghem on the Western Front. 'The life is easy, free from worry and most comfortable.' Having seen the very worst of trench warfare as an infantry officer between 1915 and 1917, Cornish, just 21 years old, considered himself 'the most fortunate of chaps' to now be a pilot in the AFC. It was, he was thrilled to report, a bit of flying, tennis for most of the day and a 'good old warm bed' in the evenings.[18]

Cornish's words do need to be understood as those of an inexperienced pilot to a concerned mother, who would have certainly taken comfort from his glowing description of aerodrome life. Still, when they weren't flying, the AFC's airmen led a life that, on the surface at least, appeared to be leisurely and comfortable.

Airmen filled in time between flights—which could be days during so-called 'dud' flying weather—with a variety of social and leisure activities. For men who were typically young, privately educated and in peak physical condition, sport was an obvious choice. There was at least basic sporting equipment on most aerodromes, and some, including Ramleh (in Palestine), even had a tennis court and cricket pitch. Clive Conrick, an observer in Palestine in 1918, wrote of having 'the tennis court rolled before breakfast' in preparation for a match between the Australian and British squadrons that shared the aerodrome. His commanding officer also organised daily swimming parties, and he was surprised to note that. 'Since I joined the squadron, I seem to have spent more time in the water than in the air.'[19] In France, Owen Lewis jogged most evenings and studied French and German with a local priest.

No. 4 Squadron's pilots were fortunate to have a commanding officer who was, according to Edgar McCloughry, 'particularly liberal with his car and squadron transport and was always keen for us to get away when there was no work to be done'. His fellow pilots spent days of bad weather 'touring by road' to towns within a day's journey and forward areas just behind the trenches.[20] The pilots also brought a variety of personal hobbies into the squadrons. Given the technical and trade backgrounds of many, it isn't surprising that they spent hours in the workshops, fashioning souvenirs from old aircraft parts and war debris. Alex Lockley, an 18-year-old engineer from Sydney, designed and built model aircraft in between patrols, a hobby befitting both his youth and vocation. At Mejdel in Palestine, some of the squadron's members even did some amateur archaeology, excavating a 'magnificent mosaic' and a number of artefacts.[21] The authors typically report these activities in a manner that suggests they were part of the everyday routine of active service. As John Harris described life in No. 1 Squadron to his son:

> For the greater part of a year the men on active service have a real good time. They play and lark about and sing and play cards and games and you would never think that the great war was on at all ... [They are] well fed and well clothed and looked after ... often he [the airman] is two and three days without being asked to do any work.[22]

Indeed, for the Australian airman of the First World War, sport, games, shopping and lunch dates were as synonymous with active service as flying and fighting.

In between the social engagements and flying, the flying officers did have some professional responsibilities, however. Some squadron commanders insisted their airmen spend time each day in the intelligence hut to remain informed about enemy positions and tactics. Flight commanders also needed to invest time in honing the skills of their pilots and training newcomers. Most aerodromes had targets for strafing and bombing practice in nearby fields, and diligent fight commanders regularly had their men do test flights and formation practice to keep their skills sharp.

Wilfred McCloughry insisted that his pilots pass examinations before they take leave. 'These tests included a general knowledge of the mechanism and working of the Vickers' gun, and the type of interrupter gear in use at the time. Also clearance of stoppages on the ground and in the air.'[23] 'Stoppages', the seizing up of a gun due to faulty ammunition or a broken mechanism in the gun, were the bane of all First World War airmen. The ability to get a jammed gun firing again in the midst of a dogfight could be the difference between life and death—a fact of which most flyers were acutely aware. Lewis described the prospect of a jammed gun as his 'eternal nightmare', and hence visited the aerodrome's firing range to practise clearing stoppages nearly every day. Still, the prospect of a 'stopped' gun haunted him. 'I went to bed early last night,' he noted in his diary, 'but did not go to sleep for a long while as my mind kept dwelling on flying and what would happen if my gun was to jam.'[24]

Considering the large proportion of pilots with technical and engineering backgrounds in the AFC, it isn't surprising that many frequented the workshops to tinker with 'their' aeroplane and equipment. Sutherland noted that his fellow pilot, Fred Haig, would spend hours on 'old 3345', his Martinsyde biplane. 'He used to fuss over her as if she were his wealthy spinster aunt.'[25]

As officers, airmen also fulfilled the more traditional duty of leader and manager. Like their counterparts in the infantry, they shared orderly duties according to a roster system. This involved censoring outgoing mail, inspecting the mens' quarters and workshops, supervising the rousing of pilots for dawn 'shows' and overseeing aerodrome work fatigues.

Nevertheless, Australian squadrons were relatively permissive in terms of military formalities. Wilfred McCloughry insisted on a minimum of drill in No. 4 Squadron, reasoning that 'little time can be spared for such details' on active service.[26] Likewise, in Palestine with No. 1 Squadron, there was no saluting on the tarmac or around the hangars. There was simply too much to do—especially for the mechanics, who were constantly overhauling, repairing and rearming the aircraft. On days of fine weather, the squadron held a single parade of ten minutes at 8.00 a.m., which was extended only if no aerial work was scheduled.

Did this lack of drill result in a poor discipline record for the AFC? Apparently not—it had fewer court martials per capita than the rest of the AIF, although the Australians' standard of discipline sometimes clashed with those of the British commands under which they operated.[27] Take, for example, the revealing comments of Lieutenant Colonel Louis Strange, British commander of the wing No. 2 and No. 4 Squadrons were attached to during the summer of 1918:

> We had our differences of opinion at times. One of them was due to the unofficial use of service cameras, and another time there was the trouble over the bartering of rations with the local inhabitants. No one minds the swapping of a tin of bully beef for a few fresh eggs, of course, but a Wing Commander has to draw the line somewhere when he finds one of his Australian Squadrons running the village grocers shop and general store. Even so, my Australians were discreet enough in the way they went about their business, so that I might have ignored it, had it not been for the inhabitants of the neighbouring villages. When the latter got to hear of the bargains, they turned our place [i.e. the aerodrome] into a sort of fair and market on Sundays, and so I was compelled to put my foot down.[28]

The social centre of the flying officer's life on the ground was the officers' mess. Whether in the Sinai Desert or rural Belgium, the airmen expended much time and effort cultivating a well-established messing culture and promoting strong fraternity within their own mess, as well as with other squadrons' messes. Australian squadron commanders were great advocates of this. They recognised the mess's key role in fostering squadron spirit, morale and the teamwork upon which aerial operations depended so heavily. The social function and class influences at work in No. 4 Squadron's officers' mess are evident in the instructions of its squadron commander:

> The officers' mess should always be comfortably furnished, well lit and cheery, a piano and gramophone being absolutely essential. The whole atmosphere of the mess should be so arranged that officers cannot help taking a pride and interest in it and the squadron. Good meals should be provided, even if it is necessary to provide a cook from outside the squadron ... I do believe that when the occasion arises to celebrate some special success of the squadron ... this should always be celebrated in a proper fashion, and a special dinner arranged with speeches, toasts and music.[29]

In the midst of war-torn economies and routed civilian populations, the squadrons often resorted to 'souveniring' to furnish their establishments. Strange noted—with some dismay—the presence in an Australian mess of a 'nice piano' from 'a deserted and half looted house'. He also explained that, 'when we others were existing on tinned milk, the Australians always had their own fresh milk from their own two cows and a spare lorry to transport the cows whenever a move had to be made'.[30]

Indeed, the Australian pilots prided themselves on their resourcefulness and proudly upheld it as part of their identity as Australian servicemen. A mechanic from No. 2 Squadron left an account of what happened when his squadron moved to Bertangles aerodrome during the chaotic days of the German spring offensive in 1918.

> True to the predatory spirit of their ancestors, the squadron, on their arrival at Bertangles ... unloaded the barest necessities of life and action from its transport, selected for themselves the best quarters available, and then set out seriously to consider the prospects of—I was going to say 'looting', but I forgot; I should have said 'borrowing'—anything of value, such as might fall into disrepair if left unused; and what a hoard of loot—I mean, abandoned material—met their gaze!

No. 2 Squadron's 'loot' that day apparently included a pig ('it wasn't starvation that killed him'), tools, pianos (apparently plural) and an 'abandoned' French aircraft that the men 'sponsored' and named 'Sophie', taking it along with the squadron on their next move to use for 'special extra duty'—that is, joy flights.[31]

In Palestine, No. 1 Squadron's messing arrangements were somewhat rougher, featuring improvised furniture built from sandbags and crates. Nevertheless, they enjoyed almost nightly revelry that was only briefly interrupted by the business of war. According to observer Les Sutherland:

> Squadron mess nights were popular, boisterous affairs. Along with the forty or so officers of 1 Squadron, the guest list often included officers from neighbouring units. Following coffee and dessert, Williams [the squadron's commanding officer] would issue orders for the following day before leaving

for conference with the flight commanders, who would afterwards return. Happenings regularly continued into the early hours, which Williams didn't mind, as long as pilots could give their best fighting on the following day.[32]

As fellow No. 1 Squadron flyer Hudson Fysh pointed out, these 'boisterous affairs' at night were a direct result of the stress of flying and fighting:

> The tension we suffered ... produced bouts of drinking and 'playing hell' in the mess. I shall always remember that bitterly cold Palestinian night when we raided a nearby British squadron mess with Verey pistols [flare guns]. Exciting duels were fought with these things. The mess was wrecked, and altogether it was a tremendous night.[33]

It says something of the perceived importance that these 'bouts' played in building morale and *esprit de corps*, and relieving tension, that Williams—the unit's rather straitlaced commander who didn't drink, smoke or swear—allowed them to continue without interference. Indeed, shortly after joining this squadron, John Harris wrote to his wife that in No. 1 Squadron's officers' mess, 'I eat good food and could get drunk every day if I wished on either sherry, port, whisky, vermouth, liquors, beer or any other beverages.'[34]

This tightly knit community of officers, who shared a similar class background, developed a uniquely egalitarian command culture. Sutherland explained how his unit's British wing commander 'gave you the impression, when he asked you to have a spot [artillery observation patrol], that he was taking you up to his rank—not that he was coming down to yours'.[35] The British historian Denis Winter noted a similar relationship between officers in the RFC. He described the relationship between pilots and their flight and squadron commanders as 'a form of democratic dictatorship, a formulation of majority opinion, a leadership of equals'.[36] Yet even among equals, there could be points of tension. Sutherland was willing to admit that:

> In many ways, we were a jealous lot. When a small body of men—our normal officer strength was 50—live so closely together, as we did in the service squadrons in Palestine, and with so few distractions; when luck plays so big a part in life all the time, when So-and-so gets assigned a job that promises

fame and promotion while you have a lousy routine task that must be done; and when there is so much time in which to brood—well, one's sense of proportion, of justice, gets weakened, and jealousy gets a toe-hold and digs in.[37]

The aerodrome's proximity to civilian populations, coupled with great amounts of free time, afforded men in the AFC an opportunity to regularly juxtapose experiences of civilian life among their experiences of war. In this, the aerodrome represented a limbo between war and peace, combat and comfort. Denis Winter considered what this meant for the flying men in particular: 'Whereas infantrymen faced sustained periods of battle and rest, for fighter pilots, there were periods of leave and going over the top perhaps each day.'[38] Indeed, it is not uncommon to find, within airmen's diaries and letters, accounts of days that began with a harrowing dogfight and finished with a dinner date in a nearby town. Observer Clive Conrick described one such typical day in Palestine:

> Nunan and I were escort to 111 Squadron RFC on a bombing raid to Aman. Before we took off I had secreted a couple of Cooper's bombs in my cockpit, unofficially, of course. There was a bit of Archie [anti-aircraft fire] about so Nunan flew down to ground level and we machine gunned the crews manning the guns. I dropped my Cooper's bombs and they fell close enough to do some damage. The gunners all ran off into a funk hole and we kept firing at them and anything that moved until all of the bombs were dropped. We spent two hours and forty-five minutes in the air today.
>
> I played a game of tennis after lunch and then went to Jaffa to a concert given by our boys at the Theatre Hall. In the evening I dined with a few mates at the Jerusalem Hotel. On the whole I enjoyed myself very much today.[39]

The uniqueness of this existence became particularly evident to those who had previously experienced life in the infantry or light horse. Bert Billings, a veteran of the trenches who transferred to the AFC in 1917, described his life in the flying corps as 'the direct opposite of my life on Gallipoli and in the Sinai Desert'. He noted the oddity of being billeted on the outskirts of a city 'where civilian life carried on in a more or less normal way'. Shops were open, *estaminets* served 'chips and fried eggs' and local women took in their washing and mending.[40] The contrasting lifestyles—in the trenches and in a flying squadron—each dished out tension and danger in strikingly different doses. Hudson Fysh should know: he experienced 'both' wars, as a machine gunner at Gallipoli and later an observer in No. 1 Squadron:

> There is no doubt that a great feeling of tension existed in an active flying squadron: a very different atmosphere to that in the land forces whose long spells of inaction and boredom were punctuated by periods of attack and defence, when brief but tremendous physical and mental effort were called for.
>
> In the squadron we might have two or three missions over the lines every week, with intensive daily flying when there was a show on, and before each mission we all wondered, more or less according to our natures, whether we would return.[41]

British pilot Cecil Lewis put it more succinctly: 'We lived therefore always in the stretch or sag of nerves.'[42]

Life on the ground, then, represented the easy-going extreme that consumed the majority of a combat aviator's hours. It was one side of what Lewis dubbed 'the extraordinary double life' of the First World War airman.[43] Richard Williams summed up this uniquely bizarre existence when he commented that 'an airman's life is one of comparative ease interspersed with moments of intense fear'. He compared the 'comparatively comfortable tents' in which he and his fellows slept with their work in the air that 'was short in duration but could mean a quick end'.[44]

'Moments of intense fear': The Australian airman in the sky

An atmosphere of perpetual tension underpinned the aerodrome's easy-going façade. Sutherland compared it with that of a 'fire brigade station' with its 'same air of alert preparedness.'[45]

The RFC was a corps within the British Army and not, until late in the war, an independent 'air force'. Like the army's other corps—the Royal Artillery, the Royal Engineers, the Royal Army Medical Corps, and so on, the RFC's squadrons had a specific and clearly defined role within the British Army's method of waging war. First and foremost, for the men of the RFC, this was intelligence-gathering. The two-seater squadrons were the

RFC's workhorses, reconnoitring and photographing enemy positions and directing artillery fire on to them by wirelessly transmitting shot corrections to the gunners far below. As an RFC postcard sent by Alex Lockley in 1917 put it:

> They call us the eyes of the army
> For we scout for the foe far and wide
> And with all information worth having
> We keep the powers fully supplied.[46]

The point is that the air war over the Western Front and Middle East was *not* about dogfights and aces. The RFC's *raison d'être* was characterised by the work of the humble two-seaters, chugging back and forth along the front lines for hours at a time snapping photographs or communicating with the artillery. It was unglamorous work, but absolutely crucial to the war's successful conduct. The scout squadrons existed to protect them and destroy the enemy's artillery and photo reconnaissance machines. In this sense, the war in the air between 1914 and 1918 was essentially a desperate struggle to get an uninterrupted view of the enemy's affairs—its defences, gun emplacements and troop dispositions. When dogfights occurred, as they certainly did on an increasingly larger scale throughout the war, it was a natural consequence of this, and this only. Of course, the role of aircraft evolved as the war went on, coming to include ground attack, strategic bombing and even battlefield resupply. But the pilot's core role from the beginning to the end of the war remained as 'the eyes of the army'. The upshot of this was that the flying corps' work was vital stuff that was inextricably linked to the success or failure of operations on the ground. It also meant that, for the pilots of this comparatively small component in the vastness of the British Army, there was always plenty of flying to be done.

The 'democratic dictatorship' commonly exercised by the squadron commander in the relaxed confines of the mess vanished when it came to flying. An order to fly was considered final, and any disinclination to do so meant serious consequences. Jack Treacy, a 23-year-old pilot in No. 3 Squadron, discovered this when he left his aerodrome for a shopping expedition instead of standing by for the artillery observation patrol for which he was rostered. On his return, the squadron commander immediately charged him, placed him under arrest and sent him before Wing Headquarters.

Such stringent measures were not necessarily frowned upon by the airmen. Treacy's roommate, Owen Lewis, who recorded the incident in his diary, appears to have agreed with his punishment.[47] The airmen, more than anyone, understood the importance of discipline and teamwork in the sky, where each man depended upon the next for survival. Those who came under suspicion of cowardice were often ostracised by their squadron mates. Cobby described a fellow pilot who, some noticed, was reluctant to cross the lines: 'He was chipped in front of the whole mess one night at dinner, and broke down. Next day, he was a physical and mental wreck.'[48] Given this culture, it perhaps isn't surprising that there are records for just nine AFC pilot court-martials during the war.

Day-to-day accounts of life in the AFC suggest airmen expected and accepted flying as part of the daily routine of active service. The strict adherence to flying orders within squadron culture may even have provided some men with a supportive foundation that enabled them to accept the inevitability of patrols and keep on going with what historian Denis Winter described as an 'oriental passivity'.[49] No. 1 Squadron's medical officer observed this shortly after joining the unit, noting: 'It is surprising how calmly the men here go about their work. They go and come just as a workman would go out to his work and come home again.'[50] The difficulty for the flying man, however, was that his work was neither regular nor predictable.

In examining the overall service lives of British airmen, Winter calculated that 'about a flight every second day' was average.[51] But this figure disguises the marked variations in air work that occurred from week to week and month to month, depending upon the weather, enemy activity and a squadron's location on the line. Take Alex Lockley of No. 4 Squadron, for example. In June 1918, he flew 41 sorties totalling 52 hours and 45 minutes in the air.[52] He flew on 25 out of 30 days, and on eleven days was airborne more than once. On average, then, Lockley did 1.36 sorties per day, each lasting about an hour and a quarter. In the following month, however, he flew on substantially fewer occasions and for less time, spending just 34 hours and 35 minutes aloft over 25 sorties. He flew on only seventeen days of the month, flying multiple times on just seven days. In July 1918, then, Lockley's average was 0.8 flights per day—with him spending nearly as many days on the ground (fourteen) as he did in the air (seventeen).

Even when he was flying, Lockley discovered there were no guarantees he would actually engage the enemy. During his first month at the front, he flew 41 sorties but rarely even saw a Germen aircraft. A typical week from his logbook recorded:

31.5.18—Very few Hun aircraft about.
1.6.18—Huns always keep over own side [of the line].
4.6.18—Fleeting glimpses of Hun planes.
5.6.18—Sighted 4 Pfalz Scouts. Nothing doing.[53]

After flying several patrols without encountering enemy aircraft, though, a pilot might suddenly be surrounded by a sky full of them. On the Western Front and in the Middle East enemy scouts tended to fight on their own side of the line, reflecting Germany's predominantly defensive strategy. Enemy pilots usually only attacked with a numerical advantage and from a position of surprise, typically out of the sun. As a result, air combat for the Australian aviator was characteristically chaotic, deadly and fought at a disadvantage. Roy King believed that what the Germans 'invariably did was to follow or wait about over our patrol in the hopes that one of our pilots would lag behind or straggle from the formation'.[54] Following a second month of encountering very few enemy aircraft, Alex Lockley was jumped by fourteen of them during an escort flight. He escaped, but his aircraft was severely damaged and he was clearly shaken by this sudden onset of enemy aggression, describing it to his parents as 'a narrow squeak' from which he barely emerged with his life.[55] Lockley and two of his comrades died six weeks later when some 30 Fokker scouts ambushed their patrol—as described in the prologue.

In spite of all the evidence—diaries, letters, interviews and official reports—it is frustratingly difficult for the historian to understand what such fighting was really like. This is because, no matter how eloquent the language, written accounts struggle to reproduce the sensory overload that dogfighting in open-cockpit aircraft must have been. Although it can only offer us a vague impression of an extraordinary reality, Les Sutherland's account's of a mid-1918 dogfight involving seventeen aircraft over Palestine is about the closest we can get:

> The formation commander signals 'attack'. After the initial dive our formation becomes 'column of lumps' immediately. It is every man for himself. We go hell for leather at those snub nosed, black crossed busses of the Hun, and they at us . . . The air is pungent with the smell of cordite; filled with the guttural, staccato chatter of the Vickers, Lewis and Spandau. Hectic work. Half rolling, diving, zooming, stalling, 'split slipping', by inches you miss collision with friend and foe. Cool, precise marksmanship is out of the question. Albatroses, Pfalzs flash across your ring sights at terrific speed. You press the triggers, and the Vickers or Lewis sprays lead. Your gunner, cursing horrifically, is shaking off a stubborn Albatros from under your tail . . .
>
> Flashing, gyrating wing, stuttering streams of lead, with only the tracer bullets, or a crackle or smack in your wings or fuselage to apprise you of where the enemy fire is going, or has gone. A Pfalz flashes by, and down, with a Bristol on his tail—t-t-t-t-t-t—bullets thud into the tail of the Hun. You can see 'em dotting, eating. Almost as if the pursued machine is voicing its anger and pain, the scream rises louder and louder—the Hun zooms, and turns in an endeavour to shake the Bristol off his tail. In vain. There is a wilder, a more violent noise. The Hun machine is hurtling earthwards, not diving or spinning. Not trying to evade its pursuer. Hurtling. Finish.[56]

'Such fighting,' thought Cecil Lewis, 'demanded iron nerves, lightning reactions, snap decisions, a cool head and eyes like a bluebottle'. The chief difference between it, and the fighting on the ground, he claimed, was the absolute 'cold bloodedness' that aerial combat required. 'You cannot lose your temper . . . see red' or 'resort to Dutch courage. Any of these may fog your judgement—and that spells death.'[57]

Lewis argued that breaking big, chaotic dogfights like the one Sutherland described down to fundamentals was really a series of turning contests: 'Two machines so engaged would circle, each trying to turn inside the other and so bring his guns into play.' Two things were critical, therefore: the aircraft's manoeuvrability and the pilot's skill at sustaining tight vertical turns—'the crucial test of a fighting pilot', according to Lewis.[58]

Another British pilot, James McCudden—a noted tactician and renowned 'ace' with 57 victories to his credit—considered marksmanship the true characteristic of a successful airman. He once told a class of young cadets: 'Good flying has never killed a Hun yet. You just get on with sighting your guns.'[59] The trick, most First World War aviators agreed, was to get as close as possible before firing. Engine vibration and turbulence—which created a firing cone roughly 15 metres wide at 220 metres range—and the effects of firing at a speeding target from a moving base (called 'deflection') made, as Sutherland has noted, precise marksmanship difficult.[60] First World War scout pilots needed to get within 90 metres and preferably closer than 30 metres for their firing to be effective. Jerry Pentland had this point graphically illustrated when he saw blood and gore spattered across a veteran British pilot's windscreen. The macabre image and its accompanying lesson remained with him. As he told an interviewer over half a century later, it 'was no good shooting at anything' unless you could 'see exactly where your tracers were going'.[61]

By 1918, most of the aircraft being flown by Australians featured the Aldis gun sight—a non-magnifying scope the pilot could use with both eyes open (see Plate 20). Sutherland claimed its concentric aiming rings allowed an airman to pick out 'the figure of a Hun pilot' and accurately estimate for deflection. When his adversary's form 'cut through' the outer ring on the lens, he would fire—and 'theoretically the Hun pilot and your bullets should arrive at the black dot [in the centre] together'.[62]

As a result, numerous private accounts and combat reports from the Australian squadrons describe enemy pilots 'slumping', 'dropping' or 'throwing their arms up' in their open cockpits. Take, for example, Cobby's striking description of killing a German pilot during a dogfight over La Bassée in 1918:

> I went round the cloud to the right and met the other chap almost head on. There was just time to press both triggers and to dive under him to get out of his way. He went down into the cloud in flames, but I had hit the pilot, too, as he almost jumped backwards out of the cockpit when I fired.[63]

The sportsmanship and chivalry so often associated with First World War air combat is conspicuously absent from such frank reports. It is absent, too, from the squadrons' kill statistics, which suggest that above anything else, aerial combat was a case of the experienced preying on the inexperience of others. Of No. 4 Squadron's claims, 112 (48 per cent of its total) were made by just six (5 per cent) of the squadron's pilots. Similar statistics are found in the records of the other Australian scout unit, No. 2 Squadron: 77 enemy aircraft (42 per cent of their total claims) came from just six pilots (8 per cent). The danger of inexperience cut both ways, though. In No. 2 Squadron, 41 per cent of casualties were pilots with less than four weeks' experience at the front.[64] Such cruel circumstances prompted young men like Conrick to consider themselves 'old hands' after just a month at the front.[65]

The result was that death—killing and dying—permeated all other aspects of life on the aerodrome. It was an ever-present shadow that lurked behind the sporting matches, shopping trips and boyish revelry of the officers' mess. The fundamental reason for this was, quite simply, that flying corps squadrons suffered the highest casualty *rates* of any service in the British Army during the First World War. One in six of all British and dominion airmen was killed.[66] In No. 4 Squadron, an airman was killed or wounded every week on average. Statistically, then, this unit's standard fighting establishment of about 21 pilots was wiped out twice over during its eleven months at the front.

Eric Dibbs witnessed the air war's grinding attrition rate while seconded to No. 11 Squadron RFC. During four months of 'tremendous' fighting in the latter half of 1917, the unit's establishment of 36 flying officers (eighteen pilots and eighteen observers) suffered 60 casualties. Dibbs emphasised the seriousness of this loss, recalling: 'They must have all been killed because it was very seldom that we had anybody wounded.'[67] Historian Trevor Henshaw's careful statistical analysis of air war casualties qualifies anecdotes such as this. In the second half of 1917, 48 per cent of allied air casualties were killed in action and a further 24 per cent were taken prisoner.[68] The reason behind these grim statistics is twofold. First, there was the British policy of not providing parachutes to its aviators. This was partially to remove a supposed temptation for crew to abandon an aircraft that might be saved but also because that era's primitive parachute designs were too cumbersome for the confines of the cockpit.[69] The other reason was the

RFC's policy of patrolling on the German side of the lines, meaning that most (85 per cent in 1918) aircraft were lost over enemy territory.[70] In this war, to be a casualty was more often than not to die or languish in an enemy prison camp. This is the reverse of the Australian infantryman's experience, who if a casualty was approximately two and a half times more likely to be wounded or taken prisoner than killed in action.[71]

Death's presence was amplified in the insular world of squadron and flight, where everyone knew each other well. Fatalities provided airmen with a striking premonition of their own deaths—or, as Winter put it, 'the man who had died had worn the same uniform, flown the same type of aeroplane and had done the same sort of work as the survivors'.[72] The prospect of dying was a constant around which all other aspects of the First World War aviator's life revolved. Some flyers responded with a fatalistic resignation, sometimes mixed with religious sentiment that became a characteristic feature of the flying corps' culture. Owen Lewis described himself as 'a poor blighter who can see no chance of ever getting home again'[73] after the deaths of several colleagues, including an old school mate. 'Trusting in providence is all you can do,' he reflected.[74] Bob Barrett, another airman in Lewis's squadron, was somewhat more fatalistic, trying to reassure his mother by writing to her: 'If Fritz has your number, it doesn't matter if you are sweeping streets in Paris, he'll get you.'[75] Through fate, providence or whatever it was, Barrett survived the war without a scratch while Lewis burned to death in his aircraft.

Witnessing a comrade fall in flames without a parachute produced a sense of helplessness that had little comparison in the war on the ground. Whereas the infantryman at least sometimes had the prospect of burying a stricken comrade and retrieving his effects, the shot-down airman was completely lost. Roy King reflected this sense of helplessness and bereavement in his description of a comrade's death. His account also suggests how quickly and unexpectedly death could strike, and the effect that a single loss had in such a small cohort:

> Before anyone could thoroughly realise what was happening, a huge, leaping ball of fire was hurtling some thousands of feet to earth ... It is a sickening sight to see one of your mates going down in a hell of flames, and to have

to sit by and not be able to render the least assistance. We went back to the aerodrome when the patrol was finished, feeling very sick at heart. We knew there would be a vacant place in the mess that night, and that the next day's cables would strike deep and remorselessly at the hearts of loving relatives at home.[76]

Eric Dibbs translated this sense of loss to a more personal level during an interview in 1976: 'I remember on at least one occasion we sat down for breakfast and we were five short—they'd all been shot down.' On another occasion, he heard two 'obviously Canadian voices' from inside his hut. But didn't get a chance to meet them. 'They went off on patrol straight away and they never came back,' Dibbs continued, emphasising how swiftly death could come to a mate. Upon embarking for leave one evening, he bid farewell to his 'great friend' and roommate, Arthur Thorndyke. The following morning while eating breakfast in London, Dibbs saw Thorndyke's name on the *Morning Post* casualty lists. Still with a touch of bewilderment in his voice in 1976, the elderly Dibbs explained to an interviewer: 'He was killed—killed in that period between the time I had said goodbye to him on the previous day and the time I was having breakfast in London.'[77]

Dibbs openly discussed his feelings during the 1970s, but he might not have done so at the time. The airmen's letters and diaries tend to deal with death in a matter-of-fact manner that is difficult for modern readers to comprehend. They rarely reveal the emotional attachments that Dibbs recalled long after the war, despite the closeness that the men had within the confines of their squadrons and flight. John Harris found it 'astonishing' how deaths were 'covered up' by the men in his squadron. 'We all feel it keenly,' he admitted to his wife, 'but no one mentions the things nearest their hearts.'[78] They instead got on with having a good time: 'they get the feeling that they may be here today gone tomorrow with the result . . . that they might as well have a merry life while it lasts'.[79] Australian airmen, it appears, perceived death as part and parcel of the job they were there to do, a literal matter of fact that at least publicly needed to be accepted with a fatalistic, religious or hedonistic resignation. 'When I went to the equipment store to draw flying gear,' wrote Uriah Hoddinott, a newly posted Australian pilot, 'I noticed two coffins and crosses with blank plates. I thought it was a rather grim advance provisioning at the time but when I found that we filled them most weeks it seemed quite a good idea in that climate.'[80]

The airman's bizarre and unbalanced lifestyle invariably led to severe physical and mental strain, meaning that, above all else, service in the AFC was often short. In No. 2 Squadron, a Western Front unit involved in fourteen months of heavy fighting, the average time served by a pilot was just sixteen weeks.[81] In Palestine, No. 1 Squadron's airmen served for slightly longer: six and a half months on average.[82] Both figures are striking because they fall far short of the RFC's standard length of tour: twelve months in a service squadron with a fortnight of leave every three months, followed by an extended break of two or three months as an instructor.

The brevity of average active service can partially be accounted for by the high casualty rate, especially among rookie pilots. But it also reflects the numbers of men who were permanently transferred from combat squadrons because of 'strain'. In No. 4 Squadron, for example, 15 per cent were admitted to hospital for 'natural causes' serious enough to end their active service careers.[83] The AIF's medical corps identified this as early as February 1918, citing in a report 'the somewhat high proportion of breakdowns among pilots and observers of the AFC in France'.[84] Yet, whereas the staff officer who wrote the report concluded this was the result of strain from prior service in the trenches, pilots like Stan Garrett might disagree. It was the flying, he claimed, that was the 'big strain on the nerves'.[85] And in his squadron it was clearly the most dangerous foe—after five months of war flying, it had lost nine men killed and three wounded; besides, in his words, 'umpteen who have been returned with nerves and heart trouble'.[86]

To borrow historian Denis Winter's fitting analogy, the Australian aviator's life was a 'Russian roulette' of comfort and combat, predictability and confusion. It was a kaleidoscopic existence unlike anything experienced by the diggers in the trenches, where something as seemingly arbitrary as a change in the weather could decide whether a man would survive for dinner and drinks in the officers' mess. Each day brought about opportunities for hot breakfasts, lunch dates with pretty French girls, tennis matches and swimming; as well as flying for monotonous hours without meeting danger or a violent tumult several kilometres above the earth and a long plummet to the ground in a burning aircraft with no parachute.

'The right backing on the ground': The air mechanic's war

Whereas the airmen experienced war in sharp, unpredictable bursts, the air mechanic's war trickled by constantly and at times tediously with little change in routine from day to day.

Ground crews in Australian squadrons were skilled tradesmen, recruited specifically for their expertise in a highly specialised field. The three main classes were fitters, riggers and armourers, positions usually filled by pre-war engine mechanics, engineers, boat-builders and cabinetmakers. The squadron also employed a range of other specialists, ranging from instrument repairers (often ex-watchmakers) to photographers, drivers, cooks and batmen.

The fitter's realm was the aircraft's engine, a true wonder of mechanical innovation in its day. His war was one long and perpetual struggle against its tendency to fail—and kill pilots—in the sky. The first step to prevent this was a careful maintenance ritual after each flight—distributor cleaned, carburettor jets given a petrol bath, oil and water drained and stored. After each five hours of flying time, the whole engine received a more thorough treatment, with care taken to detect worn components. In the days before electronics, the fitter relied upon his human senses to discern his charge's mechanical needs. An ear against the engine cowling revealed wear in the valve mechanism, a thumb stuffed into a spark plug hole indicated compression levels and the colour and smell of engine smoke would diagnose the carburettor's health. Frank Rawlinson, a fitter with No. 3 Squadron, explained how to detect a 'dud' spark plug: 'If they felt cold to touch after running the engines, they were discharged straight away.'[87]

The riggers meanwhile tended to the aircraft's intricate frame of wood, wire and fabric. Fundamentally, First World War aircraft were a series of timber-framed boxes held square by wires. Each length of wire (over 100 separate lengths capable of withstanding 120 tonnes per inch) required precision tensioning to keep the frame perfectly square and capable of straight and level flight.[88] Some 230 metres of flax fabric, doped and lacquered with a hardy—albeit flammable—nitrate cellulose finish, clothed the timber skeleton. After each 'stunt', the riggers carefully checked the airframe for bullet or shrapnel damage. Holes in the fabric were patched; damaged timber or wire required stripping, replacing and rebalancing the entire airframe. It was all highly time-consuming work, and meant that lanterns often blazed late in the hangars.

According to No. 4 Squadron's commanding officer, Wilfred McCloughry: 'The care of all machine-guns is a very important branch of work, and in a service squadron sufficient emphasis cannot be laid on the necessity for a keen and efficient Armament Officer.' He, and his dozen or so armourers—spilt up between the flights—were in charge of the squadron's Vickers and Lewis machine guns (around 80 in a two-seater squadron), ammunition, bombs, fuses, revolvers (carried by airmen) and the interrupter gears that enabled the machine-guns to fire through an aircraft's spinning propeller. The armourer's work was perhaps the most painstaking and specialised of all. The interrupter gear was extremely delicate and required constant adjustment and attention within 1/10 000th of an inch tolerance; and every single bullet that the squadron fired had to be cleaned and tested for consistency before it was fitted into a belt. A misfire of just 1/250th of a second could smash an aircraft's propeller.

All branches of work carried a weighty responsibility, as mechanical, structural and armament faults could—and did—cause fatal accidents. Rawlinson described an 'unwritten law', intended to encourage a high standard of mechanical work and reassure the officers whose lives were on the line. Pilots could, and did, order their air mechanics to accompany them aloft for test flights 'as a sort of guarantee that you had confidence in your work and were willing to take the risk with them'.[89] In a letter to his parents, Stan Nunan, an engine fitter, described how there were also 'written laws':

> I have charge of the engine of a machine. 8 cylinders, 80 HP. If it stops in the air, I would be court martialled if it was through negligence on my part. It is the very sort of job I have been dwelling on for years. I hope to be a Flight Sergeant, responsible for a dozen machines one day.[90]

As is evident from Nunan's comments, though, he perceived the responsibility with anticipation rather than trepidation. Work as an air mechanic was an opportunity for skilled tradesmen to develop unique vocational skills on some of the most complex mechanical gear of the era. Richard Williams claimed the mechanics in his squadron went home as leaders in their trade and, unlike many others in the AIF, had no trouble finding work and 'surviving' the peace.[91] It is also noteworthy that Air Mechanic Nunan, with his aspirations to become a Flight Sergeant, would within a year of writing be a distinguished pilot in No. 1 Squadron.[92] Indeed, it was possible for Australian airmen to begin their careers in the squadron workshops.

In an era preceding electronics, performing precision maintenance under active service conditions involved many hours of intensive labour. The standard working day in No. 1 Squadron over the winter of 1916–17 was seven and a quarter hours, with the caveat, 'when a machine becomes unserviceable all ranks should work overtime, until it becomes "serviceable" again'.[93] The temperamental nature of First World War airframes and engines meant this tended to be the rule rather than the exception. 'There is no forty-four hour week here,' observed Sutherland. 'These lads work night and day to keep their charges serviceable.'[94]

Squadron commanders fostered pride and devotion in the air mechanics by assigning them to specific pilots and aircraft. Riggers like Joe Bull usually had 'their' aircraft and 'their' pilots to attend to. At the end of January 1917, Bull was assigned to BE2c No. 4312. In his diaries, this aircraft ('old 4312' as he called it) received regular attention as he laboured on it, commenting with pride that 'she looks fine now, like a new bus' following an overhaul during May 1917.[95] The devotion of these specialists to their craft is further demonstrated in the memoirs of Billings, a wireless technician:

> I was fully engaged most of the time on checking and adjusting the fifty odd [wireless] sets that we had ... I am pleased to say that we never had a failure of a set attributable to mal-adjustment ... In our spare time the four of us [in the workshop] discussed technical problems and made various experiments.[96]

This commitment meant that, regardless of rank differences, air mechanics keenly felt the deaths of flying officers. Whereas empty seats in the mess and vacant beds in the officers' huts represented bereavement for the officers, missing aircraft and equipment came to symbolise the loss felt by aircraft mechanics. In his memoirs, Billings described attending 'many funerals' for pilots during his two years with a service squadron.[97] 'My wireless transmitters were kept on four shelves in our lorry and several spaces represented sets lost, and were sad reminders of men we knew.'[98]

Such feelings of dedication were recognised and reciprocated by the airmen. Sutherland, who was particularly outspoken on this subject, opened his memoir by claiming that:

> The best pilot, the prince of observers would not have been worth a burial service unless he had had the right kind of backing on the ground ... the pilot was after all, only one of a team; that there were many other chaps playing, and they all earned their Allies' guernseys.[99]

This opinion suggests an egalitarian mentality that encouraged AFC men to perceive the squadron as a community of interdependent members, united by a common cause. Sutherland, it will be recalled, dubbed it 'a kind of family team work'. Winter identified a similar mentality in the RFC, but suggested that the conventions of British class prevented officer–mechanic relationships from developing on a personal level.[100] For instance, he offers the example of handcrafted workshop souvenirs, claiming that: 'Most valued of all by the pilot, and something which by strict convention no pilot could ask for, was the walking stick made of the leather washers of petrol tin tops.'[101] Australian officers likewise valued such souvenirs, but the relaxation of formal conventions allowed them a close enough relationship with their mechanics to personally request them. Scout pilot Thomas Edols wrote to his sweetheart:

> I have got my engine mechanic making a couple of good souvenirs which if they turn out all right I will send out to you. One is a buttonhook and the other is a shoehorn. They both have fancy handles made from different materials and composites used in aeroplanes.[102]

The manner in which pilot and mechanic communicated also differed greatly between the Australian and British squadrons. Winter described the RFC relationship as bound by the 'stiffest formality', and quoted British pilot Macmillan who noticed that apologies from pilot to mechanic were rare.[103] In direct contrast to this were the experiences of Joe Bull with No. 1 Squadron:

> The Colonel went away in No. 4312 and got back just before dark. The Colonel is a fine chap and talks to us the same as he does to the Major. He always thanks us and apologises if he comes back at an inconvenient hour.[104]

Bull subsequently described several other instances of such informal exchanges between ranks. The officers of No. 1 Squadron 'shouted' the enlisted ranks Christmas dinner, there were 'officers versus men' cricket matches ('unthinkable' in British units, according to Winter) and Bull was taken on several 'stunts' (joy flights) in two-seaters: 'The Major went up to test No. 4312 and took me with him. Lieutenant Manwell kindly lent me his cap and goggles.' Bull even received food parcels from the mother of the pilot of 'his' aircraft![105]

RFC squadrons also tended to be more segregated along the lines of rank than the Australian units. Winter quoted British scout pilot Baker, who noted the 'very infrequent' visits of pilots to the hangars.[106] Likewise, Australian pilot Uriah Hoddinott, who was attached to a British squadron in Palestine, described life in the RAF as 'very different. One lost personal responsibility for, and contact with "other ranks" and did not share with them the risks and hardships of war.'[107] After spending nine months in a British squadron, Australian Stan Nunan agreed:

> A great difference is noticeable on coming back to an Australian unit. The men here have a much better time. They are not bullied by NCOs like poor Tommy [i.e. British mechanics] and are not the least bit scared of officers. The CO is the only one who is ever called 'sir'. As mechanics get 8/- and 9/- per day they put in a little towards messing and have as good a mess as the officers.[108]

Bull concurred, noting how the pilots in No. 1 Squadron treated the air mechanics like equals, 'smoking a pipe and having a yarn with them'. He claimed that, like officers in the light horse, they did not insist on 'saluting and standing to attention and all that rot'.[109]

Although relaxed compared with British conventions, rank conventions in the AFC were by no means non-existent. There was a line—usually dependent on the squadron commander's attitude—and officers were sharply reminded when they crossed it. On Christmas Eve 1916, for example, some of No. 1 Squadron's airmen celebrated in the sergeants' mess. The squadron's commanding officer paraded them in his office the following morning to reprimand and remind them of their responsibilities as leaders to the men.[110] The AFC also readily adopted 'British' conventions into other aspects of squadron life to govern accommodation, messing and fatigue duties, not to mention the exclusive social composition of the Australian squadrons themselves. Indeed, it is intriguing to consider the AFC's informal approach to inter-rank relationships among some otherwise very traditional British military conventions.

The explanation lies in the AFC's unique place within the First World War's social, cultural and military structures. Existing within the spheres of both the Australian Imperial Force and the Royal Flying Corps, the AFC developed its own unique and complex set of rules, conventions and cultural motifs. These were then shaped and transformed in the isolated limbo of the service aerodrome and by the distinctive circumstances under which the pilots, observers and ground crew of the AFC lived, worked and died.

3
'THIS GOD-FORSAKEN COUNTRY'
Egypt and Sinai, 1916

C Flight of No. 1 Squadron with a Martinsyde scout, in early 1917. From left, Frank McNamara (the AFC's only Victoria Cross recipient), Leonard Heathcote (taken prisoner, March 1917), Richard Williams (later the squadron's commanding officer), Stan Muir (claimed the AFC's first victory and killed in 1917), Eric Roberts (sent home on the verge of nervous breakdown in March 1917) and Lawrence Wackett (devised a means to drop ammunition crates from aircraft in 1918). *AWM A05340*

> Anyway, off we went, no tools no nothing, equipped as infantry, with sword and pistol to Egypt.
>
> —Captain Richard Williams, No. 1 Squadron, Australian Flying Corps

'One great British camp': Egypt, 1916

The year 1915 had been a good one for Turkey. In addition to halting two invasion attempts by the British (at Gallipoli and Mesopotamia), it had secured neighbouring Bulgaria as an ally and successfully conquered Serbia. At the beginning of 1916, then, Turkey faced no immediate threats from its neighbours or the Allies; thus leaving its military leaders to contemplate expanding their empire, from its southern limits in Palestine, across the Suez and into British Egypt.

German military planners advocated Turkish expansion into northern Africa, as it would undermine Britain's strategic position. In the century preceding the war, the Suez Canal had been a vital link between Britain and its colonies in the East. Its importance multiplied in wartime, enabling Britain's main defensive asset, the Royal Navy, fast passage between the Eastern and Western Hemispheres. Beyond the canal, Egypt itself was a hub of British communications and logistics, Australia's official historian describing it as one 'great British camp' on account of its globally central location, vast space for training and accommodation, and plentiful fresh produce.[1]

During 1915, the British defended the Suez only thinly, from trenches dug on its banks. The inadequacy of their preparations was demonstrated by a nearly successful Turkish raid in February 1915, and then pointed out quite brusquely by the British Secretary of State for War, Lord Kitchener, who after inspecting them concluded: 'Instead of you guarding the canal, the canal is guarding you.'[2] Subsequently, in January 1916, General Sir Archibald Murray took command of the British forces in this region (the Egyptian Expeditionary Force) and reorganised Egypt's defences. He reasoned that, with such meagre forces at his disposal, it would be more economical to mount an aggressive forward defence of the Sinai's main routes and oases (about a 70 kilometre front) than to passively defend the entire canal (some 140 kilometres).

On 20 February 1916, the first British forces set out to secure the wells and oases around Katia. Lying about two days' march east of the canal, these would be a vital staging point for a future Turkish invasion force. The British advance was slow, as Murray's men needed to build a railway and supply network behind them. On 7 April, the British 5th Mounted Brigade arrived at Romani, about 8 kilometres short of the Katia wells. Its commander then—quite carelessly, as it turned out—split his forces up and scattered them to a number of outposts among the region's oases. On 23 April, a bold Turkish raid isolated and destroyed those at Oghratina, Dueidar and Katia itself. Casualties among the unsupported British garrisons were extreme. Considering this the beginning of the Turkish invasion, Murray immediately sent the Australian 2nd Light Horse Brigade from Kantara to secure Romani. Intending to avoid the folly of his predecessor, Major General Harry Chauvel, commanding officer of the Anzac Mounted Division, concentrated his defences on Romani itself, intending to defend the outlying oases with aggressive patrolling. On the first anniversary of the Anzac landing, the 2nd Light Horse Brigade rode into Romani and began work on its defences. Meanwhile, back in Cairo, Australia's first military aviators were making their own preparations to meet the Turkish invasion of Egypt.

'Off we went, no tools, no nothing...': No. 1 Squadron embarks for war

The 195 men and twenty-eight officers of No. 1 Squadron boarded the transport *Orsova* in Port Melbourne on 16 March 1916. Apart from the clothes on their backs, the squadron had almost no equipment, just a couple of cars and a handful of motorcycles privately owned by squadron members. It embarked with no aircraft, as the squadron's commanding officer, Lieutenant Colonel Edgar Reynolds, expected to receive machines from the RFC overseas. 'Off we went,' recalled Richard Williams, 'no tools no nothing, equipped as infantry, with sword and pistol to Egypt.'[3]

After leaving Port Melbourne, the *Orsova* struck west, through the rough seas of the Great Australian Bight. There was a brief pause in Fremantle to pick up mail before sailing northeast across the Indian Ocean. The squadron's officers maintained a daily routine of parades, kit inspection, lectures and drill. They also encouraged physical activity, with deck cricket proving a favourite. Eric Roberts, a 22-year-old accountant from Melbourne who had been selected as a pilot because of his enthusiasm for motorcycles and engines, never forgot 'the excitement and thrill of our first touch with the tropics beginning with a magnificent sunrise over Ceylon'. No. 1 Squadron was the first contingent of Australian troops allowed ashore for nearly a year, following bad behaviour by men on their way to Gallipoli. 'We were put on our honour and the Squadron, to its credit, achieved this objective,' recalled Roberts.[4]

After four weeks, the squadron disembarked at Suez and travelled on to Tel el Kebir, where it became apparent that neither the AIF nor the RFC had been expecting it. Initially, the squadron tented down in a huge marshalling camp and the men did drill, kit inspections and route marches while the officers struggled to find out what the squadron was supposed to be doing. 'Speculation is rife as to whether we go to England or stay in Egypt,' noted Roberts in his diary.[5]

Clarification came a week later, on 21 April 1916, when No. 1 Squadron was attached to 5th Wing RFC. The men were split up between the local British squadrons (Nos 14 and 17) for some much-needed training. Practically all the mechanics had done little beyond swing a propeller, and even the most experienced pilots had done no combat training whatsoever. All observers, five of the least experienced pilots and the equipment officer went to England for instruction.

Eric Roberts was among them. He arrived at Netheravon aerodrome on 31 May, and found himself in the midst of a chaotic and overstrained training program. Under pressure to rapidly form new squadrons for front-line service while also replacing the RFC's steady flow of casualties, the RFC in 1916 was severely under-resourced. It lacked instructors and suitable aircraft, and hadn't had the opportunity to develop an effective training doctrine. The result was that, at this stage of the war, around 10 per cent of training aircraft were being wrecked each day.[6] Roberts was quickly acquainted with the dangers:

> The day after my arrival was perfect with piles of cumulus cloud and a lovely blue sky. I was out on the aerodrome in the morning sun learning Morse code while waiting for my aeroplane to come down from a height test. Suddenly I heard a screeching of wire in the clouds and looking up, saw the aeroplane I was due to fly emerge from a cloud in a steep dive. I knew the pilot, he was a Canadian and I had had breakfast with him that morning. I could see he was in trouble. He wrenched at the control column to try and right the aeroplane and when he did this a wing came off and the aeroplane dived from three thousand feet straight into the ground.

That afternoon, Roberts witnessed another crash that burned a man to death. It left a striking impression on him; 60 years later, he claimed: 'It was a terrible shock and even today I can still see the plume of black smoke mounting up into the sky from what minutes before had been an aeroplane and my friend.'[7]

Roberts survived training and rejoined No. 1 Squadron in September, but one of his mates wasn't so lucky. Twenty-one-year-old Charles Merrett became No. 1 Squadron's first death on active service in a training accident at Dover on 16 May 1916. The cycle of ineffective and dangerous training was perpetuated when, on returning to Egypt, Roberts spent time as an instructor at the RFC flying school—this before he had even crossed the front line.

Meanwhile, in Egypt during April and May, the rest of the men trained with RFC squadrons. Each of the Australian mechanics buddied up with one of his British counterparts. At the end of each week, his progress would be assessed and graded. Within six weeks, 80 per cent of No. 1 Squadron's ground staff qualified as proficient in their roles. The fact the squadron had culled Australia's most capable technical minds and hands was immediately evident, as twenty-year-old electrician Arthur Mott demonstrated during his 'apprenticeship' with a British squadron:

> Did a magneto for Lt Badgery's machine. Found it in an awful state, and yet the 'experts' who had been at work on it couldn't discover anything. One man (who calls himself an electrician and magneto expert) proved conclusively that he should be making wheel barrows rather than repairing mags.[8]

The pilots did no flying at first, but familiarised themselves with the Lewis gun, air cameras and wireless buzzer transmitters—all standard gear in a service squadron in 1916, but quite foreign to the Point Cook graduates.[9] The Australians impressed the RFC's commanding officer in the Middle East, Major General Geoffrey Salmond, who noted that their progress 'reflected great credit on the industry, keenness and discipline of officers and all ranks'.[10] With that endorsement, No. 1 Squadron came together at Heliopolis on 1 July 1916 to officially commence its active service. Major Forster

Rutledge, an Australian in the RFC, assumed command of the squadron. Since arriving in Egypt, it had been shuffled between commanding officers, but Rutledge would command the unit until May 1917. He was an enthusiastic aviator, but lacked administrative skills. His legacy is a disappointing gap in the official records relating to the squadron during his command.[11]

'An auxiliary to the troops on the ground': First steps, July 1916

The work for which No. 1 Squadron's airmen and ground crew were preparing was spelt out in a July 1916 RFC circular. Whereas later in the war squadrons were assigned specialised roles, at this stage they usually did a bit of everything:

> The Royal Flying Corps with a force of all arms [will] carry out:
>
> a. Tactical Reconnaissance
> b. Direction and observation of artillery fire
> c. Fighting against other aircraft
> d. Special missions (Long reconnaissance, bombing and incendiary raids)
> e. Offensive action against troops on the ground[12]

As Williams later summed up: 'In those days aircraft were looked upon by the army as an auxiliary ... to the troops on the ground.'[13] Initially designated a 'corps squadron', No. 1 Squadron's principal duties involved supporting the ground forces immediately on an allotted section of the front. It would do this primarily through tactical (i.e. close-range) reconnaissance—which included both observing and photographing enemy front-line positions—and directing artillery fire. Further, as the circular stated, the squadron would 'be acting in conjunction' with mounted patrols on the ground, 'drop[ping] messages to the Column if anything important is seen'. Indeed, during the latter half of 1916, No. 1 Squadron would become known as the 'eyes of the ANZAC Mounted Division'.[14]

Initially, there were not enough aircraft in the resource-starved Middle Eastern theatre to fully equip No. 1 Squadron. The Australians split up into flights (A, B, C and Headquarters) and took what they could get. Some of the unit's first aircraft came from No. 17 Squadron RFC, which was moving to Salonika. These were BE2c biplanes, fragile-looking two-seaters with

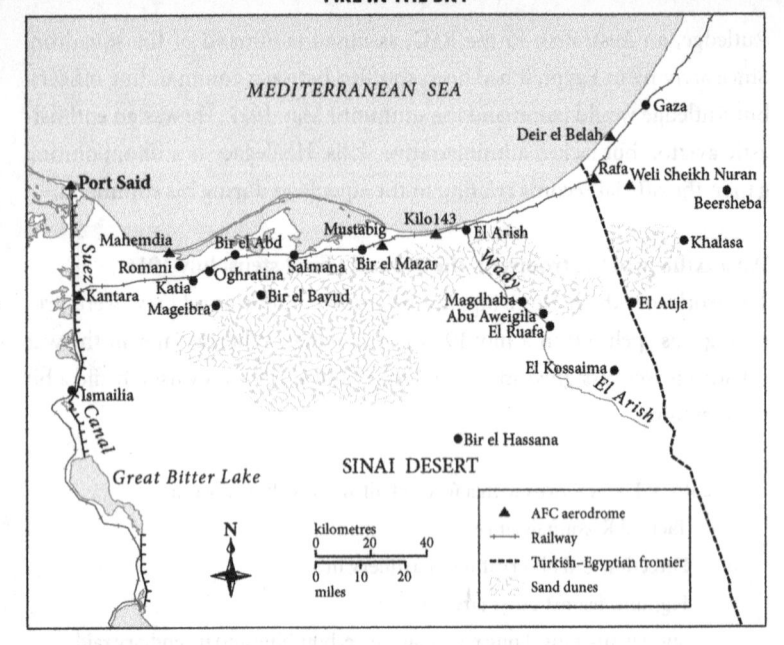

MAP 2 Egypt–Sinai, 1916

a distinctively tapered fuselage. Unlike later two-seaters, the observer sat in the front seat of the 'BE'—a disadvantage, according to Williams, who thought he could 'hardly have been in a worse position as far as gunnery, and indeed, observation, was concerned'.[15] A rear-facing Lewis gun was mounted awkwardly between the pilot and observer. Roberts considered it 'really quite useless as a defensive weapon, and was put there, I think to boost morale!'[16] The BE2c was also under-powered (it had a top speed of 115 kph), and didn't stand up well to the desert conditions (see Plate 3).

With whatever equipment and aircraft they could muster, the flights were posted to various aerodromes scattered around the Suez Canal and Mediterranean coastal areas to begin active service flying.

Captain William Sheldon, a 26-year-old pre-war professional soldier from Melbourne, led A Flight at Sherika, an oasis outpost, over 160 kilometres into the Egyptian desert west of Luxor. There, the flight waged war against the Senussi Arabs, Egyptian nationalists who were operating to destabilise British control of the Western Desert. It was A Flight's job to intimidate them with aircraft and regularly fix their location with reconnaissance patrols. One of the pilots distinguished himself as particularly intrepid when, in early November, a British Camel Corps patrol went missing. Twenty-one-year-old Allan Murray Jones, who had left a pharmacy job in Melbourne to enlist, volunteered to mount a solo search for the survivors. On 7 November, he flew 160 kilometres to Shusha where he spent the night, before making an eight-hour search over the Bahria Oasis and its surrounds the following day. Unfortunately, he found no sign of the cameleers and some months later their remains were found. This sort of conduct came to characterise Murray Jones' flying, and would later earn him a Military Cross, a Distinguished Flying Cross and bar, and the command of a squadron on the Western Front.

B and C Flights meanwhile occupied the more active canal sector. Both were commanded by men who would, over the next two years, become leading figures in the AFC. B Flight's commander, Oswald Watt, was the AFC's most experienced pilot, having flown since 1911. After purchasing his own Bleriot XI monoplane, he flew privately in Egypt and France during 1913 and 1914. At the beginning of the war, he joined the Service d'Aviation Militaire.[17] With the French, Watt experienced the pioneering days of air combat on the Western Front, when aviators fired rifles and pistols at each other. Watt's outstanding flying abilities and aggressive approach to combat earned him the Legion d' Honneur and Croix de Guerre. He ended his service with the French in 1916 and transferred into the AFC. A taskmaster with an abrupt manner ('I am an Australian and I haven't got any manners' is how he once introduced himself to a British colleague), Watt was also renowned for his dedication to the welfare of his men.[18]

Watt's flight received four BE2cs and took over No. 17 Squadron's old aerodrome at Suez. There it commenced a routine of reconnaissance flights over the forward Turkish outposts in the Sinai. The observers carefully watched for changes in the number of enemy camps, which might indicate an imminent invasion. B Flight also made some early attempts at bombing and photographing these positions. The latter proved difficult, however, due to shortcomings in the photographic equipment. At this stage of the war, cameras were bulky units attached to the outside of the pilot's cockpit. To take a photograph, he needed to remove a glass exposure plate from its light-proof packaging and load it into the camera. After exposing it, he then had to return it to its dark envelope without losing it to the slipstream, and then repeat the process. Difficulties faced by the unit's photographic section, which had to make do with an aeroplane shipping case as a darkroom, further complicated the process of getting clear pictures.[19]

As mentioned previously, C Flight's commander Richard Williams was first to qualify for his wings at Point Cook. Popularly known as 'Dicky', Williams revealed himself to be a meticulous, professional and clean-living man who didn't drink, smoke or swear. Indeed, one of his pilots remembered 'his most dashing expletive was "darn me!"'. Williams was a consummate professional: his uniform never featured personal embellishments and he was intensely serious and did not fraternise with, or have favourites among, the men. He took administration seriously—indeed, scanning through the squadron's reconnaissance reports in the archives today, Williams' stand out for their careful attention to detail. He behaved himself impeccably on leave and kept up a prodigious stream of letters to his wife. With No. 1 Squadron, Williams would prove a courageous and supremely capable officer—a 'leader born', in observer Les Sutherland's assessment.[20]

C Flight remained with Headquarters Flight at Heliopolis and, with its pair of BE2cs, spent July working with No. 14 Squadron RFC over the coastal sector. It reconnoitred the front held by the Australian light horse around Bir el Mazar and Maghara, and Turkish positions between Magdhaba and El Arish. The pilots gained some rudimentary bombing experience on operations over these targets with No. 14 Squadron, as well as some practice directing naval gunfire on to enemy entrenchments near the coast.[21]

The AFC's arrival in Egypt coincided with that of the German Air Service's first squadron, Fleiger Abteilung 300 'Pascha' (FA 300). Unlike its green and poorly equipped Australian opponents, though, FA 300 contained sixteen Western Front veterans and half a dozen brand-new Rumpler CI aircraft. With their 160 horsepower engines and rear-facing machine gun (operated by an observer in the back seat—much more effective than the arrangement in the British BE2 machines), these two-seaters, noted an Australian officer, were 'superior to any of ours in both climb and speed and could do what they wished'.[22] And so they did. Throughout June and July, the German squadron operated from an advanced landing strip at El Arish (with its main aerodrome at Beersheba). FA 300's aircraft ranged quite freely over the canal, scrutinising its defensive positions and bombing British ports and depots to disrupt supply and communication to the front. British mounted units, with their conspicuous lines of horses or camels, were particularly susceptible to air attack from enemy aircraft. On 1 June, a lone German aircraft dropped eight bombs from 8000 feet on the 1st Light Horse Brigade at Romani. They fell right among the troops' tents and horse-lines. The official historian reported that the horses broke their ropes and, 'frantic with fear, galloped for many miles; a few reached Port Said, nearly thirty miles away, and some were never recovered'. The casualties caused by this lone German raider were alarming: one officer and seven light horsemen died and another three officers and nineteen men were wounded. Recognising the importance of controlling the air above his forces, General Murray afterwards pressed the War Office to send more and better aircraft.[23]

During a visit to No. 14 Squadron's aerodrome at Kantara, Williams witnessed the unnerving result of German technical superiority on British work in the air. Upon landing, he saw a 'disconsolate-looking BE2c standing in the open, fabric torn, rigging wires cut, and with signs of having been hit by over 90 bullets'. Apparently a German scout had surprised its pilot, diving from above and behind. The first hail of bullets killed the observer and destroyed the throttle. For several minutes, it made passes on the defenceless British machine, raking it with fire before breaking off, apparently out of ammunition.[24] 'You would have found it difficult to believe,' recalled Williams, 'that the chappie could have lived in it because there were the instruments in front of him and they were shattered.'[25]

'One of the decisive battles of the war': The Battle of Romani, July–August 1916

While No. 1 Squadron commenced its first operational flights, British and Australian mounted units strengthened their bastion at Romani and patrolled the desert wells. When the expected Turkish invasion force came, the northern canal sector's commanding officer, Major General H.A. Lawrence, planned to draw them in, at the absolute extremity of their supply lines, against well-prepared and supplied defensive positions. Once they had committed their reserves, Lawrence planned to unleash a strong counter-attack to encircle and destroy them. The scheme hinged on timing: Lawrence would need a comprehensive and up-to-date picture of the battlefield to strike at the opportune moment. This was where the one weakness of the British plan lay, for Lawrence had established his headquarters 37 kilometres behind Romani, at Kantara.

The first sign of an imminent Turkish attempt to seize the wells occurred on 19 July, when a British pilot took Brigadier General Edward Chaytor (the New Zealand Mounted Rifles Brigade's commanding officer) up to look over the ground and spotted a force of some 8000 enemy troops and transport massing at Bayud, Bir Jameil and Bir el Abd. The Turks edged closer over the next twelve nights, their progress being reported by No. 14 Squadron—which Australian pilots from B and C Flights joined—each morning. They held back from bombing the Turkish columns on Lawrence's instructions, to lure them into the encirclement scheme at Romani.[26]

On 25 July, the airmen discovered FA 300 had shifted forwards to an advanced landing strip at Bir el Abd. Three days later, they spotted three columns of Turks moving towards the British lines. By evening, they were digging in between Oghratina and Mageibra, just 16 kilometres from the British front line at Romani. Over the next two days, reconnaissance flights charted movements of Turkish reinforcements in the back areas. These abruptly stopped on 31 July, suggesting the Turks were in position and ready to strike. The pilots estimated the Turkish force's strength at 13 000; later evidence would suggest it was actually closer to 18 000.

When the Turks halted on their outpost line, Lawrence lifted the embargo on air attacks. On 1 August, Australian pilots Alfred Ellis and Lawrence Wackett joined a seven-aircraft bombing raid on those positions. Richard Williams meanwhile tried his hand at directing artillery fire from an offshore naval vessel on to the Turkish positions around Oghratina. This required him to observe the fall of shell and then transmit aiming corrections to the gun crew via wireless buzzer. It was a process that would come to play a vital role in British tactics, but was still in its infancy on this front. 'They were slinging over 18 inch stuff,' recalled Williams. 'It knocked a lot of sand about but that's about all.'[27] Indeed, the Turks had further bolstered their forces there the following morning, including anti-aircraft guns. The Germans were active in the air, too. FA 300's aircraft roamed with impunity over the Australian positions, bombing the light horse at Romani on 31 July.

On 3 August there was outpost fighting combined with bombing attacks by both sides. Alfred Ellis, Wackett and a British pilot with No. 14 Squadron bombed the Turkish front line while Williams escorted them in a single-seater Bristol Scout. The British pilot's aircraft was damaged by anti-aircraft fire, but the flight suffered no casualties. In preparation for the imminent Turkish attack, General Murray sent an RFC officer to the advanced landing ground at Romani under instructions to transmit an emergency wireless signal once the battle began. On receiving this, No. 14 Squadron would send up pilots to determine the main direction of the Turkish attack, and mark it with smoke.

At midnight on the night of 3–4 August, a force of 18 000 Turks attacked the light horse listening posts in front of the Romani defence line. The Australians crumbled and began a fighting withdrawal back towards Romani. They slowed the Turkish advance considerably, but by dawn desperately needed reinforcements. At first light, Williams and fellow No. 1 Squadron pilot William Ascroft were out over the battlefield to assess the situation. They reported that the Turks had 'advanced considerably' and were shelling the Romani camp. The long telephone line between the front and Lawrence's headquarters had been cut (probably by saboteurs) during the night. So, for the rest of the day, Ascroft operated off an advanced landing ground at Romani that was under shellfire to keep the local commander informed of the Turkish movements, which included an attempt to out-flank the British positions. Williams meanwhile relayed information between the battle and Lawrence's headquarters, 37 kilometres away.[28] 'One remembers,' wrote Williams years later, 'landing at Romani after escorting a reconnaissance to find the landing ground under enemy artillery fire and our artillery in action in their wagon lines.'[29]

British pilots from No. 14 Squadron directed artillery fire from an offshore monitor on to Turkish camps, scoring four direct hits. Others patrolled behind the Turkish lines, eagerly watching for any sign of enemy reserves. They reported none. All seventeen aircraft available to 5th Wing RFC were airborne that day, with most of the aviators making two or three trips over the battlefield.[30]

FA 300 was active over the battlefield too. By flying faster and higher in their superior machines, the Germans could avoid combat and concentrate on bombing the hard-pressed defenders on the ground. At 6.00 a.m., eight Rumplers bombed the light horse lines.[31] Bert Billings, who would later volunteer for the flying corps, scribbled in his diary:

> Heavy firing. Turks in mass—can't be stopped. 8 Planes bombed hell out of this place. One of our planes sent to ground ... things serious ... The planes gave us a devil of a doing and practically no opposition from us—machine gun fire which is not up to much and few odd shots from howitzers. The planes coursed us all over the joint, one falling within fifty yds of Iky [his horse] and I but we dodge[d] the bits. It is a funny situation when you go for your life at 6–7 miles an hour and kid yourself you can dodge the plane going at 60–70mph.[32]

By mid-afternoon, though, the Turks had been fought to a standstill, and Lawrence unleashed his counter-attack. At 6.00 p.m., the first group of 500 surrendered and it became obvious that the enemy had little hope of recovering the initiative. The Australian official historian noted that, 'despite the break in communications, both Lawrence and Murray had been kept informed of the main developments of the fight.'[33] What he did not mention, however, is that it was perhaps largely due to the efforts of Williams and Ascroft that communication—and hence control of the battle—was maintained.

At dawn on 5 August, the Turkish force broke and began a fighting withdrawal. It briefly held up the pursuing British and Australian troops at Katia, Bir el Abd and Salmana before retiring 80 kilometres to El Arish. Wackett, Ellis and Stan Muir (all attached to No. 14 Squadron RFC working out of Ismailia) bombed the retreating Turks, while Williams and Murray Jones, operating from Kantara, provided commanders with regular updates on their whereabouts.

On 10 August, when the enemy had well and truly retired, the Australians attached to No. 14 Squadron returned to their respective flights. Although No. 1 Squadron had suffered no casualties during the battle, five British airmen had been wounded and one killed. The RFC had forced down a single German aircraft.

Although the Turkish invasion force was not completely destroyed, as

Lawrence had planned, the Battle of Romani was a resounding success for the Egyptian Expeditionary Force. Official historian Charles Bean regarded it as 'one of the decisive battles of the war'. It cost the Turks dearly (9250 killed or captured) and inspired the British towards a more ambitious and aggressive strategy in the Middle East.[34] It also provided some of the Australian airmen with their first experience of battle, while clearly denoting their foremost role in this theatre—that is, supporting the troops and their commanders on the ground by maintaining contact and communication across large areas of country during a moving battle. At the same time, Romani highlighted the distinct advantage held by the German pilots in their superior machines and the menace this posed for the Australian and British pilots.

'Two divisions of would-be pilots': Light horse reinforcements

Following the AFC's debut at the Battle of Romani, No. 1 Squadron at once became a centre of attraction for curious Australian troops who had never seen an aircraft up close. Williams recalled: 'We had light horsemen swarming in to have a look at what we were doing, and amongst them, were some very good tradesmen who immediately started to inquire as to how they could get into the flying corps.'[35]

One of them was George Mills, a 30-year-old dentist from Sydney who had fought with the light horse at Romani. A German aircraft had bombed his camp during the battle, and—while it caused no serious damage—it certainly left an impression on Mills, who henceforth decided to transfer to the flying corps. He was motivated by a desire to be on the giving rather than receiving end of this new force in warfare, as well as to be independent of direct command: 'Once in the air, you were your own boss,' he later put it.[36] Twenty-two-year-old Reginald Forsyth of North Sydney was another keen volunteer. Wounded at Romani, he applied for a commission in the AFC while convalescing in Cairo. Following his first entry test (riding a motorcycle), Forsyth wrote to his parents, explaining that he wanted 'to get into the air' because 'in this life is where my future lies. Aviation in Australia after the war is going to be a big thing.'[37] Shortly after he was accepted into flight training, he described the AFC as a 'splendid corps' that offered 'plenty of chance of bettering myself far past anything I could have been in the [light horse] Regiment'.[38] Such were the aspirations of these ambitious Australian volunteers for the first air war.

Williams believed ex-light horsemen were far superior to the temporary British observers the squadron had been making do with as they had a first-hand knowledge of the terrain and light horse patrol tactics. The selectors apparently felt this way too. Les Sutherland, another volunteer from the light horse, remarked that they 'chose the crack horsemen, the musicians—the men with the hands ... Fitness was a point in the applicants' favour. Not fitness bought about by hard work and hard rations, but the fitness developed by sports, like tennis, swimming and cricket.' Still, this didn't discourage many from trying. According to Sutherland, 'at times it almost seemed as if there were nearly two divisions of would be pilots waiting on our squadron doorstep'.[39]

With new observers, the Australian flights—still scattered at this time—also received more equipment and began to operate more independently. With its own aircraft, C Flight occupied Port Said and cooperated with B Flight (at Suez) to support General Murray's push along the Sinai coast towards Palestine. The advance eastward was slow, only able to progress as fast as its supplies—particularly water—could follow it. After their defeat at Romani the Turks fell back to a line extending from El Arish and Magdhaba. Screening their main bastion, they fortified outposts at Bir el Mazar and Masaid.

'The eyes of the light horse': The outpost raids, September–October 1916

While the British main force paused to wait for the construction of a water pipe and railway, the Australian airmen kept the pressure on these Turkish strongholds. Stan Muir, a 24-year-old Victorian who had trained with the RFC and joined No. 1 Squadron in Egypt in July, led C Flight to bomb Bir el Mazar on 3 and 7 September. In the first raid, he dropped twelve bombs and managed to score direct hits on tents and anti-aircraft batteries. On 17 September, C and B flights again visited Bir el Mazar, this time to support a raid on its Turkish garrison by the Anzac Mounted Division. The 1st, 2nd and 3rd Light Horse Brigades surrounded and attacked the entrenched Turks at dawn. They met stiff resistance but managed to capture some positions and sabotage Turkish communications. Overhead, No. 1 Squadron kept a vigil, watching the approaching roads for Turkish reinforcements and keeping the Mounted Division's staff informed with handwritten notes dropped on their headquarters throughout the morning. FA 300 was over the battlefield too, bombing and machine gunning the light horse with its new Rumplers, which had machine guns that could fire forward through the propeller using an interrupter gear.

Richard Williams wasn't leading C Flight over Bir el Mazar that morning because he had been reconnoitring the village the afternoon before when his aircraft suddenly began to shudder: 'The engine started to throw oil heavily and I was covered in castor oil from head to seat; it was difficult to keep my goggles clear.' Feeling obliged to remain with the light horsemen, he did so for 90 minutes until his engine seized, forcing him down near some British mounted troops. They helped him disassemble his aircraft and cart it on some mule-drawn service wagons to a railhead. From there, he rode overnight with his charge, arriving back at the aerodrome the following afternoon looking, in his words, like 'a member of the Egyptian labour corps'.[40] Williams arrived to the disappointing news that the light horse had failed to capture Bir el Mazar.

Five days after the raid, aerial reconnaissance revealed that the Turks had nonetheless abandoned their position and fallen back to Masaid. The pilots pursued them, with Williams and two other C Flight pilots bombing their camp on 5 October. Four of Williams' bombs failed to explode, illustrating the frustrating unreliability of British-made explosives in 1916. Muir had better luck, dropping twelve bombs on El Arish on the same day. Two exploded in the town's centre and ten hit the surrounding camps, all with 'good effect'.[41] Like much of the squadron's equipment at this time, bombsights were an improvised affair developed through patient trial and error by the pilots themselves. As Roberts explained: 'The method being used when I arrived at our Squadron was to line up the rear spar on the left hand bottom main plane on the target and then to release the bombs according to your height. It was remarkable how well this method worked.'[42]

On 15 October, No. 1 Squadron supported another raid led by the light horse, this time against the Turkish outpost at Maghara. An old settlement of stone houses 80 kilometres southeast of Romani, it needed clearing before Murray's main force could advance further along the coast towards El Arish.

Travelling across 'one of the most desolated and difficult expanses of dune country in all northern Sinai', the light horsemen rode through the night, arriving below the hill-top village at dawn.[43] Meanwhile, pilots from C and B Flights flew to Salmana, refuelled, 'bombed up' and ate breakfast before taking off again for Maghara. While the raiders assembled in concealed jumping-off positions, Oswald Watt flew along the two approaches up to Maghara for an hour, through heavy fog, trying to ascertain the better route for them. Foolishly, some of the Turkish garrison fired on him, revealing their positions among the rocks.[44] Watt concluded that the passes were 'being held by very small concealed forces with Machine Guns' and dropped a message to warn the light horse commander, General Dallas. His orders were not to risk capturing the position if it was heavily held, but rather to make a reconnaissance and show of force.

The 11th and 12th Light Horse advanced on foot up the rugged slopes, using the mist and rocky outcrops for cover. The scattered pockets of Turks were surprised and, under fire from some British mountain guns and the aircraft overhead, retreated into the village. The pilots bombed them as the light horsemen advanced. Roberts had a close shave when an enemy machine gunner put a bullet through the back of his seat, just behind his spine.[45]

After dropping their bombs, Williams and the other pilots kept in touch with the light horse by dropping written messages in weighted bags. The horsemen responded by laying out strips of cloth. It was a rough and ready communication system but it did the trick. As the raiders reached the edge of the town, Williams noticed them turn around and begin to withdraw. He dropped a message asking them to lay out a signal 'K' if there was a general retirement or an 'L' if it was not. They promptly showed him a 'K', General Dallas having ordered their withdrawal. As they moved back down the slopes, Williams dropped another message warning them that they represented an ideal target for enemy aircraft in their bunched formation.[46]

After refuelling at Mahemdia for the homeward journey, the crews landed in darkness, guided by burning petrol cans. For most of the pilots, it was their first night landing. Remarkably, there were no accidents.

This rudimentary form of ground–air cooperation took on increasing importance as the British sought to control the ground in front of the main enemy line at El Arish. No. 1 Squadron spent much of October and

November supporting long-range camel and light horse patrols out into the desert. Flying corps mechanics accompanied mounted units with supplies to set up advanced landing grounds.[47] In the 1970s, an elderly Roberts fondly recalled the close relationship that No. 1 Squadron had with the light horse in the early days:

> We'd go over to their mess and they'd come over to ours ... but first, in a way, we became the eyes of the light horse. Before they used to have to send out LH patrols. Well as they got to know us they began to use us as their intelligence agents to supply them with information on all the enemy movements out in the desert.[48]

'Tinsydes': First experiences of aerial combat, October and November 1916

On 16 October, C Flight inherited the squadron's first Martinsyde G100 single-seat scout. Nicknamed 'Tinsyde' by the Australians, it had much better performance than the BE2c (a top speed of 150 kph compared with 115 kph) and, perhaps more importantly, was armed, sporting two Lewis guns (one firing forward over the wing, and another off centre on the port side). It therefore took on the role of the flight's escort machine. The extra speed took at least one of the pilots by surprise. Williams cleaned up a tent on his first attempt at landing it.[49]

To counter the new German aircraft with their forward-firing guns, Lawrence Wackett, a pilot renowned for his exceptional design and engineering skills, attempted to improve the BE2c's armament. In the squadron workshops, he knocked together 'an elementary form of gun turret' positioned in the top wing, above the observer's seat. Standing up on his seat, with his head and shoulders above the top wing, he could aim the Lewis gun 'anywhere in the upper hemisphere'.[50]

Throughout October and November, the Martinsyde and Wackett's BE2c escorted the other BE2cs on photographic reconnaissance over the Turkish front line in the El Arish region. They flew in formation to take overlapping photographs of tracts of countryside below them, which British surveyors then turned into maps of the Turkish positions. After taking their photographs, the Australians regularly bombed and strafed enemy camps.

The Turks were not the only ones to suffer under No. 1 Squadron's machine guns. Williams recalled being on patrol in front of some light horse when he spotted four Arabs with camels. His observer, Turner, asked whether he could have 'a few shots at them', to which Williams agreed. Turner opened fire, and had 'great fun' until he accidentally shot part of the propeller away. Williams managed to nurse the aircraft home, but later contemplated: 'I hate to think what would have happened to us [had we been forced to land] right alongside those Arabs.'[51] This sort of behaviour must have been fairly common, as No. 1 Squadron received a circular from General Salmond on 19 October 1916 stating: 'An idea seems to have gained ground among pilots and observers that they are required to attack camels or flocks of goats in the course of their reconnaissances.' It went on to impress that pilots 'should carefully avoid attacking camels or flocks belonging to peaceful Bedouins' as they may 'at any time have to avail themselves of the[ir] services'.[52]

During the first week of November, No. 1 Squadron's photographic machines produced a comprehensive picture of the Turkish defences that now roughly ran along the wady (a dry ravine) between El Arish and Magdhaba. On 8 November, A Flight moved from Sherika to Kantara aerodrome, placing all four flights in the Sinai region for the first time. The squadron was thus able to make more concerted efforts, the first of which came on 11 November when it mounted the largest bombing raid yet to be undertaken by British forces in the theatre. Beersheba was the target, site of the Turkish Army headquarters and FA 300's main aerodrome. At dawn, nine BE2cs and a Martinsyde flew from their aerodromes and assembled at Mustabig. Eight of the BE2cs carried only a pilot so that they could take extra bombs and fuel. The Martinsyde and Wackett's BE2c escorted them. The formation refuelled and set out at 8.30 a.m. Approaching Beersheba, they were greeted with heavy anti-aircraft fire, flying 'through a flurry of white, black and green shell bursts'.[53] James Guilfoyle (who had replaced Oswald Watt as B Flight's commander in October when he went to England to establish another Australian squadron) dropped a 100 lb bomb from the Martinsyde right in the middle of the German aerodrome, while others scored hits on tents, railway buildings and tracks. Two Fokker monoplanes took off and chased the Australians as they made for home. Wackett and Turner (as observer) lagged behind, and descended to the enemy's altitude to offer an appealing target. Wackett kept their tail to the enemy, allowing Turner to stand up in the turret and fire as the Fokkers closed. 'The enemy plane,' wrote the satisfied inventor, 'was completely surprised when his attack was met by a continuous fire from this new gun location and he retired immediately.'[54] Meanwhile, Guilfoyle had turned to meet the other Fokker: 'We charged at each other firing and passed in the air less than six feet apart.' The two machines banked away from each other and taking the control column in one hand, Guilfoyle completed the tricky process of loading a new ammunition drum onto the top of his Lewis gun. Looking around to resume his attack, though, he spotted his foe heading towards the enemy aerodrome.[55]

With the combat concluded, all of the bombers made it back to their respective aerodromes, having spent almost seven hours in the air. General Murray sent a congratulatory message to Australia's Minister for Defence.

The raid marked the gradual beginnings of Australia's history of air-to-air combat. At this stage, the Germans still only had a single squadron in the theatre (FA 300). And, while it possessed vastly superior aircraft to the British and Australian squadrons, its pilots seemed reluctant to engage in air-to-air combat. Two days after the raid on Beersheba, a German machine retaliated by bombing Cairo. Several Australian pilots took off to intercept it, but the German wouldn't turn and fight, and he easily escaped the lumbering BE2cs and Martinsydes.

The AFC's official historian, Frederic Cutlack, thought this 'non-interference' by the German airmen 'remarkable', and concluded that it 'owed something to the daring of the airmen he had to meet'.[56] Certainly, the Australian and British squadrons were very active in enemy skies during this time, but Cutlack didn't consider the serious logistical disadvantages plaguing the Germans. For one thing, it took 30 camels a six-day round trip to transport FA 300's fuel from the railhead nearest its aerodrome. This had serious operational implications for the unit in late 1916, restricting them to reconnaissance flights only every other day. Furthermore, FA 300 was operating nearly 5000 kilometres from Berlin, and could only be supplied by a difficult overland route.[57] Turkey's railway system in Palestine was totally inadequate to meet the needs of a modern industrial war. It was mostly a single line, with only 1 kilometre of track for every 304 square kilometres of territory, while the squadrons in France, by comparison, were serviced by 1 kilometre of track for every 10 square kilometres.[58] For the remainder of the campaign, the Germans would constantly struggle to get aircraft parts and fuel. The British and Australian squadrons, on the other hand, would benefit from regular resupply via their much better railway system and command of coastal waters.

'A very lively time': To the Palestine frontier, December 1916

During the eight months in which the British forces were in the Sinai, General Murray never lost sight of the necessity of capturing El Arish, a coastal village marking the edge of the desert's sands and barring the way to the Egyptian–Turkish frontier. To clear the Sinai of Turks, Murray would need to capture this stronghold.

For the first fortnight in December, No. 1 Squadron prepared the way for an offensive against the Turkish positions along the Wady El Arish. The Australians photographed the enemy front line and the inland region between El Kossaima, El Auja and Abu Aweigila, through which Murray planned to outflank the fortifications near the coast. These photographs replaced the army's outdated maps and enabled the British staff officers to plan routes through the desert. On 14 December, the pilots also patrolled over Murray's three divisions as they deployed for battle.

During the afternoon of 17 December, Muir was patrolling above the British troops in a Martinsyde when he discovered a Rumpler, spying on the preparations below. From a thousand feet above, he 'dived down on him, fired ¾ of a drum, finishing the rest from underneath' (a drum contained 47 rounds which could be emptied in five seconds). Muir then chased the Rumpler for 30 kilometres, back towards the enemy lines. He finally caught up, north of Abu Aweigila, and 'again dived and fired half a drum'. The enemy observer, he saw, had collapsed in his cockpit. By the time he climbed for another pass, the German pilot had escaped.[59]

Stan Muir's 17 December dogfight left him with both a formidable reputation and a distinguishing trademark for his aircraft. The top wing of his Martinsyde had been hit and needed replacing, but the only available spare was unpainted, in its natural white fabric colour, in contrast to the other which was brown. In the coming days, the enemy would begin to associate

Muir's aggressive flying style with his aircraft's unique colour scheme. 'So impressed' became the enemy with Muir's skill, claimed a fellow pilot, that any British airman 'could ensure himself freedom of action by fitting a white wing and a chocolate wing to his machine'.[60]

As well as occasioning Muir's successful fight with the Rumpler, 17 December 1916 was the first time the whole squadron came together to operate from Mustabig aerodrome. It was an ideal location, with the men camped in tents on the side of a hill, facing a hard salt-lake bed. Although this put the pilots closer to their patrol areas, it advanced them further from supplies. Joe Bull, a rigger who had recently arrived in a pool of reinforcements from Australia, complained that: 'We get very little water, about one pannikin full a day for washing in. There is no canteen or YMCA and I have very little writing paper.'[61] Pilot Adrian Cole recalled the persistent winds that blew grit into their tents, clothes, hair, tea and food, and described the long list of things they did without—'no fresh meat, no fruit, no refrigeration, no comfort or amusement'. They lived on bully beef, he claimed, but were eternally grateful for the squadron cook who was an ex-employee of the Menzies Hotel in Melbourne and 'was reputed to know three hundred and seventy ways of disguising it'.[62] Others noted more acute discomforts—the prevalence of snake tracks around the tents and, perhaps most alarmingly, that on 21 December, two Turkish snipers were captured setting up across the road from the aerodrome.[63] It is little wonder that Jenkyn Benham referred to the Sinai as 'this Godforsaken country' in a letter to his mother: 'I wish we were out of this, we are so tired of seeing nothing but sand and a few palm trees, certainly it breaks the monotony when a machine stands on its head or a Hun machine comes over.'[64]

A break to the monotonous routine was imminent, though. On the night of 20 December, the Anzac Mounted Division and Imperial Camel Corps Brigade rode out of the Sinai's vast sand dunes and surrounded El Arish. The enemy had practically deserted it, and at dawn, they occupied it without firing a shot. As the sun rose, Australian pilots took off from Mustabig to find the retreating enemy garrison. They spotted a large force of Turkish infantry digging in at Magdhaba, 37 kilometres to the southeast along the wady from El Arish. The following morning, General Philip Chetwode (commander of Murray's advanced force, the 'Desert Column') ordered an immediate move to pursue the Turks and take Magdhaba. After lunch, ten BE2cs from No. 1 Squadron (joined by another two from No. 14 Squadron) prepared the way by dropping more than a hundred 20 lb bombs on the Turkish positions at Magdhaba. The two squadrons also raided Irgeig, northwest of Beersheba, to create a diversion. Over the target, three German scouts attacked the formation. Watching from 1000 feet above, Muir in his brown and white Martinsyde picked out a Fokker monoplane and dived. He chased it down, firing off two whole drums. 'I was very close,' he recalled, 'at times only a few feet apart.' Turning away to load a third drum, Muir saw his quarry make for the ground and land roughly on a rugged wady floor.[65] The other German pilots broke off and the raiders returned unharmed. Muir's victory is probably the first scored by a pilot in the AFC—but the RFC couldn't confirm it and German records don't record a loss, suggesting that they recovered the machine and used it again.

The light horse columns arrived in front of Magdhaba before dawn on 23 December. They had very little idea of the enemy's new positions, but knew from No. 1 Squadron's reports that a well-entrenched garrison with machine guns held the village. At 6.30 a.m., Australian pilots raided the village. After dropping their bombs the observers drew rough sketches of the enemy's positions, which by 8.00 a.m., were being read by commanders on the ground. They revealed the location of a heavily fortified redoubt and the absence of Turkish reinforcements in the area. Half an hour later, the assault units were moving into position.

The attack commenced at 9.00 a.m. with the Camel Corps assaulting frontally and the New Zealand Mounted Rifles and 3rd Light Horse Brigade flanking the village to the northeast. They had a tough fight on their hands, needing to cross open, bullet-swept ground and assault well-entrenched Turkish defenders. All morning, the air mechanics at Mustabig laboured, arming and refuelling the BE2cs to keep them over the battlefield. By late morning, rumours had reached the mechanics' workshops at Mustabig that, as there was no water at Magdhaba, 'they will probably have to retire'.[66] The attack pressed on, though, with No. 1 Squadron's machines out over the battlefield all day, strafing and bombing ahead of the troops and keeping Chauvel informed of the progress. Roberts and his observer, Ross Smith, a recent volunteer from the light horse, 'had a very lively time machine-gunning the retreating Turkish troops. They put eight holes through our machine but did no material damage.'[67]

At 4.30 p.m., after savage hand-to-hand fighting, Chetwode's troops captured the final Turkish redoubt. The column had lost 146 men, but the Turks had suffered heavily for their resolute defence: 400 dead and 1300 taken prisoner.[68] The horsemen left Magdhaba a blackened wreck and stumbled back to El Arish, desperate for water.

The following morning, Christmas Eve, No. 1 Squadron's patrols confirmed that Magdhaba remained empty of Turks, as did nearby El Ruafa and Abu Aweigila. Four days later, aerial reconnaissance reported the Turkish main force back across the Egypt–Palestine frontier and digging in on a line between Gaza and Beersheba. A smaller garrison was preparing to hold the frontier in an entrenched outpost at Rafa. During the final days of 1916, the Australians sent a couple of aircraft over the lines each morning with bombs to harass the Turks as they dug in. One pilot had a lucky escape when a bullet fired from the ground went through his instrument panel, forcing him to land on the way home.[69] The weather broke a few days before the New Year, keeping the pilots grounded.

General Salmond, the RFC's commanding officer in the Middle East, visited Mustabig aerodrome on 30 December. He congratulated the officers and men on their fine work since arriving in May, despite initially lacking aircraft and equipment. The squadron had become involved in fairly high-tempo operations, and five pilots had been mentioned in dispatches, but it was yet to suffer a casualty in combat. The New Year would bring a sharp increase in both losses and accolades, as the squadron supported the Egyptian Expeditionary Force's drive across the frontier into Palestine.

4
'AN INTENSE RIVALRY IN THE AIR'
War above the trenches, Gaza, January to August 1917

The No. 1 Squadron's motley collection of aircraft at Weli Sheikh Nuran in 1917. The closest machine is an RE8, the next one is a BE12a and the airborne aircraft is a Martinsyde G.100. *RAAF Museum*

> On the ground, one became accustomed to lethal things being thrown about, but in your first aerial action, the machine seems to take on a new fragility...
>
> —Lieutenant Les Sutherland, No. 1 Squadron, Australian Flying Corps

'Anti-aircraft shells bursting above and below us': The Rafa raid, January 1917

The foul winter weather played havoc with No. 1 Squadron's aircraft during the first days of 1917. 'Today for a change,' recorded a wry Joe Bull in his diary on New Year's Day, 'we are having a mild sandstorm.' In the first week of the year, he noted five crashes, 'scattered about different parts of the desert' as the pilots attempted to get airborne and harass the Turks as they pulled back across the frontier into southern Palestine.

There was a break in the storms on 5 January, allowing a couple of machines up to reconnoitre the Turkish front lines. They photographed 2000 Turks digging in just south of Rafa on the Sinai–Palestine frontier. Their closest reinforcements were 16 kilometres to the east at Weli Sheikh Nuran, leaving Rafa open to another encirclement on the lines of the Magdhaba operation.

Before dawn on 9 January, the Anzac Mounted Division surrounded Rafa. They were well supported by the Australian airmen, having maps and aerial photographs of the Turkish defences and wireless radio sets, mounted on sleds, to receive Morse transmissions from the aircraft. At first light, pilots signalled that the roads to the east were clear of enemy reinforcements. Chauvel ordered his troops forward but they immediately ran into difficulty. The Turkish redoubts sat at the top of a gentle slope and their machine gunners swept the open ground. The airmen used their wireless buzzers to direct artillery fire on to these points and report the battle's progress to Chauvel's headquarters.

Meanwhile, six Australians flew to FA 300's aerodrome at Beersheba to ensure that the enemy didn't get off the ground to interfere with the battle. Eric Roberts was in a recently arrived Bristol monoplane on this dangerous assignment:

> Our instructions were to fly over the main German aerodrome... to try and draw up some of the enemy machines to fight and so keep them from bombing and strafing our attacking forces at Rafa. We climbed to fourteen thousand feet to give us plenty of height. This was very high for those days and the highest I had ever been. After we had spent some time over Beersheba with anti-aircraft shells bursting above and below us, two enemy machines took off from the aerodrome but never got anywhere near us.[1]

The scouts each dropped a 112 lb bomb that left a 4 metre-wide crater on the German aerodrome.[2] Roberts admitted it was a nervewracking job, especially so because the Bristol monoplane's rotary engine (in which the propeller and engine spin as one) was reputedly unreliable. On the day before (his twenty-third birthday), he had written a 'cheerful last word' to his mother, just in case.[3]

Returning from Beersheba in the gathering dusk, Roberts' flight spotted 1200 Turkish reinforcements approaching Rafa from the southeast. They alerted Chauvel's headquarters, but before he could order a withdrawal, the final enemy garrison surrendered and the mounted troops retired to El Arish with 1500 prisoners. Williams and Muir flew over Rafa at dawn the following morning, but reported it deserted except a few Bedouins picking among the Turkish dead. It was one of the last times Muir flew with No. 1 Squadron. Before the end of January, he and a handful of the unit's most experienced pilots and mechanics were sailing to England, to help Watt prepare the new Australian squadron for service on the Western Front.

The capture of Rafa pushed the British front forward, forcing squadrons to shift their aerodromes closer to the front. No. 1 Squadron packed up and moved forward to an aerodrome near El Arish. Known as Kilo 143 (143 kilometres from Kantara), it was, in Bull's words, on 'a flat stretch of sand running pretty well to the sea'. The men certainly enjoyed the swimming, but it wasn't without its risks. In their first week there, a British officer drowned in the powerful undercurrent and two light horsemen were killed tampering with a sea mine that washed ashore. 'They could not be found afterwards,' explained Bull.[4] At Kilo 143, No. 1 Squadron received five new aircraft—BE2es. They were a welcome upgrade, with slightly better performance than the old 2cs, although the observer still sat in the front seat and was disadvantaged by a limited field of vision and fire.

The advancing front line forced FA 300's commanding officer, Helmuth Felmy, to shift his squadron too. It moved north to Ramleh, a town on the ancient pilgrim route between Jaffa and Jerusalem. Felmy chose a spot in an olive grove at the city walls, camouflaged the hangars, and set up a 'dummy' aerodrome with old canvas tents and broken aeroplanes a few kilometres away. The Australian airmen couldn't locate FA 300's new aerodrome for over a fortnight. On 28 January, though, Roberts and Ross Smith discovered it. Years later, Roberts explained that Smith—who would later emerge as one of the AFC's star pilots—had grown up on a station outside of Broken Hill, and as a result 'had a keen sense of the ground and he would pick anything out. His observation powers were far beyond that of people who hadn't had that kind of experience.'[5]

'I could not see the ground for bursting shells': Bombing and reconnaissance, January–March 1917

With the way into Palestine open to the British, the Turks fortified outposts at Weli Sheikh Nuran and Shellal to screen their main line, which ran from the sea, through Gaza to Beersheba. Australian pilots flying over the Shellal redoubts in late January described them as the most extensive fortifications they had yet seen.[6]

No. 1 Squadron reconnoitred the enemy positions nearly daily throughout January and February, noting the build-up in defences and bombing them regularly. It was especially dangerous work, as the stagnation of movement allowed the Turks to mass anti-aircraft guns at their most valuable sites. The gunners would, according to Williams, 'bracket' the aircraft by filling the air around it with high explosive shells. He remembered flying over Sheria railway station at 3000 feet and observing the first burst of four shells from the ground below and behind, and the next above and in front. The third left large holes in the wings and the fourth emptied the contents of the front petrol tank all over him.[7] Les Sutherland, an observer who transferred from the light horse after fighting at Gallipoli and in the Sinai, found anti-aircraft fire—or 'Archie', as the pilots called it, after a popular song—was an entirely new experience:

> On the ground, one became accustomed to lethal things being thrown about, but in your first aerial action, the machine seems to take on a new fragility; the ground is so far away... Imagine what would happen, I was thinking, if Archie scored a direct hit! Or if one of those tracer bullets set fire to our machine, killed the engine, or cut away the controls![8]

Jack Wright, an Australian pilot who flew in France in 1918, reckoned Archie was one of the 'hardest things' to adjust to and the chief cause of nervous tension among airmen. In his assessment, it—more than anything else—was 'responsible for the many cases of breakdown and nervous failure to stand up to front line air missions'.[9]

The reconnaissance and bombing over Shellal and Weli Sheikh Nuran quickly developed a dangerous reputation among the pilots. After doing a few trips there in January with Eric Roberts, Ross Smith pulled one of the other ex-light horse observers, George Mills, aside to explain which of his possessions he wanted sent home to his mother and which ones should be distributed among his mates. Shocked, Mills asked why. Smith replied: 'I'm not breezy, but I'm not a fool either. You just can't do Shellal so often and get away with it all the time.'[10]

Williams took Smith off operations to give him a break and assigned Mills to be Roberts' observer. On 24 January, Roberts and Mills set out to photograph and bomb Weli Sheikh Nuran. Experience had taught Roberts not to approach such a 'hot' target under 5000 feet, but low clouds changed his plans:

> As we came in just under the clouds at three thousand eight hundred feet to do our first photographic run, all hell suddenly broke loose. The anti-aircraft gunners must have ranged for height on the clouds and been waiting for us. They had our exact height and track and before we knew where we were we were surrounded by bursting shells. Then quite suddenly and unexpectedly a shell burst alongside us on the left between the wing and the tail plane. It threw us on our side and I was busy righting the plane when Mills called out, 'They've got me, Bobs!' The next thing I knew blood was seeping through on the floor from the front cockpit. Then I looked down and saw that my own hand had been grazed by a bit of shrapnel. I had to make a split second decision. I realised it was impossible to try to do any more with Mills possibly bleeding to death in the front cockpit, so I put the nose of the aeroplane down and made for home.

As he did so, Roberts looked back towards Weli Sheikh Nuran. 'I could not see the ground for bursting shells ... We were well over the lines in Turkish territory and between fifty and sixty miles from our base, that is, nearly an hour's flying time.'[11]

A shell splinter had entered Mills' wrist and exited at his elbow, breaking his arm and severing the main artery. He managed to stem the bleeding using a handkerchief as a makeshift tourniquet.

Landing revealed just how fortunate they were—every vital part of the aircraft was hit. 'Despite the worldly life I had been leading I sensed God must have been watching over us that day,' wrote Roberts. 'Before I went to bed that night, I got down on my knees and thanked Him for sparing my life, and I also prayed that George Mills ... would recover.'[12] Mills would indeed recover, but his flying days were finished. He was sent home to Australia as No. 1 Squadron's first invalided battle casualty. Roberts escaped serious physical injury, but the experience had marked him in other ways.

He noted in his diary how he had difficulty sleeping in the nights following his narrow escape.[13] A week later, he was leading a raid on FA 300's new aerodrome at Ramleh when he nearly dozed off, at 6000 feet. There was a storm of Archie over the target, and Roberts returned to Kilo 143 a nervous wreck. The squadron medical officer immediately removed him from the flying roster and 24 hours later, sent him to No. 14 Australian General Hospital. Roberts rested for a month, but continued to suffer 'violent twitching' of the right arm and insomnia. 'He is unlikely to be able to manage an aeroplane for some time,' concluded his doctor.[14] Eric Roberts' flying days were finished. In March 1917, he followed his wounded observer home, a victim of the air war's immense strain and one of dozens more to come in the AFC.

At the beginning of March, No. 1 Squadron's careful vigil over the enemy outposts indicated the Turks' imminent withdrawal. A light horse patrol confirmed this on the night of 4 March, when the Turks abandoned Weli Sheikh Nuran. Batmen shook the pilots from their sleep and told them to prepare to fly. At first light, Ross Smith and his new pilot, Norm Steele, confirmed the enemy was pulling back and reported thousands of Turkish troops cramming on to trains at Tel el Sheria. In the dawn fog, Williams led a mixed British and Australian flight of six to disrupt proceedings.

He led them in low, predicting the Turks would keep their anti-aircraft batteries at Weli Shiekh Nuran to cover the withdrawal. He was wrong, however: the enemy had moved their guns to the station. The six aircraft approached the target at 3000 feet in single file. Hell broke loose in a storm of fire, with four rounds exploding in each salvo. 'There was a terrible clatter going on all around me,' recalled Williams. A fragment tore a gaping hole in one of his wings. Another pierced Adrian Cole's petrol tank, forcing him to turn for home and crash land just across the lines. A British pilot was hit, and went down among the enemy troops.

Williams frantically hit the bomb release toggle and turned away. As the 'Archie' died down, it suddenly occurred to him that his engine had stopped. 'I started to look for a reason and my first thought was that I'd not only been hit in the wing ... but that a piece had cut my ignition or my petrol supply.'

He tried to start the engine a few times, switching between his main and reserve fuel tanks. No result. As he glided down, rifle bullets swished past. 'I remember getting very annoyed because the day before we were told that there would be a mail from Australia next day and ... we only got one every six weeks. I thought "God Damn!"'

Williams decided to land near a wady so that he could make a run for it. Suddenly he had a truly life-changing epiphany: 'I thought, it must be the ignition!' The night before, while testing his bomb release, he had bumped the switch and remarked to his mechanic, 'By jove! I'll have to watch that in the morning, that I don't knock that switch off.' He reached down, and sure enough the switch was 'off'. The engine belched black smoke and roared back to life. 'I was just about to put my wheels on the ground, you know there's never been an engine that fired so sweetly in the world.'[15]

Williams made it back to Kilo 143, his machine full of holes. In later years, he 'often thought about the effect that switch would have had on my life ... I would have returned from the war an inexperienced captain instead of a lieutenant-colonel'.[16] Such are the fortunes of war. But so as not to tempt fortune, the mechanics fitted a metal guard to all engine ignition switches in the squadron.

Raids against the retreating Turks continued at fever pitch throughout the day. At noon, a flight of Australians spotted three 500-strong units of Turkish soldiers moving along the Gaza–Beersheba road. They strafed, bombed and dispersed the enemy troops, and ran a truck off the road.[17] The bombing continued the following day, directed first at the railway traffic between Tel el Sheria and Arak el Menshiye but then shifting further north to Junction Station—the major rail hub for the Turkish front in southern Palestine. These raids cost two Australian machines, but thankfully no lives. John Tunbridge was hit by the now infamous Sheria station anti-aircraft gunners on the 7th and forced to land at Rafa. A few days later, Len Heathcote had to land with engine failure north of Gaza. He was captured and spent the rest of the war in a squalid Turkish prison.

On 7 March, Joe Bull and the ground crew had one of their busiest days yet. 'Bombing continually,' he noted in his diary, 'and during part of the night machines left hourly one at a time with a load of bombs.' The pilots, of course, had no formal training in night flying. But, as Williams explained:

> one found no difficulty in finding one's way in that country on a moonlight night provided one knew the country well enough not to require a map— the coast was a very good guide, even on quite dark nights. On night raids machines left at . . . intervals and flew on definite routes at pre-arranged heights.[18]

The bombing between 5 and 9 March was the most intense carried out by the squadron to date. Together, the British and Australian squadrons had, with their 30 machines, dropped 2.75 tonnes of bombs. Nevertheless, although harassed, the Turks managed to get the bulk of their men back to the safety of their main Gaza–Beersheba line.[19]

'A cheery, unruffled soul': McNamara, VC

The extra raiding forced the squadron to improvise when it ran short of bombs. 'Someone,' Williams explained, 'came up with the suggestion that 6-inch howitzer shells might be used until more bombs arrived.' The fuses could be set according to the altitude, and armed with a pin attached to the bomb rack. When the pilot released his 'bomb', the pin would remain behind, thus arming the shell. Understandably, this experiment initially made the pilots nervous. Williams recalled the first time he dropped one on a night raid over Gaza. 'It started to spit sparks as soon as it left the bomb rack. It gave me a scare and I pulled away but it did not explode before reaching the ground and went off with a better crack than our 20-pound bombs.'[20] The pilots became more confident with the shells, and the squadron dropped them for some months. Inadvertently, one of these shells triggered one of the AFC's most famous incidents, during a bombing raid on the Turkish railway on 20 March 1917.

Frank McNamara, a 22-year-old school teacher from Caulfield was a No. 1 Squadron original. He learned to fly on the third course at Point Cook and sailed for Egypt with the squadron in March 1916. He spent the next few months in England with Eric Roberts and the other observers, getting further instruction. He was popular in the squadron, 'a cheery, unruffled soul', yet quiet, scholarly and an unlikely hero.[21]

On the morning of 20 March, McNamara and Alfred Ellis in Martinsydes escorted Peter Drummond and a new pilot, Doug Rutherford, in BE2es to bomb a section of railway near the Wadi el Hesi, 20 kilometres north of Tel el Sheria. A light horseman who had fought at Gallipoli, Rutherford had only qualified for his wings at the end of February. This would be his third time over the lines.[22]

Each machine carried six howitzer shells with 40-second delay fuses. Ellis dropped his first, followed closely by McNamara. He flew along the railway and dropped five shells over a train. The last one exploded as it left the racks, rocking his aircraft violently and sending red-hot splinters through his seat and into his buttocks. It was, he later described, like being 'hit with a sledge hammer.'[23] Dazed, McNamara pulled up and dropped a couple of smoke flares to signal that he was hit and making for home.

Looking back at the target area, though, he spotted Rutherford's aircraft on the ground, surrounded by smoke. Ellis had seen him too and observed: 'The country appeared most difficult and from the air bodies of enemy troops could be seen advancing from all sides.' Nevertheless, McNamara banked around and dived through fire from the ground. He switched his engine off, touched down and taxied towards the downed BE2e. From above, Ellis could see bullets 'striking all around Captain Rutherford's machine and it seemed almost certain that Lieutenant McNamara must either be killed or captured'.[24]

McNamara pulled up next to the BE2e. Rutherford climbed on to the wing and held on to the centre section struts. Opening up the throttle, McNamara turned into the wind. The machine trundled and bumped across the uneven ground, but as the speed gathered, it began to veer to the left under Rutherford's added weight. With his right leg 'pretty dud', McNamara was unable to compensate with his right rudder pedal. The Martinsyde pitched into a gully, tearing away the undercarriage and shattering the propeller.[25] Rutherford pulled McNamara from the wreck, set the Martinsyde alight with a flare and helped him back towards his own BE2e. It was missing a tyre and a few bracing wires, but otherwise appeared airworthy—that is, if they could start the engine, since its failure was what had forced Rutherford down in the first place.[26]

By this time, despite the efforts of Drummond and Ellis's machine guns, Turkish troops were within 80 metres, firing at the two Australians. McNamara climbed into the cockpit and returned fire with his revolver while Rutherford swung the propeller. Miraculously, the engine fired on the first swing, and within moments the pair were lurching through the sand. 'She stuck 3 times on soft ground, then lifted off... Just in time to escape the rush.'[27] It took them an hour and a half, but they landed at Kilo 143 safely. McNamara was slumped in the cockpit in a pool of blood. The ground crew got to the machine in time to hear him make a 'classically pungent remark' before falling unconscious.[28]

'He was rushed to hospital,' recalled Williams, but ironically it was there that McNamara received his most serious injuries for the day. As his wound was full of shell splinters and fragments of timber, fabric and horsehair from the seat, the medical officers gave him an anti-tetanus shot. Moments later, McNamara had an anaphylactic reaction and fell unconscious, 'absolutely blue and cold, no pulse at all, not breathing'. The doctors started 'artificial respiration' and injected adrenaline. 'After half an hour he gave a tiny breath. We had his mouth held open wide with a gag and worked his tongue to and fro,' reported a doctor.[29] Within an hour, McNamara's breathing became regular and his condition stabilised. The alarmed medical staff packed metal hot water bottles around his body while he was unconscious. One, placed against his heel, burned the flesh off down to the bone. The wounds from the shell splinters soon healed but the burn invalided him to Australia and troubled him for the rest of his life.

McNamara received the Victoria Cross for his gallant rescue. His was the first and only VC to be awarded to an Australian airman during the First World War. As an understandably grateful Doug Rutherford observed:

> The risk of Lieutenant McNamara being killed or captured was so great that even had he not been wounded he would have been justified in not attempting my rescue—the fact of his already being wounded makes his action one of outstanding gallantry—his determination and resource and utter disregard of danger throughout the operation was worthy of the highest praise.[30]

The announcement of the award elated but also surprised his squadron mates, one of who thought him 'Quiet, scholarly, loyal and loved by all', but 'the last officer for whom that high honour would have been predicted'.[31] McNamara himself would probably have agreed, seeing his feat in pragmatic, rather than heroic terms. Speaking to a *Herald* journalist for an article published on 28 September 1917, he explained: 'It appeared obvious that if he [Rutherford] remained where he was he would either be shot or captured, so I simply turned back to meet a situation that had arisen, without at all considering what it might mean to myself.'

This hasty decision made at 22 years of age defined the rest of this country school teacher's life. The bronze cross on his chest made him something of a Melbourne celebrity. The 'McNamara story' circulated widely in the press, and in 1924 the Australian War Memorial commissioned a painting to commemorate his deed. For the rest of his life, McNamara had associations with the Empire's elite social circles and, despite his allegedly mediocre flying skills, rose through the ranks of the Royal Australian Air Force, eventually attaining the honorary rank of Air Vice-Marshal.[32]

Such is the outcome of war from time to time for men like Air Vice-Marshal Frank McNamara, VC, who may otherwise have come home and eked out an unremarkable life in Victoria's rural schoolhouses.

'An absence of mutual support and cooperation': The First Battle of Gaza, 26 March 1917

By 21 March, the British railway line and water pipe extended as far as Rafa, finally permitting the next step forward into Palestine. Knowing supply by the sea would be necessary for future operations, Murray decided to continue the advance along the Mediterranean coast. The next major Turkish stronghold in his path was the ancient city of Gaza.

Murray delegated the capture of Gaza to Lieutenant General Charles Dobell's 'Eastern Force'. Dobell planned to encircle the city with cavalry and overrun the town with three infantry divisions from the southwest. His operation orders requested six aircraft to reconnoitre and report on the progress of the battle (especially the approach of Turkish reinforcements from the northeast), another six for artillery observation and the remaining six to deal with the German aircraft. Throughout the battle, one machine would report directly to his headquarters, where a landing strip and horse would ensure a quick passage of information from pilots to the staff officers.[33]

In the week leading up to the battle, No. 1 Squadron bombed transport targets behind the enemy's front line and photographed the fortifications around Gaza. With two days to go, it shifted to Rafa aerodrome and patrolled above Dobell's troops as they assembled for battle.

In mid-March, FA 300 had been reinforced with several experienced airmen from the Western Front and eight new Rumplers, each with a forward (through propeller) firing Spandau machine gun and a rear-firing, swivel-mounted Parabellum for the observer. One historian of the campaign commented that these 'enjoyed a complete mastery over the slower British machines'.[34] They broke through the screen of British machines and succeeded in bombing and photographing Dobell's forces as they assembled. This prompted the enemy commanders to move additional reinforcements to Gaza in anticipation of the attack. On the day before the battle, the RFC lost three aircraft. An Australian pilot, Percy Snell, barely made it home after tangling with a Rumpler over Gaza for 25 minutes.[35] Bull counted bullet holes all around his seat.[36]

Dawn hardly broke on 26 March. An oppressive fog blanketed the coastline as the Anzac Mounted Division crossed the Wady Ghuzze and moved north. They advanced 8 kilometres past Gaza and then swung west towards the sea. By 10.00 a.m., the city was completely encircled. Just before noon, the British infantry divisions advanced on Gaza from the south.

As the fog lifted, all of No. 1 Squadron's airmen were over the battlefield, reconnoitring, dropping notes to troops on the ground and directing artillery fire. The German pilots were out too, and the RFC lost two aircraft—one shot down by a new Rumpler, its pilot killed. Williams reconnoitred the battlefield twice to provide updates for Dobell's headquarters. At noon, he observed that things didn't seem to be going to plan: 'Viewed from the air there appeared to be a distinct absence of mutual support and co-operation between the various units of the attacking Division.' He noted that some battalions had gone to ground and dug in, allowing the Turks opposing them to shift their fire on to neighbouring units. Also, he observed, the British gunners were missing their targets by 400 metres or more.[37]

On patrol at 4.30 p.m., though, Williams noted that things were looking up—'it appeared that darkness might not only allow the infantry to rush the Turkish positions, but it would probably find the mounted troops in Gaza itself and behind the Turkish trenches which were holding up the infantry'.[38] He was right: as darkness fell, light horsemen entered Gaza and even, in some places, linked up with the British troops advancing from the south. The Turkish garrison commander wired his superiors, stating that he was about to surrender if reinforcements didn't arrive. Before leaving the battlefield just before dusk, Williams noted that some Turkish infantry were approaching on foot from the north, but concluded that the mounted troops and armoured cars covering the encirclement could easily deal with them.

Williams landed at Dobell's command tent with his positive news. Since he had been there in the morning, however, the atmosphere had changed. He found the chief intelligence officer sitting there, totally despondent. 'This time,' explained Williams, 'when I saw him, he had his white gloves on and his stick under his arm, his table was not there, he wasn't even taking any notes.' He reported:

'It only needs nightfall and Gaza is ours.'

'Oh,' he said, 'that's interesting. Did you see any Turkish infantry coming down from the north-east.'

I said, 'Yes.'

'What about them?'

I said, 'Oh, there are only a few hundred of those and they're so far away on their flat feet, they can't make any difference to the result in Gaza. Our fellows can take Gaza, turn around and meet them.'

'Oh,' he said, 'very interesting.'

And that was that. Perplexed, Williams flew back to Rafa and spread the word: 'Gaza is sewn up. As soon as it's dark our fellows will have it.' He retired to his tent, but later in the evening Major Rutledge came to tell him that the British were retreating from Gaza. Williams was astonished; 'Retiring? I don't believe it.'

But it was true. Dobell and Chetwode had decided that unless the city fell by sunset, the need for water would be too great to keep the mounted units out. Reports of Turkish reinforcements coming from the northeast had probably further shaken their resolve. The troops on the ground couldn't believe it: their objectives were within reach when the order to withdraw arrived. But, as Williams pointed out, it was the Turks who 'were the most surprised people of the lot'.

The air fighting on 26 March had been intense: one British airman killed, two wounded, two aircraft destroyed and another six seriously damaged.[39] Joe Bull noted in his diary that the British squadron (No. 14) sharing Rafa aerodrome was left with just three serviceable machines.[40] The Germans, who sustained no losses, had dominated the sky above the battlefield. As well as providing advance notice of the attack, FA 300 made a crucial contribution to the battle, quite probably changing its course with its reconnaissance.[41] Ironically, in Williams' opinion the British lost the battle by not putting enough stock in their aerial reconnaissance: 'No air report at Gaza that day would suggest the necessity for a retirement.'[42] The following morning, the pilots were above the battlefield to cover the withdrawal of Dobell's troops. Williams described it as a 'dreary sight'.[43] 'Everyone,' he noted, 'was down in the dumps having seen the position our troops were in on that evening.'[44]

The lines had stabilised again on 27 March, and No. 1 Squadron put several machines up to direct artillery on to the Turkish counter-attack units gathering in their front line. While on this job, Rutherford—who was flying again after his rescue by McNamara a week previously—and his observer, William Hyam, were attacked by a Rumpler. Hyam, a 27-year-old fruitgrower from Gippsland, Victoria, had enlisted in the light horse in 1914 and fought at Gallipoli. He volunteered for work as an observer in the flying corps in September 1916 and had proved himself, in Rutledge's assessment, 'one of my best'. The German pilot attacked from below, his observer scoring the BE2's underside with fire. Four bullets hit Rutherford—fortunately all flesh wounds—but Hyam received a burst in the upper body. Rutherford put the machine into a dive and managed to crash land just behind the British lines. They were hospitalised, but Hyam died 24 hours later. No. 1 Squadron's first death in action hit the men hard, 'a real loss to them all', as Hyam's flight commander related to his grieving family.[45]

'An absence of "push"': The Second Battle of Gaza, 19 April 1917

General Murray cabled the British War Office following the Battle of Gaza, reporting it 'a most successful operation' that had 'filled our troops with enthusiasm'. His report could not have been further from the truth. It had, in fact, been a fiasco that seriously undermined the morale of the British troops and airmen, Murray's report was, however, believed by those in the War Office, who subsequently cabled him on 30 March, sanctioning another attack on Gaza and an advance to capture Jerusalem.[46]

If the conduct and results of the First Gaza Battle dented British morale, it had precisely the opposite effect on the Turco-German forces, who immediately set about transforming their line of outposts and redoubts into a 20 kilometre line of trenches, running from the sea to Hareira. Murray realised the days for bold cavalry encirclements had passed for the time being, and therefore planned a methodical siege, based on artillery and infantry bludgeoning their way through the enemy's trenches.

He and Dobell planned a two-stage advance. On 16 April, the three infantry divisions would capture the Wady Ghuzze. British artillery and naval vessels would then bombard the Turkish positions around Gaza before an infantry assault on the town on 19 April, with cavalry screening their inland flank. The war office refused Murray additional infantry reinforcements for the attack, but sent him six tanks and 2000 rounds of gas shell.[47]

Since No. 14 Squadron was gutted by losses during the first battle, the Australians shouldered the bulk of the preliminary air work for Murray's second attempt. Their foremost task was to reconnoitre the new Turkish front line to develop maps for the infantry and register targets for the artillery. The airmen accomplished the latter by flying up and down the line watching for flashes that would reveal camouflaged enemy batteries. By

18 April, every British gun crew had a map of Turkish batteries to fire on, although some enemy guns remained hidden.

The static trench warfare conditions and build-up of troops also presented both sides with plenty of targets to bomb. Friday 6 April set the tone of things to come over the next fortnight. Allan Murray Jones was escorting a BE2e on a reconnaissance when they ran into a flight of five Rumplers, loaded up with bombs, heading towards Rafa. The BE2e dived for home while Murray Jones stayed to fight. Bursts of machine gun fire were exchanged, and it is likely that Murray Jones scored a few hits as a couple of the Germans broke for home. His machine was soon riddled, though, and when his engine failed he landed near Weli Sheikh Nuran. The German pilots weren't finished with him yet; they bombed and strafed his machine as he ran from it. Miraculously, he escaped unhurt, and the story left a bitter taste in the pilots' mouths; from this point on, neither side would offer quarter to forced-down adversaries.

The Australian and British pilots struck back the following night with a raid on the German aerodrome at Ramleh. They scored several hits, Murray Jones getting his own back with a direct hit on a hangar. The damage disrupted FA 300's work for a few days, but the Germans retaliated in force at dawn on 12 April, a day that stuck in Joe Bull's mind and brought home the realities of being at war to the mechanics, who were usually out of harm's way:

> The first thing we heard about 5 o'clock was four bombs dropping in quick succession. Somebody sang out 'here they come' and sure enough they came before we knew where we were. We had no dugouts so had to run for it. I ran the wrong way and the next thing I knew there were four bombs bursting about 30 yards in front of me. The splinters flew down and I was fortunately on a bit of a ridge. I got down quick and lively and then went a little further on to a trench and waited in it till the other two had dropped nine between them.[48]

Bull and his mates were still in their pyjamas. After the two German machines had peppered the aerodrome with bullets, they ran back to the tent to get on their 'knicks and boots'. They then took cover as another nine bombs fell across the aerodrome. Remarkably, the raid did little damage. It

FIRE IN THE SKY

did encourage the squadrons to take air raid precautions, though, and by the afternoon there were slit trenches all around the aerodrome with a few pivoting Lewis guns mounted on up-ended truck axles.

Two hours later, seventeen machines from the two squadrons left Rafa to bomb the Turkish positions in front of Beersheba. FA 300 bombed the Rafa aerodrome again mid-morning, and the Australians replied in kind before lunch. While he was over the hotly defended Turkish positions at Sheria train station, a piece of anti-aircraft shell hit Williams' reserve fuel tank. It drenched him in petrol, forcing him to lean outside the cockpit while it emptied. Williams had an anxious flight back to Rafa, knowing a spark or bullet would incinerate him in an instant.[49]

The tit-for-tat raids continued over the next three days. On the morning of 13 April, a German aircraft dropped a note, taunting the Australians that the Germans wouldn't leave a stick standing on their aerodrome. The Australians replied with a raid on Ramleh aerodrome that afternoon and a note threatening to drop ten bombs for every one they dropped. It wasn't an idle threat. Although technically inferior, the British and Australian pilots had, just prior to the Second Battle of Gaza, 25 aircraft compared with FA 300's six serviceable machines.[50]

Dobell's assault units captured starting positions during preliminary operations on 16 April. This was followed by two days of artillery preparations, including a heavy bombardment of the Turkish front line for two hours before dawn on 19 April. Williams was over the battlefield just before the Second Battle of Gaza started. He reported disturbing deficiencies in the planning from the outset:

> It was a clear morning and I knew from where the tanks were to advance, and I was surprised when from miles away I saw huge clouds of steam coming from where the tanks were. They were boiling and giving off large quantities of steam. Of course, they could be seen from the Turkish lines and there was quite an area of open ground that they would have to traverse before they reached the Turkish positions and one imagined one could see the Turkish artillery commanders with their field glasses, ordering their gunners to stand by for targets.[51]

When the attack commenced, as Williams had predicted, the Turkish gunners easily picked off the tanks. Unsuppressed enemy machine gunners then got stuck into the advancing British troops, pinning them down far short of their objectives.

For the rest of the day, Williams observed individual units shuffle forwards in uncoordinated, isolated attacks that were easily defeated by the 'well controlled and well concealed' Turkish artillery. 'Viewed from the air,' he later wrote, 'there appeared to be an absence of "push" about this attack, a lack of cooperation between units and considerable uncertainty about the whole operation.' To him it seemed that they 'were trying to force a position by poking at it half-heartedly with one finger, instead of hitting it with our clenched fist'. He reported this to British headquarters throughout the day, but to no avail.[52] By sunset, the second British attempt to capture Gaza had failed even more miserably and completely than the first.

Despite their small numbers, FA 300's airmen were again able to dominate the skies above Gaza in their superior aircraft. They bombed and machine-gunned the advancing troops, in one notable instance hitting the 3rd Light Horse Brigade's headquarters and killing its brigade major. While the battle raged, the younger brother of FA 300's commander, Gerhardt Felmy, flew 100 kilometres into British territory, landed and blew up a section of pipe and telegraph wires, thus denying the fighting troops water and interrupting communications.[53]

A slight change in British fortunes occurred that night when a wireless station intercepted an enemy transmission, indicating that Turkish cavalry were assembling at Beersheba to counter-attack the following afternoon. The Australian flight commanders got together, and after consulting their ex-light horse observers, predicted that the Turks would need to water their horses at Hareira prior to attacking.

The next morning, Williams led five aircraft to Hareira where, sure enough, the Turkish cavalry force was watering. 'One had a view similar to a large dam with animals all around it, drinking and with another row of horses with the men behind those, ready to take their turn when those in front had finished.' Williams let his four bombs go at once. They slammed into the crowded bank, causing pandemonium:

We could watch our bombs go right into the ground, and it was extraordinary that day to watch one's bombs going down and find, when it was approaching the grounds, horses and men from some direction or another going for their lives in the direction of where the bomb was falling as though they were in a hurry to catch it![54]

Norm Steele, who was escorting the others in a Martinsyde, was hit by ground fire. One of the other pilots reported: 'His machine was seen to catch fire and sink down towards the ground over the enemy lines.' He crashed in front of the Turkish positions. A group of Bedouins found him a short while later lying next to the wreckage, trying to write a letter. He was critically injured, and died shortly afterwards. One report suggests that they buried him on the spot, but his family never received confirmation of this, and after the war the Commonwealth War Graves Commission couldn't locate a grave.[55] Twenty-one-year-old Norman Steele, warehouseman of Melbourne, is today commemorated on a memorial to the missing on the Mount of Olives, just outside of Jerusalem.

Otherwise, the Hareira raid was a stunning success. That night, the light horsemen at Shellal collected dozens of riderless horses. British intelligence-gatherers intercepted a wireless signal from the Turkish headquarters in Beersheba stating that their planned cavalry attack was unable to proceed due to an attack by hostile aircraft. As Williams observed, here was an example of what five aeroplanes could do—indeed, how 60 20 lb bombs could stop a Turkish cavalry division from carrying out its operation. 'I know of no similar instance in history,' he remarked in his memoirs.[56]

The next morning, Williams and Adrian Cole did a reconnaissance to photograph the damage done to the Turks at Hareira. The anti-aircraft guns were at it again, though, and a shell exploded right underneath Cole's Martinsyde. 'A peculiar feeling, a sudden blast between my legs, a great deal of blinding, smelly smoke and oil from the engine and when everything cleared, there was no noise, no engine, no power and in fact, no propeller—but grand—no fire either.' He glided down to land in a crop field, watched by half a dozen Turkish cavalrymen. In a repeat of McNamara's daring, Williams landed right behind him. 'It was typical of Dicky,' recalled Cole many years later, 'that upon my arrival although we were behind Turkish lines he sent me back to get my Verey pistol and burn the aircraft.' He squeezed into the front seat with Williams' observer: 'It was a crowded ride home, but we made it.'[57] For this, and the previous day's raid, Williams received the Distinguished Service Order.

'An intense rivalry in the air': Trench warfare, April–September 1917

Williams' courage, combined with the excellent leadership and administrative skills he demonstrated during a year as C Flight's commander, earned him command of the squadron when the RFC sent Rutledge to Britain in May. The men in his flight already expected him to be a tough leader. One of them described him as 'a great stickler for detail' who didn't have much of a sense of humour.[58] Another agreed, but was also quick to acknowledge his even-handedness.[59] Les Sutherland summed up these two sides of Williams with: 'If Dicky held an orderly room and some individual was punished, the squadron's verdict was always the same: "Well, he must have been guilty or Dicky would not have crimed him."' Sutherland also thought him a 'splendid judge of men', something others qualified by noting that, despite being a teetotaller himself, Williams tolerated stressed pilots, who were 'often hell bent on fun and games when off duty in the mess'.[60] Williams had, in short, the qualities of a highly effective commander: firmness, fairness and understanding, along with the discernment to know which of these circumstances required.

Following the Second Battle of Gaza, both sides dug in along a line running from the ocean to Hareira, 40 kilometres inland. For the first 13 kilometres, there were almost continuous trenches, separated by about 300 metres. Further inland, no man's land became wider (up to 3.5 kilometres) and the line petered out into a series of fortified outposts.[61] It was the most extensive trench system yet seen in the Middle East and began (especially near the coast) to resemble the stalemate on the Western Front.

As the AFC's official historian observed, this 'concentration of growing forces upon a smaller and definite front ... and the necessity which each command felt for daily information concerning the other's preparation and intentions, awoke an intense rivalry in the air'.[62] As in France, the staples of air work over a stalemated front were photography, artillery observation and bombing. In May, the RFC divided enemy territory into two areas: the tactical (the front and artillery lines) and the strategic (transport, communications and infrastructure behind the front). No. 14 Squadron was designated a 'corps' squadron, assigned to work above the lines in the tactical sector, while the Australians became an 'army' squadron, tasked with long-distance photography and bombing. To get the work done the Australians received a pair of BE12as at the end of May. They were essentially a modified version of the BE2e, with an extra large fuel tank replacing the observer's cockpit to give it greater range. Although the BE12a was deemed ineffective and withdrawn from service after only a short time on the Western Front, No. 1 Squadron's pilots appreciated its additional engine power and the forward-firing machine gun, synchronised to fire through the propeller. 'Fairly fast and good climbers,' is what Joe Bull had to say about them. They subsequently became (with the Martinsydes) the standard 'escort' machines for the old BE's during photo reconnaissance trips.[63]

As well as photographing enemy positions for intelligence, the Australians began producing pictures specifically for mapping terrain. Harry Leckie, from the squadron's photographic section, explained how the Australians were pioneers in this field:

> Our team of four was responsible for making the first 'Mosaic', jig-saw type of combined photograph. The plane took 6 photographs along a set route, then returned about ½ mile distant taking another 6 pictures at a set interval and finally retuned another ½ mile distant taking a further six photographs. After developing and printing we placed the 18 prints in their correct position and then copied the combined result and from that negative turned out the required size of enlargement in one photograph.[64]

When the British offensive resumed in late October 1917, the Australians had photographed some 800 square kilometres of enemy territory, resulting in the production of twenty new 1:200 000 map sheets. Fifth Wing's British commander thought the Australians excelled in this work, claiming, 'some of the best pictures taken from the air of the Palestine campaign were the work of the Digger'.[65]

But it was dangerous work. The photographic aircraft had to fly straight and level between 5000 and 8000 feet for several minutes at a time. This made them ideal targets for German pilots above, and Archie below. Two pilots on reconnaissance were shot down in May within days of one another. On 12 May, John Tunbridge was badly burned when a German bullet set a flare off in his cockpit and forced him to make a hasty landing. Four days later, a 'vastly superior' German machine forced Murray Jones down again and bombed his aircraft as he ran from it.[66]

The odds tipped further in favour of the enemy in June, when FA 300 received two Albatros DIII scouts. Fast, agile and armed with two forward-firing machine guns, they had accounted for a staggering 275 British aircraft during 'Bloody' April 1917 on the Western Front.[67] Here in Palestine, the performance gap between the Albatros and its RFC adversaries was even more pronounced than it was in France. It could fly 30 per cent faster and three times as high as No. 1 Squadron's workhorse, the BE2e. Reinvigorated, FA 300 established an advanced aerodrome at Huj specifically to target No. 1 Squadron's deep reconnaissance flights. 'I freely admit,' wrote Hudson Fysh, one of the ex-light horse observers who joined the unit in August 1917, 'that at this period if we were over the lines in a BE2e and sighted a hostile aircraft it was nose down for home in a hell of a hurry with bracing wires screaming.'[68]

It was a tough time to be a new pilot in Palestine. Twenty-seven-year-old Jack Brasell started flying with the squadron on 21 May 1917. An engineer before the war, he had joined the AFC as a mechanic and came to Egypt with No. 1 Squadron in March 1916. Brasell earned his wings at a flying school in Egypt and quickly gained a reputation as one of the most talented Australian pilots; indeed, Bull claimed he 'could handle a machine better than any pilot I have seen in Egypt'.[69]

Brasell and Cole were escorting a BE2e reconnaissance machine on 25 June when three German aircraft dived on them. According to one report, Brasell was 3000 feet above the other two aircraft and bore the brunt of their attack. For twenty minutes, he exchanged fire with the Germans before one of their bullets struck him in the head. 'He was seen to slowly volplane down in a spiral and landed between the lines,' reported Cole.[70] The Turks found Brasell dead at his controls. The following day, a German pilot dropped a note at the Australian aerodrome explaining they had buried him with full military honours, and regretted the loss of such a gallant and skilled pilot. In a letter to the dead man's sweetheart, Brasell's best mate, Bill Coates, described his death as an 'awful shock'.[71]

The Albatros pilots weren't the only threat to No. 1 Squadron's antiquated machines. The stifling summer climate played havoc with the aircraft, preventing the BEs from getting above 5000 feet and causing regular engine failures. On the morning following Brasell's death, the squadron lost five out of eight aircraft sent to bomb Turkish 4th Army's headquarters on the Mount of Olives. All were related to mechanical issues.

Williams took the matter to his superiors at 5th Wing Headquarters: 'If we don't get new machines I can't guarantee the morale of the squadron.' The British wing commander replied curtly that it was Williams' responsibility, as the squadron's CO, to maintain morale in his squadron. 'Yes!' replied a frustrated Williams. 'I know that and that's why I have come to you—to point out that it cannot go on like this.'[72] Williams returned to the squadron dispirited, but soon had some hope for optimism.

General Murray's abysmal failure at the Second Battle of Gaza earned him orders to return to Britain in June. His replacement was General Edmund Allenby, 'a dynamic and fit leader,' according to historian Matthew Hughes, who had 'experienced field command of everything from a troop in Zululand and Bechuanaland, through a squadron, regiment, column, division, corps and army.'[73]

The first thing the airmen noticed about Allenby when he arrived in late June was that he shifted his headquarters from Cairo to the front. Previously, Murray had commanded from the distant rear and only ever approached the front in a special train escorted by an aircraft above—'hardly an example of economy of force', as Williams wryly observed. In fact, in his assessment, Allenby was 'a different man altogether'. Two days after arriving, he made an extensive tour of the front, spending time with the troops and gathering impressions of the difficulties facing his army. The problem, he concluded, was a shortage of men and materiel—especially aircraft and artillery. Allenby cabled an urgent request to the War Office for more guns and three squadrons of the latest aeroplanes. The politicians responded with an offer of two squadrons, but not until the end of August at the earliest.

'The Hun cock-of-the-walk on our front': Gerhardt Felmy

At the beginning of July, the squadron shifted further forward to Deir el Belah. Located close behind the British front line, the men could actually see artillery and anti-aircraft shells bursting over the front. It was, nevertheless, an accommodating camp. Hudson Fysh called it 'a lovely spot, the best we ever had. Our tents were set amongst great fig trees loaded with fruit in their season and grape vines dangled their luscious clusters for picking. It was a biblical scene.'[74] Joe Bull concurred, thinking it 'a dinkum promised land after being in the desert for a few months'.[75]

At the same time, a new observer joined the unit from the light horse. Twenty-one-year-old Les Sutherland, known to his mates as 'Woodie', left his carpentry trade and enlisted as a signaller a fortnight after war was declared. Eight months later, he found himself in the 1st Light Horse Brigade on Rhododendron Spur at Gallipoli. There, during what he later described as 'blood drenched, fight for your life days', he met Ross Smith.[76] The two became mates while quarantined with typhoid, and later, after fighting in the Sinai campaign, volunteered for the flying corps. Sutherland did a fortnight's training at the aerial gunnery school before joining the squadron in July 1917. The rest was done on the job—a tough apprenticeship, given German superiority in the skies. He described his second trip over the heavily defended Sheria redoubts:

> I was the observer in a BE2e flown by Jack Potts ... With Archie filling the heavens with little balls of black wool, their concussions making the old bus stagger and tremble, I could feel plenty of moisture on my forehead and around my neck. And when white ribbons began to zip about the machine and I managed to identify them as tracer bullets, I was frankly scared stiff ...

Sutherland became fixated with the ground, trying to 'read' it for his reconnaissance report.

> 'You —— fool,' roared Potts, 'get that gun going before it's hanging in a Hun mess!'
>
> Instantly I became conscious of the split second present. It was easy to get the gun in action, but exasperatingly difficult to bring fire on the chap whose tracer bullets were flying around. He, I later learned was none other than [Gerhardt] Felmy, the Hun cock-of-the-walk on our front. Potts knew it and was zigzagging with all the cunning of which he was capable. At last

> I got Felmy in the sights and gave him a burst—and, by the way, no Lewis gun ever threw a bigger cone. Then, as opportunity offered, four or five more bursts, until Felmy broke off the fight and went home.[77]

Potts put his nose down but not before the sky around them erupted with bursting shells. Their red-hot splinters hummed through the air. One hit their engine, giving it, in Sutherland's words, 'a case of St Vitus dance, [it] shook and shuddered and seemed bent upon throwing itself off its bearers'. They made it home, but only just. In the mess that night, Sutherland listened in as the old hands discussed Felmy. He was, Williams reckoned, 'easily our most formidable opponent'—a Western Front veteran and a killer, with 'a bag' of aerial victories to his credit.[78]

The pilots also spoke of Felmy's 'sporting' side, explaining how he sometimes dropped letters from shot-down airmen on the Australian aerodrome. Just five days before Sutherland's arrival, a flight of three (a Martinsyde and a BE12a escorting a BE2e) was crossing the lines when an Albatros and a Rumpler dived on them. The Australians instantly recognised Felmy's insignia—black rings—on the Albatros's tail. The Martinsyde pilot, Charles Brookes (seconded to the squadron from the RFC) threw his machine into a violent evasive manoeuvre, but his wings collapsed and the aircraft dropped out of the sky. The German pilots then turned on Claude Vautin in the BE12a while the reconnaissance machine dived for home. Although hopelessly outmanoeuvred, Vautin turned to meet their attack:

> On opening fire with my synchronised Vickers gun, I imagine it must have 'shot up' my propeller as it flew to pieces when diving. Both Germans then closed on me and one burst from them shot away my front rudder controls. I then came to earth out of control and crashed.[79]

Two days later, Felmy dropped a letter on the Australian aerodrome explaining how Brookes had been killed and buried with full military honours and that Vautin was a prisoner—or, perhaps more accurately, a guest of FA 300. He had dined in their mess and accompanied Felmy on a tour of Jerusalem. Murray Jones took a Martinsyde and dropped Vautin's kit bag and some letters (including one of thanks to Felmy) on the German aerodrome. He came down to 50 feet and waved to the German pilots gathered on the ground. They waved back and no one fired (see Plate 6).

Violence again replaced the congeniality three days later, on 13 July, when a pair of Australian BE2es crossed the lines near Beersheba. They were alone, having missed a rendezvous with their British escorts. Just on the Turkish side, a Rumpler dived on the BE2e carrying Archie Searle and Gerald Paget. It came out of the sun and before they could react, it had fired a burst that killed Searle instantly. According to Reg Baillieu, the pilot of the other machine, their aircraft immediately tumbled out of the sky from 5000 feet and crashed, killing Paget as well. The German pilot then turned and fired a burst into Baillieu's machine, damaging its engine. He dived for the British lines, barely making it across before his engine seized. He landed safely, but was understandably badly rattled.

Felmy was over the Australian aerodrome the following morning. He approached low and fired a white Verey light—the 'agreed' signal now used to denote 'diplomatic' intentions—and dropped another message bag. He then waved, did a circuit around the aerodrome and looped—almost 'as if he were putting thumb to nose' thought Sutherland—and flew away. He also noted the Albatros's brilliant speed and manoeuvrability, 'that is,' he added, 'judged by 2e speed'.[80]

Felmy's message bag contained a letter to Vautin's mother and another to the men of No. 1 Squadron. It also included a tin of cigarettes and a playfully warm letter to Murray Jones, whom Felmy had shot down and wounded in May. His letter for the squadron, still held by the Australian War Memorial, offers a valuable insight into the fascinating and unique way that the opposing airmen perceived each other—that is, with equal measures of curiosity, respect, admiration and even affection:

Dear All Sports

My joy was very tall to receive all of your letters. Tomorrow Vautin comes to take all the things and all the letters (with photo) which were dropped. He is such well educated and genteel boy, that we do with pleasure all, what is pleasant for him. But if you write for us you must write more distinctly, because our English is not so perfectly that we can read all; the most legible writings has firstly your writing machines, and secondly Murray Jones.

Vautin has me talked very much of him. I hope to fight with this sport more oftener. I thank him for his kind letter—I thank also for the decoration of the rising sun [badge] from Mr Lex Macnaughton. Perhaps I can see the sun later in Australia. Too my very best thanks for the photo of Mr Brown and for the kind letter and many photos of R F Ballieu ...

For souvenir I have exchanged my watch with Vautin, and we have engraved our names. Where can I disperse more aqueduct? Hoping our good condition is continuing long time. With best wishes for all who have written to us! With sporty respects,

Your G. Felmy, Oblt.

I beg, this letter not to send in a newspaper.[81]

In the *Official History*, Cutlack claimed Felmy died in a flying accident late in the war.[82] This is incorrect, as Vautin—who survived the war in a Turkish prison camp—received a letter from Felmy on the eve of the Second World War. The German veteran wrote:

When one becomes older, I am now 47 years of age, one thinks more often about those years which are a long way back ... I still keep your watch in which I have your name engraved at the time you gave it to me ... Do you still have my old watch?[83]

Cutlack also romanticised the communication between opposing airmen, describing it as 'the knightly fashion in which airmen frequently treated each other between determined duels'.[84] It must be said, however, that such fraternisation was officially (that is, above squadron level) frowned upon by both sides. Felmy's request not to publish his letter is evidence of this, as is a comment in a No. 1 Squadron officer's diary that describes dropping letters and kit 'a custom on the Palestine front which, if known officially would not be allowed'.[85] In a Red Cross interview regarding a downed airman in 1918, Frank McNamara explained the system of dropping information between aerodromes but was met with the comment from an (unnamed) officer present that 'there were good, weighty reasons' for not reciprocating German attempts at fraternisation.[86] Although not elaborated on, these reasons fit in with a general British policy banning any form of fraternisation with the enemy.

The fraternisation was probably rarer than some of the veterans who Cutlack interviewed would have liked to remember. It seems to have stopped when Felmy went on leave in August 1917, and was almost unheard of on the Western Front by 1917.

In any case, the occasional—albeit remarkable—exchanges between the Australian and German airmen in mid-1917 were overshadowed by the much more routine violence of air combat. In the eight months since the beginning of the year, half the squadron's flying roster had become casualties. Nine were dead, two languished in Turkish prison cells and another five were wounded, some badly enough to be sent home.[87] Being completely at the mercy of the German pilots in their vastly superior machines was, according to Williams, having a 'ruinous' effect on his squadron's morale.[88] But steaming across the Mediterranean, in shipping containers stamped with 'British and Colonial Aeroplane Company Limited' were new aircraft set to turn the tables in the skies above the Holy Land.

5
'A REGULAR GOD DAMN AVIATOR'
No. 1 Squadron's coming of age

Captain Frank Hurley, the AIF's official photographer, in the back seat of Ross Smith's Bristol Fighter, 28 February 1918. He has fixed his motion picture camera to the Lewis gun's swivel mount ring. *AWM P04060.009*

> I am a regular god damn aviator now. I have been up to 18 000 feet and looped the loop three times and heaved my inside out over the side of the plane at 13 000 feet ...
>
> —Lieutenant Tom Prentice, No. 1 Squadron, Australian Flying Corps[1]

'Hadji': The squadron draws blood

Twenty-three-year-old Ross Smith had shown great enthusiasm and potential for flying ever since joining the squadron as an observer in October 1916. Richard Williams, who regularly flew with him, recalled how on the way home from reconnaissances, Smith would often ask to take control of the aircraft, using the spare control column in the observer's cockpit. 'He would take control of the aircraft so far as lateral and fore and aft was concerned, I had the rudder, but that's how he got his first experience of handling aircraft in the air.'[2]

In his early days as an observer, Smith (nicknamed 'Hadji') had also demonstrated superb observation skills—a product, some concluded, of his upbringing on a station near Broken Hill and his time with the light horse. He was courageous too, earning a Military Cross for his part in rescuing a comrade shot down behind enemy lines in March 1917. While his pilot landed and helped the hapless man aboard, Smith kept approaching enemy soldiers at bay with his service revolver.

For these reasons, when No. 1 Squadron lost some of its experienced pilots to form new AFC units in early 1917, Smith was among those selected for pilot training. He returned in July wearing his 'wings', and quickly established a reputation as a talented flyer. Sutherland, who flew as Smith's observer sometimes, described him as 'a leader born, he was absolutely fearless . . . he was a great pilot, a deadly gunner, and he had brains'.[3]

Smith demonstrated his marksmanship and fearlessness to all just a fortnight after rejoining the squadron as a pilot. At dusk on 3 August, an Australian observer spotted an abandoned German aircraft on the ground at Khalassa. Six machines—one a BE12a piloted by Smith—set out the following morning to bomb it. As they approached the target, fingers on bomb toggles, the pilots saw that it was a dummy, a trap to lure unsuspecting pilots. Suddenly, as Hudson Fysh recalled, 'down swooped two Albatros scouts, and soon the air was full of tracer streams as they wove in and out amongst us'.[4] Smith climbed to attack with a boldness the German pilots were obviously not accustomed to:

> He was above me and I got in a short burst with top gun. We then turned, met nose to nose, and I got in about 30 rounds with Vickers gun. We came

together again, nose on, and the hostile aircraft put down his nose and made a right hand turn enabling me to get in a good dive of about 40 rounds. He then made off with his nose well down, into his own Archies at Sharia.

Smith then turned to face the other enemy machine, one of the new Albatros scouts—probably flown by Gerhardt Felmy.[5] 'We met nose on and I got in about 20 rounds. HA made a right hand turn, under my wing, and went straight off towards Sharia.'[6]

Further evidence of Smith's abilities came a few weeks later when he and Ellis spotted an Albatros escorting a Rumpler near Beersheba. They carefully manoeuvred into the sun and dived on to the enemy scout's tail, opening fire at 40 metres. The surprised German pilot threw his machine into an about turn for his own lines, and Smith manoeuvred to make another pass. 'Zooming up over him, I again dived and then swung round head on to him.' The two machines hurtled towards each other, and both pilots pressed their triggers. Smith saw his tracers enter the Albatros, but was then dazed by an enormous blow to the face. A bullet had passed from cheek to cheek through his mouth, breaking some teeth on the way, and another grazed his forehead, shattering his goggles. Smith immediately put his machine into a spin and made towards home. Ellis fired a long-range burst at the Albatros, before it escaped.[7]

Smith was hospitalised, but elated to hear later that evening that British intelligence had intercepted a wireless message stating that the Albatros had crashed. Ross Smith, the squadron—and indeed, the Australian Flying Corps—all had their first confirmed victory.

'The turning point of their fortune': German air power ebbs, September–October 1917

The wireless message confirming Smith's victory on 1 September also indicated FA 300 was struggling to get spare parts, apparently unable to repair a dozen unserviceable machines. Confirmation of this came on 8 October when a British pilot forced down an Albatros near No. 1 Squadron's aerodrome. Joe Bull was impressed with its design, but noted that its repairs showed 'they have no proper material at hand in the field'.[8]

Sickness was also reducing enemy effectiveness in the air. In mid-August, Gerhardt Felmy went on leave with malaria. Another officer died in Jerusalem from typhus the following month and on 26 September No. 14 Squadron shot down one of FA 300's few serviceable Rumplers near Khan Yunnis.

Things went from bad to worse for the Germans when the aviation reinforcements requested by Allenby arrived in September. There were two new British squadrons: No. 113, equipped with BE2es and RE8s, and No. 111 equipped with brand new Bristol F2bs. Popularly known as the 'Bristol Fighter', or simply 'Bristol', these two-seaters are regarded by some as the finest aircraft produced by the British during the First World War. They were in a sense the world's first real fighter bombers—sporting both forward- and rear-firing machine guns and a heavy carrying capacity, yet also having the speed and manoeuvrability to be formidable dogfighters. As Fysh put it, they were 'the master of any two seater and equal to two or more scouts'.[9]

With the arrival of the new squadrons, the RFC in Palestine reorganised to improve efficiency and cooperation with the army. No. 113 Squadron joined No. 14 Squadron in 5th Wing, which became a 'corps wing' to operate over the battlefront, predominantly on artillery observation and tactical reconnaissance. No. 111 Squadron, with its Bristols, joined the Australians in the newly established 40th Wing. As an 'army wing', its pilots were responsible for the strategic area—that is, the country far behind the enemy's front line.

The Australian pilots continued in their old BE2s and BE12as until, in mid-October, some reprieve came in the form of half a dozen RE8 two-seaters. Known as 'Harry Tates' throughout the RFC, they were easy to fly—'a gentleman's bus' thought Williams—and had the observer sitting in the back seat, a significant improvement on earlier British reconnaissance aircraft designs. As Williams also explained, however, the 'Tate' lacked performance, being 'too slow, too big' and requiring protection from quick German scouts.[10]

Williams wasn't satisfied. It was, he felt, inefficient to send two-seaters out with other machines as escorts.[11] He bypassed his immediate superiors at brigade and wing levels, and appealed directly to the new head of the RFC in Palestine, Sefton Brancker. 'Give me the Bristol Fighters and I will put two men in one of those aircraft and have the reconnaissance back in no time and they can protect themselves.' Brancker refused, but promised Williams some Bristol Fighters when more arrived. Williams later admitted this was a long shot: 'I hadn't the faintest hope that they would take the aircraft from the British squadron and give them to us. They didn't do that sort of thing for Australians.'[12]

Even in the hands of No. 111 Squadron's amateur pilots, the Bristols quickly made an impression. Within a week of arriving, they shot down an Albatros, and then another a week later. By the end of September, Turkish 8th Army's German commander Kress von Kressenstein was reporting that 'the mastery of the air has unfortunately for some weeks completely passed over to the English'. He cited logistical problems and pilot sickness, but concluded that it was the 'appearance of a new type of machine which is far superior to our one seater' that was proving decisive.[13] From Williams' perspective, 'the arrival of the Bristol Fighter was the turning point of their fortune in the air in Palestine'.[14]

'The Huns are evidently not game to come over the lines now': The Third Battle of Gaza, October–November 1917

At the beginning of October, the War Office pressed Allenby to break the stalemate at Gaza and advance into Palestine. With British war plans for 1917 drowning in the mud of Belgian Flanders, Prime Minister Lloyd George wanted Turkey knocked out of the war—or at least British troops in Jerusalem for Christmas.

With his artillery and aircraft bolstered, and his railway lines almost complete, Allenby proposed an offensive against the Turkish Gaza–Beersheba line starting on 31 October. Consulting with his senior commanders, he steered well clear of the approach taken in the first two Battles of Gaza, instead deciding to focus the bulk of his forces against Turkey's apparently weaker inland flank. The initial assault would fall on the extreme left of the Turkish front, at Beersheba. With this town's vital water supply secured, the British and Australian mounted troops would then roll up the Turkish line towards Sheria. On the following day, two divisions of British infantry would move against Gaza itself, in order to capitalise on the confusion created by the attack inland.

To maintain the secrecy of Allenby's preparations, the RFC had pairs of aircraft patrolling above the marshalling areas from dawn to dusk. With

NO. 1 SQUADRON'S COMING OF AGE

their new Bristol Fighters, and a two-to-one advantage in numbers, the RFC rapidly reclaimed the skies over southern Palestine. The Turkish High Command was totally blinded, with one of its reports noting that 'the enemy has enormous superiority ... Things have got so far that no further air reconnaissance is done by the 7th and 8th [Turkish] Armies.'[15] Bull noticed the absence of enemy machines overhead as he and the other Australian mechanics toiled to get their 'buses' ready for the battle: 'The Huns are evidently not game to come over the lines now, as we never see them over this part.'[16] In fact, during the final, crucial few days of pre-battle deployment, just a single German reconnaissance machine managed to cross the lines and take photographs. A No. 111 Squadron Bristol Fighter promptly shot it down.

British artillery and naval ships began bombarding Gaza and the coastal defences on 27 October. It was a barrage, noted the British official historian, on a scale not previously seen in the Middle East—in fact, the 'heaviest carried out in the course of the war outside European theatres'.[17] Thanks to the work of the flying corps, the British gunners had the location of 131 Turkish batteries marked on their brand new artillery maps, enhancing the effectiveness of their counter-battery fire.[18]

The battle began on 31 October as planned. The British 74th and 60th Divisions captured the enemy's extreme left front line between Khalasa and Wady Saba. Later that afternoon, the Anzac Mounted Division assaulted and captured Beersheba with over 2000 prisoners taken, but found the village's water supply was insufficient—a fact that would slow their progress in the following days.

On the night of 1–2 November, British infantry attacked and captured Gaza's coastal defences. Australian pilots supported them by bombing enemy batteries at night, Williams noting the success they had aiming for the muzzle flashes. For the next five days, the action moved south, to where the Australian and British mounted troops fought a pitched battle in the hills northwest of Beersheba. The Australian airmen assisted, bombing Turkish positions among the craggy rocks and valleys. They also maintained their strategic reconnaissance work, mounting between two and three flights a day over the enemy's entire rear zone to watch for movements of reinforcements, and the eagerly anticipated Turkish retreat. During the battle, significantly improved photographic facilities at the squadron meant new images were in the hands of field commanders within four hours of exposure in the air.

The German Air Service, substantially reinforced by the arrival of four additional squadrons just prior to the battle, vigorously contested the skies above the battle. In six days, the German pilots engaged RFC flights on eighteen separate occasions.[19] They tended to avoid the Bristol Fighters, though, and only tackle the older Australian 'buses'. On 6 November, three Albatroses jumped Ron Austin and Ross Smith in BE12as over Sheria. Both pilots went into spinning dives towards the lines, only narrowly getting their bullet-riddled machines across.

Meanwhile, three British infantry divisions broke through the Turkish front at Qawuqa. They captured the formidable Sheria fortifications and advanced to Huj, 16 kilometres east of Gaza. The reconnaissance machines noted enemy hospitals and supply dumps withdrawing from behind the battlefront. Rumours began circulating at the aerodrome of an imminent Turkish retreat.

'A sad spectacle': The Turkish retreat to Nablus, November–December 1917

Joe Bull and his mates had just finished their lunch on 7 November when exciting news arrived: 'The Turks were retreating and every available machine had to go out with bombs.' They rushed to the hangars and, shortly afterwards, twelve machines, joined by 24 others from British squadrons, set out to bomb columns of Turkish troops and transport retreating north towards Mejdel. Their attacks left the roads, according to one German officer, 'a sad spectacle with material strewn along the whole road, stationary lorries, broken up carts, dead horses, camels, bullocks and sheep, lying around with fugitives and wounded here and there'.[20]

The German airmen were hamstrung. With communications to the front cut, the squadrons couldn't be sure of how far away British cavalry was. At 10.00 a.m. FA 304b at Arak el Menshiye received an alarming report. British cavalry had broken through at Sheria and were within 2 kilometres of the aerodrome. Unable to find enough lorries to carry all of its munitions, the German squadron's commanding officer ordered its aircraft to be set up around the aerodrome to act as makeshift machine gun posts.

The report proved false, but the squadron received definite orders to evacuate the following morning. While loading their equipment, Australian and British machines struck, bombing the aerodrome and nearby station. Bombs destroyed tents, trucks, aeroplanes and the telecommunications system, as well as wounding a number of Turkish soldiers camped nearby. That evening, the German squadron commander received urgent instructions to withdraw the squadron north, as the whole Turkish line was collapsing. A frantic search for transport followed, with the German pilots only securing space on a train by threatening its Turkish driver at gunpoint.[21]

They burned what wouldn't fit on the train and set off for Et Tine, where thousands of Turkish troops were converging. An Australian reconnaissance patrol reported their location the following day and 40th Wing immediately dispatched 22 bombers with a Bristol Fighter escort. They dropped over a tonne of bombs on the aerodrome and its surrounding camps, causing considerable damage to aircraft, men and munitions. In Von Kressenstein's opinion, this raid 'did more to break the heart of the Eighth Army and to diminish its fighting strength than all the hard fighting that had gone before'. He went on to describe how the bombs caused huge explosions in the munitions dump, cut all communications and 'created wild excitement'. When, shortly after the raid, rumours of approaching British cavalry circulated: 'Many formations began to retreat without orders and broke into flight. A great number of officers and men could not be stopped till they had reached Jerusalem or Damascus.'[22] A fortnight later, German military police arrested over 6000 deserters in Jerusalem.[23] The German squadrons headed north too, losing much of their equipment and rarely getting involved in the fight.

In eight days, the Turkish armies retreated 90 kilometres, harassed all the way from the air. Most of the bombs fell on choke points in the enemy railway system, such as Junction Station, to slow their retreat. The British and Australian mounted troops pursued them, but supply problems impeded their progress and prevented the decisive breakthrough and encirclement Allenby had envisaged. Instead, they advanced gradually, defeating each Turkish rear guard in turn to occupy Junction Station on 14 November and Jaffa two days later. The following day, Australian observers reported the roads outside Jerusalem crowded with enemy traffic retreating north.

By the final week of November, some of the German squadrons had re-established themselves in northern Palestine at Tul Keram, El Afule and Jenin. They began appearing over the battlefield again, bombing the advancing British columns and harassing the RFC's reconnaissance and bombing efforts. On 29 November, a flight of Albatroses bounced an Australian RE8 escorted by a British Bristol. One of the German scouts dived onto the RE8's tail, but its crew—Ron Austin and Garfield Finlay—(both ex-light horse and with the squadron for six months) used the correct tactics to defeat their assailant. Austin explained: 'I dived and then zoomed and gave my observer a clear shot. He appeared to hit the scout and it did a steep bank to the left and went down.' As often happened, though, they lost sight of it in the clouds, leaving a question mark over its fate. Nevertheless, as Austin reported: 'The other two scouts followed us at a respectable distance to the lines and then turned back.'[24]

The weather broke on 7 December, curbing flying. The British assault on Jerusalem itself began the following dawn, and within 24 hours its Turkish garrison capitulated. In drizzling rain, Australian pilots bombed and strafed Turkish troops as they fled north and established themselves on a new defensive line 20 kilometres beyond Jerusalem.

The British people received their Christmas present on 11 December when Allenby entered Jerusalem. Although not decisive, his offensive had pushed the Turks out of southern Palestine and inflicted over 25 000 casualties.[25] A large portion of them occurred during the retreat, which temporarily crippled the German squadrons, leaving the enemy troops completely vulnerable to air attack. Although the German pilots regained some initiative after reaching the safety of northern Palestine, the battle had taken a severe toll. In six weeks the Germans had lost seventeen pilots and seven observers—more than the equivalent of an entire squadron.[26] Much of their motor transport and stores lay scattered along the roads leading north from Arak el Menshiye and Ramleh. When Ross Smith inspected the German aerodrome at Menshiye, he found masses of abandoned equipment, including engines, partially built aeroplanes and a vast stockpile of bombs.[27] 40th Wing's casualties were, in comparison, slight: four British airmen wounded in action and one Australian observer killed in an accident.

'Singing songs, drinking hard and playing the goat': A doctor for Christmas

The Australian airman who died during the Third Battle of Gaza was Fred Harvey. He was, in many respects, typical of No. 1 Squadron's observers—22 years old, from a white-collar profession and with a couple of years' active service at Gallipoli and the Sinai with the light horse under his belt. Harvey had been with the squadron for eight weeks when, on 12 November, he paired up with Len Taplin, a brand new pilot. They took off on what one observer described as a 'joy ride' at 4.00 p.m. that afternoon. Taplin—through a mixture of inexperience and youthful over-confidence, it seems—had refused to let the mechanics check his fuel level. The engine stopped in mid-air and they crashed from 500 feet. Taplin emerged from the wreck with minor injuries but Harvey's skull was fractured and he died an hour and a half later.[28]

Accidents like this were part and parcel of life on a service aerodrome. Harvey's death brought the squadron's fatalities through non-combat cases for the year up to seven—as many as had been killed in combat. And while some accidents were caused by recklessness and inexperience, the incidence of mechanical failures meant that even the most experienced pilots were not immune from crashes: Ross Smith, now C Flight's commanding officer, hit telegraph wires when his engine failed during takeoff on 29 November. His machine was wrecked, but he escaped with only minor injuries.

Like most flying units in the British Army, No. 1 Squadron didn't have its own doctor. As a corps of the Australian Imperial Force, AFC squadrons in the field used the Australian Army Medical Corps' hospitals. The system was another frustration for Williams, who often had to send men away for minor injuries and illnesses. In October 1917, though, through old connections with the AIF's senior medical officer, he managed to secure Captain John Harris, an experienced general practitioner from Rutherglen in Victoria. At 48 years of age, Harris was an unusual volunteer for the AIF. He had enlisted in the medical corps in August 1917, believing that his family needed to do their bit for the Empire. He had three teenage boys, but preferred them to focus on their studies rather than enlist.

Initially, Williams was taken back by Harris's age, describing him as 'a man almost old enough to be my father'—although this probably says more about the commanding officer's youth than the experienced doctor's age. He would, however, soon come to describe Harris's arrival as 'a Godsend'. He attended to the men's physical and mental needs, practically stopping sick-leave for minor illness, and developing close pastoral relationships with the men, who treated him 'like a father and spent a great deal of their spare time talking with him'. Harris wrote to his wife that 'I am afraid all of these young men here think I am an old codger . . . Some of the boys here call me "dad" so they must like me a bit.'[29] They did indeed like him, likewise mentioning him with fondness in their own letters and diaries.

Harris's work also extended beyond the Australian men in his unit. Within a few weeks of his arrival the line outside his tent contained British men from the RFC squadrons sharing No. 1's aerodrome and shortly afterwards, local Arabs and Jews. Williams, so often a stickler for regulation, showed great foresight by permitting this, hoping to 'win over' the local population.[30]

On 5 December, just a few days before Jerusalem fell, the squadron moved forward to keep up with the front. It set up camp at Julis on a ploughed field, but moved to Mejdel when the rain turned it all into a quagmire a few days later. The new aerodrome, wrote Harris, was situated on 'beautiful sand hills and about four miles from the sea which can be seen as blue as indigo in the distance'.[31] Coming closer to the coast did have its drawbacks, though. It put the squadron in the path of the occasional waterspout that made its way inland.

On Christmas Eve, a violent storm hit the camp, before the mechanics had been able to erect the canvas hangars. Williams opened his tent the following morning: 'I looked out and here were aircraft that we'd pegged down in the open, tails in the air, one on top of the other, upside down . . . Out of twelve aircraft, I think it was nine had to be written off.'

Fortunately, a few days after Christmas, the Australians received their first pair of Bristol Fighters from No. 111 Squadron, which was converting to SE5a scouts. Williams recalled, 'you've never seen anything like how it boosted squadron morale. For the first time they had equipment which put them on an equal footing—if not a better one, than their opponents.'[32] Joe Bull was excited to get his hands on one, describing it 'as a better job than the RE8' and proudly noting that the one assigned to his flight 'holds the record for knocking three Huns in one engagement'.[33]

The Australians put their Bristols to good use almost immediately. On 3 January 1918, Ron Austin and Les Sutherland were in one, escorting an RE8, when they noticed two Albatroses diving towards them out of the sun. The RE8's pilot fired a Verey light to alert his escort, but Austin was already on the job. He hauled the Bristol's nose up and climbed steeply to meet them. They passed, with Sutherland snapping off a few bursts on his Lewis gun, and then Austin turned sharply onto one of the Albatros's tails. 'I fired a burst of 50 at fifty yards range,' he reported. 'I could see tracers going into his fuselage near the centre section and he did a sharp turn to the right and went down into a steep spiral.' The other Albatros meanwhile stalked the RE8, slowly closing in from behind and above. At 200 metres, the enemy pilot dived. The Australian observer, Oliver Lee, swung his Lewis gun on its 'Scarff' ring' and fired. The bullets appeared to strike the pilot and the Albatros went into a steep dive.[34]

'The pride of his mother's heart': Photography and reconnaissance, January–February 1918

Throughout January and early February 1918, there was little movement on the ground. In the air, however, preparations began for larger offensives later in the year. The advance following the Third Battle of Gaza had placed Australian machines within range of large tracts of previously unmapped countryside, deep in northern Palestine (see Map 3).

The squadron mounted two long-range reconnaissance flights daily, one over the coastal sector and another east of the Jordan River towards the important Turkish rail centres of Deraa and Amman. The Australian observers ranged to areas 100 kilometres behind enemy lines and, according to B Flight's commander Syd Addison, gleaned 'much information of incalculable value and striking interest ... new aerodromes, important railway centres, new railway and road works ... all these and many other things of great military significance were reported upon for the first time'.[35]

Bombing machines followed the reconnaissance patrols, targeting newly discovered camps, supply dumps and aerodromes. Having regained their footing after their retreat north in November and December, the German airmen rose to the challenge. On 4 January, following a combined raid on the German aerodrome at Jenin, five Albatros scouts surprised the

MAP 3 Palestine, 1917–18

Australians and their British escorts by diving out of the clouds. They hit a British RE8 from No. 113 Squadron; sending it spinning into an Australian RE8. Its pilot, twenty-year-old jackaroo Jack Potts, died in the crash, along with both British airmen. Remarkably, Potts' observer survived, although he

NO. 1 SQUADRON'S COMING OF AGE

was unconscious for three weeks before he woke in a Turkish prison camp. The Germans buried the three men in Jenin, and erected Potts' smashed propeller over his grave. They photographed it and dropped the pictures over the Australian aerodrome, from where they found their way back to Longueville, on Sydney's North Shore, and into the hands of a grateful but heartbroken mother. Jack Potts, thought Dr Harris, 'looked as if he might have been the pride of his mother's heart'.

According to Harris, Potts' death cast a gloomy pall over the squadron again. The mood passed just as quickly, though, as he noted a few days later:

> It is astonishing how in a squadron like this accidents and losses are covered up by the men. We all feel it keenly but nobody mentions the things nearest their hearts. The only thing one notices is that the boys might take a few drinks more for a day or two.[36]

Jack Potts' death affected one man more keenly than the others. His older brother, Leonard, was also a pilot in the squadron. He and Jack had enlisted in the 7th Light Horse Regiment in mid-1915, fought together in the Sinai, both volunteered for the AFC, trained together and then joined the squadron on the same day. They were, apparently, quite inseparable.

Leonard had the opportunity to avenge Jack's death a fortnight later, on 17 January. In a Bristol Fighter over El Lubban, he spotted a formation of five Albatros scouts 1000 feet below and another formation of two 500 feet above. He left the pair above to his escort and dived for the last aircraft in the lower formation. 'I fired a burst of 30 [rounds] into the hostile aircraft,' he reported. 'It turned over on its back and went down completely out of control.'[37] Landing, Potts told his mechanics he was 'evens with them now'.[38]

No. 1 Squadron's reconnaissance and bombing were augmented by a major photographic project in mid-January. Operations north of Jerusalem had revealed to the army commanders that their maps were hopelessly unreliable. So, on 15 January, the Australians began to photograph a strip of country extending 50 kilometres back from the enemy front line. Each day for a fortnight, four or five machines (usually Martinsydes and BE12as) escorted by a Bristol Fighter would fly in a straight line, a kilometre apart, at 12 000 feet to take a series of overlapping images.

The Germans only interfered with this work on one day, 17 January. While taking photographs southeast of Jenin, five Albatroses bounced the formation out of the sun. Before Harold Fraser knew what was happening, an enemy pilot was at his tail and tracer bullets were zipping past his cockpit. With the propeller shot through and several timber struts shattered, his prospects didn't appear good. At that moment, though, the escorting Bristol Fighter arrived and drove the Albatros away towards its aerodrome. Meanwhile, Len Taplin was also in the midst of a deadly situation. When the German scouts appeared, he had his flying stick between his knees and his camera dismantled in his lap to fix a jammed shutter. One attacked him from behind. Taplin turned to meet him, but his gun jammed on its first burst. 'I cleared the stoppage still flying towards him,' he later reported. 'We were then about 20 yards apart and the HA then put down to go under me. I immediately turned and got on his tail. I fired a burst of 20 rounds, at the range of 30 yards; the HA then went into a vertical dive.'[39] Taplin then reassembled his camera, took his place in the formation and finished the photographic run.

In just two weeks, notwithstanding some bad weather, the squadron photographed 1605 square kilometres of enemy countryside.[40] The army's survey section used the images to draft a new set of maps of the region behind the enemy front. Brigadier-General Borton (who replaced Brancker as commanding officer of Palestine Brigade RFC) congratulated the Australians, heralding the work as 'probably the highest point which has yet been reached in map making photography'.[41]

'A peep into the realm of the infinite': Captain Frank Hurley, photographer, filmmaker and flyer

On 13 February, the monotony of aerodrome life was interrupted by the arrival of Captain Frank Hurley, the AIF's official war photographer. Hurley was something of a celebrity among Australians at the time, having been the photographer and cinematographer on Antarctic expeditions led by Douglas Mawson and Ernest Shackleton. After being stranded on the ice for twelve months during Shackleton's ill-fated trip, he had, in mid-1917 gone to Europe where he accepted an invitation to film and photograph Australians fighting on the Western Front. Hurley arrived in Belgium just in time to witness the climactic phase of the Third Battle of Ypres. His work on the

Western Front is of immense historical importance, not simply because he was a master of photographic composition, but because of the lengths to which he typically went to capture an authentic sense of the fighting.

Hurley was most impressed when he arrived at Mejdel, describing the Australian aerodrome as 'the most complete I have visited' and noting that 'every branch essential to a flying squadron has its separate shop'.[42] He spent his first day there fitting a movie camera to the Lewis gun mounting in the back of Ross Smith's Bristol Fighter. The following morning, Smith took Hurley up on a tour of the region. Despite all of his previous adventures, nothing compared to this, his first trip in an aircraft:

> Oh the exhilaration of that upward climb! The powerful throb of the engine whilst on the ground now resolved itself into a whirr, and the Hangars rapidly decreased in size until they became mere specks. Up, up we go; 1000, 2000, 3000, 4000 are indicated on the gauge and still we climb heavenward. The earth below us is assuming the appearance of patchwork. Here and there, numerous villages are scattered throughout this patchwork, looking like tiny patches of honeycomb; the roads radiate from them like white ribbons, the streams and waddies might be arteries with networks of veins.

Smith flew them east, across the Judean Hills and then towards the Dead Sea and into enemy territory. 'I am powerless and utterly incapable of describing the wild and tremendous grandeur of the view now stretched before us,' Hurley wrote. They flew along the Jordan valley, 'walled in by rugged ranges', and then back west over Jericho. 'The Archies greet us but the shooting is bad.' They then followed the Jericho–Jerusalem road, 'which winds and twists among the hills almost as circuitously as the Jordan itself'. Smith flew low over Jerusalem, giving Hurley the opportunity to photograph and pick out 'familiar streets and buildings within the walls and even ... pedestrians and traffic on the highways'. They then shot up through towering clouds to 18000 feet (5.5 kilometres). The view was 'now glorified a hundredfold' as they 'flew over a billowy sea of silver mist thrown into fantastic forms by the winds and sunshadows'. Hurley shot some film in this epic setting before descending. 'This day,' he declared, 'rates as one of the salient in my life for I feel I have travelled and seen the most fascinating and wondrous area of our globe.' It was, he concluded, 'a glimpse of another world. A peep into the realm of the infinite.'[43]

Hurley spent a few more days at Mejdel, photographing and filming the squadron at work. The images and film reel that resulted are among the most important visual records of the AFC's history. The men recognised this too, some of them writing about Hurley's visit to their families. Before leaving, Hurley gave a lecture on his Antarctic expedition. Two hundred of the men attended, with Bull considering it 'very interesting and much appreciated by all'.[44]

'Bright intervals in a generally cloudy sky': The Transjordan raids, February–April 1918

In February 1918, the British front ran from the coast, 20 kilometres north of Jaffa, into the Nablus hills where it turned south to close off the flank to Turkish forces further east, in Jericho and across the Jordan. Before advancing further north, Allenby would need to deal with these enemy forces, especially the Turkish 4th Army, based at Es Salt, just east of the Jordan. Two enemy divisions operated from there out along the Hejaz Railway, a single-gauge track stretching 1320 kilometres south from Damascus to Medina.

Allenby's first step was to secure his right flank by extending it east to Jericho, on the west bank of the River Jordan. On 19 February 1918, he sent two divisions of British infantry and the Anzac Mounted Division to capture the town. For two days they fought through the 'rugged ranges' Hurley had earlier described, against resolute and well-concealed enemy. The official historian described New Zealand mounted troops being forced to leave their horses and advance through the precipitous ravines in single file, hauling each other up rocky heights.[45] No. 1 Squadron contributed with two reconnaissance patrols a day to report on progress and bomb enemy positions. In some instances, the pilots dropped notes to the struggling troops, warning them of resistance ahead and suggesting alternative, flanking routes. When, on the second day of the attack, Turkish reinforcements congregated on the Jordan's east bank, five Australian machines bombed their camps and scattered them. By the following morning, the Turks had evacuated Jericho. A few days of poor weather prevented the Australians from letting loose on another group of retreating enemy, and when the clouds cleared on 25 February, reconnaissance flights indicated that the Turks had retreated across the Jordan and entrenched themselves just inland from its eastern bank.

With his right flank anchored against the Jordan, Allenby planned a river crossing to capture Es Salt (16 kilometres east of the river) and Amman (a further 16 kilometres east). He intended to cut the Hejaz railway and interdict supplies for some 20 000 Turkish troops stationed further south. Then there was also the prospect of linking up with an Arab army which, since June 1916, had been rebelling against Turkish rule in the Transjordan. Allenby had been encouraging them to harass the Turks along the railway and provided equipment and military advisors to aid them. The best known among these was undoubtedly Lieutenant Colonel Thomas (T. E.) Lawrence 'of Arabia'—a British staff officer who had worked with the Arabs since the earliest days of their revolt.

To prepare for the raid, No. 1 Squadron shifted the focus of its reconnaissance and bombing efforts across the Jordan during February and March. Every other day, a pair of Bristol Fighters traversed the rugged country between the river and the railway, often being in the air for over four hours and needing to land at advanced aerodromes to refuel. Sutherland admitted quite frankly that 'we of No. 1 Squadron were not too keen about these jobs. Too lonely. Too far off the beaten track.' He went on to explain that, although comparatively free from Archie and enemy fighters, these routes took the Australians over terrain concealing 'unpleasant mystery'—that is, Arabs, Circassians, Bedouins and Turks.[46] The work paid off, though. By the time Allenby's raid was due to begin, the Australians had photographed 602 square kilometres around Amman and Es Salt, revealing ancient caravan routes for the attacking troops to use, and had softened up enemy strong points with 3.5 tonnes of bombs.[47]

The raiding force set out to ford the River Jordan in the pouring rain on 22 March 1918. The river's swollen torrents prevented the force from crossing at Ghoraniye as planned, and held up the troops for three days while engineers constructed a pontoon bridge. They lost the element of surprise: on the afternoon of 22 March, despite reporting 'observation impossible owing to clouds' over much of their patrol area, Addison and Fysh spotted Turkish reinforcements moving towards Es Salt.[48]

The raiders finally crossed the Jordan on 24 March. The British infantry advanced along the main road into Es Salt, while units of the Anzac Mounted Division pushed up narrow mountain tracks leading 4000 feet up to the plateau on which Es Salt and Amman lay. The going was tough, with the light horsemen leading their mounts along in single file, through the pouring rain.

Observation from the air was, predictably, limited at best. Most crews returned from their sorties with little to report owing to the cloud cover. One exception was the team of Alan Brown and Alister Kirk who, at dawn on 24 March, spotted a troop train 'moving rapidly north' towards the raiding force. They machine-gunned it, stopping the train and causing its passengers to flee from the carriages. A Turkish machine gun crew, helped by some Bedouins firing black powder muskets, shot at the Australians without success.[49]

The 1st Light Horse Brigade entered Es Salt late on 25 March without any fighting. The other two mounted columns battled on up the mountain tracks, arriving outside Amman at dawn on 27 March. In contrast to their comrades at Es Salt, they found a well-entrenched and reinforced enemy, with field guns mounted on high ground to the town's east. They attacked, and managed to destroy some sections of the railway, but were unable to capture Amman itself.

During the battle, two Australian Bristols flew overhead to report on its progress. Arriving over Amman as the sun was coming over the horizon, the pilot of the escort, Eustace Headlam, spotted a German AEG two-seater about 2000 feet below. He dived and fired a short burst. The enemy pilot immediately dived away and landed near the town. Headlam then spotted a second enemy two-seater, and approached it firing. It, too, landed immediately. He then circled overhead while his observer machine-gunned the crew, struggling from their cockpits. At nearly the same time, another two Australian Bristols attacked a lone German two-seater, 8 kilometres to the south over Kissir. They both made a pass at it, causing it to land with smoke issuing from the exhausts. The enemy crew tried to make a run for it, but one of the Australian pilots, Doug Rutherford, opened fire, 'one only going a few yards before falling'.[50]

The Anzac Mounted Division unsuccessfully renewed its attack on Amman on 28 March and then again, in freezing rain, on the night of

30 March. It made little additional ground, and by this stage the enemy had repaired the damaged tracks and was bringing in reinforcements from Damascus. The raiders received orders to withdraw. For the next 72 hours, the raiding force made a fighting retreat back across the Jordan. The airmen bombed enemy reinforcements and dropped medical supplies to their comrades who, as well as their own wounded, had a number of civilian refugees from Es Salt.

Again, though, poor visibility frustrated the flyers. When the AFC's official historian interviewed veterans during the early 1920s, he got this impression of the skies above Amman:

> The reader must imagine no clear sunny sky above, but bright intervals in a generally cloudy sky, sometimes rain storms, and an untidy and often mountainous floor below; he must imagine, too, a low lying bulk of cloud hiding some point to be reconnoitred, and the air scout diving beneath it to keep a view of the ground or to identify troops discerned, and often narrowly skimming some misty hilltop in pursuit of his quarry.[51]

The last raiders were safely back across the Jordan on 2 April.

Following the failure of the Amman raid, Allenby resolved to make a second attempt, albeit with more limited objectives. In mid-April, he ordered Chauvel to take a force across the Jordan and capture Shunnet Nimrin in the foothills and Es Salt on the plateau above. While the British infantry advanced through Shunnet Nimrin to Es Salt, a light horse brigade would dash 24 kilometres up the Jordan Valley to capture the bridge at Jisr ed Damieh, which had allowed the Turks to commit substantial reinforcements during the first raid.

The second raid, which started before dawn on 30 April, was a fiasco from the beginning. Turkish defenders held up the British 60th Division at Shunnet Nimrin and prevented the 4th Light Horse Brigade from seizing the bridge upstream. That night, over 5000 enemy troops crossed the bridge, while more massed to cross another bridgehead further south at Mafid Jozele. They struck just after 7.00 a.m. the following morning, driving the 4th Light Horse back along the Jordan. Things began to look desperate, but they managed to hold a line just north of the Umm esh Shert track, now the one remaining exit for the troops further east. Meanwhile, the British infantry renewed its attack against Shunnet Nimrin, but were again repulsed.

A pair of Australian Bristols crossed the Jordan at first light to report on the situation. Fred Haig and Dick Challinor (an ex-light horse observer) were escorted by Doug Rutherford and Joe McElligott (another light horseman who had only been with the squadron since January) over the Amman plateau. Rutherford had an 'unlucky habit of attracting trouble' that made his comrades uneasy. Since his rescue by Frank McNamara in March 1917, he had been involved in several nasty scraps, one of which resulted in him being shot down and his observer dying. Although Rutherford soldiered on throughout the difficult days of 1917, he had, according to Haig, 'found it difficult to settle down to a normal routine'. It seemed 'that Lady Luck had deserted him'.[52]

Over Amman, three German scouts appeared above the Australians. Haig fired a Verey light, signalling Rutherford to close formation. The Germans dived past firing, then zoomed and climbed away. 'I opened up the throttle,' wrote Haig, 'and climbed after them, firing short bursts from my Vickers gun while Dick Challinor hunched behind his twin Lewis guns hoping to get a chance for a shot.' One of the Albatroses spun away into the clouds and the other two outran him. Haig returned to his reconnaissance area, but couldn't find Rutherford and McElligott. He soon spotted a column of smoke rising from the ground, and on closer inspection discovered it to be their Bristol on fire. Fortunately, the two men were standing next to their machine waving. The Albatroses, Haig would later learn, had perforated Rutherford's fuel tank on their first pass, forcing him to land. He had then burned his aircraft to prevent it falling into enemy hands.

A difficult decision confronted Haig. His mates were down there, deep in enemy territory, and he could see horsemen approaching:

> I decided that I should make an attempt to carry out a rescue. But I had my own observer to consider. I shouted over my shoulder to Challinor who was sitting back to back with me and asked for his opinion. The Queensland observer had already surveyed the rough desert floor and the rapidly approaching horsemen and he shouted back, 'No, don't try it we'll crash.'

But even with the engine throttled back the wind blew the words away and it sounded to me that he said something like, 'Righto, let's give it a bash.'[53]

Haig made a good landing, taxied to the burning Bristol and ordered Rutherford and McElligott to climb on to a wing each. 'They scrambled aboard,' Haig recalled, 'but Rutherford was very shaken and put his foot through the wing fabric before he managed to get himself settled.' Haig put his arm around Rutherford to secure him and pushed the throttle forward:

The gallant Bristol gathered speed and it looked as though we would make it, but just before it was ready to leave the ground Rutherford relaxed his grip on the strut and began to fall back. I tried to hold him but the wind resistance on his body turned us to the right and I was unable to control the swing, with the result that a wheel collapsed under the added strain and my splendid 'Magpie' buried its nose in the ground and subsided into a heap of wreckage.[54]

The four airmen emerged unscathed but were promptly surrounded by Arab horsemen, who took them captive and handed them over to the next Turkish cavalry patrol that came by. Rutherford's luck had indeed run out, unable to cover another thrilling rescue attempt. He and the other three were destined to spend the rest of the war in a Turkish prison.

Australian airmen continued to report dangerous developments east of the Jordan as Turkish reinforcements massed against the light horsemen and threatened to cut off their only escape route. On 3 May, Chauvel ordered a rapid withdrawal. The Australians put every available machine in the air to help their fellows back across the Jordan once again. Many airmen were personally motivated by the knowledge that their old units, officers and mates were in dire straits. Every reconnaissance machine carried four 20 lb Coopers bombs and orders to attack any Turkish troops they spotted.

In the flurry of activity on the aerodrome, two serious accidents occurred on the day the withdrawal started. The relatively inexperienced Jack Curwen-Walker took off at dawn and, according to one witness, tried 'to climb too quickly and too steeply'.[55] He stalled and spun into the ground from a few hundred feet. Both he and his observer died instantly. Later that afternoon, a British Martinsyde from No. 142 Squadron aborted a bombing raid and crashed into some trees near the aerodrome while attempting to land. A party of British and Australian mechanics ran to help the pilot, but when they got near one of its bombs exploded, mortally wounding William Fell, a 26-year-old labourer from Queensland who worked in the squadron's photographic section.

On 4 March, as the raiders streamed back across the Jordan, No. 1 Squadron tore into enemy forces gathering behind them. They dropped 32 bombs and fired over 2000 rounds into Turkish cavalry between Amman and Es Salt. Flying low over large bodies—some as many as 700—of troops was dangerous. Arthur 'Spud' Murphy and Hal Letch faced every airman's worst nightmare when a bullet fired from the ground lit a flare in the cockpit. It quickly ignited the aircraft's fabric, but Letch was able to put it out with a small onboard fire extinguisher. By nightfall, the last raiders had retired across the Jordan and held their line there.

Bad weather during the two days following the raid grounded all but a single flight. This gave the airmen time to catch up on some sleep and sit around in the mess and conduct a post-mortem on the previous month's work: two raids, and two failures for Allenby's forces. Combined with bad news from France, as Germany's spring offensives pushed the British and French back towards Paris, it all sapped the morale of the men that had peaked earlier in the year with the advance to Jerusalem and arrival of the Bristol Fighters. 'The end,' wrote John Harris to his wife, 'seems farther off than ever and Germany seems stronger than she was in the beginning.' He described 'everything . . . at a standstill here' and predicted the war would continue until 1920 at least, and possibly 'will last for years'. For the squadron's Gallipoli veterans, it was almost too much to bear. At the end of April, Harris diagnosed four of them with the symptoms of nervous breakdown and sent them home to Australia. Among them was Leonard Potts, who it appears had not coped with his brother's death and the constant spectre of his own.

What none of the men in No. 1 Squadron could have known, though, was that the Turco-German armies were rotting at the core. Allenby's monthly intelligence reports following the raids contain several translated letters and diaries from captured enemy soldiers. They paint a picture of an army bitterly divided by religious and cultural differences, and one that was, by early

1918, lacking even 'barest necessities in the way of supplies'.[56] The news from France, which so deflated the Australians, ironically was no consolation for the Germans either. One German officer reported heavy casualties in his battalion: 'It is no wonder that our spirits become daily more depressed. Not even the news of victory from France is able to alter this. But hopes of peace exist.'[57] But these hopes lay six months away yet, with the bitterest struggle in Palestine still to come.

6

'AN EXTRAORDINARY FIGHTING FORCE'
Battle for the skies, summer 1918

A rigger and fitter working on a No. 1 Squadron Bristol Fighter during the summer of 1918. *Peter Vyner*

> Nearly always flying in twos, the Bristol Fighters present an extraordinary fighting force, and their harassing of our activities becomes more and more felt.
>
> —German squadron report, June 1918

'The flying arseholes': The observers, 1918

A visitor to No. 1 Squadron in mid-1918 would have noticed a playful rivalry between the unit's young pilots and observers. In the mess, the two groups sat at different tables and attempted to out-sing each other. They competed on the sporting field, pilots versus observers in hockey, tennis and rugby, and the pilots had a few rude nicknames for their backseat colleagues too, including the 'flying arseholes' (a reference to the winged 'O' badge they wore) and '160 pounds of baggage'—from the label on a Bristol Fighter's fuselage saying it shouldn't fly without the equivalent of a man's weight in the observer's cockpit.

But underneath the light-hearted jibes and friendly competition, pilot and observer respected one another immensely. As Les Sutherland pointed out, by early 1918 the squadron had as many observers as pilots, and 'each realised the value of the other ... the odd pilot who had no time for an observer usually was to be found shooting down his Huns in the bar of either Shepherd's or the Continental in Cairo'.[1] Richard Williams agreed wholeheartedly, explaining how in 1918 his pool of experienced observers was the unit's greatest asset.

> We had a stream of pilots, men selected from the light horse, going through for training as pilots and coming to us and the observers really were more valuable than these chaps were, because the pilots could fly an aircraft but they didn't know the country. We used the experienced observers to take the new pilots out and to teach them the country and to look after them whilst they were doing it.[2]

These veteran observers were mostly ex-light horsemen, who had joined in early to mid-1917 and cut their teeth during the arduous days above the Gaza–Beersheba trenches. They typically arrived with just a fortnight or so of training at the school of aerial gunnery and did the rest 'on the job'. As well as 'knowing the country', they added a formidable sting to the tail of their Bristol Fighters. The pair of Lewis guns in the back seat could rotate 360° and fire about eighteen bullets a second, from specially modified double-capacity drum magazines containing 97 rounds.

Some of the Australian observers would do remarkably well with their Lewis guns over the summer. They included men like Garfield Finlay, a

FIRE IN THE SKY

22-year-old labourer from Sydney who, with an assortment of pilots, would manage to bring down eight German planes. Quite the 'backseat flyer', Finlay could, as Sutherland recalled, 'always be depended on to point out to such and such a pilot that he certainly would have got his Hun if he had done this and that'.[3] Sutherland himself was also involved in shooting down eight enemy machines while fellow ex-light horseman, Alister Kirk, an Irish motor mechanic who had been in Australia when war broke out, helped get seven. Some of the observers flew with various pilots while others formed enduring partnerships. As Hudson Fysh recalled, his more discerning comrades tended to jostle to get on board with the crack pilots and 'fought shy' of those who had crashes, rough landings and bad luck attached to their reputations.[4]

'Their harassing of our activities becomes more and more felt': Skilled adversaries, May–June 1918

Things became quiet again after the Amman and Es Salt raids. Allenby's operations were constrained by the stifling Palestinian summer and the filleting of some of his forces to stem the German offensive on the Western Front. In June, he lost the equivalent of three divisions in infantry, yeomanry and guns. Summer operations on the ground would therefore be limited to seizing some small pockets of high ground between Nablus and the Mediterranean coast and preparing for a major offensive in September.

In the meantime, the squadron shifted north to the old German aerodrome at Ramleh. Close behind the front again, its Bristols came within range of the very depths of the enemy's railway and transportation system in Syria which, throughout May, the airmen reconnoitred and photographed relentlessly. In four weeks, they made 29 strategic reconnaissance flights and photographed 466 square kilometres to produce new maps of the Damieh and Samaria regions.[5]

These deep incursions into enemy skies brought Australian crews into regular contact with enemy aircraft. The crews devised tactics to take advantage of the Bristol Fighter's assets—namely, its fast climbing performance and the double Lewis guns in the backseat. As a rule, the ideal killing position for enemy scouts was above and behind, whereas two-seaters needed to be stalked from below to avoid exposure to the enemy observer's gun.

In just one of several engagements during May, in which the squadron accounted for sixteen enemy machines, Ross Smith and his regular observer, Alister Kirk, demonstrated how it was done. They were on a long-range reconnaissance when they spotted an Albatros scout over Nablus, about 1000 feet above them. Despite holding an obvious tactical advantage, the German pilot turned to escape, but Smith swung his Bristol into a climbing turn to engage them. He was shortly within range, Kirk firing over the top wing as they closed. 'I got right under his tail,' reported Smith, 'and [Kirk] put in a full double drum at 50 yards range, a puff of smoke came out of the enemy aircraft and he started to glide. I then dived on to his tail and fired 40 rounds with front gun at close range.' This finished the Albatros, sending it spinning through the clouds out of control.

In early June, the reconnaissance machines noted Turkish troops concentrating east of the Jordan. Although some appeared to be harvesting crops, large groups of soldiers and cavalry were camping and building up materiel around Amman, Es Salt and the Wady Fara. German aircraft were also appearing with alarming frequency over British positions in the Jordan Valley, giving rise to fears at Allenby's headquarters that the enemy might soon attempt to recapture the river crossings it had lost during the raids in April and May.

The RAF dramatically ramped up its patrol efforts in the regions most frequently visited by German aircraft. Each squadron became responsible for patrolling a particular patch of sky throughout the daylight hours. No. 1 Squadron's workload escalated, growing from 32 hostile aircraft patrols in May to 133 in June. The patrol work brought the Australians into contact with some veteran German flyers who had recently arrived in Palestine, following Russia's surrender on the Eastern Front.

On 4 June, Albert Tonkin and Richard Camm were over Damieh when they spotted a German Rumpler further south, flying towards the Jordan Valley. Tonkin carefully manoeuvred through the enemy crews' blind spots to arrive in a killing position just below and behind them. Camm had an ideal line of fire into the Rumpler's belly, but his guns jammed. Tonkin then climbed slightly to bring his forward-firing Vickers to bear. Again, an ideal shot presented itself. 'I pressed the Bowden control but [the] gun did not fire. Apparently everything was in order . . . so I reloaded—but a second

FIRE IN THE SKY

pressure of the control gave no results.' Suddenly, the German pilot banked. His observer lashed the Bristol's engine with fire. 'Water sprayed over me,' claimed Tonkin, 'my engine went rough and was obviously badly hit.' He threw the Bristol into a sharp diving turn, but not before a bullet shattered Camm's wrist. Tonkin landed at Bireh hospital, where surgeons saved Camm's hand and invalided him to Australia. Their Bristol was so badly shot up that the squadron had to send a party of mechanics out to Bireh to replace its engine.[6]

Although gun stoppages were inevitable, Tonkin and Camm were immensely unlucky. In June, the squadron fired 43 000 rounds, experiencing, in the equipment officer's words, 'no trouble ... beyond a few minor stoppages'.[7] Two armourers maintained the squadron's guns and ammunition, checking for faults that could cause a jam. Many airmen also paid careful attention to their arms. Sutherland described tent mates Ernest 'Pard' Mustard and Alister Kirk as 'fanatics' who 'set out to know every bit of the gun by its Christian name ... [until] bolts, ejectors, return springs, gas chambers and firing pin had no secrets'. They obsessed over ammunition, arguing about the right composition—regular, armour piercing and incendiary—and meticulously preparing their drums: 'each drum after it had been fitted, with every bullet hand picked and polished, would be carefully wrapped up to keep out the sand and the dust'.[8]

A week after Camm's injury, Carrick Paul and Billy Weir, with Ron Adair and a new observer, Lawrence Smith, responded to an enemy aircraft sighting at 4.00 a.m. After taking off, they followed a trail of friendly anti-aircraft bursts for fifteen minutes that led them to an enemy two-seater, about 2000 feet above them. They recognised it as the one that had shot down Tonkin and Camm.[9] Its pilot turned for home, maintaining his altitude. As a testament to the Bristol's superb performance, Paul was able to catch up to him just north of Nablus while nearly doubling his altitude. From here the enemy pilot dived towards his aerodrome at Jenin, his observer firing widely from 270 metres. Paul replied with a short burst and flew underneath the enemy to give Weir a clear shot from the rear guns. For twenty minutes, the two machines jostled to get below each other's tail. When they had descended to 5000 feet, Paul got in a burst that hit the German observer. He then climbed above and dived on to the enemy machine, raking it with fire. It tumbled out of control and slammed into a hillside. They returned to Ramleh, the numerous bullet holes in their Bristol testifying to their opponent's skill.

At dawn on 19 June, Ross Smith and Kirk bounced another veteran Rumpler crew prying on British doings in the Jordan Valley.[10] 'While on patrol over Jericho,' reported Smith, Kirk 'pointed out a machine a long way away and about 500 feet above me'. He followed the Rumpler, 'keeping under his tail'. Suddenly the enemy pilot pulled up sharply, allowing his observer to fire at the Australians. The German pilot then kicked his rudder hard and brought his machine around to bear down on the Bristol's tail. 'For the next five minutes,' Smith explained, 'we flew around in circles, the enemy aircraft doing numerous "Immelmann" turns, apparently with the object of getting on my tail.' But Smith kept underneath the enemy's tail, allowing Kirk a line of fire while denying the German observer the same. The high-speed turns pinned the four men into their seats and blurred their vision, making accurate shooting difficult. Nevertheless, one of Kirk's bursts managed to knock the German observer down in his cockpit. The enemy pilot, apparently losing his nerve, then attempted to dive away. Smith seized the opportunity and latched on to his tail, firing a devastating burst at close range. The enemy aircraft went into a spiral dive, with Smith in hot pursuit. Reaching speeds in excess of 320 kph, he had to disengage to avoid losing his wings. Levelling out, they saw the enemy aircraft crash land just northwest of Damieh. Smith circled the hapless machine, while Kirk fired 300 rounds into it. 'Judging by the tracers, his shooting appeared to be very accurate,' noted Smith, 'only one man was seen to run away from the machine.'[11]

Although the German airmen devoted their greatest attention to the Jordan Valley area (in preparation, it would turn out, for a raid there in July), they also mounted daily patrols and raids over the central and coastal sections of the front. On 23 June, Sydney Addison and Hudson Fysh were on an early hostile aircraft patrol when they spotted a tight formation of four Albatros DVas southeast of Bireh, nearly 24 kilometres behind the British lines. Addison dived from 1000 feet above, scattering them across the sky. Falling at over 300 kph, Fysh was pinned to his seat 'with the aircraft shaking so vigorously that I expected the oscillating tailplane to come adrift any minute'.[12] Addison wheeled around and fired a 30-round burst into the rearmost scout, but had to break off when the engine showered his face in oil. After cleaning his goggles and clearing a gun stoppage, he again dived on an enemy scout, firing as he went. 'I saw several tracers enter the fuselage,' recalled Addison. The Albatros 'then reeled over and spun into the clouds'.[13] German documents later revealed that it had broken up before hitting the ground. The other enemy scouts scattered and escaped through the clouds.

The battle to keep German machines out of British territory intensified during the last week of June, when enemy machines crossed the lines over 100 times. The fighting took its toll on some of No. 1 Squadron's less experienced airmen. On 26 June, Arthur Murphy and Wally Farquhar, a light horse volunteer who had joined the squadron in May, were returning from a patrol when they engaged a German reconnaissance machine close to Ramleh at 18 000 feet. It had just bombed the Australian aerodrome. Murphy chased it down to 5000 feet, exchanging fire all the way. He hit the enemy observer, who slumped over his guns, and was forcing the German pilot to land on the Australian aerodrome when he noticed Farquhar unconscious in the rear cockpit. Murphy's gun jammed and the enemy pilot used the opportunity to escape. By the time Murphy landed, Farquhar was dead, a bullet through his heart.

The following morning, another new crew in the squadron, Gordon Oxenham and Lawrence Smith, was escorting Alan Brown and Finlay on a reconnaissance of El Kutrani when they spotted two heavily armed AEG two-seaters about 4000 feet above them. The two Bristols roared off in pursuit. Brown manoeuvred to within 150 feet behind and below one of the enemy machines. Finlay aimed his twin Lewis guns over his pilot's head and raked the underside of the German machine's cockpits. 'The enemy aircraft then went down in a vertical nose dive, belching forth huge clouds of smoke from underneath the pilot's and observer's seats.'[14] Oxenham and Smith were meanwhile in a turning contest with the other AEG. They were gradually losing height when it broke away and led the Australians over a 'well-fortified' enemy outpost. The sky around their Bristol erupted with fire from the ground, as Smith recalled:

> they fired everything they had about the place. Gordon was hit through the head. One bullet ... hit me a severe blow on the cheek bone, rendering me

unconscious ... As we dived to earth our plane turned on its back, I fell out, then as it straightened out again I was suspended [by a seatbelt] to the side of the plane. The terrific force of the crash plunged the engine right through my cockpit.[15]

Brown and Finlay circled the crashed Bristol for several minutes, but saw no one emerge from the wreck. The squadron initially assumed that both men had been killed, but on 29 June a German aircraft dropped a letter on the Australian aerodrome explaining that, miraculously, Smith had survived and was a prisoner (see Plate 9). Still, his parents had the crushing experience of receiving a telegram erroneously reporting his death. Williams passed the good news onto them, though, assuring them that he was likely to receive 'very good treatment indeed at the hands of both Turks and Germans'.[16]

Smith was indeed being treated well. As he later pointed out, despite being allies, the Turks and Germans 'hated each other's guts'.[17] The German airmen of FA 304b hid him at their aerodrome rather than hand him over to the Turks. 'Every time the Turks came to claim me they would shove me down into a hole and there I would stay, perhaps for two days,' he explained.[18] The Germans fed him well, provided books and even disguised him in a German uniform for excursions into Haifa. 'As we walked about the streets, the path was cleared, and I took my turn saluting, much to the amusement of my friends ... We made many trips all over the country, visiting all the Army Headquarters about the place.' The squadron threw Smith 'a large party' for his 21st birthday. 'Officers from everywhere seemed to arrive. I played and sang several songs, and the amount of talent these German chaps had made a most enjoyable evening.'[19] Not surprisingly, Smith came to greatly admire his German 'hosts', noting their bravery as they carried on flying against increasingly steep odds. After two months, though, the game was up. Turkish authorities 'crept in' and arrested Smith. He was sent to Turkey, where he spent the remainder of the war fighting off life-threatening illnesses in a squalid prison camp.

Farquhar, Oxenham and Smith left a hole in the squadron's tightly knit community. When a replacement observer, Clive Conrick, arrived at the aerodrome a fortnight after their loss, he added 'a sad note' to his diary,

FIRE IN THE SKY

describing how 'Gordon Oxenham's little dog raced up to us and sniffed each of us in turn, hoping to find that one of us was Gordon, coming back.'[20]

Another newcomer to the squadron avenged Oxenham the day after his death. Twenty-six-year-old Stanislaus Acton Nunan from Melbourne was a fighter pilot straight out of the mould. A motorcycle racer, he had enlisted in the 5th Field Company Engineers in early 1916 and arrived in France in time for a bitter winter in the Somme trenches. 'This life is most depressing,' he wrote to his mother a few days before Christmas 1916, adding that trench warfare had reduced him to caring little about anything or anyone. Having recently lost his two best mates—one to dysentery and another to enemy fire—he told her that he planned to transfer out of the infantry to 'another branch', where he would at least 'have a shooting chance of hitting back'.[21]

The flying corps offered Nunan precisely what he was after. He arrived at No. 1 Squadron in March 1918 after flying with a British unit known as 'X' Flight in the Sinai to support the Arab revolt. Back among his countrymen, he immediately gained a reputation for his impressive mechanical skills and as a 'confirmed souvenir hunter'. He was cavalier, dashing and supremely confident—in Les Sutherland's words, as 'game as a soldier ant'.[22]

On 28 June, Nunan and Finlay flew across the Jordan with Adair and Charles Vyner to reconnoitre the growing number of Turkish camps. They were over Amman when six Albatros scouts dived on them out of the sun. Adair and Nunan hauled their machines up to meet them and the air filled with tracer as all eight aircraft opened fire. They passed, and wheeling around Adair latched on to an Albatros's tail and blasted its centre section. It rolled and tumbled out of control. Suddenly, another Albatros was on Adair's tail, tracer zipping past his cockpit. He hauled the Bristol into a climbing turn, giving Vyner a clear burst from his twin Lewis guns. They finished the loop on the German's tail and fired off a long burst, shredding fabric and shattering timber until it too spun away out of control.

Nunan was meanwhile revelling in his first experience of aerial combat with two other Albatroses. It left quite an impression, which he conveyed vividly that night in a letter to his family. It captures both the thrill and violence of such encounters, as well as something of Nunan's jaunty character and his acknowledgement of the squadron's strict gentlemanly conventions regarding ostentations:

Dear People,

I have not heard from you since the last couple of letters I have written. This is just to tell you that I have had my first air fight and got my man. I will tell you how it happened on the understanding that it is strictly private and confidential.

... I glanced around and could not see them for a moment and then Holy Sailor, there loomed out of the sun six lovely big fat Albatros scouts ... We pulled our noses up and went straight into the Hun formation ... They split up all over the sky. I followed two who kept together. Put a long burst into one of them with my front gun. He put his nose down vertically. I followed him down at 200 mph. My observer brought both guns to bear on him and ripped them into him. I could see his tracers (flame bullets) gleaming off his machine. The Hun burst into flames and crashed into an orchard.

Nunan then got into a turning fight with another pair of Albatroses:

I circled with them for 15 minutes and had the time of my life. Between us (observer and I) we put into them nearly 1000 rounds of ammunition and got so close at times that we could almost see the colour of their eyes. I feel as if I should have got them both. While I was concentrating on one the other would be getting into a firing position behind me. Had we got one the other would have been cold meat for us. But together they were a pretty strong combination. I was not going to leave until I got them as I was sure to do shortly; but two of the other Huns came above a couple of thousand feet above us. As we were only 50 feet above the ground ... I broke off the fight.

... I enjoyed it immensely as soon as I got past the first touch of stage fright. The others were awfully bucked too.

... It is not considered 'the thing' to give a detailed account of one's exploits like this. You will of course remember this please.[23]

Nunan's debut kill brought the squadron tally to 26 since the beginning of May. The enemy was feeling the strain, with one German officer describing the Bristol Fighter as 'an exceptionally fine machine' that 'nearly always flying in twos ... present an extraordinary fighting force, and their harassing of our activities becomes more and more felt'.[24]

'Excellent fun for the airmen': Ground attack, July–August 1918

At the end of June, Richard Williams was promoted to temporary lieutenant colonel and given command of the 40th (Army) Wing, which contained the Australian as well as two British squadrons (No. 111 and No. 144). 'I really was surprised,' he later revealed. 'There had been ... instances when British officers were put in command of Australian forces but I knew of none in which an Australian officer was put in command of a British formation.'[25] Because a dominion officer could not, at the time, exercise disciplinary measures against British servicemen, Williams received an RAF commission. B Flight's commander, Captain Sydney Addison, a 30-year-old journalist from Franklin, Tasmania, replaced Williams as No. 1 Squadron's commanding officer.

With the German airmen becoming reluctant to fly at low level and engage them, some of the airmen in No. 1 Squadron began searching for targets on the ground. Although specific ground attack sorties had been ordered from time to time since 1916, in June 1918 pilots on any operation—reconnaissance, escort or photography—began to attack targets of opportunity whenever and wherever they could be found. The more colourful characters of the squadron even took to sneaking a couple of 'unofficial' bombs onboard for reconnaissance and escort flights. According to Cutlack, this 'offered excellent fun for the airmen and wrought demoralising damage upon infantry, cavalry and transport alike'.[26]

On the morning of 21 June, during a reconnaissance to Nablus, Ross Smith and Kirk, with Paul and Weir, set the tone for things to come. The two Bristols took off at dawn and followed the Lubban–Nablus road north, as usual counting enemy camps, transport columns and troops. They flew over Nablus and continued along the railway line to the German aerodrome at Jenin. All was quiet and, as was becoming increasingly common, no German aircraft challenged them as they circled the airfield and took notes. Smith and Paul then turned their Bristols back towards home. Near Samaria, they spotted a body of Turkish troops boarding a train. The Bristols roared in low and raked the station with fire. Smith recorded that: 'Panic ensued and troops ran everywhere. Train started north and we flew alongside of it firing at close range with apparently good result.' Paul and Weir joined in, firing 450 rounds into the train as it made its way north towards Jenin. They then followed the railway line south, firing at anything that moved. After a brief pause to strafe troops waiting for transport at Messuide station, they continued on to Naurah and machine-gunned a motor transport depot, camp and station. 'Troops ran from tents and dumps seeking cover in all directions, apparently very demoralised,' wrote Smith in his report.[27]

In Cutlack's words, such attacks henceforth became 'the rule'.[28] On 9 July, Ross Smith and Kirk, again with Paul and Weir, wrought further havoc, this time at the enemy's Jenin aerodrome. They circled it at 2000 feet, with Smith snapping off photographs while Paul and Weir followed behind, dropping bombs and firing into the hangars. The German ground crew wheeled out five scouts and began warming their engines but Kirk sent them running for cover with his Lewis guns. The two Bristols circled Jenin aerodrome for the next twenty minutes, firing bursts at anyone who emerged on to the aerodrome, and dropping a bomb directly on to the squadron's workshop.[29]

Three days later, the same two crews shot up Balata aerodrome and camps at nearby Nablus. Smith reported that the Turkish troops 'became panic stricken, and ran in all directions'. They flew home along the busy Lubban road, sending horses stampeding and enemy vehicles careering off the road. Meanwhile, Nunan and Edwin Mulford shot up a group of 500 horses and camels in the Wady Fara. They reported its position and the squadron sent another two machines out late in the day to attack it again.

The brazen ground strafes continued right across the front. East of the Jordan, along the Hejaz railway, long-distance reconnaissance crews shot up trains carrying troops and supplies to the remote Turkish garrisons along the line. It was exciting but dangerous work, as one pilot recalled:

> There was a thrill diving on a train filled with troops or munitions and seeing your bullets hitting the engine until it came to a stop in a cloud of smoke and steam, with the crew running for cover followed by any soldiers who were aboard. But often we experienced severe anti-aircraft fire from the ground, and if you were hit and survived the probable crash landing you were faced with all the horrors of capture. The Turks were not well disposed towards airmen who had just been machine gunning them.[30]

Carrick Paul and Billy Weir emerged as a particularly aggressive—if perhaps unlikely—ground strafing partnership. They had both enlisted in the light horse on the same day in Sydney, in September 1914, and then fought in the same unit at Gallipoli and in the Sinai. They parted ways temporarily in April 1917 when Paul was accepted into flying school, but they met up again at the squadron in January 1918 when Weir arrived as an observer. It was perhaps a foregone conclusion that they would arrange to fly together. Paul was unusual among the pilots in that he was married. He was also not quite the towering, bronzed Anzac effigy we might imagine. With a light complexion, slight features and quiet temperament, Harris thought 'you would hardly pick [him] out as a fighter at all'.

Paul gave a much different impression at the controls of his Bristol Fighter—a yellow machine the squadron nicknamed 'Yellow Peril'. According to Sutherland:

> the speciality of the Yellow Peril was a cavalry camp, and when it swooped down hectic things used to happen ... Paul and Weir could use their guns. Because of it, this anti-cavalry turn of theirs earned them a unique distinction. They were specially mentioned in Turkish orders as follows: 'All ranks are instructed to take immediate cover upon the approach of the yellow English aeroplane.' Paul and Weir certainly wrote that name on the Turkish memory in letters of fire—machine-gun fire.[31]

They lived up to their reputation on 14 August when they attacked a Turkish cavalry camp discovered that morning on the coast at Mukhalid. Working with Brown and Finlay, they started with the horse lines, sending them into a wild stampede. Brown reported that then the whole camp erupted into chaos. They then turned their attention to the beach, where some 300 soldiers were bathing with their horses. Under heavy fire from the cliffs above the beach, the Australians roared in low over the sand, machine guns clattering. Turks bounded in and out of the water and the horses bolted. The two Bristols left after expending 2350 rounds. Both were perforated with bullet holes, the riggers counting 27 in the Yellow Peril alone.

'Feeling like dead icicles': Battle preparations, July–August 1918

Photography and reconnaissance again became the squadron's priority during July and August, as Allenby's headquarters planned for a major offensive in September. In eight weeks, the Australians flew 68 long-distance reconnaissances and photographed almost 1400 square kilometres. Of particular importance were images of roads and the coastal plain, where Allenby hoped to break through with cavalry and motorised units and roll up the entire enemy front.

On no occasion did enemy aircraft prevent the photography machines from doing their job. When met, the camera-carrying Bristol Fighters (working in pairs) would pause to meet their assailants, deal with them and then resume their important work. On 3 August, four enemy aircraft attacked a photo reconnaissance flight containing another renowned pilot–observer partnership. Paul 'Ginty' McGinness joined the squadron from the light horse in March. 'A superb pilot, full of dash and adventure', he quickly became veteran observer Hudson Fysh's 'pick'. The two struck it off and shaped a formidable partnership that they would carry into the postwar aviation industry as the founders of Qantas. McGinness's flying skills were evident from the beginning, as Fysh related from their 3 August fight:

> We and our escort ran into four Albatros two seaters and promptly took them on. I remember in the melee firing a long burst at a two seater as it flashed past, but with no visible result. Then McGinness, making a sharp wheeling manoeuvre, was on his tail and diving fast, his front gun flat out to keep the German rear gunner quiet.
>
> A few close shots zipped past, the Albatros careered up in a great towering loop with McGinness on its tail close behind. Up and up we went in an eyeball and guts flattening manoeuvre with the ground careering away, stripping off 200 mph with the blue sky dizzily taking its place as we reached the upside down position.
>
> 'Ginty' shot the two seater down at the top of its loop with us also in the inverted position, the enemy then plummeting straight into the ground to end up a heap of smoking debris.[32]

In mid-July, to keep his battle preparations secret, Allenby ordered the RAF to stop enemy observation altogether. Each unit received an area to patrol, with No. 1 Squadron taking the sky between Bireh (north of Jerusalem) and El Auja on the Jordan. Three pairs of Bristol Fighters patrolled the sector each day, for about three and a half hours each. According to Fysh, it was physically debilitating work:

> Dressed in fleece-lined top boots, heavy leather coat and gloves, we would fly up and down getting colder and colder till I remember on occasions being unable to press the triggers of my machine guns, my thumbs limply doubling over. The enemy aircraft used to come over at their extreme altitude, which meant that we were for long at 16000 feet without oxygen, and used to come home feeling like dead icicles.[33]

The patrolling achieved results almost immediately. On 16 July, the Australians claimed seven victories in two separate engagements. On the dawn patrol, Brown and Finlay with George Peters and James Traill, engaged four German machines near Tul Keram, forcing all of them to land. An hour later, Tonkin and Ashley McCann had just finished their patrol over Bireh when they spotted three Albatros scouts flying towards British lines. Tonkin pushed his throttle forward and climbed to meet them. They spotted him and began to dive away. 'I followed with engine full on,' reported Tonkin, 'but had difficulty in drawing sights on them as they went down in a kind of spiral dive. When about 1000 feet from the ground I got a good burst of 30 rounds into the enemy aircraft at about thirty yards from his tail. He went down vertical.' Tonkin followed the other two Albatros scouts down to 200 feet, 'firing odd short bursts' at them as they landed.[34]

In addition to the daily patrols, the squadrons each kept a pair of fighters on standby throughout the day to respond to 'hostile aircraft alarms'. Wireless stations at the front alerted squadrons when enemy machines approached the lines. Les Sutherland described how this kept everyone on their toes:

> those two [Bristol Fighters] out there on the tarmac are 'standing by' for a Hostile Aircraft alarm. The two men in attendance on each machine are the

engine-man and the rigger. When the alarm sounds, their job is to start the engines immediately. You can see the flying-kits of the pilots and observers hanging over their cockpits. Yes, it is something like in a fire brigade station—the same air of alert preparedness.[35]

When the klaxon by the hangars sounded, continued Sutherland, the airmen would dash to their machines 'at full gallop. They grab their flying kit but don't stop to don it—that's done while they are climbing to gain their height.' The ground crew would fire the engine starters while the wireless operator yelled the direction and height of the enemy aircraft. The Bristols then took off and climbed steeply, following a trail of friendly Archie bursts ('pointers') towards the enemy.[36]

With the patrolling and alarm system, and their photography and reconnaissance for Allenby's headquarters, the squadron clocked up a remarkable 727 hours in the air during August. It weighed heavily on the ground crew, who laboured long and hard in the heat and dust to keep the aircraft serviceable. With the aircraft clocking up so many hours in the air, there was always something to be fixed, adjusted or tested. It was a considerable responsibility, as mechanical failures cost lives. Ern Stooke and Paul Krieg were taking off on a test flight on 19 August when their engine started missing. Stooke committed the cardinal mistake of trying to turn back. The engine seized and the machine plunged, colliding with a locomotive. Conrick described how 'there was an awful explosion and the plane burst into flames which were about thirty feet high. When help arrived they were just dying'.[37] As was the custom, the squadron dealt with the deaths swiftly to leave little time for the kind of reflection that could undermine morale. The other officers buried Stooke and Krieg in the cemetery behind the aerodrome almost as soon as their blackened bodies could be untangled from the wreckage. As squadron doctor, John Harris attended numerous funerals. He described them in his diary as 'a very matter of fact affair' and explained 'the work always goes on. The deceased man is sewn up in his blanket with his uniform on and is consigned to the dust by perhaps four or six of his comrades.'[38]

The hostile aircraft alarm sounded daily during the latter half of August. Given the tight screen maintained over the front by the British and Australian squadrons in the morning and afternoon, the Germans began sending their reconnaissance machines over at 18000 feet during the middle of the day, when the heat reduced the Bristol's climbing performance.

Williams decided to set a trap. He put two patrolling aircraft in the sky and another two on the ground, 'where they could easily be seen. These took off as [the German machine] approached and when we were expecting him to be watching the aerodrome rather than the sky.' The trap worked, but at a cost for No. 1 Squadron.

On 22 August, Brown and Finlay, together with relative newcomers Johnny Walker and Hal Letch, were airborne to spring the trap. When a German LVG came over the aerodrome, the other two 'bait' Bristols took off and the whole squadron came out to watch. Williams craned his neck up and shouted 'No!' as Walker dived at the LVG from above and behind, right through the enemy observer's field of fire. The Bristol was almost instantly alight and slowly gliding towards the earth. Williams understood what this meant for the two young men at its controls:

> Both were at once faced with death by fire if they remained in the aircraft or by contact with the earth if they both jumped. They jumped, and it was a trying experience to see one's own fellows faced with such a decision.[39]

Meanwhile, Brown positioned himself ahead of and slightly above the LVG to give Finlay a clear shot. After firing 400 rounds, Finlay's gun fell off its mounting. Brown turned sharply and came in behind the German two-seater. He closed inside 50 metres and pummelled it with bullets. It spiralled down and made a bad landing near the aerodrome. According to Major Addison, the enemy crew were remarkably fortunate to survive: 'A bullet had passed through the pilot's glove, and three more had punctured a map board that was resting on the observer's knees. Their machine was riddled.'[40] Nevertheless, it was a trophy for the squadron, being the first German machine it shot down in friendly territory in the Middle East. Accordingly, the men raided it for souvenirs and snapped photographs with their vest pocket cameras, which officially they weren't supposed to have (see Plate 10). Conrick was 'lucky enough to get a German cross which I cut from the fuselage.'[41] Brown and Finlay took their own laurel from the fight: both receiving the Distinguished Flying Cross.

The dogfight's proximity to the aerodrome meant that all were confronted with the horrible fate of their mates. Harris wrote in his diary how they found Walker and Letch's 'frightfully injured' bodies some distance from their wrecked aircraft.[42] From what Joe Bull could tell, 'Letch jumped out as he was not burned but Walker was badly burnt so he must have controlled the machine until the tank burst and then threw him out'.[43]

Remarkably, the Australian officers extended the full hospitality of their mess to the two captured German officers. They dined there twice in the week following, joined the officers on swimming leave and at a picture show, and attended Walker and Letch's funeral. Conrick's appraisal of the men who had just killed two of his mates as 'quite decent chaps' is evidence of lingering attitudes from an earlier era of warfare.[44] Such fraternisation with those they were trying to kill in the sky produced confused and contradictory feelings, though. After another pair of shot-down German airmen visited the aerodrome for afternoon tea in May, Harris considered them 'very nice young men', prompting him to admit in the privacy of his diary, 'the thought that occurred to me was why are we fighting and killing one another?'[45]

There was little place for chivalry at 10 000 feet, however. Two days later, in one of the German Air Service's last serious attempts to discover the progress of British preparations on the ground, the German pilots employed a deceptive ruse. The hostile aircraft alarm sounded at 8.00 a.m., sending Peters and Traill, together with McGinness and Howard Fletcher, running to their Bristol Fighters. They climbed over the aerodrome and followed a string of British Archie bursts northwards. Sure enough, over Jelil they spotted an LVG at 9000 feet. Seeing the Australians, its pilot turned towards home and fired a string of Verey lights. 'Almost immediately,' reported McGinness, 'six enemy scouts appeared from the north-west flying about 1000 feet above us.' The LVG had been the bait in a trap.

Peters made the quick decision to press on after the LVG while McGinness climbed to meet the six enemy scouts. The German flight leader, distinguished by the red loops around his fuselage, came straight at McGinness's machine, but broke away when met with hot fire from Fletcher in the back seat. Two others followed, and Fletcher's well-aimed bursts saw them off too. The remaining three German scouts shied away, and gave McGinness a wide berth as they dived past. He set off after the middle one, pressing the firing button at 45 metres range. It rolled and spiralled down trailing smoke, exploding as it hit the ground. McGinness then chased another one down to 200 feet, firing as its frightened pilot attempted to land on a road. The German scout lurched and collided with a truck. As they zoomed past, Fletcher gunned down the pilot, as he struggled from the wreck.

Peters, meanwhile, continued to pursue the 'bait'. He fired at it, first diving from above and then pulling up below. It quaked and shuddered as bullets tore through its fabric and timber frame, and then 'went down like a leaf and crashed'.[46] Two of the scouts that had dived past McGinness now bore down on Peters and Traill. From 130 metres away, Traill coolly snapped off carefully aimed bursts at each in turn, sending both spinning away. The first one disappeared into clouds, but Peters chased the second one down, firing until it slammed into the ground. With mere feet to spare, he hauled the stick back into his stomach to avoid hitting an enemy anti-aircraft gun. They skimmed over it, spraying the crew with bullets as they went. The two Bristols returned to Ramleh triumphantly, with only a single bullet hole through Peters' tailplane.[47]

The day had been a disaster for the German Air Service. Out of the seven aircraft (six Pfalz scouts and the LVG), only a single Pfalz made it home. Major-General Salmond and General Allenby congratulated the four Australians and approved a Distinguished Flying Cross for each.

'A lot of rabbits searching for a funk hole': A funeral for the German Air Service in Palestine

By the final week of August, the German squadrons were practically incapable of offering any resistance in the sky. Since March, they had lost 59 pilots and observers.[48] FA 301's losses were such that it suspended all flights over certain sectors, while those on 'the rest of the front will be attempted to be maintained occasionally'.[49] The vulnerability of their aerodromes invited a swift and ignominious end to German air power in the Middle East.

Five successive bombing raids on 21 August—one of them by six Australian Bristol Fighters—hit the German aerodrome at Amman. It was wrecked and then abandoned. Stan Nunan, in his characteristically brash and aggressive manner, smashed up the Jenin aerodrome a week later. His observer, Clive Conrick, described the raid, capturing something of the extent to which the British and Australian airmen controlled the air, and subsequently everything that moved underneath it. It began with a hostile aircraft alarm at noon:

> Nunan and I rushed for the bus, Allan Brown's, and flew off for Deir Alla, climbing all the way. From Deir Alla we flew to Jenin, patrolling over the [German] aerodrome at four thousand feet. There was no Archie so we came down to seventeen hundred feet. Still no movement down below, so down we came again, but this time to a hundred feet or so, from which height we machine-gunned the seven Hun scouts and one two-seater on the ground, as well as the hangars. There were troops and mechanics dashing all over the place, looking, for all the world like a lot of rabbits searching for a funk hole. I had great fun and used up four hundred rounds of ammunition and Nunan used a hundred rounds. We dived into an air pocket and the plane dropped and I came half way out of my cockpit and broke the bolt on the right hand side of my gun mounting. On the way home, we flew over Nablus where we were 'Archied'.

They returned to the aerodrome. Conrick had nearly been thrown from his aircraft, flown through a storm of exploding Archie and had, in all likelihood, killed dozens of enemy ground crew. He finished his diary entry for the day not with reflection on these things, but instead: 'I had two sets of tennis before dinner and won both of them, only just.'[50] Such was the bizarre 'double life' of the First World War aviator.

The Germans made a final attempt at discovering where Allenby's battle preparations were occurring on the last day of August. McGinness and Fysh were on the afternoon patrol when they discovered a pair of LVGs spying on British forces below. McGinness skirted around to the north, cutting off their escape route, and closed in. He used the tried and tested tactic: 'I dived at one enemy aircraft from in front and fired a short burst of 15 rounds. I then turned under the tail of [the] enemy aircraft and Lieutenant Fysh opened fire at 100 yards getting in a very good burst.' The enemy pilot made evasive manoeuvres and started to dive, but McGinness kept below and behind, in its rear gunner's blind spot. Fysh blasted the machine's underside from close range and the LVG pitched into a steep dive and went to pieces. McGinness then pursued the second LVG, again diving underneath to let Fysh tear into it from close range with his Lewis guns. It too went into a vertical dive, losing its wings before crashing.

'It was a fantastic sight,' recalled Fysh, 'as the fuselage with the wings gyrated down while the two starboard wings with interplane struts attached floated off in another direction.' Everyone on the aerodrome had watched the fight, and cheered as they pulled up on the tarmac. Fysh was ecstatic; he dubbed it 'the greatest day I have had in the war'. The following one was sobering, though, when he helped bury two of the dead German airmen.[51] In a letter to his mother shortly afterwards, he admitted: 'It is a funny thing to go to the funeral of two men you have actually killed yourself,' although he tried to assure her that it hadn't affected him as he was 'used to' seeing dead people.[52]

In a metaphorical sense, the funeral was for more than just two aviators. It effectively marked the end of German air power in the Middle East. In eight weeks, the Australians had claimed 38 enemy machines (including at least seventeen definitely destroyed). The Germans, who had been crossing the line 100 times per week in June, managed to get just four machines across in the first week of September.[53]

The British official historian recorded the significance of this, emphasising that the RAF's dominance of the skies would have 'a powerful influence' in Allenby's coming offensive. Although he acknowledged the contribution of 'all' British squadrons, he maintained that 'it would hardly be an exaggeration to say that the Bristol Fighters of the Australians kept the sky clear'.[54]

The result of this was a sky that was practically empty of enemy aircraft. As Allenby himself later claimed, come September the Turkish command had little idea of where his armies would strike. Despite major logistical preparation involving tens of thousands of troops and transports on the British front near the coast, where he intended to attack, the Turks spread their forces right across the front, including east of the Jordan River.

The near-wholesale destruction of the German Air Service in Palestine during July and August 1918 achieved another result, though. As of 1 September 1918, the Australian and British airmen were practically free to roam about enemy skies unmolested, shooting up anything on the ground that caught their attention. And this they would do in the coming weeks, wreaking devastation only previously imagined in the pages of the Jules Verne and H.G. Wells science fiction which the airmen had fed their imaginations with as schoolboys.

7
'NINE MILES OF DEAD'
The Battle of Megiddo, September and October 1918

No. 1 Squadron's bombs falling on El Afule railway station on 19 September 1918, the first day of the Battle of Megiddo. *Peter Vyner*

> I can think of no word to convey the dreadfulness
> of this action ...
>
> —Lieutenant Les Sutherland, No. 1 Squadron Australian Flying Corps

'The open gate': Allenby's battle plan

While the airmen battled for control of the skies throughout the summer, the British high command put together a plan to bring the whole campaign to a decisive close. On 11 August, General Allenby revealed the scheme to his corps commanders.

It was a bold proposal designed to exploit the Turks' thinly held front line and acute lack of reserves. Allenby intended to attack with the majority of his forces (XXI Corps) in a 13 kilometre-wide corridor between the main Turkish railway and the Mediterranean coast. The infantry would break through the Turkish trenches and, like a gate, swing northeast towards Tul Keram to roll up its front. The cavalry would then charge up the coast through the 'open gate', and swing inland across the heights of Samaria and out on to the Plain of Esdraelon at Megiddo. From there, the cavalry could paralyse the Turkish command and control system by capturing the key transport and communication centres at El Afule, Nazareth, Jenin and Beisan. If this could be achieved quickly enough, the cavalry would be in a position to completely cut off the retreat of the two Turkish armies (8th and 7th) stationed between the Jordan River and the coast.

While XXI Corps attacked on the coast and sent its cavalry on a breakthrough charge into the Turkish rear areas, XX Corps (in the centre) would advance north towards Nablus. A smaller force under General Chaytor, would meanwhile make feint attacks in the Jordan Valley to deceive the Turks into maintaining substantial forces there. East of the Jordan, Lawrence and the Arabs would cripple Turkish rail transport by advancing along the Hejaz and capturing key junction towns.

Allenby gave the RAF a crucial role. If all went to plan, the battle would move rapidly and intelligence would date quickly. Therefore, his headquarters would need to rely on the pilots to keep them in touch with the action at the front. Zero hour was scheduled for 4.30 a.m. on 19 September.

'Nothing unusual to report': Deception tactics, 1–18 September 1918

In the three weeks preceding the offensive, Allenby needed to move three divisions across from the Jordan Valley to the coast, where they would attack. It was imperative that this be done in absolute secrecy to ensure surprise for the cavalry and a clean breakthrough up the coast.

The greatest threat to the secrecy of British preparations should have been German reconnaissance aircraft. But the entire German Air Service in Palestine could, according to one German source, only muster three aircraft by mid-September.[1] The marshalling areas were nevertheless patrolled vigorously. Paul McGinness and Hudson Fysh were the only crew in 40th Wing to engage an enemy machine prior to the offensive, on 14 September over Jenin. They forced it down and strafed it.

Below, the army was engaged in its own efforts to blind the enemy. British agents deliberately started rumours in town bazaars that the offensive would be directed along the Jordan Valley. The story was given credence by 15 000 timber trestles, dressed as 'dummy horses' that replaced the real ones in the valley's camps. At night, thousands of fires burned in empty British camps and during the day, donkeys dragged sleds around the Jordan Valley to create the huge dust clouds typically associated with masses of cavalry.

It was a convincing ploy. A captured German map dated 17 September placed the Australian Mounted Division in the Jordan Valley where it had spent the summer—not over on the coast where it in fact was waiting for zero hour. Another report, found on a captured German airman just four days prior to the start of the battle, stated that despite some 'regrouping' of British cavalry units on the coast, there was 'nothing unusual to report'—this despite the fact that, over the past fortnight, the British had in fact deployed two mounted divisions and an infantry division, and tripled their artillery there.[2] That the Turks believed the offensive would be directed along the Jordan was confirmed beyond doubt when, just prior to the offensive, an Australian reconnaissance flight indicated that the Turks were working hard to strengthen their defences in that region.

On the afternoon of 18 September, Richard Williams visited the squadrons in 40th Wing to explain the plan. Stan Nunan was 'fairly knocked' by the 'audacity' of Allenby's plan to outflank the entire Turkish front with cavalry.[3] Each British squadron, Williams revealed, had a specifically designated part to play in the offensive—a sector to patrol or targets to bomb. The Australians, however, were to maintain their broad, strategic role and keep a general oversight over the entire battlefront. The observers would report any Turkish retreats to RAF HQ via wireless, which would in turn arrange raids to rout the enemy. Ross Smith and Pard Mustard would undertake special bombing missions in a Handley Page bomber, which had recently arrived from England. With its twin engines and 30.4 metre wingspan, the 'HP' was a behemoth compared with the Bristol Fighter. It was the only one of its kind outside of Europe, and its assignment to No. 1 Squadron (and Ross Smith) was a considerable accolade (see Plate 12).

Knowing the whole squadron would be stretched, Williams also addressed the mechanics and warned them to be prepared to 'work all hours' during the coming days.[4] The men were pleased with their important role in the scheme. 'It seems,' noted Conrick proudly, 'that we are No. 1 Squadron in fact as well as in name.'[5]

Sutherland captured the tension and restlessness that beset the mess that night.

> At dinner that night . . . we talked of targets. Talked and talked. But not over drinks. Mustn't be any thick heads or shaky hands next day. What the deuce *was* going to happen? Some brooded; some wrote letters—you could tell by their air that this might be the last words to their dear ones. Nearly everyone bought extra cigarettes and chocolate. Handy things, those, if one is forced down in the wrong place.[6]

'Child's play for those in the air': 19–20 September 1918

The roar of two 375 horsepower Rolls Royce engines woke Sutherland at about 1.00 a.m. on the 19 September. It was Ross Smith, his observer Pard Mustard and two other crew in the Handley Page bomber, on their way to make the opening strike of what historians would dub the Battle of Megiddo, one of the most spectacularly successful offensive actions of modern military history.

Smith bombed the Turkish army group telephone exchange at El Afule. A few hours later, British DH9s hit it again, and also raided the Turkish 7th and 8th Army telephone line junctions at Nablus and Tul Keram. According to the commander of the Turkish forces, Lieutenant General Liman von Sanders, by 7.00 a.m., 'telephonic and telegraphic communication between Tul Keram and Nazareth [his headquarters] ceased . . . the wireless headquarters of the 8th Army also failed to reply when called.'[7] The enemy commanders were blind and deaf before the battle had even really started.

The British artillery barrage began at 4.30 a.m. Fifteen minutes later, five infantry divisions of XXI Corps left their trenches with the cavalry close behind.

No. 1 Squadron's first machines were aloft at 5.25 a.m. to report developments to RAF headquarters via wireless. McGinness and Fysh, with Eustace Headlam and William Lilly, flew a wide circuit over the Turkish back areas. They found most of the camps between El Afule and Tul Keram quiet, apparently unaware of the British attack. Flying towards the front, though, they spotted British cavalry breaking through on the coast as planned, and Turkish infantry beginning to fall back.

Harold Maughan and Sutherland were airborne just before 6.00 a.m. to escort a large flight of British DH9s to bomb the main Turkish railway junction at El Afule:

> Dawn was just showing in the east. The earth was a dim dark mass; not a light showing anywhere ... Even from our height of 10 000 feet the sight was magnificent. We could not hear the guns but we could feel the percussions.[8]

The aircraft dropped their bombs with devastating effect but encountered heavy anti-aircraft fire. One DH9 was hit and came down within sight of the German aerodrome at Jenin. Maughan and Sutherland circled in their Bristol and landed nearby to rescue its crew. Suddenly, as Sutherland put it: 'Hundreds of natives seemed to appear from nowhere.' They were Bedouins from a nearby village, apparently interested in the £40 reward the Turks were offering for captured British airmen. As the two British officers sprinted towards the Bristol, Sutherland swung his Lewis guns around and fired into the charging line of Bedouins: 'Rat-a-tat-tat-tat. It was impossible to miss. Gaps appeared in the Bedouins' ranks and down they went, wounded and unwounded to take cover.' Maughan meanwhile tossed out everything they didn't need—spare ammunition, camera, photo plates, rations—to lighten the machine. He directed the British observer to crouch on the floor of Sutherland's cockpit and the pilot to sit up on the Lewis gun mounting and hold on to the top wing struts:

> The Bristol with her double human load, moved slowly forward at full throttle. The machine rolled, staggered and lurched over the rough ground ... up

came the tail and the pace increased, up to flying speed. She was off! Cheers from all concerned!

Maughan set a course for Ramleh and, after barely clearing a 3000 feet-high mountain range, landed safely.[9]

At 9.45 a.m., a flight of three Bristols led by Colin Cameron and Howard Fletcher over the main front spotted the first sign that the Turkish 8th Army's front was collapsing. Over 7000 troops with transport and guns were making a 'general and disorganised retreat' north along the road from El Tireh towards Tul Keram.[10] The crews bombed and machine-gunned the mass, blocking the road and scattering the men and horses. They returned to Ramleh with the news. Sutherland was waiting by his aircraft, having just returned with his British 'passengers':

'Stand to!' calls the Flight Commander.
    A last puff of the gasper. Sandwiches are stowed away; we'll finish 'em upstairs. Off on the second flip, feeling good. This time we'll see some real war. And targets.

At 11.40 a.m., five Bristols set off towards the road, by this time choked with enemy cavalry and transport. In Sutherland's words:

We gave the cavalry our bombs. From a height of 1500 feet. We blew them to blazes. Then zoomed on the enemy and chopped them to ribbons with our guns. We couldn't miss. Emptied our belts and drums ... The Turkish survivors were in disorderly flight all over the countryside.[11]

Some of the Turks stopped and raised their rifles. Dudley Dowling and Edwin Mulford were hit and they crash-landed near the road. The Turks seized them, but within three hours were 'prisoners' of the advancing British cavalry themselves. Dowling and Mulford were back at the squadron that night, the latter with a nasty shoulder wound that finished his flying for the war and nearly cost him his left arm.

The pilots returned to Ramleh, refuelled and rearmed, then set out again at 12.30 p.m. 'The ground staff,' observed Clive Conrick were 'like a goanna at water, continually occupied with servicing and bombing-up returning aircraft'.[12] The Australians made another three raids on the retreating column during the afternoon before losing sight of its scattered remnants in the evening's gathering gloom.

By nightfall, No. 1 Squadron's Bristol Fighters had dropped 3 tonnes of bombs and fired over 20 000 rounds of ammunition into the retreating Turkish 8th Army. They left the roads leading north from the enemy front crammed with a tangled mess of shattered horses, men and transport. The 8th Army's morale, like its front line, had disintegrated. Von Sanders reported that 'the repeated attempts of officers to rally at least some of the men were made in vain as the men were entirely indifferent and were concerned only for their own salvation'.[13]

Progress on the ground was outstanding. The British cavalry were 50 kilometres beyond the enemy's front line by sunset. They had taken 700 prisoners and were on the outskirts of the first major Turkish railway junction at Tul Keram. The final Australian reconnaissance for the afternoon reported that, remarkably, the enemy camps east of the Jordan were still blissfully unaware of the catastrophe befalling their comrades on the coast. Allenby's plan was progressing to the letter.

The officer's mess at Ramleh was lively that night as the pilots and observers celebrated and spun tales about the day's events. John Harris thought it 'great to see the keenness of our boys ... all vying with one another to see who should do ... the next job'.[14] There was excitement as news arrived that the Turkish retreat was spreading; the 7th Army (occupying the inland sector) had begun to withdraw towards Nablus. 'They'd be there for us the next day. No doubts for targets now,' thought Sutherland.[15] Ross Smith and Pard Mustard didn't indulge in too much revelry, though; they were scheduled for two night raids on Jenin in the Handley Page bomber before morning.

Two pairs of Bristols left Ramleh at dawn on 20 September. Carrick Paul and Billy Weir, on the eastern reconnaissance, confirmed that the Turkish 7th Army was indeed retreating towards Nablus as the advance of the British XXI Corps on the coast rolled up its line. Columns of troops and transport were crowding the road leading north from Jenin to El Afule.

Across the Jordan, however, it was a different story. There, the Turkish 4th Army remained quiet, still apparently unaware of the disaster developing over on the coast. It appeared Turkish high command in Nazareth was still unable to communicate with the 4th Army on account of the bombed-out telephone junctions. Stan Nunan and Clive Conrick meanwhile reconnoitred the coastal sector. They found most of the Turkish camps between Anebta and Deir Sheraf burnt or abandoned. The troops were trying to board trains at Messudie railway station or were cramming the road leading north from Burka. The Australians flew north, noting that the German aerodromes at Jenin and El Afule were also abandoned. From El Afule, they flew west, passing over the British cavalry, by now advancing quickly across the Plain of Esdraelon towards El Afule. They entered this town at 8.00 a.m. and captured Nazareth a few hours later. The Turkish general staff, including von Sanders, were surprised and only narrowly escaped.

Once the reconnaissance flights returned, six Bristols left to attack the enemy columns retreating along the central, Jenin–El Afule road. For the rest of the day, the Australians worked back and forth along the crowded roads, alternating with the British squadrons. Sutherland described it as 'sheer butchery', claiming, 'there was no need for pre-offensive heights. We flew just high enough to keep clear of our bomb splinters. That was about 150 feet. Child's play for those in the air.'[16] Altogether, the RAF dropped 10 tonnes of bombs and fired 40 000 rounds of ammunition on 21 September, turning the Turkish 7th and 8th Army's retreat into a rout.

Returning from a bomb run, Sutherland had a sudden onset of dysentery, 'chlorinated water having done all manner of unkind things' to his bowels. His pilot Ted Kenny—who was sympathetic, having recently suffered the same ailment himself—landed near Jiljilie, in a supposedly deserted area. Sutherland leapt out of the cockpit and bolted behind a nearby sand dune where, to his great surprise, he startled a Turkish officer. Instead of dropping his pants, Sutherland pulled his revolver and directed the Turk towards the aircraft. Kenny forced him to sit on the floor of the rear cockpit while Sutherland made another trip behind the sand dune. Arriving back at Ramleh, they discovered that their captive was in fact a Turkish corps commander who had in his possession comprehensive plans of Turkish troop dispositions along the whole front. Sutherland claimed the officer's Zeiss field glass as a 'souvenir of his being caught short'—a souvenir that spent numerous Saturday afternoons at Randwick racetrack after the war.[17]

FIRE IN THE SKY

The British 4th Cavalry Division captured El Afule during the morning and, almost immediately, the RAF established a forward landing ground there. 'That is to say,' wrote the British official historian, 'about thirty hours after the British offensive had been launched, aircraft of the Royal Air Force were operating from an aerodrome which was forty miles inside the Turkish lines when the attack had begun.'[18] The rapidity of the British advance combined with the wrecked communication system threw Turkish command into chaos and gave rise to a number of ludicrous incidents. Pard Mustard related one:

> Lieutenant Paul & Weir were just about to land when they noticed an enemy two seater about to land too. The German seeing about six of their machines on the ground didn't think that we had possession of the place. On seeing the German landing, Lieutenant Paul stood by to attack. While this was going on, an armoured car on patrol on the Jenin-Afule road moved towards the machine. The pilot, finding himself among strangers thought it was time to leave and opened up his throttle to take off again. As soon as the machine began to move the armoured car opened fire with its machine gun wounding the observer and bringing the pilot back to earth [who] ... promptly surrendered with both hands.[19]

The German machine had onboard a bag of mail for the Turkish staff at El Afule. Peters and Mustard explored the abandoned El Afule aerodrome the following day and discovered a wagonload of sealed crates. 'We found one,' recalled Mustard, 'full of [currency] notes ... We filled our pockets and shoved them away till the box was empty.' They returned to Ramleh and taxied up to their hangar where the mechanics were eagerly waiting for news from the front. One of them asked Peters if he had found any souvenirs at El Afule. Peters and Mustard stood up in their cockpits and showered the mechanics with bundles of cash. 'They got it, showers of it. We must have had a few hundred pounds of Turkish paper between us. I finished up with less than ten pounds.' The resulting scramble, recalled Peters, nearly smashed the aircraft's tail.[20]

By sunset on 20 September, the British cavalry, which had been pressing east all day, captured Beisan, just 6 kilometres from the Jordan. This effectively sealed off the entire Turkish front between the Jordan and the coast. Only a few river crossings to the east remained open for the Turkish 7th Army, and these could only be reached by narrow tracks running through rough mountain and wady terrain.

For Conrick, it all made 'Gallipoli seem like a bad dream'. He wrote in his diary that it seemed 'incredible that the Turco-German forces could sustain such casualties and such defeats in just two days'.[21] Others were disturbed by the carnage they had left strewn along the Jenin–El Afule road. According to Sutherland:

> It was a gloomy night in the mess. Gone our excitement of a few days previously. Gone the elation of having Jacko where we wanted him. Targets? No one wished to discuss them. We were weary of the slaughter. On the trips to and from the aerodrome there was time for thinking—too much time for the kind of thoughts we had ... Thank God for a bath—that helped—it seemed to wash some of the invisible blood off our hands. Only the lucky ones slept that night.[22]

For the Australian airmen and their retreating Turkish adversaries, the worst by far was yet to come.

'Nine miles of dead': Bombing the Wady Fara, 21–22 September 1918

At 5.00 a.m. the following morning, Brown and Finlay, with Nunan and Conrick, reconnoitred the enemy's 7th Army sector (between Nablus and the Jordan). Finlay had a special wireless set to broadcast significant targets to RAF headquarters.

As the sun rose, the pair of Bristols flew over Balata and followed the narrow track that wound precariously along cliffs above the Wady Beidan, then along the Wady Fara and, finally, to a rough track heading northeast to the only Jordan River crossing not occupied by British cavalry. Conrick found 'the whole length of the road jammed tight with troops, motor transports, gun carriages and horse transports, all of which were moving at a snail's pace'. Following these were thousands more, pouring into Balata from the south. The road they clambered and lurched along was in fact a 2000-year-old Roman construction 'built along the sides of steep hills rising out of the

FIRE IN THE SKY

Wady, with, on the eastern side, a sheer precipice from the edge of the road to the bottom of the Wady Beidan'. In other words, some sections of this road hemmed the traffic in, confining it to forwards or backwards movement only.[23]

Finlay transmitted this and the two Bristols dropped their bombs on the narrowest sections of the road—creating, in Sutherland's words, 'a traffic jam on a one way street'. They then got to work on the trapped masses with their machine guns. The pilots roared in low, firing their forward Vickers before pulling up steeply to allow their observers to open up with the back guns. Conrick described one pass in his diary:

> They had little chance of escape from my guns as we were so close to them. As I fired I saw chips of rock fly off the cliff face and red splotches suddenly appear on the Turks who would stop climbing and fall and their bodies were strewn along the base of the cliff like a lot of dirty rags. When Nunan was climbing again to renew his attack, I had a better opportunity to machine gun the troops and transports on the road. I saw my tracer bullets hit the lead horses pulling a gun-carriage. As they reared up, they turned away from the cliff side of the road and their heads were turned back towards me, so that I could see the terror in their faces as their forefeet came down and, missing the road altogether, they plunged over the cliff dragging the carriage with them. Their driver, realising what was happening, jumped back towards the road, but he was late, far too late. He seemed to float just above the gun carriage, as it rolled over and over with the horses until the transport hit the cliff face, when he was thrown far out into the valley and his body disappeared in the haze far below . . .[24]

With their ammunition belts empty, they headed for home, passing three Bristols already on their way in response to Finlay's wireless message. The British squadrons joined in too—the DH9s of No. 144 Squadron, and the SE5as of No. 111 and No. 145 Squadrons. Even the corps squadrons raided the column in between their other sorties. For the rest of the day, there were hardly fewer than half a dozen aircraft above the crammed road at any time.

Les Sutherland was over the road in the afternoon. He called it 'A bomber, a machine-gunner's paradise. A giant, greyish-black snake, nine miles in length'. By this time, its narrow passes were choked with shattered men, horses and transport. The slaughter was overbearing for the airmen, who usually killed at a distance and fired at 'machines', not human beings:

> It had been sheer butchery on those previous two days. But I can think of no word to convey the dreadfulness of this action. As our bombs rained down scores, hundreds of motor lorries, guns and wagons were literally lifted off the road and smashed to pieces ... One could see the expressions on the faces of the poor devils below; could read the agony and the anguish in front of the gun-sights. One second it would be a team of horses; the next a bloody mass of shattered legs and carcasses.[25]

By mid-afternoon, the Turks were totally demoralised. The pilots began reporting white flags and groups sitting with their heads bowed, totally resigned to their fate. Like Sutherland, Conrick was overwhelmed by the carnage he and his fellows were causing below. With cold determination, though, he got on with the job:

> Jacko is totally demoralised and has had a gut full of the fight as whenever we came near them, they waved white flags of surrender. It was quite impossible for us to accept the surrender of the enemy, so we just kept on destroying them. While I kept firing my guns I had to close my mind to all that I could see, to the abject terror on the faces of the Turks, to the dead piling up on the road, to the burning transports, to the horses stampeding over the cliff edge or being crippled and trying to stand up again and again and always falling back until they died in the heat and the dust and the flies along the roadside.[26]

The squadrons pursued the scattered groups of survivors on the following day, as they made their way northeast along a track towards the Jordan River crossings. The targets were much fewer, though, with No. 1 Squadron only expending a quarter of the ammunition that it had the previous day. Nevertheless, the slaughter continued, as Sutherland recalled:

> The 22nd. Raid. Bomb. Guns. 'Drome ... Many of those poor devils were killed a dozen times over. The bombs continued to raid down. And hundreds

of Turks just stood—stood awaiting the bullets and shrapnel splinters that were going to end their days of war ... 'Drome. Sandwiches. Coffee. Maybe a bottle of ale to take back in the plane. Against 'regs' but—maybe mail to read while flying back ... This flying to the butcher's shop had got to be as much a matter of routine as getting the tram or train to work ... But, oh, that nauseating smell of cordite, the pools of blood we could see, the debris framed by those barren desolate hills of Samaria.[27]

By sunset on 22 September, the Turkish 7th Army ceased to exist as a fighting formation. All that was left were scattered remnants fleeing overland towards the Jordan. They would be rounded up within the next 48 hours by General Chaytor's Jordan Valley force. They were indeed the fortunate few. Remarkably, this entire army had been all but annihilated by a comparatively minuscule force of pilots and observers. It was a new thing in warfare, and it struck the pilots with an awesome sense of their destructive capability. As Sutherland realised: 'Alone we had to deal with a force that outnumbered us by thousands to one.'[28] The demoralised state of the Turkish army and the terrain had certainly contributed to the situation, but the key ingredient was British air superiority. Here, in central Palestine on the 21 and 22 September 1918, was history's first example of the calamity that could befall a retreating force without air cover.

RAF records indicate that on these two days its squadrons dropped 13.5 tonnes of bombs and fired 86 000 rounds into the choked roads north east of Balata. A few days later, when the light horse advanced along these passes—which came to be known as 'the nine miles of dead'—they counted more than 100 abandoned guns, 55 destroyed trucks, 912 wagons and innumerable heaps of rotting, putrid flesh (see Plate 13).[29] General Salmond visited No. 1 Squadron to congratulate the airmen, but he quietly advised Williams 'not to encourage pilots and observers to go and see the results of their work'.[30]

'A British colonel with Arab headgear and a handshake like a fish': Lawrence of the flying corps

Since May, No. 1 Squadron had been in semi-regular contact with Lawrence and his Arabs as they operated in the desert, east of the Hejaz railway. The squadron flew special reconnaissances for him during the summer, sometimes dropping reports at his remote headquarters. He also occasionally used the Australian Bristols as a taxi service to ferry him from his Transjordan outposts to Allenby's headquarters at Bir Salem, just outside of Ramleh.

Most of the Australians first came into contact with Lawrence personally on 16 May 1918, when Ross Smith flew him back from a meeting with Allenby to his desert base near Kutrini. Some, like Sutherland and Bull, were awed by his presence, noting his chest full of medals and striking appearance in 'Arab togs'.[31] Williams, on the other hand, was underwhelmed by the supposed living legend:

> I expected to see a man of some impressive stature or one that would make an impression on you, instead of which I met a smallish man with pale blue eyes and fair hair, dressed in the uniform of a British colonel with Arab headgear and a handshake like a fish. I was very surprised.[32]

Out in the Transjordan desert, Lawrence had the assistance of X-Flight, an ad hoc unit of the RFC containing a few mechanics (some of them Australian) and a couple of old BE12a machines. In August 1918, No. 1 Squadron had supplemented this meagre establishment with a Bristol crewed by Arthur 'Spud' Murphy and Fred Hawley. Murphy was well suited to the role, having served with X-Flight in late 1917, along with Stan Nunan.

In September, Lawrence moved his force to El Umtaiye to begin raiding the Hejaz railway, in support of Allenby's offensive. The few remaining German aircraft in the theatre, based at Deraa, began harassing them immediately. Murphy and Hawley destroyed one of them on 15 September, but were 'badly shot up' in the process.[33] They returned to Ramleh for repairs, 'very rough and lean and ... sick of living in the desert with Lawrence and his Arabs', by Conrick's account.[34]

Murphy and Hawley's absence left the Arab raiders vulnerable, and the Germans bombed them heavily on the following two days. Lawrence pulled their camp back to Umm Es Surab but the situation became precarious, as many of the Arabs threatened to go home.

On 21 September, Lawrence flew to General Allenby to urgently request more air support. On the following morning it arrived in the form of three

Bristols flown by Peters and Traill, Ross Smith and Mustard, and Headlam and Lilly. The Australian crews had just sat down to breakfast with Lawrence when the sound of aircraft engines reached their ears. They dashed to their machines and took off to intercept an approaching enemy DFW with three Pfalz escorts. Smith attacked the two-seater and forced it to land. As its crew ran from the wreck, Headlam machine-gunned them: 'I dived at them from about 500 feet and observed one of them fall, but he was helped to his feet by his companion.'[35] Smith meanwhile circled their machine so Mustard could shoot it up with his Lewis guns. It started burning, and then exploded as the bombs ignited. Mustard looked at the two German airmen, standing in the open after surviving Headlam's strafing run. 'Having burnt their crate, I felt kindly disposed to them,' explained Mustard. 'We just gave a wave and returned to camp to finish our breakfast.'[36]

Lawrence had kept their porridge warm. They were just starting on the marmalade and bread when the sound of aero engines reached their ears again. Smith and Mustard bolted for their aircraft. Lifting off, they spotted the three Pfalz circling low over the burning DFW. Smith dived, scattering them in all directions. He chased one, but it landed and taxied to a Turkish outpost. They then took off after another, but it too landed and its pilot ran for cover. Smith then chased the third Pfalz across the desert at 20 feet towards Deraa. The German pilot tried to land at full speed on his aerodrome, but piled up on the tarmac in a cloud of dust. 'Without waiting to see the result,' reported Smith, 'we returned to the other scouts and found them still at the same places. 50 rounds were fired into each of these machines.'[37] A more pitiful picture of German morale is difficult to imagine.

After breakfast, Smith and Mustard flew back to Ramleh to get the Handley Page bomber. They returned to Lawrence's camp with a tonne of fuel and supplies, and Brigadier General Borton (commander of the RAF's Palestine Brigade) as a passenger. Tonkin and Les Climie escorted them in a Bristol, and when the two machines landed the Arabs erupted in awe and excitement, reputedly firing volleys into the air and remarking: 'Indeed at last they have sent us THE aeroplane, of which these things [the Bristol Fighters] were foals.' Mustard recalled: 'They were afraid to approach. It was an aeroplane beyond all their dreams. After a while, they came closer, and timidly touched its wings, just to make sure it wasn't a mirage.'[38]

The Australians attached to Lawrence's flight completed the destruction of the German squadron at Deraa over the next 24 hours. Late in the afternoon, Peters and Traill forced another DFW down and machine-gunned its crew. That night, Smith dropped a tonne of bombs on Deraa aerodrome from 1000 feet in the Handley Page and the following morning two Bristols on the eastern reconnaissance finished the job with a load of 25 lb Coopers bombs. When British troops occupied Deraa a few days later, the aerodrome was a blackened mess of burnt aircraft and stores. A detachment of Australian Bristol Fighters and crews remained with Lawrence's force until 27 September, cooperating with his Arab fighters to blow up sections of the railway line between Amman and Deraa, thus completely trapping the Turkish 4th Army that garrisoned this remote section of the front.

'One Turk left alive could mean another Australian light horse casualty': The fall of Damascus, 23–30 September 1918

The Turkish 4th Army's headquarters remained oblivious to the disaster unfolding on its front west of the Jordan until late on 22 September. An afternoon reconnaissance by a pair of Bristols discovered that the Turkish camps, which since the beginning of the offensive had remained remarkably quiet, had begun to stir. At 11.35 p.m. that night, RAF headquarters ordered all squadrons to stand by for massed bombing attacks should the 4th Army begin a general retreat.

At dawn, two Australian Bristols reported Turkish columns retreating along the Es Salt–Amman road. They were heading towards the only means of escape from this isolated section of the front—the Amman railway station. At 7.00 a.m., six Bristols left Ramleh and attacked the column as they had near Balata two days previously. The pilots aimed their bombs at choke points on the road to block traffic and then swept the trapped men and transports with machine gun fire. The carnage was not quite what it had been on 21 September—the terrain being more open—but the 4th Army's orderly retreat became a rout nonetheless. At 2.50 p.m., ten Bristols attacked Amman, where thousands of retreating Turks were converging. The Australians fired 15 500 rounds and dropped 3 tonnes of bombs during the day. The British squadrons, working relays with the Australians, expended as much again.

By the following morning, General Chaytor's force (including the Anzac Mounted Division) had crossed the Jordan and was within 11 kilometres of Amman. The airmen switched their attention to Marfak, 45 kilometres further north on the railway, where the Turks were now converging in their mad dash north. At dawn on 25 September, ten Australian Bristols hit the crowded station, freezing all rail traffic. One stick of bombs hit a train that 500 troops had just boarded. Australian and British airmen circled the town all day, hitting each new train that arrived from Amman. Four tonnes of bombs rained on to Marfak in twelve hours. The survivors abandoned the trains and fled north on foot. These pitiful remnants of the Turkish 4th Army—numbering between six and seven thousand—faced an even more dreadful prospect, though, as they attempted to walk 65 kilometres to Deraa with no food or water, the light horse behind them and the RAF above.

By 26 September, a week after zero hour, Allenby's forces were north of Lake Tiberias—that is, over 100 kilometres from their starting lines. The Australians continued to rove over the eastern sector, bombing the scattered parties of fleeing Turks, but the work began to slacken. Conrick noted in his diary on 27 September: 'Nothing much doing today from the squadron as we seem to be waiting for more reports of the progress of the war, which has moved almost out of our reach.'[39] Reconnaissance flights over the rapidly advancing front now required fuel stops at forward landing strips.

The break was welcome. No. 1 Squadron had flown 416 hours in the week since the offensive had begun. Although the burden was not shared with complete equality, most airmen had spent several hours a day in the air. Nunan seems about average with a total for the week of just under 32 hours. On most days, he flew three sorties and the average length of each of these (which increased as the week went on, as the patrol zones and targets moved forward with the front line) was just under two hours, although there were some longer flights, such as the raids on Marfak on 25 June that lasted for almost four hours and required a fuel stop.[40] Les Sutherland probably spoke for the entire squadron when he finished his account of this period with a sigh of relief: 'Thank God for a drink.'[41]

On 26 September, Allenby ordered his forces to advance alongside the Arab army to capture Damascus. On the same day, C Flight took its six

Bristols to Haifa to operate as an advanced reconnaissance unit. During the next two days, as Allenby's troops approached Damascus, the Australian crews watched the town for signs of an enemy counter-attack. As he peered down on it from 6000 feet, Sutherland was pleased to note that, although 'Damascus was a hive of industry that morning', most of the traffic was headed north, not south—'away from Allenby'. After finishing their reconnaissance, Kenny and Sutherland spotted a German two-seater several thousand feet above. As Kenny climbed towards it, Sutherland noticed there was no rear gun in the cockpit and that the observer had apparently fainted.

Kenny closed to within 50 metres and fired a burst. As Sutherland recalled, the German pilot 'looked amazed, dumbfounded . . . He could not use his front gun—and he had none at the rear . . . he was "cold"'. Flying level with the German aircraft at a distance of 10 metres, Kenny pointed towards the British lines and patted his guns. The message was loud and clear. The enemy pilot banked with the Bristol hovering behind, 'like a sheep dog edging an erring sheep back into the fold'. As the two aircraft crossed into British territory, the German pilot suddenly threw his machine into a power dive. Kenny followed close behind and opened fire. The enemy aircraft spun and crashed into the ground.[42] Later that afternoon, four Bristol Fighters destroyed the remaining German aircraft on the ground at Damascus.

Australian airmen noted signs of evacuation beginning at Damascus on 29 September, and the following day the town was shrouded in dust from Turks fleeing to the north and Allenby's cavalry bearing down on it from the south. The airmen worked closely with the horsemen to help them overcome the enemy rear guard on the outskirts of Damascus, as Conrick related:

> On a road at the south west entrance to Damascus we saw a small machine gun defence post which was holding up the light horse advance. We machine gunned the area wiping out the defence post and then patrolled along the south of the town, machine-gunning enemy positions. Nunan then flew low over the light horse regiment while I dropped a note telling them what we had done.[43]

The airmen then set upon the enemy troops fleeing north. But as Harold Maughan found when he flew towards them, they just sat by the road, absolutely dejected. Maughan apparently could not bring himself to kill such utterly helpless men and flew away without firing a shot. In the *Official History*, Cutlack generalised: 'The Australians, in pity, restrained from firing on them.'[44] Yet the personal records reveal a different story. After helping the light horse, Nunan and Conrick flew north of the city. Conrick revealed in the privacy of his diary:

> Our next job was to machine-gun Turks fleeing along the Beirut road north-west of Damascus, following them as far as Rayak. When we caught up with the first of them, they sat on the road with their heads bowed, thinking perhaps that we would let them be, but they soon got a move on when our bullets started smashing into them. I know that some of our blokes had had enough of the slaughter, but for me the war wasn't finished as I knew that, until they surrendered, one Turk left alive could mean another Australian Light Horse casualty. Since I had landed at Gallipoli, I had seen enough casualties to last me a lifetime, but to me they weren't beaten soldiers down there, they were the enemy who had to be destroyed before we could go home and get on with our lives.[45]

By the end of the day, the Turks had abandoned Damascus. Allenby's forces and Feisal's Arabs occupied it the following morning.

'Not the least bit like war now': Haifa and the armistice, October 1918

The rest of No. 1 Squadron moved north to join C Flight at Haifa two days after the fall of Damascus. The airmen flew up there, but for the ground crew it was a rough overland journey through a landscape ravaged by battle. For the past fortnight, they had been loading aircraft with bombs and ammunition belts, now they got to see the results of their work. At Tul Keram, Joe Bull described 'thousands of prisoners coming in and a large number of captured guns and transport'. Further north, there was 'motor and horse transport scattered all over the road and dead horses and men near the roadside'.[46] They camped by the road at Nablus and ate breakfast among the smell of decomposing corpses. The journey took two full days, and perhaps it's not surprising that, as Conrick observed, 'most of the men [were] drunk on our mess supplies' when they arrived.[47]

The squadron established itself on an aerodrome just south of Haifa, in the shadow of Mount Carmel. The hangars overlooked the wide Bay of Acre. It was an excellent spot for the war-strained men of No. 1 Squadron to set up camp. Stan Nunan described it as 'a very picturesque spot and not the least bit like a war now. We have a good time of evenings in Haifa. It is the best place we have struck yet in Palestine.'[48] Others wrote of swimming in the bay's serene waters, catching bream and mullet (with Mills bombs) and going to shows and parties in the town. A typical diary entry came from Conrick, who reported: 'It was such a fantastic day today that I went for a swim before breakfast and again after dinner. Billy Weir and Nunan spent their day looking for nurses. They must have had a bit of luck as they had not come back by the time I turned in.'[49] McGinness and Fysh shot grouse on the Mount Carmel heather, close to where Elijah had called down the fire of heaven.[50]

Others spent their time looking for souvenirs, with Nunan observing, 'The fervour of getting something for nothing has beset everyone.'[51] Joe Bull and his mate explored the monastery atop Mount Carmel and were delighted to score a brand new German officer's camp bed and an Iron Cross. Some of the mechanics spent their down-time mounting a truck engine into a boat they had 'souvenired'. On 10 October, four of the pilots drove out to the recently abandoned German aerodrome at Kuskus to hunt for an especially valuable souvenir—German Z7 aeroplane magnetos that could fetch £20 each in the Cairo bazaar.

Ross Smith and Sutherland flew out to the abandoned German aerodrome at Jenin to look for magnetos. On landing, they were confronted by gratifying, if not disturbing, evidence of their aerial attacks on Jenin: shattered aircraft and vehicles, abandoned munitions and fuel stocks, and what Sutherland referred to as 'Exhibit As': the decomposing remains of those caught under the bombs. Treasure was not in short supply, either. Sutherland noticed large quantities of abandoned fuel and spare parts, and they filled a sandbag with magnetos.

Yet this loot paled into insignificance when they spotted a cave at the aerodrome's edge. It was crammed with cases of 1904 champagne: 'cases an' cases of it . . . my lips twitch at the memory,' recalled Sutherland twenty years later. The two Australians had some samples right away and, deciding 'it was great stuff', loaded the cockpit with as many bottles as they could carry. Sutherland recalled that 'had there been a popularity competition that night' in the mess, 'we were an odds-on bet'. Over the following days, the crews inconspicuously requested flights to Jenin to, as they told Major Addison, requisition German fuel. 'These strictly business trips', as Sutherland explained, 'always had a spot of alcoholic colour ... we called the homecoming planes "Silver-top Expresses", because the observer's cockpit always wore a kind of hedge-hog coat of silver tops'.

Soon, however, impatient with a lack of fighting action and driven by an imbalance in supply and demand, Ross Smith planned a large-scale raid to secure the rest of the Jenin cave's treasure. He recruited Sutherland and Nunan to accompany him in a motorised railway truck named 'Agnes' to recover the cache from Jenin. According to Sutherland, Smith 'purchased' the truck by bribing a series of railway officials with currency that some of his friends in the light horse had 'found' in an abandoned Turkish cache at El Afule. The four officers made it to Jenin, pulling rank to get through checkpoints along the way. There, after bribing the guard on the railway, they recruited several 'gypos' to load the alcohol. When they tried to leave, however, Smith realised that the cart could not go backwards. So they putted south, hoping to find a turntable, or alternative transport. After crashing 'Agnes' on a piece of broken track, they hailed down a British clerk and bribed him with a couple of bottles and some cash to take them, and their stash back to Haifa. Arriving there just after dinner, the Wineburg '04 disappeared rather quickly. Sutherland reasoned, 'It was hot weather, and we were scared that our cache would be discovered. So—well what would you do? Agnes's cargo lasted one night.'[52]

Still, there was some fighting to be done. After Beirut fell to the British on 7 October, Allenby ordered his troops north, towards Homs and Tripoli. No. 1 Squadron scouted ahead of the armoured cars to maintain contact with the remnants of the Turkish armies that were scattered across wide expanses of Syria. The flights were some of the longest ever conducted by the unit—upwards of 800 kilometres and involving three stops for refuelling.

British XXI Corps captured Tripoli on 13 October and the Desert Mounted Corps took Homs two days later. A Flight established an advanced landing ground there, and began long-range reconnaissance flights as far north as Alexandretta. On 19 October, Ross Smith and Ashley McCann, with

Headlam and Lilly, spotted a DFW over Maarit el Naaman. They attacked it together, the two observers catching it in a crossfire. Almost immediately, the German pilot landed and he and the observer fled. Ross Smith landed nearby. The two Germans watched from a distance as McCann climbed out of the Bristol, walked over to their machine and fired a flare into its fuel-drenched cockpit. At that moment, a tribe of Bedouins came galloping over a nearby rise. McCann ran for the Bristol and got away, just in time. For his daring, the 25-year-old Victorian farmer received the Distinguished Flying Cross, the unit's twentieth.

On 22 October, C Flight moved further north again, to Hama, to keep up with Allenby's rapidly advancing forces. The next morning, Stan Harper, who had just joined the squadron from a training school, fought the squadron's last dogfight. Over Muslimie, just north of Aleppo, he and Lilly met a pair of DFWs flying above the German aerodrome there. After a short exchange of fire, both enemy aircraft landed on their aerodrome, where there were four other machines about to take off. Harper dropped his bombs among them and machine-gunned the fleeing pilots and ground crew. Later that day, Conrick flew over the aerodrome and found it burnt out and abandoned. On 26 October, some Australian machines cooperated with Allenby's armoured cars and the Arabs as they cleared Aleppo of its last remaining defenders.

Turkey signed an armistice on 30 October and the war in the Middle East finished the following day.

'The perfect bender': Armistice and homecoming

Immediately after the armistice, most of the squadron got leave passes to Cairo where there was, in Sutherland's words, 'a colossal binge ... the perfect bender'.[53]

The job wasn't quite finished yet, though. There were rumours that No. 1 Squadron would be sent to join the other three Australian squadrons on the Western Front, where the war was still going. This never eventuated, but in late November, while the rest of the squadron prepared to go back down the coast to Ramleh, A Flight went north to monitor the Arab occupation of the region and to ensure the Turks left their equipment behind, in accordance with the armistice terms. They went to Rayak, a town high in the mountains east of Beirut. Stan Nunan was not enthusiastic about spending a month up

FIRE IN THE SKY

there, 'totally isolated' at 3000 feet above sea level as winter closed in. 'We were cursing the "heads" for keeping us up there so long,' he wrote to his parents after rejoining the squadron at Ramleh in December.[54] For Nunan, like thousands of others in the AIF, with peace also came the anxiety of going home, finding work and readjusting to civilian life. A week before Christmas, he wrote a candid letter to his father, contemplating what he might do after the war. Given his flying experience, he hoped to avoid returning to his pre-war occupation as a motorbike mechanic. Commercial flying, he considered, might be an option—although he predicted the industry would be small, under-funded and highly competitive. As he realised, his financial situation would probably leave him with limited options. 'One disadvantage of army life,' he wrote, 'especially in peace time, is that it is very difficult to save out of the pay. Not that saving was ever my particular love. Still I defy anyone to live with 50 other young men and spend considerably less than them without getting the reputation for meanness.'[55]

As it turned out, Nunan returned home with empty pockets to his motorbikes. He was killed three years later in a racing accident on the Aspendale speedway near Melbourne. 'To his squadron pals,' reflected Sutherland, 'his end seemed like an anti-climax.'[56]

The squadron remained at Ramleh until February 1919. Some of the men who had been on active service since late 1914 got to go home in December. Among them was the slightly built Carrick Paul, half of the squadron's famous ground-strafing partnership in the 'Yellow Peril'. Gallipoli, the Sinai, two wounds and a year of flying had taken its toll on his health. Gaunt and nervous, he was put on a boat home on 13 December 1918. Sadly, Paul didn't make it to meet his wife at the dockside. During the voyage he was playing tennis—a pastime of so many hours at Ramleh—when he fell overboard and drowned. It was another 'anti-climax' for his squadron pals, and the beginning of a lifetime of bereavement for another young Australian woman.

For those who stayed in Palestine, there wasn't a lot to do and discipline slackened as the officers tried to enforce military routines. In December, Conrick was greeted with muttered comments like 'The bloody war is over mate' when he inspected the men's tents.[57] There was also an increase in men going absent without leave, and on 3 January it all came to a head when Major Addison ordered a pre-breakfast parade. The men assembled

THE BATTLE OF MEGIDDO, SEPTEMBER AND OCTOBER 1918

but then walked off, leaving 'the Sergeants and Sergeant-Majors to themselves'.[58] When word reached Williams, temporarily in command of the RAF's Palestine Brigade, he was furious. But not, as one might assume, at the accused mutineers:

> Now the war is over and this commanding officer, moved back from the front, equipment handed over, nothing to do but wait and go home and he orders a physical training parade before breakfast! Now can you imagine such a blooming idiot? I don't think I can. So I said 'This is an absolute disgrace, this is out of character with the squadron all together. Mutiny? I've never heard of anything of the sort. I want to see the officers and NCOs.'

Williams got the officers and NCOs together and told them to assemble the men immediately. He then ordered Addison to dismiss the parade and told him there would be 'no more silly damn things like that'.[59]

The squadron relinquished its much-loved Bristols to No. 111 Squadron and moved to Kantara in February to prepare for embarkation to Australia. Just before leaving Ramleh, one pilot managed to get a last 'flip' in his Bristol. He dropped a bundle of poppies over the cemetery for the men who would not be going with them. They fluttered down over the graves of the 21 Australian airmen and five mechanics who had died during the campaign. In all, 168 pilots and observers had flown with the unit. Nineteen had been killed in action or accidents, two died of other causes, 23 were wounded and twelve were taken prisoner. Without including those who were invalided home to Australia (for sickness and combat stress—24 in total), the squadron's casualty rate was 33 per cent.[60]

Just before the squadron embarked for Australia, General Allenby visited and addressed the men with a fitting assessment of the unit's remarkable service record: 'You gained for us absolute supremacy of the air, thereby enabling my cavalry, artillery and infantry to carry out their work on the ground practically unmolested by hostile aircraft. This undoubtedly was a factor of paramount importance in the success of our arms here.' He also made a special mention of the squadron's ground crew, 'because although the officers did the work in the air, it was good work on the part of your mechanics that kept a high percentage of your machines serviceable. I wish you all bon voyage and trust that the peace now attained will mean for you all future happiness and prosperity. Thank you and good bye.'[61]

'Leaving the lesser and the fortunate to carry on': Ramleh War Cemetery, 1961

Forty-three years after the armistice, Hudson Fysh was back in Palestine. With his wife, he travelled the old battlefields and aerodromes, marvelling at how things had changed. Sprawling cities, development and progress had transformed the biblical landscape.

At Ramleh, it pleased Fysh immensely to see that the Commonwealth War Graves Commission had transformed the dusty field corner with makeshift crosses of his memories into a neatly manicured lawn, flanked by flower beds and Australian eucalypts. Among the rows of headstones, white and rectangular in their military uniformity, were names that conjured up in the old man a kaleidoscope of emotions and memories long tucked away in the recesses of his mind. Before him, standing at attention, were the graves of Vesper and Haendly, the two Germans he had killed and buried here during the thrilling days of August 1918. Beside them lay John Walker, Hal Letch, Wally Farquhar, Ern Stooke and Louis Krieg. Four decades had transformed the surrounding landscape almost beyond recognition. But there they lay, still in their early twenties, still with cap and goggles. Still peering over the cockpit of a Bristol. Still in a land far from their own.

In 1918 there had been too little time to mourn. Theirs had been a loss grieved quickly, if acutely, in the insular world of the squadron. Military efficiency, masculine stoicism and the perpetual flying roster pushed things forward before anyone could dwell on a dead mate too deeply. Yet 43 years, a remarkably successful business, another world war, a wife, children of his own and retirement gave the old man a renewed sense of their loss as he stood before his old flying mates in the cool shade of the eucalypt branches:

> They represented the flower of youth in our day, and the sight of their graves induced thoughts of the grief of their parents, and of what these young fellows' futures might have been had they lived. Such has always been war, which has taken of our best and most promising, leaving the lesser and the fortunate to carry on.[62]

8

'SURVIVAL OF THE LUCKIEST'
Training in Britain, 1917–18

AFC cadets studying aerial gunnery at the Australian training aerodrome in Minchinhampton. *AWM D00497*

> It's absolutely essential to smoke a cigarette after crashing an aeroplane.
>
> —Cadet James Ross, No. 48 (Training) Squadron, Royal Flying Corps

'Not used to that kind of hospitality': The Australian Flying Corps in Britain

The shivering commuters waiting for a train home at London's Waterloo Station on the evening of 29 January 1917 beheld a positively bizarre sight, even for wartime London, flooded as it was with troops from all corners of the empire and living in the grip of rationing and the threat of air raids. There, piling off the 7.30 train from Southampton were some 180 dishevelled and unsoldierly looking Australians. Their hair was unbrushed, whiskers 'an inch long' and they wore the uniform of a dozen different units. Each had his swag strung around his shoulder and looked, admitted one, 'like the tramps at home in the bush'. The emu plume of the Australian light horse bobbed here and there among the throng as the few officers present tried to get them into some semblance of military order. Perhaps the most striking thing to Londoners heading home on that bleak winter's evening, though, were the soldiers' dark complexions.

Just a month before, these tanned men had been sweltering in the Sinai desert. They were now in England to establish the Australian Flying Corps' second operational squadron. Most were tradesmen, volunteers from the ranks of the light horse, but a few—including some of the officers—wore the AFC's distinctive blue and red triangle on their shoulders. These were No. 1 Squadron men, there to provide experience and leadership in the new unit, which had formed in Egypt on 20 September 1916 following an offer from the Australian government to raise additional squadrons for overseas service. It was their job to organise this motley crew of diggers and light horsemen into No. 2 Squadron, Australian Flying Corps and prepare them for the war on the Western Front. This, they had heard, was where the real fighting was: Palestine was just a sideshow compared with the titanic struggle in France and Belgium.

While the Australians waited for their train, English women pressed 'huge mugs of steaming tea and coffee' and sandwiches into their grateful hands. After a short trip by Underground to Charing Cross, they boarded a northbound train for Harlaxton training aerodrome. To men long accustomed to the Middle East's exotic ways, London's rail system represented a return to a more comfortable and familiar world. Ex-light horseman Vern Knuckey wrote in his diary:

The trains were fairly full and as we boarded it men and women would jump up to make room for us, young ladies would demand that we took their seats whilst they stood. Our boys were not used to that kind of hospitality and many an argument would crop up. All along the train would be seen a dirty dilapidated Australian sitting with some children and in many cases young ladies dressed in the latest fashion sitting on their knees, whilst old men were pressing cigars and cigarettes on us and as usual plenty of laughing and talking... Snow was falling outside and everything was lovely and white in the brilliant moonlight.[1]

When the weary members of No. 2 Squadron arrived at Harlaxton the following morning, they learned another new Australian squadron, 'No. 3', had also recently arrived in Britain and was training in nearby South Carlton. Unlike No. 2 Squadron, it had been formed in Australia from Point Cook graduates and tradesmen volunteers from the army. A fourth squadron, also raised at Point Cook, was due to arrive in Britain shortly. The three AFC squadrons in Europe would spend most of 1917 training before playing their part in the war above the trenches.

'A tremendous amount to learn': The British training system

During the war, about 410 Australian officers flew as pilots in the AFC. Of these, only 126 trained at Point Cook and another 50 or so at the New South Wales State Aviation School at Richmond near Sydney. Most Australian airmen, then, learned to fly from scratch at overseas schools. A few did so in Egypt but the overwhelming majority went through the RFC's training system in Britain. In fact, with the exception of some of No. 1 Squadron's 'originals', even those who had done courses in Australia needed to complete the British training course. As James Ross, a 21-year-old telegraphist from Moruya, discovered when he reached England in mid-1917: 'Our Australian Certificate doesn't stand for much and they generally start all over again when they reach here.'[2]

For the first two years of the war, however, the British training system wasn't much better than the Australian one. The rapid and totally unprecedented expansion of the flying corps, combined with high casualty rates at the front, stretched the RFC's limited training resources thin. Edgar

McCloughry, an engineer from Adelaide who trained as a scout pilot in 1916, recalled, for example, that 'the standard of flying was then very low ... and as long as it was possible to take the aeroplane off the ground and put it on again without damage, one was considered a good pilot'. When McCloughry went to France, he had 'no real idea of flying' and 'little conception of such manoeuvring as is required in air combat'.[3]

In late 1916, though, the RFC began overhauling its training system. Robert Smith-Barry, a talented squadron commander and one of the RFC's original pilots, developed a new training doctrine to prevent novices like McCloughry leaving England so poorly prepared. The bulk of the AFC's pilots were fortunate to train during 1917 and 1918 under this improved 'Smith-Barry' system. Although individual pilots had slightly different experiences, the new training course had five stages and took roughly eight months to complete.

Prospective Australian pilots began the course with two months of theoretical instruction at the School of Military Aeronautics, either at Oxford or Reading. There, irrespective of their former rank, all reverted to 'gentleman cadet'. The school at Reading had an improvised air about it. Cadets stayed in a camp on the edge of town and attended classes in a variety of public buildings. As Donald Day described it: 'One would start with say signalling, and as the next lesson, bombing, was 200 yards away, we would have a pleasant little march between studies.' Day also noted that, while pleasant enough in autumn, winter transformed the campsite into a bleak, boggy quagmire.[4] The Oxford school's cadets were better accommodated. They stayed in one of the university's colleges and attended classes in the lecture rooms. At Oxford, around 1000 flying corps students—men from all over the empire—would attend the course at one time, although classes were usually small—say, a dozen cadets to each lecturer.[5]

The school's syllabus was crowded and covered a broad range of theoretical subjects relating to aviation and its application in warfare. Students attended lectures on aeronautical theory, meteorology, map-reading, aerial photography, artillery observation and Morse communication. In most instances, lecturers presented the information while cadets took notes to review during prep periods in the evenings. Twenty-year-old Dick Howard likened it to his 'old uni days'.[6] Most cadets found the amount of information bewildering. Jack Weingarth told his family that 'there is a tremendous amount to learn here. It is almost as hard as the Matriculation examinations. There is not a moment to spare all day.' Stan Nunan claimed he had never worked so hard in his life: 'My old brain feels like a wet rag.'[7]

A reprieve from the dry lectures was practical work—which Howard, among others, found 'the more interesting'. In these subjects, cadets went into workshops and tinkered with engines and aircraft rigging, and did navigation exercises outdoors. Howard described doing mock artillery observation up a tree with a Morse buzzer and steering wheelbarrows with compasses attached to them around paddocks. The goal, he recognised, was to 'make us good pilots on the ground before venturing to send us into the air'.[8]

Many of the school's subjects could at best be described as esoteric. At worst, it could be argued, they were of little relevance to men who had limited time to learn much about surviving in the skies above the front. The lecture notebooks of Australian cadets are jammed with meticulously detailed, hand-drawn diagrams and notes on all manner of subjects of dubious relevance to a combat flyer. The lecture notebook of Harold Cornell, for example, has over 200 pages of handwritten notes on the rigging of various aircraft (including the gauge of wire used in each part of the machine and the step-by-step process of how to rig them), the intricacies of the internal combustion engine and magneto, and even the alloys which valves were made of.[9] Perhaps the school should have re-evaluated its syllabus in light of comments made by one of its more pragmatic instructors, who taught Francis Penny in 1917. When Penny asked him to explain in more detail the function of a magneto, he replied that, as one couldn't get out and repair it at 5000 feet, 'all you can do is to hope that you are a good enough pilot to land your machine without crashing it and killing yourself'.[10]

The syllabus, crowded as it was, resulted in a hectic schedule for cadets as they rushed from one lesson to the next, with little time to consolidate their understanding. Days began with Reveille at 6.30 a.m. with cadets falling in at 7.00 a.m. for roll call and physical drill. They ate breakfast at 8.00 a.m. before attending classes until 12.30 p.m. Following lunch and sport, cadets returned to class until 5.30 p.m. Mandatory sporting matches were followed by dinner at 7.00 p.m. On weeknights, cadets were confined to barracks to study.[11]

In addition to the heavy workload, Australian cadets typically found the school's British 'old army' ethos a shock. Discipline at Oxford and Reading was far more stringent than a cadet was likely to have experienced in his Australian infantry or light horse unit. Douglas Ferguson wrote to his sister that everything at Oxford had 'to be done on the double, boots and belts not only cleaned, "but highly polished"'.[12] Things were similar at Reading where, according to Donald Day, 'discipline was especially strict and we had a maximum of drill'. He saw it as all very 'British', and explained that being under RFC authority, he and his fellow cadets had to 'mind their Ps and Qs and comply exactly with all regulations relative to behavior, hours and habits'. Meals, he explained, were a stiffly formal affair in the College Dining Hall—'an imposing looking place with beautiful stained glass windows and paintings of old chaps who were evidently of some consequence a few hundred years ago'. The cadets, in their best dress uniforms, marched 'solemnly' to their position at the dining table.[13] Conventions such as this introduced the young colonials to the etiquette of gentlemen officers—or, as Stan Nunan put it to his mother, 'they are teaching us to "swank"'.[14] According to one source, some of the Australian cadets lashed out at the stringency one night, throwing their British sergeant major off a bridge into the River Kennet.[15]

The eight-week course concluded with written and medical examinations. Those who failed faced the disappointment of going back to the trenches, or perhaps of staying with the AFC as a mechanic or driver. Successful cadets went on to elementary training squadrons where, for the next three months or so, they would learn to fly.

British cadets passed out of the School of Aeronautics with their commission. Owing to an AIF policy, though, Australian cadets didn't become officers until they earned their wings at the end of elementary flight training. Nevertheless, at the training squadrons the privileges of life as an officer were available to the Australian cadets. Ross, who had enlisted in the AFC as an air mechanic before transferring to pilot training, described the advantages suddenly available to him at the No. 48 Training Squadron at Waddington:

> We have all the privileges of officers. I am writing this in a big beautiful lounge filled with easy chairs and lounges, writing tables etc. All daily papers etc are provided . . . For breakfast we get porridge and something like bacon

and eggs or steak and mushrooms with the usual padding of marmalade etc. Then lunch usually runs into 3 and perhaps 4 courses ... We have batmen to clean the tent and make the beds etc. If one requires a drink of any sort while in the lounge, ring the bell and the waitress hops out.[16]

But these privileges came at a price, which quickly soured the experience for many cadets. Until 1918, when the AFC had its own training squadrons up and running, Australian cadets were usually posted to British training units alone, or with perhaps just a couple of other colonials. Otherwise, all the other students in the squadron would be British and, by this stage of the course, commissioned officers. This presented the Australians with two distinct disadvantages. First, it put them in the socially awkward position of being a few cadets among a majority of officers who were, essentially, at the same point in the course. Day, for example, found himself as one of 'two cadets, amongst about 150 officers, some of whom were not advanced as we, but prepared to come at the "salute an officer" stunt'.[17]

A far more serious issue created by this curious administrative oversight was that of finances. Officers in the RFC received a £50 allowance to finance their uniform and kit upon graduating from the School of Military Aeronautics. The Australian cadets, meanwhile, had to get by on an AIF allowance of £8. Nunan summed up the problem succinctly: 'We have to live like gentlemen—on privates' pay.'[18] Forsyth 'went all over London trying to make the £8 spin out'. After pricing uniforms at a dozen places he realised he couldn't afford anything and was forced to cable some family friends to borrow the money.[19] The training squadron mess bills further impoverished the Australians, as they far outstripped the AIF's cadet wages. Stan Nunan wrote of having 'a rotten time for money lately' in August 1917 on account of a 35 shilling per week mess bill 'on an AIF 24/6 allowance'. Nunan complained to the AIF's administrative headquarters and the allowance was subsequently increased to just cover mess bills, without any extra for leave or sundries. This all contrasts with the typical picture of well-paid, spendthrift Australians on active service during the First World War.

While these personal dramas unfolded in the background, the cadets made a rapid transition from the theoretical to the practical in their training. Dick Howard arrived at his elementary training squadron on 19 February

1917. The next afternoon, his instructor took him on a joy ride to gauge his reaction to flying. He was in the pilot's seat the very next morning.

> I took the front seat with the control. The instructor took the dual control to check me, should I do anything rash. Before dinner I did half an hour's flying making three proper landings. I took full control in the air, keeping the machine at its proper flying speed over sixty miles, and counteracting bumps etc. After dinner I was up again, for three quarters of an hour, making five landings.
>
> This time I made the landing myself, although the instructor was ready to check me. Once, I flattened out a bit too soon, which would have resulted in a 'pan-cake'. He immediately shoved his control forward, saving us.

Within 48 hours of arriving, therefore, Dick Howard had spent almost two hours in the air, controlled the aircraft all by himself and made eight landings. The result was precisely what Smith-Barry had envisaged. 'The effect of a few days flying,' reported Howard, 'was to show conclusively how simple it was to manage the machine and, at the same time, to give me confidence in myself.'[20] An important part of the system was suitable training equipment—namely, an easy-to-fly two-seater with dual controls like the Avro 504 and the 'Gosport tube', a rubber hose allowing verbal communication between instructor and pupil.

The rite of passage for each cadet was his first solo flight. The number of hours of dual instruction required before going solo varied throughout the war, and with the instructor's discretion. In March 1917, Howard went solo after three and half hours of dual instruction. Later that year, Jack Weingarth had an hour and fifty minutes' dual flying before going up by himself. In any case, it was for all cadets a nervewracking but ultimately exhilarating experience. Rolf Brown described it as 'survival of the luckiest'—a cadet's life being completely dependent on there being no engine failure or stall from which he would not, at this stage of instruction, know how to save himself.[21] Not surprisingly another young Australian pilot described it as surely 'the most trying thing on your nerves'.[22]

As Day explained, though, most instructors didn't give their students prior warning of the solo, 'so as to prevent prior worrying or "wind up"'.

PLATE 1 Cadet George Merz climbs aboard the Bristol Boxkite during the first course at Point Cook Central Flying School. Merz was killed a year later in Mesopotamia—the AFC's first death on active service. *AWM A03918*

PLATE 2 Half Flight air mechanics prepare a Maurice Farman F.27 for a sortie in Mesopotamia. White and Yeats-Brown flew their disastrous mission to Baghdad in a similar machine. *AWM A04138*

PLATE 3 The BE2e pictured here, and its predecessor the BE2c, were No. 1 Squadron's main aircraft in 1916 and 1917. Unlike later British two-seaters, the observer sat in the front seat, limiting his field of vision. *AWM P00588.023*

PLATE 4 No. 1 Squadron's makeshift enemy aircraft warning system at Weli Sheikh Nuran. The Australian and German airmen raided each other's aerodromes aggressively in the middle of 1917. *Charles Betteridge*

PLATE 5 The commander of FA 300, Helmuth Felmy (left) in an AEG CIV at Huj. Felmy's younger brother Gerhardt was well known to the Australians for his outstanding flying skills and chivalrous behavior. *US Library of Congress*

PLATE 6 Lieutenant Claude Vautin (left) with German pilot Gerhardt Felmy. After being shot down in July 1917, Vautin enjoyed the hospitality of the German squadron. *AWM P02097.002*

PLATE 7 Major Richard 'Dicky' Williams, No. 1 Squadron's commanding officer from May 1917 to June 1918. Williams went on to command the squadron's senior formation, 40th Wing, and take temporary command of the RAF's Palestine Brigade. *AWM B02060*

PLATE 8 'The flying arseholes'—observers of No. 1 Squadron in early 1918 with a couple of squadron pets. Back row, left to right: lieutenants Howard Fletcher DFC, Hudson Fysh DFC, Charlie Vyner, Harold Letch MC, Ern Mustard DFC and Les Sutherland DCM MM. Front row, left to right: lieutenants Fred Hawley, Walter Kirk, Richard Camm, Garfield Finlay and Edward Beaton. *Peter Vyner*

PLATE 9 Australian observer Lawrence Smith with a group of German and Turkish officers after he was shot down and captured in June 1918. As evident in this photograph, Smith had a lucky escape when a bullet grazed his cheek during the action in which he was shot down. *Horst W. Laumanns*

PLATE 10 Alan Brown (left) and Garfield Finlay (right) stand with Major Sydney Addison in front of the German LVG they shot down near the Australian aerodrome at Ramleh on 22 August 1918. *Peter Vyner*

PLATE 11 Despite being against standing orders, some Australian airmen flew with personal cameras. Charlie Vyner took this photograph of another Bristol Fighter during a long-range reconnaissance over northern Palestine in mid 1918. *Peter Vyner*

PLATE 12 The giant Handley Page bomber, which Ross Smith flew during the Battle of Megiddo, and a pair of Bristol Fighters. The aerodrome is at the foot of Mount Carmel, near Haifa, where the No.1 Squadron spent the war's final weeks. *Peter Vyner*

PLATE 13 A section of the 'nine miles of dead'. Abandoned transport and equipment litter the narrow road north of Ferweh where the Turkish 7th Army was caught and decimated by British and Australian aircraft on 21 September 1918. *Peter Vyner*

PLATE 14 The wreckage of a Sopwith Camel of No. 8 (Training) Squadron AFC at Leighterton Aerodrome on 30 September 1918. The accident killed 22-year-old cadet Patrick Walsh. *AWM C04684*

PLATE 15 No. 3 Squadron armourers load bombs onto an RE8 at Savy on 22 October 1917. *AWM E01176*

PLATE 16 No. 3 Squadron took this photograph of the front line near Arras on 2 October 1917, a few weeks after it arrived at the front. By the end of the war, No. 3 Squadron had taken thousands of these images to create mosaic maps for the Australian Corps headquarters. *National Archives, United Kingdom*

PLATE 17 A German Albatross DVa scout on No. 3 Squadron's aerodrome at Baileiul in December 1917. This machine was forced to land during the dogfight in which James Sandy and Henry Hughes were killed by a single bullet. It is now part of the Australian War Memorial's collection. *AWM E01684*

PLATE 18 A de Havilland DH5 of No. 2 Squadron. Its reverse staggered wings gave it a unique appearance and a good field of vision forward, which was convenient for ground strafing. Its underpowered engine and obstructed rear vision made it a poor dogfighter though. *AWM C01858*

PLATE 19 A No. 2 Squadron SE5a. With high altitude performance and the ability to dive at high speeds, they spent most of their war patrolling above 15 000 feet. This was the regular machine of 24-year-old Francis Howard. He was killed in it on 27 October 1918. *Colin Owers*

PLATE 20 The 'office', as pilots called it, of a No. 4 Squadron Sopwith Camel. The optical Aldis gun sight sits between the two Vickers .303 machine guns. The pads on the gun butts were intended to protect the pilot's face in the event of a crash. *AWM E04899*

PLATE 21 A No. 2 Squadron SE5a overturned on Savy aerodrome in March 1918. This was the regular machine of Captain Henry Forrest DFC, who claimed 11 victories in just over 10 weeks. *AWM E01882*

PLATE 22 Both sides made prodigious use of static observation balloons during the war. Despite their benign appearance, they were incredibly dangerous targets for pilots. Nevertheless, No. 4 Squadron became something of a specialist balloon busting unit during the summer of 1918. *AWM E01173*

PLATE 23 The elaborate grave No. 3 Squadron provided legendary German pilot Manfred von Richthofen in Bertangles cemetery. French civilians vandalised it shortly after the burial service. *Les Parsons*

PLATE 24 No. 4 Squadron's A Flight at Clairmarais, 16 June 1918. In the centre, without a hat, is Harry Cobby, the AFC's highest scoring pilot with 29 victories. To his left is Bo King, who was second with 26 victories. Second from the right is 20-year-old Alex Lockely, who was killed in September in the large dogfight described in the prologue. *AWM E02661*

80 WING R.A.F. SQUADRON	IN FLAMES	CRASHED	O.O.C.	DRIVEN DOWN	BALLOONS DESTROYED
4 A.F.C.	19	57	36	7	22
88	20	33	53	15	
2 A.F.C.	10	30	48	16	
92	4	15	8	1	
103	5	12	30	3	
46	3	11	5	4	1
54	2	2			
TOTALS	63	160	180	46	23

PLATE 25 80th Wing's scoreboard, probably on the wall of a mess at Serny aerodrome just after the end of the war. Squadron commanders cultivated a competitive spirit in their units to encourage aggressive flying. *AWM P02163.016*

PLATE 26 During the Battle of Hamel on 4 July 1918, a digger snapped this image of a British RE8 moments before it crashed. It was attached to No. 3 Squadron to drop ammunition and was probably struck by an artillery shell. *AWM E03912*

PLATE 27 No. 3 Squadron mechanics overhauling an RE8's engine in one of the squadron's portable canvas Bessonau hangars. The table on the left no doubt used to be the property of a French family. *Bill Pomroy*

PLATE 28 A pair of No. 3 Squadron mechanics with a pilot and observer at Premont in October 1918. The squadron received a pair of Bristol Fighters on 23 October 1918 to supplement their war weary RE8s. *Bill Pomroy*

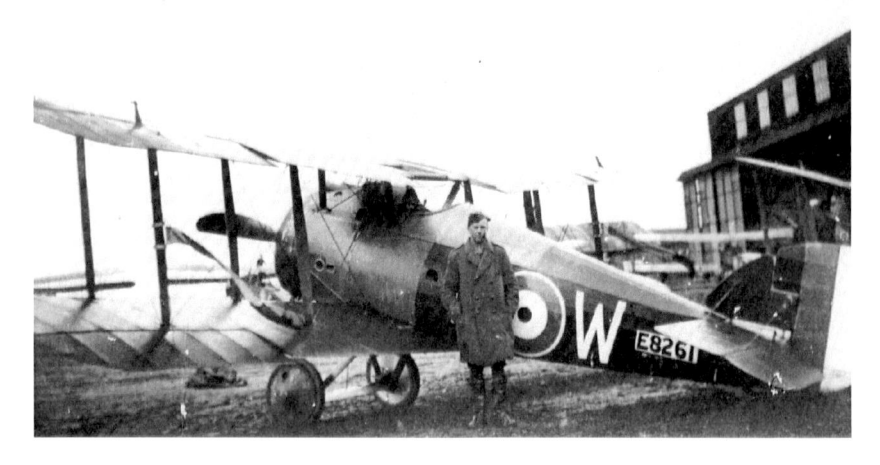

PLATE 29 Captain Jack Wright with one of the Sopwith Snipes No. 4 Squadron received in the war's final month. The Snipe was the pinnacle of British fighter design in the First World War, but lacked some of the Camel's whippy maneuverability. *Brian Wright*

PLATE 30 Henri Hemene, the French orphan who showed up at No. 4 Squadron's mess on Christmas Day 1918. He is pictured with Tim Tovell, the mechanic who smuggled him back to Australia and adopted him. Tovell hid Henri in this oats bag for the voyage across the Channel. *AWM H13589*

His turn came suddenly after his eleventh flight with his instructor: 'We had just landed and he stood up in the cockpit, stretched himself, got out of the bus, came alongside me and yelled out above the roar of engine, "Now go up—and if you make a bad landing you'll break your fucking neck. Cheerio."' Without time to consider what he was about to do, Day obediently pushed the throttle forward and trundled off across the aerodrome. The DH6 bounced once and was suddenly airborne. It then suddenly occurred to Day that he was alone in the air. A rush of exhilaration was quickly tempered by the cold realisation that he now had to get down again. 'I am positive if aeroplanes could remain aloft forever,' he wrote afterwards, 'there would still be hundreds and hundreds of first soloists tootling around England above their aerodromes thinking "Will I chance it?" ... "No, just another round."' Day did a few circuits of the aerodrome before finally willing himself to land.[23]

Whereas, earlier in the war, dual instruction would have all but ceased after the first solo, instructors under the Smith-Barry system continued flying with students throughout the training program to fine-tune and correct their technique.

Elementary training usually lasted between ten and twenty hours. Pilots then progressed to a course in higher instruction—or, as Ross quipped to his mother, 'higher destruction'.[24] Here they graduated to a superseded service machine like the BE2e or the Sopwith Pup, to learn some advanced manoeuvres and do cross-country flying. The instructors would also introduce them to some basic combat manoeuvres such as vertical turns, rolls and loops—'so important for taking evasive action when an enemy machine got on your tail,' as Wright's instructor told him. Wright also learned to spin his aircraft to evade enemy fire. Just a year before, British instructors had been telling their pupils to avoid spinning at all costs because it was too dangerous.

By the end of higher instruction, pupils would be flying a service machine—a Sopwith Camel or SE5a for scout candidates and an RE8 for their two-seater counterparts. After clocking up five hours on a service machine and completing a series of tests—cross-country flight, engine off landing from 8000 feet and a night landing—they graduated as pilots. They could sew the 'AFC' wings on their tunic, wear a Sam Browne belt and, most importantly for the majority, draw a pay rise to finance their new, gentlemanly lifestyle.

It was a momentous occasion for a young Australian man to become an officer *and* a qualified pilot. 'I'm a full flying officer now, and can do anything at all in a bus,' Weingarth proudly reported to his parents. 'Fly upside down, side loop, spin, dive vertically and over etc.' He went on to regale his parents with descriptions of hurtling along the streets of Salisbury, whipping around the Cathedral spire and racing trains across the countryside. One wonders how his parents back in Sydney—who may well have never laid eyes on a 'flying machine'—might have taken all of this. If they were concerned, then they actually had good reason to be. Even under the Smith-Barry system, training was still as dangerous as combat. Historian Denis Winter has calculated that about 8000 out of the 14 166 RFC pilot casualties during the war occured in England while training.[25] The Australian statistics tell a similar story—50 AFC pilots died in training accidents compared with 44 who were killed in combat.[26] In 1917, RFC pupils were wrecking 3.11 per cent of aircraft they flew each day, a marked decrease from pre-Smith-Barry days (when it was more like 10 per cent), but nonetheless striking when one considers that the average cadet made close to 100 separate flights during their half-year or so of training.[27] Indeed, it would not be an exaggeration to say that few, if any, Australian pilots didn't crash, or at least make a forced landing, while training.

Jack Wright was fortunate when it was his turn. He choked the engine of his Avro trainer while landing at Turnberry. The machine's tail caught a telegraph wire and, acting like a spring, slammed it backwards into the ground: 'The fuselage folded up and bent at right angles to the front portion just behind my seat, leaving me lying on my back with my legs in the air.' When Wright's commanding officer arrived at the scene moments later, he told the shaken pilot not to worry about the accident and invited him to lunch. 'He sat alongside me while we had some lunch,' recalled Wright. 'He talked about everything under the sun except flying and my recent crash.'

After the meal, Wright's commanding officer told him to get back into his flying gear and deliver a new aircraft to another aerodrome. This 'back on the horse' mentality was widespread and effective. Years later, Wright claimed he 'never gave a second thought to the incident', and only regretted being ushered away from the crash before getting a souvenir from the wreckage.[28] So common were accidents, apparently, that certain customs grew up around them. Ross, for example, told his family he had taken up smoking because 'it's absolutely essential to smoke a cigarette after crashing an aeroplane. This creates a great impression and everyone accordingly wonders and marvels at the coolness of the daring aviator.'[29] There was a somewhat more macabre convention in Francis Penny's training unit, where each pupil paid a levy of two shillings and sixpence to purchase wreaths for those who wouldn't survive the course.[30]

Graduation from higher instruction was followed by a fortnight at the School of Aerial Gunnery. Wright went to the school at Turnberry, situated on one of Scotland's most prestigious golf courses. After learning about the mechanics of the Vickers and Lewis guns, pupils did target shooting on the range. They fired at both fixed and moving targets as well as clay pigeons to develop their reflexes and deflection shooting skills. Airborne training involved pupils sitting in the back seat of an RE8 and firing live rounds at a canvas drogue towed by another machine, and targeting aircraft with a camera-fitted Lewis gun.

A pilot's training finally concluded with a week at the School of Aerial Fighting, colloquially known as a 'finishing school'. Pupils received instruction in the latest air fighting tactics from veteran combat pilots. In many respects, the finishing schools encapsulated Smith-Barry's philosophy that training should instil pupils with absolute confidence in their flying abilities—not the youthful, ignorant confidence that killed so many keen young flyers, but a confidence informed by an intimate understanding of aerobatic flying techniques. 'Nothing that a pupil may do in the air is dangerous,' he wrote, 'if he knows what he is doing and what the results will be.' Rather than teaching pupils that spinning and looping were dangerous, Smith-Barry argued that they should be taught how to do them properly—'his instinct of self preservation will do the rest,' he predicted.[31]

Even after six months of training, the flying at a finishing school awed most pupils: 'They do the most reckless things here,' wrote Weingarth, 'such as looping straight off the ground and follow the leader through trees and between houses and up and down streets.'[32] Just one week in this environment transformed pupils from competent aviators into fighter pilots with the skills fundamental to surviving their first few weeks at the front.

Weingarth remarked seven days after arriving: 'I take a machine and fly for miles around about 10 feet from the ground. We call it hedge hopping or contour chasing.' Wright noticed a marked improvement in his confidence, too—although it was an exceptionally steep learning curve. In eight days, he did six hours of formation flying at the touch-sensitive controls of a Sopwith Camel. His flight flew at hedge level with only 4 or 5 metres between their wing tips. 'I can remember how tense we were while doing this, one had to be, you couldn't drop your intense concentration for a fraction of a second.' At the end of it, though, he explained: 'I felt I really could fly.'[33]

In spite of this sense of confidence and achievement, training ended with an anti-climax for most pilots. After finishing school, they went to a pilot's pool to wait posting to a service squadron. Wait times varied from a few days to several weeks, depending on the supply and demand of pilots. Wallace McDougall captured the mood of this limbo between training and action in his diary: 'One of the observers [is] going to France today and Roberts and I are the next to go. May be tomorrow, may be a week or two. Nothing definite is known.' In McDougall's case, the wait would be a tedious three weeks of 'loafing around'.[34] The inactivity, wedged between the stress of advanced training and the tension of anticipated combat, affected morale. With little to do, conversation inevitably drifted towards speculation about the casualty rates that would determine their postings. It created, recalled McCloughry, 'a morbid atmosphere'.[35]

As he 'loafed around' at the pilot pool, the new pilot would also inevitably wonder whether his training and mettle were sufficient for the dangerous and stressful job ahead. Just how well prepared was he? Without a doubt the Australian pilot who trained in 1917 or 1918 was immeasurably better equipped than his British counterparts had been earlier in the war. Still, the perpetual demand for pilots at the front meant corners were sometimes cut. Harry Cobby's unit was posted before he could do the gunnery course and so he went to France before firing a machine gun in the air.[36] Others, such as Uriah Hoddinott, reported finishing training early to replace losses at the front.[37] Nunan was rushed through the School of Military Aeronautics' two-month course in just three weeks.[38]

Even when the training appeared more or less sufficient on paper, some cadets were still not ready to make the leap to service flying. James Baxter, for example, went to France with just under 58 hours of solo flying in his logbook. In his first three weeks at the squadron, though, he crashed three times and was, according to his commanding officer, so dangerous in formation that 'the morale of the other pilots of the patrol is seriously affected'. Leigh McCulloch was a similar case. His commanding officer described him 'of no use in a service squadron' and promptly sent him back to Britain for additional training.[39]

In any case, no matter how extensive or effective flying instruction was, tumbling around England's peaceful skies and shooting at fabric targets was one thing; anti-aircraft shells, small arms fire, improvised and barely sufficient landing grounds and of course enemy pilots would all add precarious dimensions to the already dangerous business of piloting a 'flying machine' in the First World War.

'Fire eaters': On-the-job training, June–August 1917

In the summer of 1917, the most advanced cadets from the AFC's first cohort of pilots went to the front for some on-the-job training with British squadrons. It was expected that these men would then form an experienced nucleus for the three Australian squadrons, which were due to go to France later in the year.

The timing made for a tough apprenticeship. They arrived at the front in late July 1917, just in time for the main British offensive for the year, around Ypres in Flanders. The German Air Service had recently changed tactics, grouping its scout units (Jastas) into Jagdgeschwaden (or 'hunting squadrons') of 50 aircraft. The first of these, Jagdgeschwader Nr I (JG I) was commanded by a young ex-cavalry officer named Manfred von Richthofen. Already known as the 'Red Falcon' and later the 'Red Baron', on account of his all-red Albatros, Richthofen was well on his way to becoming the highest scoring pilot of the conflict, and undoubtedly the best-known fighter pilot in history. His Jagdgeschwader would make life very dangerous for the inexperienced Australians who cut their teeth in the skies above the Third Battle of Ypres in the summer of 1917.

No. 3 Squadron sent about a dozen airmen to British two-seater units at the front. One of them was Owen Lewis, a 22-year-old student from Melbourne University, who had enlisted in the Engineers in 1916 and served briefly in the trenches. Impatient to get a commission, he used his family's influence—his father was friends with Australian divisional commander Major General John Monash—to secure a transfer to the AFC as an observer. Lewis was attached to No. 7 Squadron RFC (flying RE8s) at Proven in Flanders in early August 1917. He was paired up with an experienced British pilot named Norman Sharples, who thought his new protégé 'a raw looking Australian'.[40]

The demands of battle flying meant Lewis was in the air just a few hours after arriving at the squadron. Following takeoff, though, his inexperience was immediately apparent. As Sharples described: 'He had let the wireless aerial out with a rip, broken the handle on the reel, and the lead weight had dropped off.' After returning to the aerodrome and fitting a new aerial, the pair again embarked on their artillery patrol. Lewis had little time to absorb his first view of the Western Front, though. As they arrived over the line, a German scout was on their tail. As Sharples put it, Lewis 'rather lost his head' and failed to return fire. Putting the RE8 into a steep dive for friendly territory, he lost the enemy scout and managed to return with nothing worse than torn fabric and a rattled observer. Before unpacking his bags, Lewis had received a jolting initiation into the air war, an experience that his British mentor thought 'useful', adding: 'I bet he will not delay in getting his gun to work next time.'[41]

'Next time' came scarcely twelve hours later. On the following morning, Lewis and Sharples took off on another artillery shoot. Again, the pair ran into opposition over the line. Sighting eight enemy scouts, Sharples put the machine into a dive for the British lines but was cut off and caught in a hail of fire that sounded 'for all the world like a boy drawing a stick along iron railings fairly rapidly'. Applying his minimal experience, Lewis brought his gun into action in a period that seemed to Sharples 'like an age'. Returning fire, Lewis kept the German scouts at bay while they escaped into friendly skies. The RE8 was riddled from nose to tail with bullet holes. After nursing the aircraft back to Proven, Sharples inspected it, noting that 'a bullet had gone right through my compartment from side to side ... even the propeller is hit and bits of explosive bullets are discovered in another blade'. Lewis had a slight wound in the foot and the doctor ordered him not to fly for two days. 'Lewis winks at this,' noted Sharples.[42]

They were airborne again the following morning. For the third time in as many days, German scouts intercepted them over the line. This time Lewis was ready. To Sharples' satisfaction, the rear gun was 'ripping away in no time', compelling the enemy pilots to dive away. The patrol continued unhindered and successfully bombed enemy positions. During the return to Proven, though, they became lost in fog. Hopelessly disorientated, the pair flew around until Lewis recognised trenches that he had previously occupied with the 10th Field Company. Gathering his bearings, Lewis directed them home safely.

In the following few days, Sharples and Lewis were shot up another two times. The other airmen started referring to them as 'fire-eaters', a title that bothered Sharples, who complained: 'Lewis and I seem to get the sticky end of the stick every time.' In six days, they had been in five aerial combats, and were twice badly damaged.[43]

On 14 August 1917, just a week after arriving at the squadron, Lewis started his sixth flight with Sharples to direct artillery fire in preparation for the offensive at Langemarck. It was a misty morning, but breaking through the cloud ceiling revealed a bright and clear day. Just as they were crossing the line, three German scouts attacked 'most aggressively'. As Lewis brought his gun to bear, enemy bullets knocked it out of action and tore into his legs and chest. Throwing the RE8 about violently, Sharples dived into the fog and escaped back across the line. With his observer bleeding severely and the aircraft badly damaged, Sharples barely made it back to Proven. Lewis had gunshot wounds in the chest and both legs, and had lost most of his right foot. Sharples drove the critically injured Australian to a field hospital where, over the following days, his condition stabilised.[44] Lewis was then sent back to England. In the chaotic stream of casualties from the offensive, Sharples was misinformed, instead hearing that his observer had died. He remarked that 'Lewis's death has been a vital loss on me', a clear demonstration of the bond that formed between pilot and observer during the week's fighting. August 1917 had taken a heavy toll on the aviators of No. 7 Squadron RFC. By 17 August 1917, Sharples was one of only two airmen left from the previous month's flying establishment. 'Our dinner table shows many empty seats and an absence of popular and familiar faces,' he noticed.[45] A month later, he too was dead, after a British artillery shell struck his RE8.

By the end of August, all of the Australian pilots who had emerged unscathed from their apprenticeship over the front had returned to their respective squadrons in Britain to complete final preparations for active service. Half a dozen had become casualties (four dead and two prisoners)—a figure probably not out of proportion with the rest of the RFC, which suffered a staggering loss of 287 airmen and 251 aircraft during August alone.[46] Von Richthofen's Jagdgeschwader, or 'flying circus' as the British pilots nicknamed it, was responsible for about 37 of these. The 'Red Falcon' himself had only claimed two, as he was grounded with a head injury for most of the month. These nevertheless raised his personal score to 59.

'The one earthly ambition which these boys cling on to ...': Bean confronts the air war

In September 1917, Australia's official war correspondent, Charles Bean, and his assistant, Henry Gullett, visited some of the British squadrons to which Australians had been attached over the summer. He knew the AFC units would soon be arriving at the front, and he was eager to find out how the young airmen had fared, and what this air fighting business was all about.

At No. 32 Squadron at Proven, the unit's young Canadian commander, Captain Joy, greeted Bean and Gullett. 'A fine modest chap', Joy was 'most warm' about the Australians who had spent a few weeks in his unit. 'What one most liked about them,' he told the correspondents, 'was that they were always ready for any job you suggested to them, whatever it was.' Joy spoke at length in glowing, if general terms about the Australian pilots. When Bean asked him for some 'definite stories to be published', however, the squadron commander became uneasy. He couldn't do that, he explained. It wasn't the RFC way—they were a modest corps that, as a matter of policy, didn't publicise the exploits of individuals. He did, however, agree to introduce the two Australian correspondents to 'Edwards', an Australian in the squadron (a member of the RFC) who might be able to share a few 'unofficial' stories with them.

After a few minutes, a young pilot shuffled into the mess. He looked, thought Bean immediately, like 'a typical man from one of the big Victorian public schools'. In fact, it turned out he was. Edwards was a Melbourne Grammarian. On closer inspection, though, Bean saw that Edwards was nervous. He moved about jerkily and as he sat down the correspondents noted how his neck twitched.

Bean asked the young Australian pilot how the AFC men fared. They had, he replied in a quiet, direct tone, 'done a lot of real good work'. Bean asked him for some of their names and examples of their exploits. Edwards produced the squadron's record book and began leafing through the pages. 'Funny,' he murmured absentmindedly as he ran his finger across the pages, 'I flown with 'em all but I can't remember names now—things seem to go too fast . . .' He trailed off vaguely. Suddenly it dawned on Bean that he was speaking to a man with a 'new disease'—a man whose nerves were being 'wrecked within a few whirlwind weeks by a new craze—a new craving'.

Bean and Gullett continued gently conversing with Edwards to draw out his own story. Gradually, the young man began to open up, showing them his logbook and speaking about the war the pilots fought high above the trenches. Bean was astonished at the impressions of this 'new craze' Edwards revealed with a disturbing detachment and nonchalance. There were the dogfights—high-speed affairs fought at 'point blank range' that sometimes resulted in mid-air collisions. Then there were the explosive bullets the Germans fired, which would set an aircraft alight and burn its pilot alive. And there were the ground-strafing sorties he had done during the Ypres campaign. Edwards shuddered as he recounted flying *through* a barrage of British artillery shells to strafe enemy troops. 'You can see 'em, you know?' he explained quietly to the correspondents. 'Didn't mind 'em at first—hardly knew what they were. But I don't like them now.'

Bean was certain of one thing. No man could live at that tempo for very long. Indeed, the proof was sitting before him. 'He was already out of touch with the world—his memory going, his nerves twitching. He could not give it up—yet in a way he dreaded some things in it.'

Edwards was careful not to boast—but it was obvious to Bean that he wanted to tell his story. 'I suppose the chances of immortality for their deeds and name is the one earthly ambition which these boys cling on to,' considered Bean. 'They must see the next few weeks ahead of them as the short crammed hour, a short straight blind alley . . . and then flash, out.'

The meeting left the two war correspondents with no illusions about what the airmen of the AFC were getting themselves into. As they drove away from Proven aerodrome, leaving Edwards to his fate, Gullett asked Bean whether he had seen the rows of liquor bottles and recipes for 21 cocktails on the squadron's mess wall. Bean hadn't. 'I wish you had seen it, it was awfully significant,' said Gullet. 'Poor chaps,' replied Bean, 'I expect it is. That pace can't last. It must be either death or a breakdown—and a breakdown probably means—well, those bottles show what.'[47]

9
'A RED KANGAROO ON THE COWLING'
The Australian Flying Corps on the Western Front, 1917

Pilots of No. 2 Squadron AFC at Baizieux on 7 December 1917, the day the Battle of Cambrai ended. In the past 17 days the unit had sustained 50 per cent casualties. *RAAF Museum*

Then as you look on the ground the battered houses,
earthworks, huge shell holes and craters come into view...

—2nd Lieutenant Stanley Garrett, No. 3 Squadron, Australian Flying Corps

'Here we are within a few miles of the line': No. 3 Squadron's induction to war flying, September–November 1917

Western Europe was uncharacteristically blanketed with rain and fog during the last week of August 1917. It was bad news for the hundreds of thousands of British troops struggling through the quagmire at Ypres. It wasn't much good either for No. 3 Squadron's pilots and observers who were preparing to fly across the Channel and become the first AFC squadron to begin active service on the Western Front.

For nine months, No. 3 Squadron had prepared for this occasion. The pilots and observers trained for the work of a two-seater squadron—that is, reconnaissance, artillery observation, photography and bombing. The unit

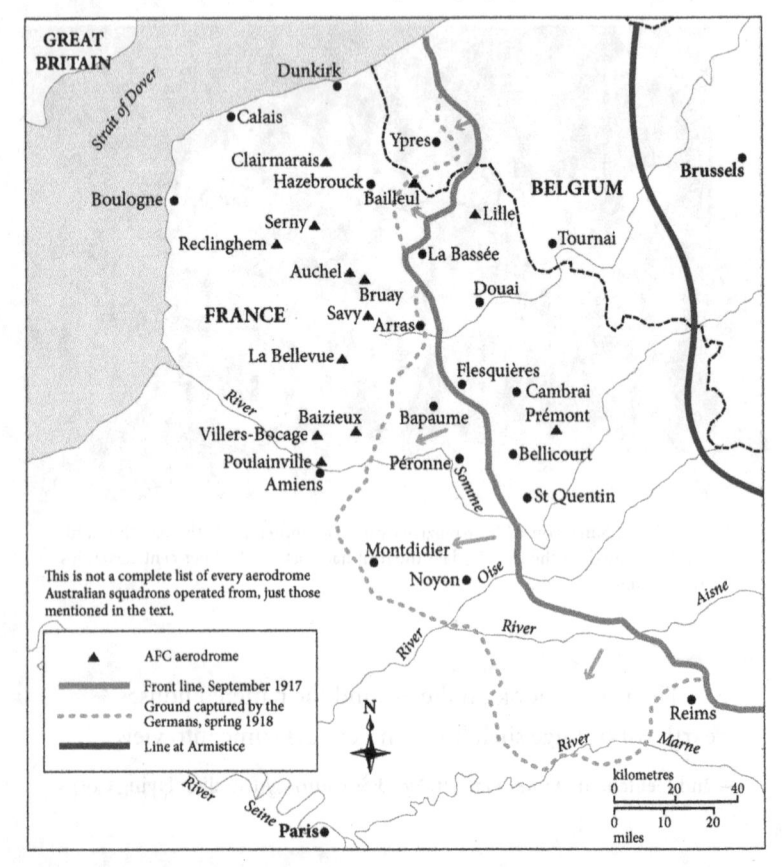

MAP 4 The Western Front, 1917–18

was equipped with the RFC's latest two-seater, the RE8, otherwise known as the 'Harry Tate'. Although already dated by the time it made it from the drawing board to the front line, the 'Tate' was at least armed (forward-firing Vickers and a Lewis gun for the observer), and it was incredibly stable and easy to fly.

No. 3 Squadron's airmen took off in their RE8s to cross the Channel on 21 August 1917. It wasn't a good day for flying. Pilot Stan Garrett described how the 'clouds were very low and very heavy', forcing him to fly by the compass. The squadron hit a storm over Margate and had to abort their crossing. They all landed at Lympne, except for Frank Shapira and his passenger 2nd Class Air Mechanic William Sloan, who were both killed when their RE8 crashed en route. Shapira, a 29-year-old station overseer from western New South Wales, was particularly unfortunate to die like this after having survived injuries at Gallipoli and in France before volunteering for the AFC.[1]

The RE8s and their crews would remain at Lympne for three weeks, grounded by foul weather and a mechanical defect that revealed itself on a number of the machines during the first leg. It was an anti-climax for the pilots, who spent the time playing cards in a hotel lobby and listening to the distant rumble of artillery in the Ypres Salient that made the building 'quiver from top to bottom'.[2]

In the meantime, the rest of the squadron crossed by sea. Fifty-seven trucks carried the unit's gear, with the men 'stacked away on top of the loads and in the tenders, just anywhere that was big enough to squeeze into'.[3] They disembarked at Le Havre, and after a two-day journey arrived at Savy, the squadron's first service aerodrome. To men who had only ever known Britain's well-established training stations, this must have appeared an inauspicious place to start an active service career. Situated on the edge of the tiny village in some muddy paddocks, the aerodrome's previous squadron had stripped it of almost all comforts and amenities. All that remained were half a dozen corrugated iron hangars and a few 'leaky huts'.[4]

With the aircraft still held up in Britain, the ground crews set about improving the facilities. They spent their first night under the squadron's portable canvas hangars but soon managed to erect corrugated iron Nissen huts to accommodate either fourteen men or four of the officers. A few lucky air mechanics found bunks left by the aerodrome's prior occupants, but most had to make do with what they could find. Stanley Tuck, an instrument fitter, pilfered a door from an old shed near the aerodrome. 'I will sleep on that until I can make a bunk,' he noted in his diary.[5]

Building materials were in short supply, but the resourcefulness, initiative and loose discipline for which 'colonials' were renowned made up for the shortfall. When the men realised that a unit of British troops camped nearby were moving, they saw an opportunity. 'As soon as we heard they were leaving,' Tuck recorded:

> we raided their huts and walked off with bunks, chunks of timber, roofing iron etc. anything that would be useful and right under their noses. The Tommies were so surprised at the audacity of the Australians that we got away with all we needed before they gathered themselves together and blocked us. Then someone discovered some abandoned store sheds about a mile away, very soon there was a stream of fellows carrying boards ripped off the floor. We had a clear day at that before it was found out and stopped. After that we went too and fro in the shelter of some trees and hedges. We got all we wanted and a bit to spare.[6]

When the airmen finally arrived with their machines on 10 September, Savy aerodrome, although ramshackle and improvised looking, was a much more accommodating place from which to fight a war.

The aerodrome was about 12 kilometres behind the front, in the sector between the River Scarpe and Lens. Although heavily fought over earlier in the year, it was now a quiet sector used by both sides to rest units from the fighting in Flanders. It was therefore an ideal place for No. 3 Squadron to have its induction to war flying.

No. 3 Squadron was designated a 'corps' squadron, meaning that it was permanently attached to one of the British Expeditionary Force's army corps. Each corps contained between two and five infantry divisions (each 18 000 men strong at full strength) and was responsible for a specific stretch of front line. Corps were self-sufficient military formations by late 1917, having their 'own' tunnellers, signallers, transport, heavy artillery and, of course, a flying squadron. As a 'corps squadron', No. 3's job was to supply its corps headquarters with photographs and reconnaissance reports, and help the artillery hit targets by transmitting shot corrections to the gunners. To begin with, No. 3 Squadron shared the work of the two British squadrons supporting the Canadian Corps and British XIII Corps in its sector.

There wasn't much experience to speak of in No. 3 squadron to begin with. The background of its commanding officer, 29-year-old Major David Blake, was in staff work, not war flying. He was a pre-war regular soldier who had gone to Egypt with No. 1 Squadron's administrative staff in March 1916. To meet the urgent need for trained pilots, he was one of those sent to Britain for pilot training before the squadron even started operations. Blake earned his wings in September 1916 and was subsequently selected to command No. 3 Squadron when it arrived in Britain in December. There were three observers in the unit who had fought in British squadrons and a dozen of the officers had done on-the-job training with front-line squadrons during the summer.

The airmen began flying on 12 September 1917. They initially practised formation flying well on their own side of the line, over the old battlefields around Arras. After a few days came familiarisation flights along the front line itself. Stan Garrett, a 23-year-old architect from Melbourne, recorded his first impression of this most iconic and terrible landscape:

> The first thing that you would see is the captive balloons either side has there. They are generally about 1500 feet up and take the shape of a huge sausage. Then as you look on the ground the battered houses, earthworks, huge shell holes and craters come into view, then above the line the white crusted trenches, with on either side, their wide stretch of barbed wire. Here and there gun flashes show up and amidst it all the dull booming of our guns is heard punctuated now and then with the sharp grunt of Archie.[7]

Rolf Brown's impression was similar, but he was shocked by how quiet and peaceful everything appeared from 8000 feet during the daytime. He found 'no sign of movement except for a few trains in the far distance' behind the 'Hun' lines. 'The false air of peace and security was so impressive that it will always live in one's memory,' he explained.[8]

The first real work the squadron attempted was the line patrol. Probably the most basic and mundane of a corps squadron's tasks, it involved flying back and forth along the corps' front to report on artillery flashes and movement on the enemy's side of the line. A fortnight after arriving, the airmen also began photographing the front line. At least once a week, corps squadrons were expected to supply their headquarters with a complete mosaic of the trenches. The work was similar to that undertaken by No. 1 Squadron during its early days in Palestine, although by the time No. 3 Squadron's crews started, the equipment was far more sophisticated. Jack Treacy, a No. 3 Squadron pilot, explained the procedure.

> Your aerial gunner is watching all the time for the enemy and he lets you know if you are about to be attacked. Photos were taken with a camera mounted in the rear at the aircraft behind and under the gunner's seat. The camera for oblique and map making plates was automatically driven and it changed the plates itself. All the pilot had to do was to count the time for exposure and overlap on his stop watch and press the button, the camera did the rest itself. The aerial gunner would change the magazines in the camera on signal from the pilot.[9]

Despite the simple process Treacy described, it took some time for No. 3 Squadron's amateur crews to get it right. Eric Dibbs, one of the few observers with prior war flying experience, recalled trying to arrange photographs from these early patrols into mosaic maps to send to corps headquarters. 'As these had in many cases been taken at varying altitudes,' he explained, 'it really was hardly possible to do a good job.' To improve things, Major Blake sent Dibbs and the other two experienced observers up with the green pilots to act as instructors.

Dibbs recalled another 'amusing' mark of inexperience during the squadron's first few weeks at the front. The RE8's radio set was equipped with a wire aerial that swung below the aircraft on a lead weight. It was the observer's job to unwind it after takeoff and retrieve it before landing. One observer forgot to wind his aerial in, though, and when the aircraft pulled up at the hangars, the weight was dragging behind, covered in blood and hair. 'There was a first class flap about it,' explained Dibbs, 'till analysis revealed that they were animal and not human traces. Some poor old cow must have got a terrific whack from that weight as the RE8 glided in at low level for its landing.'[10]

The squadron's first five weeks passed uneventfully, with only fleeting glimpses of enemy machines. The airmen flew a sortie most days, and spent the rest of the time with the war just beyond the horizon. The peculiarity of it wasn't lost on Garrett:

> In the distance we can hear the dull booming of the guns. How little one realises that with each boom men are being knocked to pieces and yet here we are within a few miles of the line and all is quiet and peaceful, only the drowsy hum of the engines as they are warming up prior to taking off.[11]

The workload stepped up considerably in mid-October when the two local British corps squadrons allocated part of their artillery observation work to the Australians. This was the cornerstone of a corps squadron's work, and indeed one of the principal ways the RFC supported the army. The most common targets were enemy batteries that had been identified by the photographic and flash reconnaissance patrols.

It was the pilot who did the actual observation and shot corrections—as well as flying the machine, of course. With a map board resting on his knees, he would fly figure-of-eight circuits between 'his' battery and the enemy target, observing where shells landed and then signalling aiming corrections in Morse on a wireless transmitter.

Of course, artillery aircraft chugging back and forth across the lines at 5000 feet for around three hours straight were inviting targets for German scouts. On 21 October, A Flight's commander, William Anderson, and his observer, John Bell, were in the middle of a shoot when five enemy Albatroses dived on them in succession. Despite being 'too scared to think', Anderson's resolve held and he resisted the temptation to dive away and present the enemy pilots with a more vulnerable target.[12] He kept the RE8 steady while Bell, crouched at his Lewis gun, fired at them. The German pilots rallied for a second pass, but then thought better of it when another pair of Australian RE8s arrived to help. Anderson then called up his battery again and resumed the shoot. Ten days later, Anderson found himself in a similar bind. He was again directing artillery when four enemy scouts set upon him. Again he kept his cool and manoeuvred to keep the enemy machines in his observer's field of fire. Nearby, Eric Dibbs was showing a new pilot, Ernest Jones, the line. Despite being his first time out, Jones didn't hesitate to dive into the fight. Dibbs later recalled what it was like for the observer—who, unlike the pilot, wasn't strapped in:

> Those were unforgettable moments—as the pilot dived, the observer was flung on his back with his feet pointing up to the blue sky. He was reassured by the sound of the front gun firing and the smell of the cordite fumes. When the front gun stopped firing, you were in suspense, wondering whether the pilot had been killed, till either he fired again or the machine lurched out of its dive ... Each time the pilot pulled out of a dive, the observer had to clamber to his feet against the centrifugal force, swing both Lewis guns in the direction of the nearest enemy aircraft and let fly. Masses of tracer and hundreds of unseen bullets would be flying in all directions and the opposing aircraft would be wildly dog fighting in a mad, whirling mass.[13]

Despite being far from outstanding dogfighters, the lumbering RE8s gave the German pilots sufficient cause to break off and leave. Jones and Dibbs' machine was shot up quite badly and they had to make a forced landing. Once again, Anderson resumed his position, called the battery up and recommenced his work. It was this kind of initiative and quiet devotion to their work that made the humble two-seater crews the unsung heroes of the air war. It would also see Anderson later take command of his squadron and, after the war, become an Air Vice-Marshal in the RAAF.

The weather deteriorated in October and accidents increased. Remarkably, there were no fatalities—even when two RE8s collided on the aerodrome on 12 October. They approached the airfield at right angles and met up just after touching down. 'There was an awful crash,' recalled Tuck. 'They were each travelling at about 60 miles an hour and were both smashed completely and rolled over several times.' One of the observers was thrown clear and landed on his head. 'By some remarkable freak both pilots and observers got off scot free!' The observer who had been thrown clear, John Blair, was fortunate indeed. The collision was the thirteenth accident he had walked away from since arriving in France.[14]

The weather cleared on 6 November and, just before lights out, orders arrived for the squadron to support a trench raid on its corps front the following day. 'Orderlies were dashing around and our mechanics were working on our machines most of the night,' explained Garrett. By 9.00 a.m. the next day, the squadron's eighteen RE8s were lined up in front of the hangars alongside those of the two neighbouring British units, all fitted with bombs.

In No. 3 Squadron, each flight had its own objective. A Flight would drop smoke bombs to screen the raiders from German machine-gun positions on high ground, while B and C Flights bombed a village just behind the German front to keep enemy reinforcements away.

Corps headquarters set 'zero hour' for midday. The pilots synchronised their watches with the infantry and only crossed the line five minutes before them to maintain surprise. Stan Garrett led B Flight:

The air was just alive with machines and at 11.55 they set out for their objectives. As we passed over the town I dropped my bombs and each other pilot in succession dropped his bombs. There was not a Hun in the sky and although Archie did fire his shots were awfully wide. I suppose there were so many machines that he did not have time to engage anyone in particular. At the same time of our bomb dropping every gun in the sector opened fire and Fritz's side was one mass of explosions. After we had dropped our bombs we came back and watched the show from about 3000 feet. There were smoke shells fired to hide the infantry movement and a gas attack launched over his trenches. We believe that we put a proper wind up the Hun.[15]

Garrett had a rough trip home. His RE8 was buffeted by British artillery shells passing close by and he flew into a hailstorm, forcing him to land in a paddock. He made it back to Savy that afternoon, giving the squadron a perfect sortie. The raid provided No. 3 Squadron with a fitting graduation to fully operational status. It also serves as a perfect illustration the importance the RFC, and in particular the corps squadrons, had to army operations by 1917.

Five days later, the squadron received orders to pack up and prepare to move. Its apprenticeship was over and it was now headed north to a sector and corps of its own.

'We can better an equal number of the best German machines': No. 2 Squadron goes to France, October 1917

The dishevelled and unsoldierly mob of light horsemen who had arrived at Waterloo Station in January 1917 had come a long way in nine months. British training schools had transformed them into specialists: engine fitters, riggers, armourers and fighter pilots. By September they were ready to become Australia's first operational scout unit, No. 2 Squadron, ready for war on the Western Front.

The squadron was equipped with Airco De Havilland DH5s, a relatively new biplane with an unusual design feature (see Plate 18). The top wing was staggered backwards from the bottom one, giving the pilot uninterrupted forward views but restricting it to the rear. The Australian pilots initially liked their new machine. It was nimble and easy to fly, and as Dick Howard reported, robust, being able to 'be dived at 180 miles an hour without the wings dropping off'.[16] But the DH5 also had some blemishes. It was under-powered for a scout of its generation, and it performed poorly above 10 000 feet. The squadron's confidence in its new machines took a hit when one of its most experienced and respected flight commanders died in an accident just prior to leaving for France. Stan Muir, it will be recalled, had distinguished himself in 1916 with No. 1 Squadron in his white- and brown-winged Martinsyde. He had scored what was probably the AFC's first aerial victory. Muir was testing one of the new DH5s at Harlaxton when it suddenly shed its wings and plunged to the ground. 'When the onlookers went to the smash,' reported Vern Knuckey, 'the man was unrecognisable, every bone in his body must have been broken.'[17]

Fortunately, Muir wasn't No. 2 Squadron's only experienced pilot. When the unit formed in Egypt in September 1916, a handful of mechanics and airmen joined it from No. 1 Squadron to provide experience and leadership. Muir's best mate, John Bell, also came from Palestine (along with his pet monkey) to take a flight to France, and Oswald Watt, who flew with the French Air Service during the earliest days of the war and commanded a flight in the Middle East, was No. 2 Squadron's commanding officer.

Watt was an excellent choice to command the new squadron. In addition to being one of the most experienced pilots in the British Empire, his leadership style was ideal for volunteer citizen soldiers, who responded well to a just and commonsense approach to discipline. Take, for example, a speech he made to the squadron while training in England after some of the air mechanics refused to do an early morning drill:

> You boys have had a hard time on Gallipoli and Sinai, most of you have been through hell, now I want you to have as good a time as possible during your stay in England but I want you to remember that I am Major and anyone up before me will find I'm no milksop.[18]

No milksop indeed. When 80 of the men snuck into Marseilles against orders during a stopover on the voyage from Egypt, he docked their pay for a month and put them at the bottom of the squadron's leave roster. 'In things that mattered,' explained one of Watt's fellow officers, 'his men knew he stood for absolute obedience. They also knew that when discipline could be safely relaxed he would be quick to grant them some relief from the strain.'[19] Harold Brinsmead fondly recalled Watt's care for the men under his command, his personal interest in their lives and his deep concern for their welfare. He was, concluded Brinsmead, 'a born leader of men' who ran an extremely tight-knit and efficient squadron.[20]

The rest of the pilots were rookies who learned to fly in England during 1917. Out of the eighteen 'originals' who went to France with the squadron on 21 September 1917, just under half had enlisted in the first six weeks of the war and another seven did so in 1915. The majority had fought at Gallipoli or the Western Front before volunteering for the AFC, sometimes in the light horse, but more usually in the engineers or infantry. In the trenches, nearly all of them had been enlisted or non-commissioned ranks. Fairly typical among them was 22-year-old Dick Howard. Athletic and intelligent, Howard had left a degree at Sydney University to enlist in the engineers in September 1915. His father needed to write him a permission note because he was not yet 21. Howard fought on the Somme in 1916 at Pozières and Flers, where he was wounded by machine gun fire. When the AFC advertised for volunteers late in 1916, Howard applied, hoping for a commission and a way out of the trenches.

No. 2 Squadron's first posting was Baizieux, just west of Albert and close to the 1916 Somme battlefields (see Map 4). The aerodrome was on a farm, the officers sharing the house with the farmer and his family while the men slept in the barns and stables. Knuckey explained they were 'right away from towns of any sort', Baizieux being 'just a collection of smashed up houses'.[21]

The squadron's first priority was to prepare their aircraft for work over the front. In the days before air to air radio communication it was difficult for pilots to distinguish each other, so each machine was personalised. 'Mine is in "A" Flight,' wrote Howard of his new DH5, 'and red is the distinguishing colour, so I have a red kangaroo on the cowling, a red propeller boss, red bands round the gun and fuselage and red numbers to distinguish each pilot. I am No. 4.'[22] Flight commanders also attached pennants to their wing struts and worked out hand signals with their pilots.

The routine job of scout squadrons at this stage of the war was the 'offensive patrol'. According to the RFC's tactical manual, *Fighting in the Air*, it had the 'sole duty' of finding and destroying enemy aircraft over their own territory so British corps squadrons could do reconnaissance and artillery observation above the front line unhindered. The squadron started work on 28 September. Three days later, Dick Howard described the routine in a letter to his family:

> An offensive patrol means that for two hours you are patrolling up and down a strip of the line, 20 to 30 miles [about 30 to 50 kilometres] long and anything up to 10 miles behind the German lines. Today we did not sight any Hun machines, so there was nothing exciting in that line, but we were continually being 'Archied'. There seems to be one crack 'Archie' battery near Cambrai and each time we get near him his shooting is very accurate and gives us a little 'hurry up'. Holden got one of his planes pierced by a splinter from one of these shells, which burst just in between him and me. Also another chap in our Flight got his plane hit.[23]

The DH5's shortcomings as a dogfighter were soon evident. On the day Howard wrote his letter, the squadron flew seven patrols over enemy territory. Five of them encountered enemy reconnaissance machines, but each time the Germans easily outran the under-powered DH5s.

A patrol the following morning also revealed that the pilots had much to learn. When A Flight's leader, Wilfred McCloughry, dived on an enemy two-seater 500 feet below them, all the other pilots followed with guns blazing. Howard wrote: 'I could see my tracer ammunition entering the fuselage and suddenly the observer who had been firing at me stopped, so I presume I hit him.' The German pilot made a steep dive and quickly outran the Australians. The flight returned to its patrol altitude and soon came across another enemy two-seater. Its pilot threw it into a tight corkscrew and dived back east, but this time the Australians showed a little more discipline. Howard and Les Holden chased it while McCloughry and Ivo Agnew remained above to cover them. They chased him down to 3000 feet, exchanging fire, 'at which point he was going straight for the ground with smoke issuing from him'.[24]

A Flight returned to Baizieux, but landed without Agnew, who had gone missing. Although a milestone success in the squadron's history, the patrol revealed some obvious inexperience. For one thing, the entire flight should not have dived upon the first German machine. This was simply inviting German scouts, which sometimes used lone two-seaters as 'bait', to dive on their exposed backs. Second, nobody in the flight, including McCloughry, could account for Agnew's disappearance. Later Red Cross reports would reveal he had crashed with engine failure and was a prisoner. Nevertheless, Major Watt was proud that his squadron could claim its first two machines 'driven down' and granted A Flight a tender for the afternoon to go shopping and sightseeing in Doullens.

Patrols continued with the predictable routine of two per day, but encounters with the enemy were sporadic, reflecting the German Air Service's practice of shifting scout units around the front as local conditions dictated. The result was that after roaming about the enemy's skies for a week with complete impunity, a pilot might suddenly find himself among a swarm of recently arrived German scouts. This occurred on 13 October, when four pilots from C Flight were returning from an early patrol. They hadn't seen a German aircraft all week, but when Douglas Morrison, a 22-year-old orchardist from rural Victoria, developed engine trouble and lagged behind the others, four Albatroses pounced and shot him down into no man's land. Some British soldiers rescued him under a white flag, but Morrison died a fortnight later following the amputation of his right leg.[25]

No. 2 Squadron's first serious dogfight happened on 16 October. Four members of A Flight were 10 000 feet above Gouy on the enemy's side of the line when eight Albatroses surprised them from 2000 feet above. It was a 'battle royal' according to Howard:

> We made our machines twist and twirl to outmanoeuvre the Huns. At one time I was tackled by three of them; one in front, which I had turned round on suddenly and was firing at, and two others, which dived on me from behind. Our only chance was for our four machines to stick together for, if one got separated, it would be attacked by all the Huns and brought down.

It seems A Flight was learning from experience. McCloughry gave his pilots 'the greatest credit for the manner in which they stuck together in good formation throughout' and covered each other's tails.[26] When he went to the assistance of the flight's newest pilot, Howard and his partner stayed above to protect him. The dogfight only lasted a few minutes before the German pilots made off. The Australians all landed safely, although Howard only just made it back to Baizieux with his aircraft 'riddled with bullets'. 'In fact,' he wrote to his family, 'it was a "write off" ... five out of eight main spars were hit, one so badly by an explosive bullet that it was a wonder the wing did not break'.

Despite being indecisive, the dogfight was a clear indication that No. 2 Squadron was settling into the war above the Western Front. 'Consequently,' wrote Howard, 'we are filled with confidence and consider that, on our comparatively slow and dud machines, we can better an equal number of the best German machines.'[27]

'Their work was really magnificent': The British offensive at Cambrai, 20–27 November 1917

While No. 2 Squadron was learning the ropes at Baizieux, events were unfolding at British General Headquarters which would have a significant bearing on its experiences in the weeks to come.

With the Ypres offensive petering out in the quagmire around Passchendaele, the BEF's commander, Field Marshal Sir Douglas Haig, approved a new offensive to finish off 1917 with, he hoped, more positive results for the British public. Third Army, under General Sir Julian Byng, had collaborated with the nascent Tank Corps to plan for a 'tank raid' against the important enemy transport and communications hub of Cambrai. Despite being protected by the formidable Hindenburg trench system and the St Quentin Canal, the country surrounding Cambrai suited tanks and was only thinly garrisoned. With Haig's endorsement, Third Army's final plan grew from a hit-and-run raid into a determined offensive. The final plan aimed to punch holes through the first and second German trench systems with tanks and infantry, and send cavalry galloping through to capture Cambrai and cut off large pockets of enemy troops.

The tanks weren't the only innovation in the Cambrai plans, though. By late 1917, the science of artillery aiming had evolved to a point where gunners could fire at points on a map with a reasonable chance of accuracy, obviating the need to give their positions away with 'registration' fire in the days before an attack. For Cambrai, Third Army's 1003 guns would deploy in secret and hold fire until the infantry left their trenches at zero hour, to maintain surprise. A third unique feature of the plans involved the RFC. Operations at Arras and Ypres during 1917 had suggested the effectiveness aircraft could have in assisting the infantry directly on the battlefield by attacking ground targets ahead of their advance. At Cambrai, the RFC would contribute fourteen squadrons (289 aircraft), three of which were specifically detailed for ground attack work. No. 2 Squadron was one of them. Byng set zero hour for 6.00 a.m. on 20 November 1917.

Rumours of a big offensive did the rounds at Baizieux. 'For weeks now there has been a kind of suppressed excitement,' recorded Vern Knuckey in his diary. He and the other mechanics fitted bomb racks to the DH5s and watched with curiosity as the pilots practised dropping dummy bombs in a field next to the aerodrome. Each night, endless columns of troops, cavalry and guns moved up past the aerodrome towards the front.[28]

By 19 November, everyone knew it was close. An advanced landing ground had been established at Bapaume and the pilots from the ground attack squadrons gathered there that evening. Spirits were high and after the briefing the pilots went into Amiens for the 'gaiety of the café and the humour of the picture shows'. One pilot, Harry Taylor, missed the tender back to Baizieux and had to walk home. He arrived just as the other pilots were being woken to prepare for their first sorties.[29]

FIRE IN THE SKY

Dawn didn't break on 20 November 1917. As pilot Gordon Wilson explained: 'A heavy fog—an airman's worst enemy—enveloped the "drome".' He considered it 'impossible to fly in', but at 7.05 a.m., John Bell, the Palestine veteran, led C Flight out on the squadron's first ground attack assignment. Because of the fog, they flew in pairs rather than a six. None of the men from this flight left their impressions of the approach to the Cambrai battlefield, but one of their British colleagues, Arthur Lee, whose squadron was also flying low sorties that morning, wrote a striking description in a letter to his wife:

> Everything flashes by like a dream, and as we rush forward at over ninety miles an hour, twenty feet up, I get split second glances that remain vividly in my memory. I see the ragged line of grey, diamond shaped monsters, thirty to fifty yards apart, stretching into the mist on either flank, rolling unevenly forwards, their tracks churning round, their exhausts throwing out blue grey smoke. I see, behind each tank, a trudging group of infantry, casually smoking, looking up at us . . . The ground slopes upwards, trapping us under the clouds, so that our wheels almost touch the grass. I have to rise to clear the tank ahead, skim over it, dip down in front. It seems to be standing still. Then we've passed them, we're ahead of the advance and approaching the Boche. Smoke shells burst ahead, a flash of red flame and masses of belching cloud, which we speed through—nauseous smelling stuff that stings the eyes. In patches, where smoke merges with smoke and cloud, we fly blind.[30]

John Bell and Robert McKenzie flew into this maelstrom to bomb German artillery positions around Cambrai. They crossed the two enemy trench systems and scattered gun crews with a hail of bombs and machine gun fire. The reply from the ground was equally intense, though, and Bell took a bullet in the chest. He managed to fly back across the British line before crashing, but later died from his wounds. In John Bell, No. 2 Squadron had lost its most experienced and able flight commander. But, as they would soon learn, that's how ground strafing worked. As Lee—himself a veteran—realised, when pilots exposed themselves 'to the concentrated fire of dozens of machine guns and hundreds of rifles', skill and experience counted for nothing: 'Trench strafing is all chance, no matter how skilled you are.'[31]

The other two flights left Baizieux at 8.00 a.m. B Flight's leader, Gordon Wilson, paired up with Harry Taylor, who after some black coffee had recovered from his night in Amiens. 'The fog hung about 30 feet off the ground,' recalled Wilson. 'Below that it was clear and above as dark as night.' Wilson and Taylor crossed the Hindenburg Line and passed over some advancing British infantry. Ahead, they saw enemy troops. 'Close together we dived down and opened our machine guns on the Germans,' wrote Wilson, 'before pulling up to the level of the fog again and letting a bomb drop as we rose.'

Wilson had just finished a strafing run when he spotted two red Verey lights streaking up through the mist. Descending, he spotted Taylor's machine 'down on the ground, wrecked and among the enemy'. Wilson scattered the Germans with a few bursts from his machine guns, giving Taylor time to take cover behind a small mound:

> He pulled out his automatic and fired at the Huns who rushed towards him as I pulled up ready for another dive. Then as I dived he dashed back a few yards, dropped to the ground, and fired again. He repeated this until he had got back, maybe, 60 yards from his machine, and nearer to our own men, and then I saw him surrounded by a small band of British soldiers.

Wilson flew circuits and watched as Taylor picked up a rifle and joined the British infantrymen in a fight against the Germans, who 'were gradually creeping up and spreading out fan shape to surround them'. Wilson dived to scatter them, but a bullet shattered his windshield, blinding him with glass dust. He climbed away and it was several minutes before he could see again. When he returned, the area was overrun with Germans. Wilson assumed Taylor had been captured and flew back to the advanced landing ground. 'We gave up on him for lost,' he noted.

But Harry Taylor wasn't 'lost'. He took charge of the British troops and led them in a fighting withdrawal back to their own lines. At one point, he found a wounded teenage Tommy, crying for his mother. Despite his bantam stature, Taylor slung the boy over his shoulder and carried him to safety.

From the British line, Taylor trekked back towards the advanced aerodrome. He came across Bell's machine in a field but couldn't get it started, so he kept trudging, making it back in time for dinner. Wilson fondly recalled his partner 'grinning, merry and boyish, clinking his glass at the mess table, forgetful of the day's adventure and seeking only the fun in life which he always found'.[32]

While Taylor's adventure unfolded, Les Holden led A Flight to bomb communication trenches full of German reinforcements streaming forward to the battle. He landed a bomb in a crowded trench and his partner, Robert Clark, machine-gunned the survivors as they clambered out and ran for shell holes. Les Ward was 'shot down out of control' during the strafing runs. He crashed, but survived with a broken leg to be taken prisoner.[33]

The weather deteriorated and all flying ceased at lunchtime. Losses for the first day, during just five hours of flying time, were seven aircraft destroyed, two pilots wounded (one mortally) and another captured. It was a similar story throughout the RFC, with all the ground attack squadrons averaging 30 per cent casualties. At this rate, they wouldn't survive the week. In purely military terms, though, the yield was high. Byng's Third Army had advanced 8 kilometres punching through the enemy's outpost system and two trench lines. On both flanks, things had gone almost perfectly to plan. The tanks had battered a path for the infantry to follow and dig in on their objectives. Closer to the centre, however, there were some difficulties. British tanks couldn't get across the St Quentin Canal (a bridge collapsed under the weight of one) and German field gunners knocked out some 40 British tanks and held onto the tactically important Flesquiéres Ridge. This subsequently prevented Third Army from securing its most important objective for the day: the dominating heights of Bourlon Ridge, to Cambrai's southwest.

The battle's second day dawned with even worse weather than the first. The decision about whether or not to fly was ultimately Major Watt's. It was a responsibility that weighed heavily on him, as he related in a private conversation with the official war correspondent, Charles Bean:

> He often had to send four of his youngsters out on days when we knew that flying was perilous. He had to make the order for these friends to go. It was not as if they were a battalion or even a company say of 120 men. They

were four boys who sat at the same table every day for six months and had become exceedingly well loved friends. 'You can just imagine the feelings with which I used to sit there during two hours waiting for them to come back,' he said.[34]

In the end, Watt cancelled flying for 21 November and the fog stranded most of the airmen at the forward landing ground. The offensive continued without air support, although with German reinforcements arriving British progress slowed. They took Flesquiéres before dawn, then Cantaing and Fontaine during the day but were again frustrated in their efforts to capture Bourlon Ridge. In the evening, Haig authorised the offensive to continue so Third Army could seize the ridge and secure its commanding views of enemy-occupied country to the east.

Third Army spent 22 November preparing for an all-out assault on Bourlon Ridge. The main obstacle was Bourlon Wood, which dominated the high ground, a tangle of broken timber and barbed wire hemmed with machine gun nests. Throughout the day, the ground-attack squadrons pounded them to make way for the infantry.

Fred Huxley, a 25-year-old veteran of the trenches on Gallipoli and the Somme, was among five pilots who left the advanced landing ground at 10.00 a.m., bound for Bourlon with a rack of bombs. He dropped them on a column of enemy reinforcements marching up towards the wood. Returning to strafe them, all he found were two holes and 'two heaps of dead'. As Huxley flew away, he spotted a German two-seater chugging along through the mist just below him. 'It was a gift,' he realised, so dived on to its tail and gave it a burst from 15 metres out. It plunged into the ground.[35] Just an hour later, Roy Phillipps, also 25 and an ex-digger, forced another one down into a family's garden in Cambrai. Before lunch, Dick Howard had got one too.

Throughout the morning, the pilots of damaged machines tried to get from the advanced landing ground back to Baizieux for repairs. The mechanics fired up Verey lights through the fog all morning. 'At about 11.00 a.m.,' wrote Knuckey:

we heard away in the distance the deep drone of a DH5 engine and away went the lights into the air again, the machine was right on us and only one hundred feet in the air but we could not see him until he shot over our heads and into the fog again, but he saw our signals and a few minutes afterwards returned and landed safely.

Exhausted pilots trickled back in their shot-up 'buses' throughout the afternoon. 'To see some of them,' thought Knuckey, 'one would wonder how on earth they got back at all.' The pilots brought snippets of news, including word that pilot David Clark had been shot down over Bourlon Wood. The news particularly affected his brother, Robert—also a pilot in the squadron. 'The two brothers are never apart... and one cannot help feeling sorry as he sees the other brother walking round on his own,' noted Knuckey.[36]

The British IV Corps commenced its assault on the Bourlon heights the following morning. The pilots supported the infantry directly and had opportunities throughout the day to influence the battle on the ground. At 10.30 a.m., for example, Huxley found the attack held up in the eastern corner of Bourlon Wood by a pair of German field guns. He dropped his four Coopers bombs among them and then had the satisfaction of watching the tanks resume the advance. Crossing over to the right flank of the British attack, Huxley then found British troops pinned down by a German strongpoint in front of Fontaine: 'Dived on this several times firing 500 rounds and each time I dived infantry advanced.'[37] According to one German defender, they 'flew so low that we had the feeling they could reach out of their machines, grab us by the collar and whisk us away'.[38]

Clearer weather made the aircraft equally visible to those shooting back at them from the ground, and the squadron lost another two men that day. Albert Griggs, an American-born pilot, was killed at around 4.00 p.m. by ground fire. The squadron didn't know what had happened to him; nor did his family who, through the Red Cross, searched in vain until mid-1919 without closure. The answer appeared in *The London Times* In Memoriam column, in a notice put there by the grateful troops Griggs died assisting:

> To the unknown airmen shot down on 23rd November 1917 whilst attacking a German strong point south west of Bourlon Wood, in the effort to help out a company of the Royal Irish Rifles, when other help had failed.[39]

Another pilot, Sydney Ayers, was also hit by ground fire while doing similar work. He landed in no man's land and made a run for British lines, but was felled by a bullet in the back and died soon afterwards. Acutely aware of the perils of his work, Ayers had premonitions of his death. When his fellow officers went to pack up his kit to send it home, they found everything put in order, including a new will and final letters to his family.[40]

It wasn't just from below that the pilots faced danger on 23 November, though. That afternoon, Richthofen arrived in the Cambrai sector with JG I and took command of German air operations over the battle. Over Bourlon Wood that afternoon, he claimed his 62nd victim, a British DH5. The Australians managed to avoid tangling with the Baron but did run into German scouts from Jasta 5. At midday, Holden had a narrow escape from a flight of Albatroses over the ridge. He made it back to the aerodrome with bullets in almost every part of his machine.

By the end of 23 November, the British had secured Bourlon Wood at the cost of about 4000 casualties. The slugging match on the heights wore on over the following days. British troops captured Bourlon village on 24 November and Fontaine on 27 November, but then lost both to German counter-attacks. The RFC pilot Arthur Lee described it as 'tricky in a battle like this, where ground is won and lost and won again every day'. Front lines changed 'from hour to hour', and the only way to identify troops was to fly low over them, in order to look before firing. 'You may not know you're over Boche troops until they open fire on you,' he explained.[41]

During this struggle for the high ground, the weather returned to rain and mist, grounding No. 2 Squadron for two days. On 26 November, a couple of contact and ground attack sorties reported that things had reached a stalemate on the ridge. Pilots dropped a few bombs on enemy positions and Harry Taylor managed to force down a DFW two-seater.

There was no flying on 27 November, and the following two days were fairly quiet, with the squadron doing some line patrols. During a low-altitude patrol on the morning of 29 November, an incredibly game enemy DFW crew attacked Dick Howard. He was only flying at 400 feet when the enemy pilot dived on him, firing with his front gun. Howard whipped around and got on to the DFW's tail, but the pilot climbed steeply, stalled and shot up Howard's underside as he passed above. Howard banked and came at the DFW from side on. 'After 30 rounds I saw the observer hanging over the side,' he reported. Howard then latched on to its tail and fired until the aircraft went into a steep dive and landed north of Cambrai.[42]

That afternoon, British reconnaissance crews reported the enemy's back areas a hive of activity. A German counter-attack, it appeared, was imminent.

'Diving into a black bottomless pit': German counter-attack at Cambrai, 30 November–7 December 1917

At 7.30 a.m. on 30 November 1917, a German bombardment crashed down on the newly won British line between Masnières and Vendhuille. It was brief but incredibly intense, and promptly crippled communications between forward troops and their commanders. Before anyone seemed to know what was happening, German assault units were surrounding British strong points and pouring through the gaps. Within 30 minutes, they had overrun the Banteaux Ravine, which the British had captured on 20 November. By 9.00 a.m., German troops were in Gouzeaucourt, 3 kilometres behind the original British front line.

This hurricane strike against the weakly held eastern flank of the British salient was accompanied by a simultaneous one from the north, against the high ground between Bourlon and Moeuvres. Having predicted that the enemy would strike here, General Byng's men were much better supported, and succeeded in holding their ground against five successive waves of German infantry.

Aircraft from both sides filled the sky above the counter-offensive. Like the RFC, the German Air Service had perceived the value of supporting troops directly with aircraft during the 1917 battles and sent its infantry into action accompanied by low-flying Schlachtstaffeln (battle flights). They bombed and machine-gunned British troops while the Jastas covered them from above. The RFC met them in kind, and there were at least a hundred aircraft fighting over the battlefield throughout the day.

No. 2 Squadron had its busiest day so far, making low-level attacks against both axes of the German advance. The fifteen available pilots, including several rookies who had replaced men lost earlier in the offensive, flew 33 sorties during the day. Most did one or two, but five pilots crossed the line three times. The advanced landing ground at Bapaume became congested as pilots stopped by to replenish fuel and ammunition in between sorties. According to Lee, 'there was an oppressive feeling' as pilots waited silently for their 'buses' to be rearmed and refuelled. 'Almost everybody had been winged in the previous jobs, and I felt that people were inwardly asking, how long can my luck last out?'[43]

It was a tough first day on the job for Harry Cornell. A 25-year-old electrician from Tasmania, he had only been with the squadron a week and was scheduled to do his first patrol on the morning the German counter-attack began. He was just starting breakfast when the aerodrome's klaxon sounded. A and C Flights assembled on the tarmac and their flight commanders explained they had to be airborne in 30 minutes. C Flight would be strafing German infantry while Cornell's flight covered them from above.

The two flights headed for Bourlon Wood. Cornell found it 'all very confusing'. He could pick out the tangled remains of the forest and Cambrai's ruins in the mist but was 'uncertain all the time' who occupied which sections of the battlefield. The only indication that he was over Germans, he quickly discovered, was when Archie burst around them. 'A tremendous amount of firing was going on, both machine guns and shelling.' In any case, Cornell had little time to look at the ground as keeping formation with his flight leader, who was 'dodging about everywhere', consumed his attention.

Suddenly, a German two-seater shot past Cornell. Gripped with excitement, he broke formation to pursue it, but almost immediately lost it in the mist. Turning to rejoin the others, he found himself alone in the soupy sky for a few moments before coming across another separated member of the patrol, Robert Clark. 'I followed him round for a few minutes when my engine suddenly spluttered and stopped.' Cornell turned and glided west, being 'fired on heavily' all the way down. 'I was coming down cross wind and in my anxiety to reach our lines, left it too late to turn up wind.' The DH5 hit the ground heavily, sheared of its undercarriage and flipped over. Cornell was 'pinned tightly' under the aircraft with blood 'flowing freely' from his face. 'After some difficulty, I unfastened the belt, managed to worm my way backwards and out of the machine between the struts.' Dumbstruck, he stood in the deserted landscape trying to wipe mud from his brand new flying suit. Shells exploding nearby snapped him back to his senses and sent him running for a nearby village:

> Though it appeared to be under heavy shell fire I thought it might be safer than the open. The village was quite deserted but I found a comfortable basement in one of the largest houses and settled down to recover myself. The shelling of the village appeared to increase in violence and a couple struck the place I was in, though without harming me.

Cornell sheltered for three hours before building up the courage to make a run for it. He grabbed a few German souvenirs—a chess set and a 'Hun bible'—and ran through the curtain of shellfire ringing the town. Unsure of where he was, he struck south and trudged through a kilometre of deserted shell-torn landscape before spotting British helmets bobbing about above a trench. After he had convinced their officer he wasn't a German, they made him 'very welcome'. He spent the afternoon sheltering in a dugout from a heavy bombardment and when night fell was escorted out of the trenches. He walked almost 5 kilometres to Ribbecourt, where he began an all-night journey, hitching rides all the way back to the aerodrome. A doctor diagnosed Cornell with shock and Major Watt organised five days' leave in Paris for him.[44]

The German offensive continued in foul weather on 1 December. At first light, eight Australian pilots went out in pairs to bomb enemy troops around Villers-Guislain. Over the target, Huxley found himself behind yet another 'gift':

> On emerging from the mist I saw an enemy aircraft (two-seater) on my right about 100 feet below and 100 yards away. I did a diving turn onto him and his observer opened fire. I passed over him and did an Immelmann turn to the left, and opened fire at 50 yards before the observer had time to swing his gun to the right. Almost at once the observer dropped and his gun remained still pointing to his left. I then swung my machine to the right and after about 100 rounds the enemy aircraft nose dived, striking the ground and turning on its back.[45]

Later in the morning, Huxley was over this part of the battlefield again. He found a crowd of enemy soldiers gathered around the wreck and dropped a bomb right among them.

Twenty-one-year-old Henry Forrest, who arrived in France on 23 November to replace John Bell as A Flight's commander, led its three surviving members on a low sortie to the same area at noon and came across the unusual sight of a German bomber in the daylight. He and his three pilots attacked it and some escorting scouts. During the fight, McKenzie got an Albatros but 22-year-old Lawrence Benjamin, another raw replacement, was badly shot up, and had to make an emergency landing at the advanced aerodrome. He was one of four Australians forced down by enemy fire on 1 December.

Strong German counter-attacks continued to drive the British southern flank back over the next couple of days. Although the Bourlon front held, the enemy drive across the base of the salient from the east made it increasingly untenable. On 4 December, Haig ordered Byng to withdraw to a good 'winter line'. Byng settled on a more modest salient that stretched out to Marcoing at the tip of Flesquirés Ridge and ordered a withdrawal from the hard-won Bourlon heights. No. 2 Squadron covered the troops as they fell back on 5 and 6 December by bombing German troops and doing higher altitude patrols to keep enemy aircraft away. Huxley maintained his hot streak by shooting down another two-seater late on 6 December. It brought his personal tally up to three, and took the squadron's to eight.

The Battle of Cambrai was over on 7 December. The British had withdrawn to a line about halfway back to their original 20 November starting positions. They held a 4 kilometre deep salient, which included part of the Hindenburg front and support lines, although the Germans had captured almost as much British territory in the other direction, making the Battle of Cambrai something of a tactical draw.

The battle is today almost unknown to the Australian public, as none of the AIF's infantry divisions took part. But it was a defining event for the AFC. Six No. 2 Squadron pilots received the Military Cross and two mechanics got Military Medals for recovering crashed aircraft from the battlefield, under fire. The squadron also received the highest praise from British and Australian commands and was lauded by the press in both countries.

But its sixteen days over Cambrai had worn the squadron threadbare. Nearly half the squadron's establishment of flying officers had been shot down (four of them killed, two wounded and another captured) and a staggering 23 aircraft were destroyed or severely damaged. The constant perils of low flying over the battlefield left the survivors with frayed nerves, including three of the Military Cross recipients. Gordon Wilson, who had led B Flight so resolutely throughout the battle, was sent back to England three weeks after it finished with a 'nervous debility'. Huxley, clearly one of the unit's rising stars, took over his job but only lasted six weeks before he too went to England with 'aero-neurosis'.[46] Even the tenacious Harry Taylor couldn't handle the strain. He left the squadron in January 1918 after fainting in the air and crashing. Significantly, these three men were all veterans of the trenches. A medical inquiry in early 1918 would draw 'attention to the somewhat high proportion of breakdowns among pilots and observers of the AFC' and highlight as the cause the fact that many had 'already served many months in combat units, and have experienced the strain incidental to such arduous campaigns as Gallipoli, Egypt and the Somme'.[47]

The British pilot Arthur Lee (incidentally, also a soldier before joining the RFC) recorded the descent into nervous breakdown in his diary and letters during the battle. First he got 'the shakes', then lost his appetite and began suffering stomach cramps. For much of the battle, he subsisted on brandy and milk. By the end of the German counter-attack, he was having trouble sleeping. A couple of days later, he noted that one of his roommates had to wake him when he started screaming in the middle of the night. 'I was shaking and sweating with it,' he wrote. 'I was diving, diving into a black bottomless pit with hundreds of machine guns blasting up endlessly at me.'[48] A few weeks later, Lee too went home on the verge of nervous collapse, another casualty of the 'low sortie'.

After his ordeal in no man's land, Paris did Harry Cornell the world of good. In a characteristic demonstration of his care and devotion to his men, Major Watt arranged for his niece, who lived there, to show Cornell around and recommended an excellent hotel in which he could stay. The hot baths, meals, shows and shopping soothed his frayed nerves and after five days Cornell returned to the squadron refreshed and eager to fly again. In his diary he noted—surprised, it seems—that there had been no 'amendments' in the squadron—that is, casualties—since he left. Things had changed on the 'Cambrai front', though: 'The place where I landed near Cantaing is now two or three miles behind Hun lines.'[49]

At 2.20 p.m. the following day, Harry Cornell took off on what the squadron record book described as an 'air test'. The taciturn, bureaucratic note that follows is almost all that exists in the squadron's official records of this pilot, who only ever flew one operational sortie:

> Lt Cornell in 9324 left the aerodrome at 2.20 pm and crashed at 2.25 pm at Baizieux. Pilot killed. Cause flat turn and stall and nose dive at 500 ft. Machine struck off.[50]

Cornell's logbook, training card and the short diary that he used to describe the eighteen days he had at the front are practically all the evidence we have that this ordinary Tasmanian pilot ever existed. When they found their way back into the hands of his wife, Jessie, in Queenstown, they revealed a bitterly—indeed, tragically—ironic and unfair story. Her husband, who had left home just over a year before, survived three accidents while learning to fly in England, a crash in no man's land and an enemy barrage to be killed on an 'air test', four days after the Battle of Cambrai ended.

10
'ABSOLUTE HELL LET LOOSE'
The German spring offensives, 1918

A line up of No. 4 Squadron Sopwith Camels at Bruay aerodrome on 26 March 1918. The German offensive is in full swing and the aircraft are being refuelled and rearmed for yet another sortie. *AWM E01878*

> It was absolute hell let loose; fires burning everywhere, oceans of smoke, roads choked with transports and troops.
>
> —Lieutenant Jack Weingarth, No. 4 Squadron, Australian Flying Corps

'Today has been what we call a snifler': No. 3 Squadron at Messines Ridge, Winter 1917–18

Its apprenticeship in the Arras sector complete, No. 3 Squadron moved north to Bailleul near the France–Belgian border in mid-November 1917. There the squadron was attached to the headquarters of the newly formed Australian Corps, which was holding the line running south of Ypres from Messines Ridge down to Armentières. Although Australian troops had been on the Western Front since early 1916, they had not previously had Australian airmen to work with. The aerodrome at Bailleul was soon crawling with curious diggers, wanting to see the flying men and their machines up close. 'Naturally,' considered Stan Garrett, 'the first Australian squadron is a novelty to most of the Australian troops.'[1]

The aerodrome at Bailleul was a busy and well-established affair on the edge of town. No. 3 Squadron shared it with two other squadrons, but unlike at Baizieux, accommodation was abundant and comfortable. Officers had half a Nissen hut each, and being so close to town meant plenty of food, drink and sundries were available. Looking at a survey map, fitter Frank Rawlinson discovered they were stationed at the base of the infamous Ypres salient—a bulge in the British front line around the medieval town of Ypres. 'Every village, road and farm,' he noted, 'was named, mostly after famous units or happenings, and contour lines of the country were accurately plotted in.' The famous happenings to which Rawlinson referred were from the three major campaigns the British had fought in the salient since 1914. The most recent, 'Third Ypres' was just winding down as No. 3 Squadron arrived.[2] It was still an active sector, though, its proximity to the Belgian coast giving it strategic importance to both sides. 'All day and every night, the guns boomed and rumbled away, and night time was a flashing flicker of light that never stopped right around the line. Tables and things vibrated with the rumbling,' wrote Rawlinson.[3]

Winter weather prevented No. 3 Squadron from doing much work for the Australian Corps in November. However, the pilots and observers, conscious that their work directly assisted the diggers in the trenches, got airborne as much as possible—even in dangerous conditions. On 2 December, in response to an urgent request for artillery observation support, B Flight's commander, Henry Storrer, took it upon himself to go up despite gale-force winds. William Scott, an artilleryman who had fought at Gallipoli, answered Storrer's call for a volunteer observer. As their RE8 left the ground, it was caught by a gust of wind and, in one witness's words, was left 'literally standing still in the air'. The aircraft stalled and crashed into a brick wall on the edge of the aerodrome, killing them both.[4] The other pilots buried Storrer and Scott quietly in the cemetery next to the aerodrome that afternoon. Garrett had the sad task of packing up their kit to send home. 'Naturally a gloom is upon the other officers,' he wrote, 'for undoubtedly Captain Storrer was one of the best liked fellows I ever met. His observer was also a great favourite. It will be an awful blow to his mother, for she had already lost a son on the Peninsula.'[5]

While the weather was bad, airmen visited local artillery batteries to meet the gunners. Garrett started his 'tour' at the battery's billet, where he immediately discovered the close working relationship between pilots and artillerymen: 'We formed a happy party and before dinner was over we were chatting away as though we were old friends.' After spending the night in a 'very dingy dugout', he took a respirator and steel hat and accompanied an artillery captain through 3 kilometres of trenches to the gun positions. The artillery officers enthusiastically showed Garrett around the battery's twelve guns and explained how each had its own particular firing characteristics, which were further determined by wind, temperature and barometric pressure.

Garrett's hosts then took him up to a forward observation post where he could 'see well into Hunland'. He peered through a slit and watched as the outpost crew transmitted shot corrections back to the gunners, who were firing at a church held by enemy troops. They eventually scored a direct hit, but Garrett quickly discovered that, despite the scientific calculations, gunnery was still an imprecise art. 'Peculiarly, the same gun with the same range etc. was quite a 100 yds away next shot.' Garrett remained with the battery for four days and 'gained quite a lot of useful information'. The excursion also developed a 'mutual confidence' between the airmen and gunners, which, Garrett thought, 'for aerial work is half the battle'.[6]

Most days in December had just fleeting moments of suitable flying weather, and into these the squadron squeezed as much work as it could. On 6 December, for example, in 'a brief spell of good visibility at midday', the crews accumulated 24 flying hours, knocking out three enemy batteries and dropping two dozen bombs into German trenches.[7] On this occasion, No. 3 Squadron claimed its first aerial victory when William Anderson and John Bell—the pair who participated in some sharp dogfights in October—shot down a German two-seater. They were ranging artillery fire when they spotted it below them. Anderson dived and manoeuvred to allow Bell to fire almost a full 97-round drum into it. The German machine crashed in the enemy trenches.

During another 'fine spell' on the afternoon of 17 December, the squadron sent out nine crews on artillery observation patrols. James Sandy, one of the unit's more experienced pilots, was taking new observer, Henry Hughes, on his first artillery shoot. Rawlinson recalled how anxious Hughes looked as he fixed his Lewis gun to its mounting before the patrol. He and Hughes had been on leave together in Scotland a few months before when, at a dinner party, 'a very fey lady' read their palms and predicted that one of them would soon be killed.

Sandy and Hughes took off and had just called up their battery when six Albatroses attacked. Back at the aerodrome, Rawlinson and some of the other mechanics watched 'the scrap' in the distance.[8] Sandy turned and engaged the enemy scouts. He hit one and it landed with a pierced petrol tank inside Australian lines. Ern Jones and Keith Hodgson were patrolling nearby and came to Sandy and Hughes' assistance. For ten minutes, the two RE8s fought the remaining five Albatroses, Hodgson firing all of his ten drums of ammunition at them. At this point, a third RE8 appeared and the Germans broke off and flew away. Jones reported that Sandy and Hughes were 'apparently all right and passed our machine flying north'. He flew home to replenish his ammunition.[9]

By sunset, though, Sandy and Hughes hadn't returned. The squadron fired Verey lights in the gathering darkness but they didn't show up. The German scout they had shot down was recovered as a trophy for the squadron, but anxiety tempered the mood in the mess that evening. Most assumed they had crash-landed and were prisoners. The suspense carried on until the following evening, when a phone call from St Pol, 80 kilometres away, reported that Sandy and Hughes' machine was sitting in a field, both men dead in their seats. A post-mortem indicated that a single armour piercing

FIRE IN THE SKY

bullet had passed through both men, killing them instantly. The RE8 had then flown by itself for two hours, gradually being pushed northwest by the wind until its petrol ran out. Charles Bean, who investigated the aircraft, concluded that 'it steeply bounced and flew 60 yards [55 metres]. When the tip of the propeller hit the ground, the propeller broke, and the machine swung round to a standstill'.[10]

Artworks and news stories made the Sandy and Hughes incident famous in Australia during the war. It was further guaranteed posterity by the Albatros they had shot down, which the AIF claimed and shipped to Australia. Today it is on display in the Australian War Memorial's *Over the Front* exhibition, one of only two of its kind left in the world (see Plate 17).

The weather continued to deteriorate over Christmas. It snowed heavily and a wind, which according to Garrett 'seems to blow right through you', cancelled flying for days at a time. 'Today has been what we call a snifler,' he wrote on 29 December, 'otherwise very good for the flying corps. A beautiful day but very heavy ground mist making the visibility very bad and so washing out flying.' To fend off the chill, the airmen even took to sleeping in their flying suits. Some built brick stoves in their huts, but inevitably smoked themselves out in the process. Garrett described how his roommate, Alf Barrow, 'clears out until bed time then he comes back and puts on his goggles and gets into bed going crook all the time'.[11]

The winter weather had operational benefits, though. On 1 January, six RE8s photographed the entire corps front and discovered a number of hidden enemy batteries on account of the tracks and blast marks they left on the snow-covered landscape. Anderson also recalled how snow assisted artillery observation, as 'short' shells left clearly discernible markers around the target, making it easier to calculate corrections.[12]

Aside from photography and routine artillery shoots, the most common jobs for the squadron in January and February were 'trench' and 'flash' reconnaissances. These usually involved a lone RE8 patrolling back and forth along the enemy's lines for three hours or so. On a 'trench' reconnaissance, the pilot would report on the enemy's positions, carefully noting the state of wire, changes in the trench lines, numbers of visible enemy troops and so on. They yielded valuable and highly detailed intelligence. A trench reconnaissance on 21 February, for example, indicated a particular enemy pillbox in front of the Australian positions was likely to be filled with troops during the day on account of the numerous walking tracks leading to it that had not been there on the previous evening's patrol. On flash reconnaissances, crews watched the area behind the enemy's front line for the flash of enemy guns or concentrations of troops and transport. If a pilot saw an opportune target, he would notify all friendly batteries in the area via wireless. Known as a 'zone call', this made the humble RE8 one of the RFC's most potent weapons, allowing its pilot to rain down destruction and potentially kill dozens of enemy troops at the tap of a buzzer.

The work was sporadic and completely at the mercy of the weather, which remained indifferent until well into March. Observer Owen Lewis joined No. 3 Squadron in February after recovering from the wounds he had received during on-the-job training the previous summer. He described waiting around for hours each morning for the clouds to clear: 'It's a poor game this standing by—I would much prefer to get to the job and get it finished.' When he did get airborne the first few times, Lewis found the responsibility of watching for enemy machines while the pilot did the reconnaissance or photography demanding, especially in the grey winter haze. Despite being 'bang on the lookout the whole time', he was only able to distinguish other machines when they were 'quite close'. He described it in his diary as 'a really nerve [w]racking job' and predicted it would 'tell' on him before long: 'I hope to be able to do a few months before my nerves really go.'[13]

Within a few weeks, Lewis was settling in, though. Key to this was a passive resignation to things like changes in the weather, flight rosters and casualties in the unit. Bad weather, as he came to accept, even had its advantages. 'This morning I was pleased to hear that the weather was fairly dud—I am afraid that I am always pleased when that is so.'[14]

'About the most ignorant bunch of pilots that you could find in France': No. 4 Squadron's induction to war fighting

When the pilots of No. 4 Squadron landed in France a few days before Christmas 1917, they bore almost no resemblance to their fellow scout pilots in No. 2 Squadron. Whereas No. 2 Squadron had been formed overseas from infantry and light horse volunteers, most of No. 4 Squadron's men were fresh from civilian life in Australia. Aside from their commanding officer, Major Wilfred McCloughry, who had flown with No. 2 Squadron at Cambrai to get some experience, and a couple of flight commanders on loan from British units, No. 4 Squadron's pilots were, acknowledged one, 'about 100 per cent novices'. In fact, he admitted, they were 'about the most ignorant bunch of pilots, as far as knowledge of air fighting went, that you could find in France'.[15]

The man who wrote this was Arthur 'Harry' Cobby; 23 years old, an ex-clerk from the Commonwealth Bank in Melbourne and at war because of pressure from 'patriotic but blundering flagwaggers'. Although he was destined to become the AFC's top-scoring fighter pilot, in December 1917 he was full of feelings of 'smallness and trepidation' and felt quite sure his squadron contained 'very few who could in cold blood be regarded as a hero'.[16]

For the first fortnight at the front, No. 4 Squadron settled in with familiarisation and practice flights. It was equipped with Sopwith Camels, an idiosyncratic aircraft that, in the apt words of British historian Peter Hart, 'made a virtue out of its main defect'.[17] Nearly all of the machine's weight was concentrated in its nose and this, combined with its high-torque rotary engine and small wingspan, made its controls highly sensitive. Flown with anything more than a feather touch, the Camel was prone to violent spins, a trait that killed scores of novice pilots during the war. In the hands of a veteran, though, the Camel was a whippy, manoeuvrable aircraft that could turn tighter than anything the Germans put in the sky. The Camel's Achilles heel became apparent above 12000 feet, though. Any higher, explained Jack Wright, and the Camel was 'practically useless'. The controls 'all became sloppy and we would not have been able to do much in a fight'.[18]

The Camel's sensitivity and penchant for killing inexperienced pilots was illustrated while the squadron practised formation flying around its aerodrome at Bruay. On 6 January, C Flight was doing formation exercises when two Camels collided and then fell on to another. All three men died. Before the month was out, another pilot from this same, unlucky flight was killed when his Camel hit the ground during a gunnery exercise.

War flying began on 9 January 1918 with a close offensive patrol and an escort to a neighbouring squadron's photographic machine. Despite being 'a rather prosaic task', in Cobby's words, the sortie was etched in his mind and left his whole flight feeling 'bucked' at having ventured into enemy skies.

Not surprisingly, the inexperienced Australian pilots were somewhat anxious about meeting the enemy. Their first experience of him came through 'Archie' as they crossed the lines on offensive patrols, or 'o-pips', each day. On his first time over the line, Jack Wright suddenly found that 'German AA shells were all around us, above and below and the "crump" of the burst was a sound that made one jump'.[19] It actually claimed very few victims in the air but was, according to Cobby, 'the bug bear of new pilots'. It 'had a kind of hoodoo on beginners' and was responsible for 'the cracking up of quite a large number of the chaps who were invalided back to England'.[20]

Archie wasn't the only dangerous thing being slung about in the sky, though. By early 1918, the front was lined with literally thousands of artillery pieces, which fired day and night, pitching shells to heights of several thousand feet. Reports from pilots of seeing them as they slowed down at the top of their trajectory and being buffeted as they flew past are quite common. Instances of aircraft being hit by shells in mid-flight weren't unheard of either. In this respect, 17 February 1918 was a truly unfortunate day for the AFC on the Western Front. Charles Martin, a 23-year-old builder from Melbourne, was flying above Lille when an artillery shell broke up his Camel in mid-air. Remarkably, just two hours previously a shell also hit one of No. 3 Squadron's RE8s over Messines Ridge, killing its crew as well.

Bad weather throughout January and February limited No. 4 Squadron's opportunities for meeting enemy formations. It was 20 January before the squadron claimed its first victory. Arthur O'Hara Wood, one of the experienced British flight commanders on loan to the squadron, shot down an enemy two-seater near La Bassée. The Australian pilots were anxious to know how he had done it, but were disappointed by O'Hara Wood's demure response that all he had done was fire a couple of bursts and watch it spin to the ground.[21]

On 3 February, after a quiet fortnight above the line, O'Hara Wood invited Cobby and Elliot 'Tab' Pflaum to accompany him across the line to see whether they could entice some German machines to fight. Cobby admitted to feeling 'a bit uneasy' about this, 'knowing what an aggressive kind of cove old O'Hara was', but decided he couldn't do anything but 'look the part, even if not consumed by eagerness'.

The trio crossed the line at 12 000 feet and kept climbing east. Cobby and Pflaum found it difficult to keep up with the British veteran and stalled several times. They had just made it to 17 000 feet when O'Hara Wood rolled his Camel over into a steep dive. With 'no idea what the business was about', Cobby and Pflaum followed close behind. As they plummeted, Cobby suddenly saw the enemy machine O'Hara Wood was leading them down on. He saw another one too, 'scooting east for all it was worth', and sheared off towards it.

It was 2000 feet below, but Cobby was on top of it in a matter of seconds. 'Suddenly, there appeared to be too many things to do at once,' he wrote. He had to ease back the throttle, work the machine gun cocking handle and bring the Aldis sight to bear on the enemy machine. 'I pressed the triggers when only about twenty feet away and just managed to get one burst in before pulling out of the dive and skimming across with my wheels a few inches above the wings of the enemy.'

The German observer, who was snapping off shots at Cobby as he dived, dropped in his cockpit. Seeing the way clear, Cobby half rolled and came down right on his opponent's tail. He fired four bursts and broke away, but was disappointed as it 'just tootled off on its way home'.

Back on the ground, O'Hara Wood was furious. He thought the two younger pilots had left him alone in the fight. They appealed to him, saying they had both attacked separate two-seaters. Pflaum was, in fact, certain he had shot his down. The British flight commander was unconvinced, though, telling them they needed to go back to England for more training—'You are no dammed use out here.' Cobby and Pflaum went away indignant, but were vindicated that evening when news arrived that all three enemy machines had crashed, including Cobby's, which made it all the way to Douai before igniting in the air.[22]

The victories had an electric effect on the squadron, and on Cobby and Pflaum in particular. They also illustrated the value of having a cranky old hand like O'Hara Wood around when '100 per cent novices' were starting out.

'Everyone is getting ready for a big "to do" in the spring': Offensive patrols, February–March 1918

Following the Battle of Cambrai No. 2 Squadron spent December and January refitting and retraining for its part in the air war of 1918. The first significant change came just days after the battle, when the squadron replaced its DH5s with a newer and vastly superior scout, the SE5a. With almost double the horsepower, an additional machine gun and better performance up high, the SE5a was a first-class dogfighter. Although it couldn't turn as sharply as the nimble little Camel, it lost no performance above 15 000 feet (although, without oxygen, its pilots usually did) and could dive at 400 kph without losing its wings. In this sense, the SE5a and Sopwith Camel complemented each other perfectly—the 'SE' as a high-altitude cruiser that could swoop down on its enemies, while the Camel flew circles around them at lower altitudes.

The other major change experienced by No. 2 Squadron during the winter was the loss of its commanding officer, Major Oswald Watt. Although not flying, he had maintained a punishing schedule since arriving at the front. He routinely worked in the squadron's office until well after midnight and was always awake to see the dawn patrol off. The pilots idolised him for his devotion, but at almost 40 years of age, and with three years of war experience weighing on him, he couldn't maintain the pace. When Charles Bean visited No. 2 Squadron in December, he thought Watt looked 'very worn' and noted in his diary how he fell asleep immediately after dinner in front of the mess room fire: 'It was not a cold night but he was shivering.'[23] Watt went to Britain in February to command an Australian Training Wing, which was then forming. His replacement was William Sheldon, who had commanded one of No. 1 Squadron's flights in the Middle East.

The final change for No. 2 Squadron over the winter was a shift north to Savy aerodrome, where No. 3 Squadron had started its active service career in 1917. This placed it close to No. 4 Squadron at Bruay. Both scout units were attached to First Army on the sector between Armentières and Arras.

As the two Australian scout squadrons settled into their new sector at the end of January 1918, the RFC's reconnaissance units began reporting 'widespread and abnormal railway movements' and numerous new aerodromes behind the German front.[24] British General Headquarters suspected the Germans were planning a major offensive for the coming spring and ordered the RFC to 'watch for symptoms of attack'.[25]

Despite the lingering winter conditions, the two Australian scout squadrons patrolled First Army's sector as vigorously as possible in February.

Their tactics matched their hardware, with No. 2 Squadron's SE5as patrolling above 15 000 feet while No. 4 Squadron's Camels worked at lower altitudes. George Jones, a 20-year-old motor mechanic from Melbourne who had experienced the worst of trench warfare at Gallipoli, did his first 'o-pips' with No. 4 Squadron in early February:

> This was the middle of winter, and at that height the cold was intense. We all wore knee length leather coats, fur lined leather flying helmets, goggles, fleecy lined boots, and silk gloves beneath our leather gauntlets, but even with all that we suffered, and found it very difficult to concentrate at times because of the cold.[26]

Above 15 000 feet, No. 2 Squadron's pilots had it even worse. Archie Rackett came down from one patrol with a frostbitten nose. 'When the blood started to circulate when I landed, it was very painful,' he explained.[27]

Both units encountered enemy aircraft in the first fortnight of February but found them frustratingly timid. Fairly typical was Roy Phillipps' patrol report of 3 February: '4 enemy aircraft seen. On approach they spun down and were lost sight of.'[28] Grounded for a week in the middle of the month, No. 2 Squadron's pilots spent their time debating the best tactics. They agreed to patrol in pairs, rather than full flights (six), to entice the German pilots. When the sun came out on 18 February, the results were immediate. Early in the morning, Fred Huxley and a rookie, Anthony Paxton, surprised four brightly painted Albatroses over Lille. Huxley picked out the leader and dived. He 'turned on his wingtip and fell out of control after I had fired about 50 rounds at 150 yards range'.[29] Later in the morning, another pair, Dick Howard and Les Holden, bounced some unsuspecting Albatroses from above:

> We dived down on them, each singling out one of the leading machines, at which we fired our guns. The one Holden fired at put its nose down and dived straight into the ground, the pilot apparently having been shot. The one I fired at spun down, but flattened out near the ground. We then turned on the other four, but they flew off and landed on their aerodrome, near Lille, before we could inflict more damage.[30]

Three days later, in clear, bright sunshine heralding spring, No. 4 Squadron got among the action too. Working at lower altitudes, though, its pilots were the ones much more likely to be surprised. Half a dozen Albatroses fell on George Jones' flight of four from out of the sun: 'Their leader dived onto ours, I dived onto him, another Albatros onto me, and so on all down the line.' The whole line of aircraft circled, trying to turn inside each other. The Camels, with their whippy performance, had a distinct advantage. Jones closed on the Albatros chasing his flight leader:

> I got so close to him that he filled the whole lens of my Aldis sight and I shot him. He slumped over his controls and went into a vertical dive with his engine full on. After falling from about a thousand feet his right hand lower wing broke off and floated down separately. That of course was the end of him—no parachutes in those days. But immediately afterwards one of the other Germans was firing at me from behind so I circled as quickly as I could and in as smaller radius as possible to avoid his fire and one of the other members of our formation attacked him and drove him off.[31]

It was indeed an exciting day for Jones, who was not yet 21—his first dogfight, his first kill and the gratitude of his flight commander! In 1980, an elderly Jones described it in detail to an interviewer: 'It stuck out very, very vividly in my mind.'[32]

By the last week in February, it was clear to the pilots that an enemy offensive was imminent. Their messes buzzed with gossip and speculation and they wrote about it in their letters and diaries. 'Everyone is getting ready for a big "to-do" in the coming Spring,' Howard told his family. 'Behind their lines the Germans have massed guns [and] several divisions of men from the Russian Front.'[33] On orders from the RFC's Headquarters, No. 4 Squadron's planes began taking bombs on their 'o-pips' to drop on German billets, to 'interfere' with the enemy's preparations. The Camel pilots discovered what their opposite numbers in No. 2 Squadron had learned at Cambrai the previous November: attacking ground targets, as Cobby noted, was always 'full of incident':

> The flight would be flying under the clouds at a few hundred feet, shooting up ground targets, and getting in return all the 'hate' the enemy could throw

up at us with machine guns, field guns and flaming onions... We nearly always came home with our machines shot about.[34]

No. 4 Squadron wrote off several Camels on these low sorties, and on 24 February it lost a pilot, Wentworth Randell. He had only been with the squadron for four weeks when he was hit by Archie and caught fire at 1000 feet. His Camel dived into the ground but he managed to jump clear just before the crash. Enemy troops took him to their billet, strip-searched him and then sent him to Lille where he was interrogated and locked up alone 'in a filthy room for two days'. For the next week, Randell shared a cell with Alec Couston, another No. 4 Squadron pilot shot down the week before. The discovery of hidden microphones in their cell made them careful of what they discussed. After a week, during which Randell claimed they revealed nothing, the two men were sent to a prison camp in Germany, where they would spend the rest of the war.[35]

On 7 March, the German Air Service began a concerted effort to photograph the British front, prior to launching its offensive. 'Two-seaters were continuously being met, escorted by protective fighters,' recalled Cobby.[36] They were still reluctant to fight, though, having orders to get the photographs and avoid tangling with the RFC.

Once again, No. 2 Squadron adapted its tactics to suit. Dick Howard, now a flight commander, studied the 'method of attack' used by British ace James McCudden, and came up with a way to surprise the enemy two-seaters.[37] He would patrol high above their aerodromes and attack from the east, out of the morning sun. 'His machines hardly expect us to come from his side and also, if one flies in the sun, the glare prevents him from seeing you,' he reasoned.

Howard took his flight up early on 8 March and crossed the lines at 15 000 feet. They flew 16 kilometres into enemy territory before spotting some enemy two-seaters taking off from their aerodrome. Howard led his flight down and attacked these unsuspecting victims right over their home turf, shooting down one and scattering the others. They returned to 15 000 feet to seek more unwary victims:

> We next surprised another Hun two-seater which was just approaching the lines, flying in a westerly direction. As we were further over the German

lines than it was, and as the sun was behind us, we could dive at it and take it by surprise. Lieutenant Paxton and I fired at it and it rolled over and spun down out-of-control to the ground. The observer had had time to fire a few shots at me, some of which went through my plane. Next, I came up behind an Albatros scout, which was leisurely flying along, thinking himself secure—being so far over Hunland. This machine was taken completely by surprise and after I fired a few rounds at it, it turned on its back and fell to the ground. I was so close to this machine that I almost bumped into it and I could recognise the figure of the pilot, who I think must have been killed.[38]

Using the same tactics, Howard claimed another two scouts the following day and a third the day after. A week later, he destroyed a German reconnaissance machine over Lille, making him No. 2 Squadron's top scorer, with seven victories.

These challenges to the German reconnaissance machines compelled the Jastas to be more aggressive. Again, it was the Camel pilots, working at lower altitudes and weighed down with bombs, who bore the brunt. On 15 March, five Pfalz scouts surprised a No. 4 Squadron flight of four, 9 kilometres across the line. George Jones had the most terrifying experience of his young life when he ran out of petrol in the middle of the fight. He put his nose down and turned for home, with a Pfalz close behind. Bullets zipped past, severing bracing wires around the cockpit. 'I nearly broke the rudder bar trying to make that aeroplane go further and faster,' Jones recalled. He crossed a trench line at 100 feet and crashed in a shell hole:

I was half stunned, but I managed to crawl out. We knew that we had to burn our aircraft if we landed n the wrong side of the lines, so I grasped my 'Verey' Pistol, and watched anxiously to see what colour uniform would appear. Luck was with me. It was khaki, not field grey.[39]

Although he returned to the squadron a few days later, Jones was in a fragile state. 'My nerves were badly shaken up,' he explained. 'Every time I thought of it I could hardly hold a knife and fork if I were having a meal ... they would always fall out of my hands.' It took a week and a tremendous amount of willpower before Jones could manage an aircraft again.[40]

'Absolute hell let loose': Operation Michael, 21 March–5 April 1918

In Cobby's words, March 1918 'came with an ominous sign'.[41] There were indications all along the front that the Germans were about to launch a major offensive. The problem for the British and French generals, however, was that it remained unclear exactly where they would strike first. There was strong evidence pointing to the Somme sector, where the British line was weakest, but German deception tactics clouded this with other possibilities. In Flanders, for example, where No. 3 Squadron was working with the Australian Corps, on 13 March it appeared the Germans were kicking things off with a preparatory barrage. Shells hit Bailleul, forcing No. 3 Squadron's men to sleep in dugouts. By 21 March, the shelling was so intense that they were forced to move to an aerodrome further back.

But this was only a distraction. The German Army's leaders, Field Marshal Paul von Hindenburg and his Chief of Staff Generalquartiermeister Erich Ludendorff, were planning to unleash the first stage of their spring offensive ('Operation Michael') on an 86 kilometre front between Vimy Ridge and the Oise River. There, they had managed to mass an overwhelming 76 infantry divisions and 730 aircraft against the thinly held front of the Third and Fifth British Armies, which between them had just 26 infantry divisions and 579 aircraft.[42]

Operation Michael started at 5.00 a.m. on 21 March. For four hours, 10 000 German guns deluged the British front with high explosive, shrapnel and gas, destroying strong points and severing communication between units. At 9.00 a.m., specialist German 'stormtroopers' surged forward in heavy mist and quickly overran the British outpost line. Most British troops first knew of the attack after they were already surrounded. By 10.00 a.m., the British were falling back along the entire battlefront.

At Bruay, just north of the German right flank, ten No. 4 Squadron pilots were roused at dawn to see what was happening. 'It was bitterly cold and the whole landscape was blotted out by mist,' recalled Cobby. The pilots hung about despondently, listening to the rumble of the German artillery down south until 8.00 a.m., when the mist appeared to be thinning. They took off, and climbed to 4000 feet to emerge 'under a clear sky with nothing but a sea of what appeared to be white cotton wool below'. Using his compass, Cobby led the patrol southeast towards Bapaume. After an hour, though, the ground was still completely obscured and he had no idea where they were. Spotting a line of observation balloons poking out just above the mist, he decided to follow them north, back towards Bruay.

They were cruising above the balloons when a string of colourful Albatroses and Pfalz emerged, climbing up from the murk below. Cobby rocked his wings to signal 'attack' and dived into the centre of their formation. The German pilots were completely surprised. Cobby picked out a yellow and black Albatros, and with a couple of bursts sent it spinning through the clouds trailing smoke. He then saw one chasing Tab Pflaum and blasted it from 3 metres away: 'He heeled over and went straight down through the mist all "arsey tarsey".'[43] In the chaotic moments that followed, Pflaum and another Australian each sent a machine spinning down too.

In just two minutes, the sky was strangely empty again. The Camel pilots regrouped and flew home, believing they had just shot down four of Germany's elite fighter pilots. 'They were, beyond any doubt, the famous Circus of Baron von Richthofen, from the gay colours which their machines were variously painted,' wrote Jack Wright.[44] Cobby claimed the same in a letter to the official historian after the war and then in his 1942 memoir. Cutlack reproduced Cobby's letter, word for word, in the official history.[45]

The 'fog of war' was literally clouding the facts, though. German records indicate the enemy unit was actually Jasta 35, which in fact reported no casualties that day.[46] The four Australian claims probably spun through the clouds to escape and then flew home.

By noon the following day, the situation on the Somme was critical. Gaps were opening in Fifth Army's line as units lost contact and retreated independently of each other. The German pilots dominated the battlefield with their numerical superiority, while local RFC units busily evacuated their aerodromes and retreated. RFC Headquarters ordered all scout units north of the battlefront to fly south and get involved in the fight: 'The enemy must at all costs be prevented from operating over our lines.'

No. 2 Squadron's pilots spent the morning waiting for the mist to clear. 'We stood about in excited, nervous groups,' recalled Robert McKenzie. 'Out, somewhere in the haze, drowning out all other sounds could be heard the punching detonation of the tremendous artillery barrage which had commenced before dawn.' He looked around at his fellow pilots, 'some standing by their machines, some going over every detail of machine and engine, others nervously puffing cigarettes' and wondered who might not be around for tea in the mess.

At 2.00 p.m., Henry Forrest and Roy Phillipps of No. 2 Squadron led their flights down south to help stem the tide. Eighteen thousand feet above St Quentin, they ran into eight Albatroses escorting a lower formation of five Rumplers. The Australians engaged the escorts first. 'In a second,' recalled Robert McKenzie, 'both formations had disintegrated and the battle royal became a series of individual duels. Pretty soon it became a dogfight of the worst kind.' McKenzie spotted a 'fat glistening' Albatros dive out of the fray and gave chase. The German zoomed and fired a stalling burst underneath the SE5a, but McKenzie met him with a half-roll that came out right on his tail. 'A pressure of a thumb, a short burst, a puff of smoke, a flash of flame, a hole on the clouds—and it was over.' It was his fifth victory—and, as it turned out, very nearly his last.

With the other escorts engaged, McKenzie followed his flight leader, Forrest, down on to the two-seaters. 'Half a mile from the Rumplers,' related McKenzie, 'we separated.' Forrest plunged past the back of the formation and zoomed up underneath it. He closed to point blank range and fired. McKenzie watched as the Rumpler went down 'like a burning meteor'. He overshot the formation, did a 'spin turn' and attacked it head on. 'Just as I was all set to do a neat bit of execution,' explained McKenzie, 'both guns jammed.' He thumped his Vickers in distracted frustration, allowing a German observer to draw a bead on him. 'His first burst sprayed my machine from nose to tail, shattering the windscreen and instrument board and cutting the joystick clean in two.' McKenzie's SE5a went into a violent spinning dive, pursued closely by a German pilot, intent on completing the kill. Bullets whizzed past: 'A good pair of goggles went by the board followed by bits of Sidcott suit. With only 3000 feet of altitude and the lines immediately below I prepared to give up the ghost.' At that moment, though, Forrest arrived and drove the enemy machine away, allowing McKenzie, with some 'frantic juggling with the controls', to level out. 'The SE came out of the spin so violently as to almost throw me out of the cockpit.' Improvising with the rudder, tailplane and throttle he managed to get down on his own side of the line, ending what he later dubbed 'my most thrilling flight'.[47]

Later in the afternoon, Dick Howard led his flight down after an innocuous-looking pair of German two-seaters over Honnecourt (south of Cambrai). Halfway down, one of Howard's pilots noticed they were being 'hotly pursued by about 30 enemy scouts'. The six SE5as wheeled around to meet them and quickly became broken up in a chaotic dogfight. Everyone was concentrating on keeping the enemy off their own tail, but Greg Blaxland noticed Howard streaking away from the dogfight towards the British line. Everyone else made it home but Howard never showed up. German documents suggest he came down behind enemy lines and died of his wounds in a field hospital near Cambrai. He was buried in a military cemetery, but the Imperial War Graves Commission couldn't locate his remains after the war.[48] The members of Howard's flight were shocked that their talented leader had fallen for such a trap. 'Dick certainly could not have seen them or he would not have placed himself in such a position,' considered Archie Rackett. 'For an old pilot of such experience it was not done.'[49]

The British Third and Fifth Armies, and the French further south continued to fall back in complete disorder. On 23 March a critical situation developed to the east of Bapaume, where a gap opened in the British line. The Germans exploited it relentlessly, driving a wedge towards Bapaume. The RFC ordered scout units from neighbouring sectors (including No. 4 Squadron) to fit their bomb racks and attack them from low altitudes.

For three days, No. 4 Squadron turned the crowded roads leading to Bapaume into killing zones. It was 'almost impossible' to miss, explained Cobby. 'One only had to fly straight over a road for a few seconds, and let the bombs go one after another as quickly as possible, and they fell amongst masses of marching troops.'[50] Each day, the Germans advanced, making locating the front line 'a dicey business', as Wright put it: 'We sometimes had to wait until we were fired on from the ground before turning our guns on the troops below us.'[51] The Camel pilots found themselves with frayed nerves. 'It was not long before we were all starting to show signs of the strain,' recalled Cobby, who had his wicker seat shot out from underneath him during one strafing run. 'My principal trouble was that I could not eat, but champagne and brandy, with an odd biscuit seemed good enough.'[52]

Wright did three sorties on 25 March and reckoned he fired 'at least' 1500 rounds and dropped a dozen bombs into 'the masses of Germans on the roads'. It was, as one of his fellow pilots put it, 'absolute hell let loose; fires burning everywhere, oceans of smoke, roads choked with transports and troops'.[53]

Wright backed this up with another three low sorties the following day. On the third one, he landed a pair of bombs fair on to a column of marching infantry. Wheeling his machine around, he dived at the survivors with both guns blazing: 'I became so engrossed with keeping my stream of bullets on the target that I suddenly found myself off my seat and dangling in my belt.' His machine had gone beyond vertical, and was careering towards the ground. He hauled the stick back but nothing happened: 'It just flapped uselessly in my hands, my elevator was in a vacuum and failed to get a grip on the air.' With the ground rushing up to meet him, Wright forced himself into his seat and pushed the stick forward, and then 'gently and steadily back'. The Camel zoomed with about 30 metres to spare—'so close to the troops on the road I could almost see the whites of their eyes,' as he put it. Levelling out, Wright spotted a stream of tracer coming up at him from a gun mounted on a lorry. 'A moment later,' he wrote, 'I felt as if I had been kicked in the backside by a giant mule and would have bounced out of my seat had my belt not held me.' The Camel's engine spluttered and petrol flowed into the cockpit. Wright switched to his reserve tank and flew back towards the line, kicking his rudder from side to side to dodge the streams of tracer arching up from below. As the din died away, he became acutely aware of the 'excruciating pain' of his petrol-drenched wound. He made it to Bruay, the engine dying at the aerodrome's edge. 'I made a reasonable dead stick landing and rolled to a stop.' The next thing he recalled was being on an operating table in a casualty clearing station—'then, oblivion'. He woke in great pain, and drifted in and out of consciousness for twelve hours. When he finally came to, he was pleasantly surprised to find George Jones in the next bed. Jones had also been wounded in the buttocks by ground fire the evening before, meaning they had a few months of convalescence in England together to look forward to.[54]

While the Camel pilots raced around just above ground level, No. 2 Squadron protected them from above. The SE5a pilots found plenty of action higher up and claimed sixteen victories in the first ten days of the offensive. As was typical, the lion's share went to the flight commanders, who always got the first shots in when diving to attack. The leaders of A and B Flights, Roy Phillips and Henry Forrest, claimed five each. Phillips' effort and his 'skill and determination when escorting low flying bombing patrols' earned him a bar to the Military Cross he had received following the Battle of Cambrai.[55]

On 25 March, with the Germans approaching the Ancre River and a gap between Third and Fifth Armies opening, RFC Headquarters ordered scout units to 'bomb and shoot up everything they can see on the enemy side of the line. Very low flying is essential. All risks to be taken. Urgent.'[56] No. 2 Squadron abandoned its high patrols and went out 'loaded up with ammunition and bombs'. Archie Rackett's flight found the Germans had abandoned their 'infiltration tactics' and were advancing in 'massed formation'. The aircraft decimated them. 'Just to cheer them up a little we three dived on them and put about 200 bullets in amongst them.' There were no German aircraft about to stop them, and Rackett reckoned the enemy troops were 'having one hell of a time'.[57]

On 27 March, the situation began to stabilise. The British and French came together under the supreme command of French general, Ferdinand Foch, and reinforcements from other parts of the front deployed in the threatened sectors. On that date, the Australian Corps arrived from Flanders and plugged the gap between the Somme and Ancre Rivers. The RFC was also getting on top of things. Thirty-seven out of its 60 squadrons on the Western Front were on the battlefront by 27 March. That day, they mauled enemy troops between Albert and the Somme with over 310 000 rounds and 50 tonnes of bombs.[58] One German general claimed these air attacks caused half of all German casualties on that date. An exaggeration perhaps, but nonetheless, a reflection of how effective the Germans considered the RFC's ground attack sorties to be.[59] After 27 March, enemy troops made no further progress north of the Somme.

On the following morning, however, the Germans launched 'Operation Mars' against the northern part of Third Army's sector, on the River Scarpe. The plan was to capture Arras, but the German attacks stalled almost immediately in the face of reinforced British units on the ground, and of course a fusillade of bombs and machine gun fire from above. Forrest led a dozen SE5as out in the morning to shoot up German troops along the

Arras–Douai road. Fire from the ground remained intense, and this time fate picked 25-year-old Thomas Hosking, another 'original Anzac' who had recently joined the squadron as respite from a long stint of trench warfare on Gallipoli and the Somme. As Forrest wrote to the young pilot's family:

> We were diving on the enemy trenches from about 1000 feet and Hosking was a couple of hundred yards from me when I suddenly saw his right top wing and his tail break off, apparently a direct hit from a shell. He crashed in a hopeless mess just behind the German front line. I circled around his machine for a few minutes but there was no movement near it.[60]

At noon, another flight of SE5as escorted No. 4 Squadron to shoot up German reinforcements advancing along the Arras–Cambrai road. The aptly named Oscar Flight, another rookie, became separated in clouds and rather brazenly dived down by himself and began machine gunning German troops. For fifteen minutes he laid into them, drawing immense amounts of fire from the ground. All of a sudden, it stopped: 'On looking around I saw three enemy Albatros machines.' He pulled around in a climbing turn to meet them but they had too much height on him. 'The fire was more or less incessant for a minute or so.' Flight managed to evade their bullets, but at this point four Fokker Triplanes joined in. He was 150 feet above the ground and 'bullets were coming in all directions'. They ripped through his SE5a, severing flying wires and knocking off timber struts. The wings collapsed together and the aircraft fell out of control: 'I switched off and held on to the front of the cockpit. The machine then dived into the ground tearing down a number of enemy telephone wires. I was rendered unconscious.'

Flight woke up beside his wrecked aircraft. Some German medical orderlies were bandaging his head. They allowed him to go to the machine to get his watch, and while there he grabbed his Verey pistol and fired a flare into the petrol-soaked cockpit, setting the aircraft ablaze. Nearby German soldiers opened fire, and would certainly have killed him on the spot if an officer hadn't intervened. Flight ended up at Landshut POW camp in southern Germany with a No. 4 Squadron pilot named Cecil Feez, who coincidentally was also shot down the same day. An attempt by the two to tunnel out of the camp was foiled when an Italian prisoner informed on them.[61]

Operation Mars was stillborn and thereafter the fickle Ludendorff again switched the weight of his offensive back to the Somme in an attempt to seize the important British logistical hub at Amiens. For another week, the exhausted Germans made small, local gains, but were ultimately held short of their objectives. The Australian Corps (supported by No. 3 Squadron) provided instrumental defence astride the Somme at Villers-Bretonneux, Morlancourt and Dernancourt. By 5 April, Operation Michael had petered out altogether and both Australian scout squadrons resumed normal offensive patrols further north, in their own sector.

'Every time we go out somebody's machine gets it': Operation Georgette, 9 April–29 April 1918

In the midst of all this chaos, there was a bizarrely timed reorganisation of British military aviation. On 1 April 1918, after a year of political and high-level military wrangling, the two separate British air services, the Royal Flying Corps and the Royal Naval Air Service, were amalgamated into the Royal Air Force (RAF). The change would have significant consequences for the British squadrons as they struggled to integrate two different service cultures and operational styles, but it was hardly noticed in the Australian squadrons.

On 4 April, No. 2 Squadron moved south to La Bellevue aerodrome (20 kilometres west of Arras) to help re-establish British air superiority over the front north of the Somme.

Meanwhile, No. 4 Squadron remained on First Army's front at Bruay, where signs pointed to a renewed enemy offensive. From 31 March, RAF reconnaissance detected the movement north of troops and guns from the Somme. On the afternoon of 6 April, aerial photographs confirmed a definite buildup of enemy forces in front of the River Lys, immediately to the northeast of No. 4 Squadron's aerodrome.

The following morning, all the pilots went out with bombs 'on a whole squadron affair' to disrupt the enemy's preparations near La Bassée. They met a storm of Archie just after crossing the lines. Cobby noticed one of the other flight commanders, John Courtney, suddenly dive out of formation and start burning up. He could just make out part of the engine falling ahead of the blazing machine and surmised that an artillery shell had shot the nose clean off his Camel. 'There was practically nothing left of his machine by the time it reached the ground.' The rest of the machines bombed and machine-gunned enemy troops, and then repeated the sortie again before lunch.[62]

The Germans unleashed the next stage of their offensive, named 'Operation Georgette', at dawn on 9 April. They attacked between Bois Grenier and La Bassée, directing the full weight of their barrage and infantry assault on an unreliable Portuguese division, which buckled and retreated in disorder. Thick mist again shielded the German stormtroops and added to British confusion. Garnet Malley led No. 4 Squadron's only sortie for the day in the late afternoon, a flight of five to bomb bridges over the Lys before the Germans could use them. Jack Weingarth painted his parents a harrowing picture of the sortie, explaining that 'we had to fly as low as 200 feet on account of the heavy ground mists and the clouds of smoke from shells and burning towns and villages; in fact, the whole country was ablaze'. At this height, the pilots were literally flying through the artillery barrage. They dropped their bombs and had 'a pretty hot time' getting home. Weingarth landed with his Camel 'riddled with bullets' but was pleased as it meant a brand new replacement machine. A bullet had gone through Malley's leg and smashed the watch on his instrument panel. A squadron orderly dressed the wound and sent him to the closest field hospital in Major McCloughry's car. According to Vern Knuckey, Malley was a favourite among the air mechanics in his flight: 'As he sat in the back seat of the car waving to the boys everyone hoped he would soon return.' They weren't disappointed. Malley stayed in hospital for two days before insisting he get back to the squadron. Six days later, he was on the flying roster again. The bombing reports from Malley's sortie don't survive, but it is clear they didn't have a decisive result. A British reconnaissance flight at 6.00 p.m. confirmed that the Germans were across the River Lys, some 8 kilometres from their starting line.

The Germans widened their offensive the following morning, attacking with another army immediately to the north. They punched through the British lines at Armentières, and Messines Ridge, and advanced through the southern part of the Ypres salient. Despite another oppressive ground fog, No. 4 Squadron began sending out bombing relays at 6.00 a.m. Being so close to the front augmented the workload and the strain. Pilots could take off from Bruay, empty their bomb racks and ammunition belts and be back on the ground again to reload within 40 minutes.

Weingarth's flight was in the air before breakfast. They bombed German infantry sheltering in a wood and then swept along a road strafing horse-drawn transports. 'We tore into them,' he wrote, 'it nearly made me sick, killing all those horses, but it had to be done.' Rifles and machine guns 'chattered' at the Camels as they swept back and forth. 'The Bosche threw everything at us except the grand piano,' described Weingarth. He saw his good mate, Howard Love, hit and pile up into a hedgerow. Moments later, the flight's leader, Fred Woolhouse (Malley's temporary replacement), also ploughed into the ground. Both pilots' families faced months of uncertainty before the Red Cross could confirm their fate. The tension was broken for Love's fiancée when she received word after eight weeks that he was a prisoner. The Scottish girl 22-year-old Woolhouse had met and married while on leave in Edinburgh had six months to wait. A letter then arrived confirming Fred's death.[63]

The German drive across the Lys continued on 11 April, reaching Merville and Nieppe by evening. With the British artillery forced into a rapid retreat following the initial breakthrough, the pilots took the place of the gunners in breaking up enemy troop concentrations. In drizzling rain, No. 4 Squadron made 33 bombing sorties. The battle reached a climactic phase the following day as the Germans closed in on Hazebrouck, a major British transportation hub for Flanders. Its loss would cripple the British Expeditionary Force's ability to commit reserves to the battle from other parts of the front and leave the way open to the Channel coast. With just remnants of one tired, strung-out British division dug in outside of Hazebrouck, the RAF played an instrumental part in averting a disaster. With the good fortune of clearer weather, No. 4 Squadron's Camels joined an armada of 137 aircraft on low attack sorties over the front at first light.[64] They targeted choke points in villages such as Merville and Roberque from 'point blank range'. On one of the three sorties Cobby flew that day, his flight of six, each with four bombs slung below its wings, spotted a column of German reinforcements marching along a road towards the front. 'Every one of the twenty four landed on the roadway, and as the troops who were left took to the fields, we turned and machine-gunned them.' Of the survivors, he predicted, 'it would be some time before they stopped shivering when an aeroplane came near them'.[65]

By the end of the day, the RAF had flown more hours and expended more ordnance than at any other day in the war so far. The ground attack formations had dropped 750 bombs and fired 60 000 rounds into advancing German infantry. The German drive on Hazebrouck was blunted and, by evening, reinforcements (including the 1st Australian Division) were deploying in front of the German advance.[66]

As the German advance lost momentum, No. 4 Squadron shifted its sights to German supply dumps and artillery positions behind their front line. The flying hours didn't slacken, nor did the danger from ground fire. 'Every time we go out somebody's machine gets it,' wrote Weingarth on 15 April. 'I had a wing smashed this morning. I have to fly another machine in about half and hour, while they are fixing my bus up.'[67]

The usual respite the pilots enjoyed on the ground in between patrols wasn't available to them either. By 14 April, Bruay aerodrome was in range of German heavy artillery. A gun the men nicknamed 'Gentle Annie' intermittently shelled the aerodrome and town. The damage wasn't significant, but the random shells rattled the strung-out pilots and overworked mechanics. 'One never knows when or where the next one will arrive,' explained Knuckey, 'and the large majority of this squadron have never heard a shell burst until now.' Far more distressing to Knuckey, though, was the 'great mass' of French refugees who jammed the roads all around the aerodrome. It was a spectacle, he predicted, 'that will stay in my mind for the rest of my life'.

The chaos in the countryside gave rise to rumours about German spies. One suggested enemy agents were dressing as priests to move about undetected. One evening, some of the mechanics noticed three priests standing across the road from the aerodrome with a map. After dinner, they set off into town armed with revolvers and went from church to church, hunting down the suspected spies in what afterwards became known in the squadron's folklore as 'the parson hunt'.

Knuckey was in his tent when he heard a 'great uproar'. Along the street leading up to the aerodrome was coming a 'huge crowd' of 'men, women and children by the hundreds'. At their head, in the custody of two Australian mechanics, was a terrified-looking priest. They had barged into his church during mass wielding their revolvers, ordered him to say 'amen' and come along with them.

With most of Bruay's population milling about on No. 4 Squadron's aerodrome, 'yelling and awfully excited as the French always are', Major McCloughry sent for an interpreter. When one finally arrived, it emerged the priests were planning to build a mission on the aerodrome's site after the war. Their 'map' was in fact a blueprint for the structure. 'For days afterwards,' claimed Knuckey, 'I never saw a priest in the streets of Bruay.'[68]

This comical interlude was followed by a much more serious one. On 21 April, the German shelling of Bruay intensified. Harold Stone, a fitter who had the misfortune of joining the squadron the day before, scrawled his initial impressions of the aerodrome in his pocketbook. 'Fritz shelling our place all day and night,' he wrote. 'Could not sleep.' Like Knuckey, he found it 'heartbreaking' to see the suffering of French civilians. 'House blown up right in front of our 'drome. Little boy had his arm blown off. Awful sight.'[69]

The shelling got worse as the week wore on. Knuckey was trying to get to sleep on 24 April when a red-hot shell splinter tore through the roof and went right through the unoccupied bed next to his. 'There were a lot of empty beds in camp that night,' he wrote. One of the squadron's few ex-diggers, Knuckey took a more fatalistic view: 'It did not shake my opinion that I was as safe there as anywhere.'[70] Of course, no one was safe and on 28 April the squadron packed up amid falling shells and prepared to move to a new aerodrome further back. The Germans called off Operation Georgette the following day. It, like Operations Michael and Mars, had broken into the British lines but had failed to break out of them and bring the war to a decisive close.

The German offensives in March and April 1918 presented No. 2 and No. 4 Squadrons' airmen with some of the most intense fighting ever experienced by Australian combat flyers. For almost six weeks, they flew multiple sorties every day—usually at low level and well within range of small arms fire. Although the Germans had air superiority at the beginning of Operations Michael and Georgette, within a few days they lost it due to logistical difficulties and the ability of the RAF to shift reinforcements to the threatened front. Indeed, the Australians experienced minimal interference from the air. Of the ten Australian pilot casualties—four killed, three wounded and three captured—only three were the result of enemy aircraft. The other seven were hit by ground fire.

FIRE IN THE SKY

At the time, things didn't look good from the perspective of the average pilot or mechanic. The British and French had lost a quarter of a million men and well over 2500 square kilometres of territory. Unknown to most at the time, though, was the fact that the German military had played its last hand. There were no more reserves and the war-strained German home front was edging closer to revolution. As Harry Cobby commented after the war: 'It was the beginning of the Allied victory, although we did not realise it at the time.'[71]

11

'THE NEAREST THING TO A HOLIDAY IS A WET DAY'

From German offensive to British counter-offensive, April to July 1918

Manfred von Richthofen's wrecked triplane at No. 3 Squadron's aerodrome at Poulainville on 22 April 1918. Souvenir hunters have all but picked it clean, despite the presence of the guard on the right. *AWM E02044*

> Windy and wet. No flying. The nearest thing to a holiday is a wet day.
>
> —Air Mechanic Stan Tuck, No. 3 Squadron Australian Flying Corps

'The foundation of our world had melted away': Death and bereavement in the Australian Flying Corps

During the German offensive on the Somme, No. 3 Squadron followed the rest of the Australian Corps south to shore up the line in front of Amiens. It arrived at Poulainville on 7 April, an aerodrome conveniently close to the Australian Corps Headquarters in Bertangles.

By this time, Owen Lewis was counted among the squadron's veteran observers. He had done almost ten weeks at the front and was just a fortnight shy of getting a leave pass to England. On 11 April 1918, he woke to find the weather 'dud' for flying, so he and another observer took the opportunity to walk into Bertangles to see if there were any field canteens. After asking around, they were directed to 'a couple of boxes of stuff under a tree' where they could purchase cigarettes and a few other luxuries. Lewis bought a toothbrush and can of boot polish ('a great rarity') for his tent mate, 22-year-old George Best. A Tasmanian draper, Best had only just joined the squadron from pilot training in England. He and Lewis got on famously right away and arranged to fly together.

The sun came out in the afternoon revealing a glorious spring day. Lewis wasn't rostered to fly so he spent the time improving his tent. He aired blankets and tidied up and then set about building a makeshift table. A rough timber crate did the trick, with a few odd boards nailed across the top. He then kicked a football around with some of the other airmen and finished with a bath. 'I feel absolutely splendid,' he noted in his diary. A large mail arrived from Australia in the late afternoon and Lewis was delighted to receive a bundle of letters. He pored over each one, relishing the news from home. Lewis's older sister Phyllis, who he was particularly close to, had become engaged to a Melbourne University law student named Bob Menzies. His older brother Ralph, recently wounded, was safely home in Australia and his 16-year-old brother Neil had done well in his school examinations. He would probably receive a scholarship—a real boon for an aspirational middle-class family like the Lewises.

After dinner, Lewis and Best went for a stroll in the countryside surrounding the aerodrome. They left the narrow country lanes and struck across fields that were bursting with spring colour. It was immensely enjoyable. Lewis was glad he and Best had been assigned to fly together. Returning to their tent, Lewis sat at his crude crate table and recorded the day's events in his diary. It had been splendid, full of simple pleasures that only men on temporary reprieve from the tension and violence of war can ever really savour.[1]

The following morning at 11.00 a.m., Owen Lewis and George Best were burned to death when their RE8 burst into flames shortly after taking off. According to Jack Treacy, their bodies were unrecognisable. He went to Albertville Hospital to identify the remains and was only able to do so because he knew Lewis so well. Five decades later, he would remember it as 'a sad sight'—and indeed, one that could have been avoided. The RE8 in which they were killed had a reputation for having a bad engine, and an examination of the wreckage found that a twisted camshaft had probably caused the accident.[2] Lewis and Best were buried beside each other in the flying corps manner, 'very short and simple', as his brother Athol, an artilleryman, reported, with a handful of their fellow airmen in attendance.[3] Their mates cleared their tent out and boxed their personal effects up for shipping home. New men would be there to replace them within a day or so.

Five days later, in a quiet, leafy street in Melbourne's inner southeast, Owen's 12-year-old brother, Brian, was sitting on his bed with some mathematics homework when Phyllis rushed in: 'Owen's been killed.' She collapsed on the bed next to Brian and wept. The young boy joined her. 'The foundation of our world had melted away,' he later explained. 'Of course, it was happening to others every day, but this was to us, and this was Owen.'

The rest of the day was a trial for the Lewis family. They met and tried to eat a meal through lots of tears. The news quickly travelled around family and community. Aunts seemed to almost relish the opportunity to wear black armbands and people they hardly knew made nuisances of themselves, calling by to see whether it was true. At Wesley College, the principal announced another old boy was dead. Not as many as Scotch or Grammar yet, Brian recalled, but a respectable number nonetheless. 'Sorrow,' Brian thought, was being 'vulgarised by publicity.'

The Lewis family shied away from public rituals of mourning. They wore no armbands and didn't bother to place In Memoriam notices in the newspaper or purchase Owen a £5 memorial chair at Wesley College. Mrs Lewis abruptly stopped wearing her 'mother with sons on active service' badges and she refused a relative's offer to commune with Owen's spirit via séance. The rhetoric of public mourning was found wanting by those at the sharp end of bereavement. 'Owen had not laid down his life,' concluded Brian. 'It had been snatched from him and from us.'

Letters posted by Owen before his death continued to arrive for another six weeks. Each Friday they would come, nagging at the family's grief with their ironically cheery and upbeat tone. Mr Lewis read these letters out, along with those from Owen's surviving brothers, after tea each Friday evening. He then carefully stored them away in file boxes, one for each of the boys.

Although Owen's letters soon stopped, his file stayed open for several months. Then, one Saturday morning, Brian collected a large envelope from the mailbox and brought it into his mother. She was sitting in a sun chair, about to begin her morning prayers.

'Open it,' she instructed him, 'What is it?'

Brian stood there staring, unable to speak. She reached across and took it. It was a photograph of Owen's grave, a simple timber cross in a distant town she had never heard of and would never have the chance to visit. She got up, went to her desk and put it in Owen's file box. She then closed it and returned to her prayers. Owen's file was now complete.[4]

'The sky was red with Huns': Fall of the 'Red Falcon', 21 April 1918

When No. 3 Squadron started flying over the Somme in mid-April 1918, there were indications that the Germans had plans to kick-start their offensive. The Australian pilots reported German troops and guns marshalling east of Villers-Bretonneux and met aggressive resistance from enemy scout formations. In its first fortnight on the Somme, No. 3 Squadron was attacked six times and had a crew shot down and wounded. Rumour had it that Jagdgeschwader Nr I, 'Richthofen's Circus', was in the sector.

The German offensive resumed on 24 April at Villers-Bretonneux. Although the enemy captured the town, the Australian 13th and 15th Brigades successfully counter-attacked the following morning, Anzac Day 1918, and drove them out. No. 3 Squadron attempted to support the diggers with a few contact patrols but poor visibility excluded them from playing a significant role in this, one of the AIF's most celebrated actions of the war.

FROM GERMAN OFFENSIVE TO BRITISH COUNTER-OFFENSIVE, 1918

Three days earlier, though, on 21 April 1918, No. 3 Squadron was involved in another famous event—indeed, possibly the most discussed and written about incident in the history of aerial warfare. Just after 10.00 a.m. that morning, three Australian RE8s left Poulainville. Stan Garrett and Alf Barrow, together with Thomas Simpson and Edmond Banks, had orders to photograph the Australian Corps' front. John Duigan and Alec Paterson in the third machine would act as an escort and drop a few bombs.

Half an hour later, the Australian RE8s were 7500 feet over Hamel taking photographs when Barrow slapped Garrett on the shoulder and shouted 'Huns!' Garrett looked up and saw two flights (nine in total) of Fokker triplanes closing in. Two peeled off and bore down on them.

Garrett closed ranks with Simpson's RE8 for protection and fired flares to attract the attention of some nearby British scouts, but within moments a triplane was on their tail firing: 'It was a gaudy red one and seemed to be all over us at once, but Barrow was pouring in lead at 800 shots per minute and apparently the Hun got fed up, for we last saw him in a funny roll, with Barrow firing for all he knew.'[5] The other triplane made firing passes at Simpson's RE8 but Banks and Barrow kept it at bay with their interlocking fields of fire. 'He took a bad battering,' recalled Banks, 'and after splinters were seen to fly from his wings he pulled out of the fight.'[6] According to Duigan, who—weighed down by his bombs—was a few hundred metres behind the other two, 'the sky was red with Huns' around them, 'but they seemed to disappear as quickly as they came along'.[7] The Australians resumed their photographic work.

Returning to Poulainville, the three Australian crews found 'all excitement'. The triplanes had apparently been from Richthofen's Circus and according to Paterson, 'mechanics rushed out to meet us and wanted to know who shot down the Baron'.[8] They explained that, at about 11.00 a.m., an all-red triplane had crashed on the Morlancourt Ridge, and its dead pilot was the legendary 'Red Falcon', the Baron Manfred von Richthofen ('Red Baron' was popularised after the war). Garrett and Barrow filed their claim for the 'gaudy red' machine they had hit, but took a prosaic view of the whole affair, admitting they had lost sight of it and couldn't verify it had actually crashed: 'We were met by generals, doctors and goodness knows whom, who asked us about the fight but it was such a mix up that we could

FIRE IN THE SKY

not give a very good account of it.' Garrett was sure 'there would be other claimants'.[9]

Unknown to any of the Australians at this time, Garrett and Barrow's victim was not the 'Falcon', but rather Hans Weiss, one of his deputies.[10] When the Germans spotted the RE8s over Hamel, Weiss and another pilot (some claim it was Richthofen, but evidence for this is thin) attacked while the rest of the Circus stayed above to cover them. Barrow's fire severed one of Weiss's rudder cables, forcing him to spin away and return home. The other German pilot pressed the attack but was driven away by Banks' burst. He left the Australians alone and rejoined his flight.

Minutes later, Camels from No. 209 Squadron arrived and drew the Germans into an all-in dogfight above Cerisy. Wilfred May, a Canadian rookie, had instructions from his flight leader to dive home if a fight started. He did this, but was pursued in a steep dive west by Richthofen. Seeing the plight of his young protégé, May's flight leader and fellow Canadian, Roy Brown, took off after Richthofen.

The trio went down low across the Australian lines at Sailly-le-Sec and along the Somme valley towards Corbie. They skimmed over the rooftops of Vaux and then Brown came into range and fired a 'long burst' at the red triplane and pulled away, seeing his target apparently go 'down vertical'.[11]

Brown was mistaken, though. Richthofen continued to pursue May away from the Somme, up the Morlancourt Ridge's steep slope. The whole area was teeming with Australian troops in billets and artillery positions. Norman Nicolson, an Australian artillery captain, was just one of hundreds of spectators of the breathtaking pursuit. 'There was a great crackling of machine gun fire,' he recorded, 'not only from our guns but from the machine gun companies and infantry.'[12] May barely cleared the crest, with Richthofen following and snapping shots off at him. Passing over the ridge, he came under heavy fire from Australian Lewis gunners concealed behind the ridge. Richthofen abruptly broke off the chase and began a sharp climbing turn back towards German lines. Part-way through the manoeuvre, his aircraft swerved and crashed suddenly into a beet field beside the Bray–Corbie road.

Excited diggers were swarming around the wreckage within moments, eager to get souvenirs. Their enthusiasm was augmented when an intelligence officer examined the dead pilot's papers and announced his identity.

A padre unsuccessfully tried to stop the frenzied looting while a signaller from the 3rd Division and some of his mates unscrewed the propeller and made off with it.[13] Others tore off sections of fabric, pulled dials out of the instrument panel and even 'ratted' Richthofen's pockets for loot. The souvenir grab was cut short when the German shells began landing in the exposed field. It was night before a mechanic from No. 3 Squadron could crawl out and attach cables to drag the wreckage and Richthofen's corpse away.

Both were taken back to No. 3 Squadron's aerodrome at Poulainville, where the red triplane continued to draw souvenir hunters. Guards were posted on it overnight but, according to Nigel Love, they didn't do a good job because 'by the time the morning had arrived there was scarcely a bit of the red fabric left on the frame of the aircraft'. He did confess, however, that he got 'his share'—including a piece of fabric, a turnbuckle and one of the stars from Richthofen's epaulette.[14] Second Class Air Mechanic John Alexander remembered, 'we all got something as a memento'.[15]

Richthofen's corpse also drew considerable curiosity, and a stream of pilots and mechanics visited the tent where his body was laid late that night. 'He was badly hit,' recalled Love. 'They tied him up against the tent pole, while they cleaned his face up, opened his eyes, then they took two or three pictures of him.'[16] Paterson was struck that, although dead, he had a smile on his face,[17] while Garrett thought he 'had a distinguished appearance' but looked like 'a typical Hun'.[18] Frank Rawlinson was disappointed, though. 'He looked very insignificant, lying there in his plain stained overalls.'[19]

Souvenir hunters got to Richthofen's body too, despite guards being posted on the tent. Private Joe Porter entered the tent at about 11.00 p.m., and with the approval of the guards (probably his mates) 'ratted' Richthofen's clothes for souvenirs. To his great surprise, he discovered a bundle of cash tucked away in one of the Baron's pockets. Just at that moment, an officer entered the tent and ordered Porter to hand it over. He begrudgingly did—and never heard anything more about it. Nevertheless, the opportunistic Porter didn't leave empty handed. He found Richthofen's boots a perfect fit and swapped them for his own.[20]

Six medical officers visited Poulainville to examine Richthofen's body. Their methodology was crude; the body wasn't opened and one doctor probed the wound with a piece of fence wire. The resulting reports, not surprisingly, therefore have some discrepancies and suspect conclusions. All six did, however, agree that Richthofen was killed by a single bullet that entered on his right side at the ninth rib and exited six centimetres higher, just below the left nipple. Apparently it had gone through a lung and struck his heart. But the doctors drew different conclusions concerning the bullet's origin. Lieutenant Colonel George Barber, the Australian Corps' deputy director of medical services, concluded: 'I am *sure* he was shot from *below* while banking.'[21] Major Blake and No. 3 Squadron's recording officer, Errol Knox, who also examined the body, concurred.[22] Two British doctors from the RAF disagreed, however, arguing it was caused by another aircraft, firing from roughly the same plane, 'slightly behind the right' of Richthofen. His death, they thought, 'could not have been caused by fire from the ground'.[23]

In the event, the RAF credited the Canadian Camel pilot Roy Brown with the kill and in 1934 the British official historian did likewise. Three years later, the Australian official historian, Charles Bean, investigated the matter further and collated more than 60 accounts from a diverse range of eyewitnesses, including British and German soldiers. Examining this mass of evidence today, it is clear that we will never know for certain who fired the fatal shot. The most likely candidate to emerge, though, is a carpenter from Queensland's north coast named Cedric Popkin. Firing a Vickers gun from the bank of the Somme, about 1000 metres west of Vaux, he claimed to have hit Richthofen as he turned over Morlancourt Ridge.[24] But Popkin was just one of dozens of Australian soldiers all firing the same .303 projectiles at the triplane as it zoomed over their positions.

What we can be almost certain about, however, is who *didn't* shoot down Richthofen. It was not Roy Brown, or any other airman for that matter. The traditional view is that Brown fired his 'long burst' from the northeast (Richthofen's right) just as they passed Sailly-le-Sec, and therefore almost a minute before the crash.[25] The physician and medical historian Dr M. Geoffrey Miller, takes this view, but negates Brown's claim by arguing that Richthofen's cardiovascular injuries would have rendered him unconscious within 20 seconds or so. 'Certainly,' he concludes, Richthofen 'could have not continued to fly his aeroplane and fire on Lt May for over a minute.'[26] The most recent study of the Baron's last flight also discredits Brown, but on different grounds. It presents a strong case that Brown actually fired his burst from the southeast (Richthofen's left side) between Vaux and Corbie—that is, much closer to the crash site but on the wrong side to inflict the entry wound on Richthofen's right side.[27] In either case, Brown emerges a very unlikely candidate for the kill.

Old myths die hard, though, and it remains difficult for some to believe that history's most famous fighter pilot was felled by a fluke shot by a very ordinary carpenter from a small country town in Queensland.[28] Yet if the AFC's experiences on the Western Front have revealed nothing else so far, it should be clear that ground fire from masses of troops was no respecter of a pilot's skill or reputation. The simple fact is that flying low over a valley packed with automatic weapons was extremely perilous, even for an expert with 80 victories to his credit.

It was Major Blake's conviction that No. 3 Squadron should honour their fallen adversary. On the afternoon following his death, the squadron gave Richthofen a lavish funeral in Bertangles cemetery. A squadron tender conveyed the coffin, crowned with wreathes and Germany's colours, through the town's crowded streets. Six Australian airmen acted as pallbearers and fourteen air mechanics formed a firing party. The event was filmed, photographed and attended by a number of high-ranking British and Australian officers. An Anglican minister conducted the ceremony among the silent crowd to the distant rumble of gunfire. The pallbearers then carefully lowered the coffin into the ground. The grave was filled and covered with a mound of wreathes. One, from the 5th Australian Division, read: 'To our worthy and gallant foe.'[29] A cross fashioned from an RE8's propeller marked the grave (see Plate 23).

Most of the squadron was glad to extend this respect to their fallen enemy, in keeping with the notions of chivalry and honour that many of them still held on to (despite having looted his body). One air mechanic, for example, told his family: 'The Baron was given a good funeral as he was a good airman and a clean fighter.' He rationalised that the honour was deserved, as Richthofen was 'a good soldier for his country and never went to London or Paris killing women and children'.[30] Others were more cynical, though. Why should a German pilot get such pomp and ceremony when their own men—the likes of Owen Lewis and George Best—were sewn up in a blanket and buried quietly? Another mechanic, John Alexander, expressed this view in his diary: 'Of course it seemed a down right shame that such a fuss should be made over an enemy airmen,' he wrote. 'I would be one to pass him by like they are known to treat our boys.'[31]

The gulf between these two views of the Richthofen funeral illustrates the tension—indeed, the crisis—the First World War presented for the ordinary civilian men who fought it. They had been raised on the understanding that war was an honour-bound thing, fought between 'gallant foes', who mutually respected one another. The Western Front was swallowing up that innocent view before their eyes though, along with thousands of their mates. For the French civilians whose homes were being swallowed, there was no such moral crisis. At dusk, following the funeral, the citizens of Bertangles entered their little cemetery. They knocked down the cross and tore apart the wreathes covering Richthofen's grave.

'The trouble was that he was too brave': No. 2 Squadron's flying circus, April–June 1918

As things on the Somme settled down in the wake of Operation Michael, No. 2 Squadron moved south to La Bellevue (20 kilometres southwest of Arras) to form a 'circus' with a pair of British Camel Squadrons (Nos 43 and 80). The move was part of the RAF's response to the appearance of larger formations (30 plus) of enemy scouts, operating at high altitudes. The three squadrons would patrol together, stacked in layers for mutual protection. The Australians in their SE5as would be on top at 16 000 feet, with the two squadrons of Camels staggered below at 2000 feet intervals. Their patrol sector was large, spanning from the Somme up to the Nieppe Forest in Flanders.

The change forced the Australian pilots to abandon the small patrol tactics they had used so effectively in February and March. Flying in circus formation locked them into prearranged routes, and restrained the initiative of individual pilots. This might have been bearable if the circus tactics yielded results, but they didn't. In April and May, No. 2 Squadron made just eleven claims. It encountered few large German formations, and the smaller ones tended to flee at the sight of the British circus. The explanation wasn't, as the Australian pilots typically assumed, that their foes were cowardly. They were, in fact, short on fuel. At the beginning of May, resource shortages forced the German high command to ration fighter units with enough fuel for only ten individual flights per day.[32] In the conditions, No. 2 Squadron's commanding officer questioned the validity of circus tactics. He considered that better results would be obtained with a return to the flexibility of smaller patrols.[33]

May was an inauspicious month for the squadron in other ways too. On 8 May, four SE5as were patrolling in hazy conditions above the Nieppe Forest when their flight leader, Leslie Primrose, spotted three unfamiliar-looking machines below. Assuming they were Germans, he waggled his wings and dived. Two of his pilots, Ern Davies and Greg Blaxland, followed. Before coming into range, Primrose recognised the machines were in fact French Spads, and accordingly pulled out of the dive. The other two Australians evidently didn't see him, and opened fire. Davies' gun jammed, but Blaxland hit one of the French machines, killing its pilot and sending it down to crash well behind the British line.

Back on the ground, the flight reported they had seen some French machines but didn't mention anything about firing at them. Within 48 hours, though, the commanding officer of 51st Wing (No. 2 Squadron's senior formation), Lieutenant Colonel R.P. Mills, had identified the responsible pilot as Blaxland. Things didn't look good for the young Australian. On inspecting No. 2 Squadron's record book, Mills found no mention of the incident whatsoever. When pressed, Blaxland admitted he had fired at a machine but claimed it wasn't a Spad—something he maintained even when Mills took him to see the wreck. Blaxland's story unravelled, however, when Mills read a report from his flight commander, claiming: 'Lt Blaxland states that he dived onto the tail of one of these machines and it was not until he fired a short burst that the machine banked and the red rings became visible.'[34] It seemed that Blaxland *had* recognised the machines as French after firing. The squadron's commander, Major Sheldon, confirmed this when he explained to Mills that the flight had reported seeing some French machines after its patrol, but had not mentioned firing at them.[35]

This all pointed to an initial attempt within the flight to cover up the incident and an ongoing attempt by Blaxland to do so, even once he was confronted with the evidence. The wing commander was angry and embarrassed. 'One of the most regrettable features of the occurrence,' he wrote to Major Sheldon, 'is the fact that none of the pilots appear to have reported the engagement to their Squadron Commander, or if they did so, no report was made to these Headquarters.' It wasn't a good look for the RAF, trying as it was to placate the angry French flying service. In order to make 'an example' to other pilots and conciliate the French, Mills concluded that Blaxland had 'displayed culpable negligence' and should be sent home immediately.[36] On 12 May, he was relieved of his duties and sent to Britain to work in a training unit.

Just a few days later, Major Sheldon was very suddenly removed from command of the squadron and sent back to Australia. It is unclear whether this was linked to the Blaxland incident—at least one group of historians think it was—but Sheldon went home to take command of the flying school at Point Cook.[37] In any case, his replacement was Alan Murray Jones of No. 1 Squadron fame. After recovering from the wound Felmy had given him in May 1917, Murray Jones served in Palestine as a flight leader until, at the end of that year, he went to England to help train the new Australian squadrons. His reputation preceded him when he took command of No. 2 Squadron in May, and in spite of his fresh-faced appearance (he was just 24) he immediately had the respect and confidence of his pilots. Adrian Cole, who followed Murray Jones from Palestine and joined No. 2 Squadron at the same time, remembered him as 'a leader by nature and the embodiment of confidence and energy'. Murray Jones took advantage of the RAF's newly relaxed policy of forbidding squadron leaders to fly and quickly impressed the other pilots with the aggressive flying style that had distinguished him in the Middle East.

At the end of May, ironically just after Murray Jones wrote his critical report on the ineffectiveness of circus flights, they proved their worth. Large formations of German scouts aggressively began contesting the skies in No. 2 Squadron's sector, and within 48 hours the squadron claimed seventeen enemy machines down. Three went to Henry Forrest, making him the squadron's leading scorer with eleven victories. Major Murray Jones immediately recommended him for a Distinguished Flying Cross, the RAF's new award for 'gallantry during active operations against the enemy'. He cited the 23-year-old Melbourne clerk's 'great dash and determination' and noted that 'as a flight commander he has set an excellent example to the squadron'.[38]

The spike in enemy activity suggested that another offensive was imminent. Intelligence indicated it would fall against the French between Noyon and Montdidier within days, and on 3 June No. 2 Squadron went south with the circus to Foquorolles to help shore up the line. The Germans launched Operation Gneisenau four days later. The bombardment was characteristically fierce and enemy infantry advanced 9 kilometres on the first day. No. 2 Squadron went into action that morning, sending out pairs on low-altitude bombing and strafing attacks. It was misty and, for the few Cambrai veterans left in the squadron, there must have been a sense of *déjà vu*. In the first three days of the offensive, the squadron slung 86 bombs on to enemy troops and artillery positions, and provided French infantry commanders with reports from the battlefield.

On 11 June, the French launched a powerful counter-attack, supported by low-flying aircraft and 144 tanks. No. 2 Squadron's circus switched to high-altitude offensive patrols to cover it. In the middle of the day, Forrest's flight of five spotted half a dozen enemy two-seaters flying south far below them. It was 25-year-old James Hammond's first patrol. An impetuous and aggressive young man, a boxer, he rather recklessly dived on to the enemy formation alone. He finished up 30 metres behind one of them, blazing away. The enemy observer collapsed in his cockpit and the machine 'healed over to the right and went past the vertical and then went straight down in a nose dive'.[39] Forrest confirmed that the two-seater did indeed crash, but probably had a few curt words for Hammond about sensible tactics.

The French counter-attack continued the following morning, blunting the German offensive. Forrest's flight was airborne at 9.00 a.m. and ran into a dozen enemy scouts just north of Noyon. Hammond again impulsively chased an enemy machine down below the others, making himself an easy fifteenth victory for veteran German pilot Hans Pippart. The other Australian pilots didn't see what happened, but in 1920 an exhaustive search by the Red Cross for his bereaved parents confirmed that his machine 'crashed down burning and smashed' and that his killer, Pippart, was subsequently shot down and killed too. Forrest tried to explain to them what had happened: 'The theory we hold is that he, being a new man, did not realise how many Huns were there, and was so keen on getting his Hun that he went down and probably got some Huns onto him in doing so.' Forrest graciously assured Mr and Mrs Hammond that their boy was one of the most courageous pilots in the squadron. 'The trouble was that he was too brave', he explained—words they would no doubt cherish.[40]

The tragedy was followed by a triumph later in the morning. Roy Phillipps led his flight of six on a circus patrol south of Noyon. Over Ribbecourt, he surprised half a dozen triplanes unwittingly diving to attack a layer of Camels beneath them. In minutes he had shot down two, observing them both crash. Twenty minutes later, the circus came upon a pair of reconnaissance machines. Phillipps dived on to one of the machines and hit it, sending it down to crash and burn in an artillery barrage. Half an hour later, another flight of German scouts attempted to attack the lower level Camels. They were Fokker DVIIs—the latest German scout design. Their high-compression engines and incredibly good handling allowed them to perform at 20 000 feet with no loss of performance and climb more rapidly than anything in the sky. Phillipps led his flight down to rescue the British pilots. He positioned himself behind and above a DVII that was chasing a Camel and fired. It 'zoomed up and went into a spin'. Phillipps couldn't watch it because he had to evade another one on his tail, but a British pilot confirmed its crash. Although probably never known to Phillipps, German records suggest his victim was Jasta 26's commanding officer, Fritz Loerzer, who had shot down eleven aircraft.[41]

Roy Phillipps landed a squadron record holder. He had shot down four enemy aircraft in a day, all confirmed destroyed by other pilots.[42] He was now equal with his fellow flight commander, Forrest, with eleven confirmed victories and was also recommended for a Distinguished Flying Cross. They had the opportunity to celebrate as, after 12 June, the battle wound down and 'dud' weather scrubbed flying. While the Germans came to grips with another failed offensive, the Australians made friends with the French pilots on a neighbouring aerodrome and started drinking in their mess.

The French offered to take some of them to Paris on a dud afternoon. Murray Jones consented as long as they were back for the following morning's patrol and lent them a car. 'Our French friends excelled themselves,' remembered Adrian Cole. 'They knew their Paris and their Paris knew them.

Consequently we were feeling distinctly "jaded" when we assembled at 5.30 a.m. to return through the chilly mist.' Cole was driving and soon became lost. With all the others snoring in the back, he had to rely on his 'schoolboy French' to get directions. They arrived at the aerodrome just after dawn to find the skies clear and the mechanics running up their machines for a patrol. 'I am sure that Murray Jones' blunt choleric words could be heard in London, but the upshot of them was that I should "get weaving at once and get off the ground"', explained Cole. They pulled Sidcott suits over their dishevelled dress uniforms and took off right away. The patrol was uneventful, fortunately, because Cole fell asleep at the controls. 'It was probably the only patrol ever led by an unconscious flight commander, as was pointed out by the rest of the formation who had difficulty in following engine spins in formation.'[43]

'Bringing home the bacon': Balloon busting with No. 4 Squadron, May–July 1918

After being shelled out of Bruay at the end of April, No. 4 Squadron moved to Clairmarais North. Situated on the Flanders front, it became part of the 11th Wing attached to the Second British Army, then holding the line in front of Ypres.

The new aerodrome was literally a breath of fresh air. After the coal pits and brick stacks of Bruay, Clairmarais was, thought Knuckey, 'like coming from the city to the country, the atmosphere is beautiful and fresh'. The countryside was in spring bloom, and quaint villages, lanes and canals flanked the landing ground. Although an old aerodrome, it did have one welcome addition. Previous residents had built a washhouse over a creek that ran past the aerodrome. The men could get a hot shower there—a strange luxury, considered Knuckey, to have 'within earshot of the gunfire'.[44]

Another welcome addition was a neighbouring unit, No. 74 Squadron. It was home to a number of outstanding British pilots, including Captain Edward 'Mick' Mannock, one of the top scorers of the day (32 and counting) and a renowned tactician and teacher. 'He took upon himself the task of making all the pilots around him keen and aggressive,' recalled Harry Cobby. 'Several talks of his to the Australian pilots there were responsible for some fine aggressive shows against the enemy.'[45] Several veterans later saw Mannock's brief association with their squadron as a watershed in its development. Edgar McCloughry thought he 'played a great part in the success of the squadron' and that there wasn't an Australian pilot who didn't look up to him.[46]

Like the pilots in No. 2 Squadron, the Camel pilots found it difficult to draw enemy machines to fight during May, but unlike them weren't locked into the rigidity of circus work. Imbued with Mannock's influence, they worked hard to coax the enemy pilots to fight.

Cobby had the idea of attacking German observation balloons. Since the earliest days of the war, both sides had flown these lumbering, gas-filled dirigibles above their front lines, tethered to the ground by cables. Two observers occupied the basket, and from heights up to 4000 feet could telephone intelligence and shot corrections to artillery liaison officers below. A balloon was a tempting target to an amateur scout pilot, suspended there, huge and motionless above the front. But their benign appearance was deceptive. Scores of Archie batteries and machine-guns usually guarded them and the Germans sometimes packed the basket with explosives to detonate when British aircraft approached. It is little wonder Jack Wright considered balloon busting 'almost a suicide job'.[47]

Nevertheless, Cobby took a flight out on 21 May, determined to shoot one down. He arranged for the other pilots to stay 'upstairs' and cover him while he dived on to a line of balloons from 5000 feet above. To skew the German gunners' aim, he planned to head for one, fire from long range and then change tack and head for another. With a hand signal, he dived. 'Then the hate started. I think everything that could point upwards was hurling stuff at me.' Cobby's vertical descent made it difficult for the gunners to aim. He snapped off a quick burst at his 'decoy' and then turned on another, following it and firing as its crew winched it down. The gasbag refused to ignite and Cobby only broke off when it was almost on the ground. 'I fired a few bursts at the crew for luck and bolted across country to the lines before attempting to climb again.' Ironically, Cobby learned after landing that his decoy had gone down in flames. It was the squadron's first balloon, and started a trend for 'balloon strafing'.[48]

Cobby was promoted to command A Flight on 25 May, and five days later got another balloon. Having decided their patrol formations were too large, making it easy for the Germans to avoid them, he arranged to go out with just two other experienced pilots, Garnet Malley and Gillies Watson. They crossed the lines at dawn and went a long way over before turning around to work their way back. The first enemy machines they saw were a pair of Albatros scouts patrolling at 12 000 feet, 'not looking for anything harmful to arrive from the east'. Cobby led the trio in out of the morning sun, and moments later both enemy machines were spinning down out of control. Coming back across the lines, they dived on a line of balloons near Estaires. Cobby attacked three in succession, setting one alight. Malley got another.

On 1 June, Cobby and Watson tried out their tactic again. After bombing St Maur with eleven Camels, they left the formation and climbed above some balloons. Watson waited 'upstairs' while Cobby dived on one. It burst into flames at 2000 feet. He was climbing away when he noticed a lone German scout chasing a British Camel. He stalked it, Mannock style, keeping above and in the sun: 'I pulled the stick back and kicked on "hard boot" and dived flat out towards him, opening fire when at some twenty yards range.' Cobby was certain he had hit the pilot, as it went 'badly out of control'. He chased it, firing short bursts until it sideslipped down, sheered its left wings off on a balloon cable and spun into the ground. At this point Watson joined him, and the two pilots set upon another line of balloons near Merville. They didn't 'flame' any, but when the observers bailed out Watson fired at one, severing him from his parachute. 'It wasn't pleasant to see him finish the last couple of thousand feet by himself,' remarked Cobby.[49]

Cobby's exploits shaped the way other flights did business. Balloon busting came into vogue, although it remained extremely dangerous. Two experienced pilots were killed trying to emulate Cobby and Watson's tactic when they collided while diving on a balloon. Then, on 17 June, a new flight commander, Edgar McCloughry (the squadron commander's younger brother), tried it out with adverse results. He selected Jerry Martin, the flight's senior pilot, to dive on the balloons with him while the others covered them from above. They arrived over the enemy balloon line at 7000 feet. The sky appeared empty, so McCloughry gave the hand signal for Martin to dive with him:

I ground my teeth and went straight on to the balloon and then fired about 200 rounds from about 200 yards and the balloon went up in flames. Looking around I saw the one Martin tackled, smoking. I suddenly wondered why no Archie was firing at us, but soon found the reason: 17 Huns were coming down at us and already the remainder of my flight was mixed up with them.

An 'awful scrap' followed. McCloughry spotted a Pfalz following Martin down and went to his assistance, but had to break away when another appeared behind him. Hauling the Camel into a tight climbing turn, he wheeled around on to its tail and fired a long burst 'from almost on top of him'. The Pfalz tumbled, broke up and went down in pieces. Suddenly the sky was empty. The remaining German scouts had 'vanished almost as quick as they came' and Martin was nowhere to be seen.[50] McCloughry led the others home. That night, news arrived that Martin's Camel had ditched in no man's land but was riddled by German machine gunners before he could escape. Australian infantry crept out that night and retrieved his body.[51]

Cobby was furious about the whole affair. He began to harbour a simmering resentment towards Edgar McCloughry, suggesting in his 1942 memoir that his appointment as a flight commander over other, more experienced pilots in the unit was the result of nepotism.[52] Yet this seems unlikely. Although Edgar McCloughry had less front-line experience than some of Cobby's mates, he was in fact senior in rank to them all. He had held a commission since late 1915 and commanded a flight at a training unit in England. What's more, when McCloughry found out he was being posted to the squadron his brother commanded, he attempted (unsuccessfully) to transfer to No. 2 Squadron instead.[53]

Nevertheless, Cobby's resentment of 'the two brothers', as he referred to the McCloughys, continued for years. In the early 1920s, he wrote to the AFC's official historian alleging that Edgar deliberately fabricated claims. This doesn't really stack up either, though—other pilots in the squadron witnessed all but four of the 21 claims he eventually made—and Cutlack judiciously avoided the issue in the official history. Even more acrimonious perhaps, was Cobby's judgement of Major Wilfred McCloughry's command of the squadron:

> I feel it is beholden on me to mention that the CO of No. 4 Squadron had nothing, whatsoever to do with the handling of either his squadron or the formation as a whole. The squadron was led by myself—and the handling and leading of the whole organisation devolved upon me, this, at the strict injunction of the brigade headquarters.[54]

This is certainly a gross and most ungracious over-exaggeration, which has no currency in the official documents at all. Wilfred McCloughry's command style was indeed flexible, but this was appropriate given the initiative and enthusiasm of the pilots he commanded. To satisfy his superiors at wing headquarters, each day, the squadron was obliged to make double flight-sized (a dozen or so machines) 'OP and BPs'—offensive and bombing patrols—to sweep the skies behind the German line and then bomb troop billets along the Lys on the way home. Beyond these, though, McCloughry allowed his flight commanders to plan their own sorties. Ironically, this flexibility allowed Cobby to do, as he put it, 'a little private hunting' to augment his personal score. Following his promotion to flight commander (which he felt was 'long deferred'), he regularly took one of his good mates, Malley, Watson or a promising newer pilot named Elwyn 'Bo' King, on 'special' missions.[55] 'We did not always disclose what we were going to do on these occasions, in fact we did not always know ourselves, but relied on something turning up.'[56]

Indeed, with the latitude McCloughry allowed him, Cobby's score rose dramatically in June. Of the squadron's 28 claims, nine went to him. 'Our new tactics were bringing home the bacon,' he explained. Five enemy aircraft fell to his guns between 17 and 26 June, but his best streak came on 28 June. That afternoon, he did a 'special mission' with King over Merris. Coming around a bank of cloud, they spotted an LVG 100 feet below. Cobby dived first. His initial burst missed, but he then zoomed up underneath and fired into the floor of the pilot's cockpit: 'The machine swayed sideways into a steep sideslip and piled up just outside of Outtersteene.' Within moments, three Pfalz scouts had dropped out of the clouds above. Cobby 'splitarsed' about as they swept past firing. With the exception of one, they made it a 'hit and run' and kept diving for home. The one who was game to fight turned around and climbed back towards Cobby, firing as he came: 'I flicked my bus over into a half roll so quickly that he was directly under me as I came out, hastily pressed the triggers, and put in a long burst at him. He started to spin and almost instantly burst into flames.' Cobby and King returned to Clairmarais separately, each thinking the other had 'gone west'. They met up there, enjoyed a celebratory drink and took to the sky again at 6.30 p.m. Crossing the line at Merris, they found the sky dotted with small groups of German reconnaissance machines. Picking out a pair over Messines Ridge, they dived together and zoomed up underneath, firing. Cobby's target pitched forward and spun until it hit the ground. King's 'heeled over and dived'. He followed it down to where it crashed, near Cobby's kill.[57]

Four days later, Cobby shot down a balloon and a triplane while on a solo balloon hunting 'flip'. In six weeks, he had destroyed fifteen enemy aircraft, bringing his personal score to 20 and cementing his place as the AFC's most successful scout pilot. Fittingly, on this day—2 July 1918—he was gazetted for a Distinguished Flying Cross, and was, along with Henry Forrest and Roby Manuel of No. 2 Squadron (who had both claimed three enemy machines in June) and Thomas Simpson of No. 3 Squadron, in the first cohort of 39 pilots to receive this award.[58]

Harry Cobby was, without a doubt, among the AFC's truly outstanding figures. He was a superb pilot and marksman, and demonstrated exemplary initiative and fighting aggression over the summer months. This, along with his commitment to training and developing confidence in new pilots, made him a model flight leader.[59]

It is a shame, then, that Cobby couldn't recognise the talent of some of the men he served with. Edgar McCloughry was an impressive pilot and flight leader too, and despite some early mistakes he certainly proved his skill and courage as the summer wore on. His brother, Wilfred, was likewise a very capable flyer and commanding officer. His leadership of No. 4 Squadron earned him a Distinguished Service Order after the war and one of the few commissions issued by the post-war permanent RAF. Wilfred McCloughry eventually rose to the rank of Air Vice-Marshal and may have gone higher, had he not been killed in an air accident in 1943. On the other hand, it is ironic that Cobby, who joined the RAAF after the war, ended his career with an inauspicious leadership failure. In 1945, he was commanding the First Tactical Air Force in the Pacific when eight of his officers tendered identically worded resignations as a protest against the type of operations they were being ordered to fly. Cobby was relieved of his position and in the inquiry that followed, deemed to have 'failed to maintain a proper control over his command'. It was, as air force historian Alan Stephens recognised, 'a personal and institutional tragedy that a genuinely great figure of RAAF history had to end his career in such circumstances'.[60]

'A truly glorious fourth': No. 3 Squadron and the Battle of Hamel, 4 July 1918

By the beginning of May 1918, things were once again settling down on the Somme. Along the Australian Corps front, which ran between the Ancre River and Villers-Bretonneux, conventional trench warfare began to replace the chaos created by the German offensives.

The return to stalemate conditions reintroduced No. 3 Squadron to the traditional work of a corps squadron—that is, artillery observation, 'spark crawls' (flash patrols) and photographing their corps front each week. The return to routine by no means represented an easing of the pressure, though. The onset of summer, with its longer daylight hours and more consistent flying weather, produced a much more demanding flying roster. An airman's flying day in the summer of 1918 typically stretched from 3.30 a.m. to 9.30 p.m., seven days a week. As Stan Tuck put it, 'the nearest thing to a holiday is a wet day'.[61]

In addition to the longer hours, the RE8 crews found themselves hard pressed in the skies over the Somme Valley in May and June 1918. The German Army opposite them had a large concentration of enemy scout units, including JG I. Although Richthofen was dead, it still contained some of Germany's most talented pilots, equipped with Fokker triplanes and the new DVIIs. Both made the lumbering old 'Harry Tate' look very antiquated indeed.

On 6 May, C Flight's leader Henry Ralfe and veteran observer Bill Buckland were patrolling over Morlancourt when five scouts from JG I attacked and shot them down.[62] Jack Treacy was nearby and saw their 'machine come through the mist in flames'. Buckland jumped out before the RE8 buried itself 15 feet into the soft ground of the Somme. 'It was a bad show not having parachutes in those days,' reflected Treacy in 1970.[63]

Richthofen's circus struck again three days later. B Flight's leader, John Duigan, and Alec Paterson were photographing Villers-Bretonneux from 8000 feet when a pair of German scouts shot them down. Their first burst smashed Paterson's Lewis gun and the next one knocked him down. Duigan dived for home. Each time they made a firing pass, he would 'swing the machine about as much as possible and when they had finished ... make a little nearer to our lines'. At 4000 feet, the RE8's petrol tank (situated just behind the instrument panel) was hit and emptied fuel all over Duigan. He then felt 'two awful blows' as bullets went through his leg and shoulder and 'could hear the bullets striking the machine all over the place'. Putting the nose down, he crash-landed near some French trenches. 'Crawling from the machine,' he later told Garrett, 'he couldn't see a soul so in like Aussie custom he cooeed out.' Some French soldiers emerged and carried him and Paterson to a dugout. They had to stay until night because German snipers were covering the communication saps leading back. Nonetheless, Duigan convinced a French officer to send a runner to deliver their photographs to Australian Corps headquarters.[64]

Losses among the flight leaders mounted over the coming days. On the next attempt to photograph the line, A Flight's commander, Ern Jones, and Roy Hainsworth were savaged by six German scouts and were only narrowly saved by an intervening squadron of Camels. Jones' luck didn't hold out, though: four days later, on 20 May, he was attacked in the middle of an artillery patrol. His observer, 21-year-old Bert Taylor, was shot through the head and killed. Jones was wounded, but managed to get the RE8 down safely near the aerodrome. On 2 June, an Archie burst wounded Thomas Simpson, Duigan's replacement to lead B Flight.

The loss of flight commanders was always destabilising for a squadron. Losing four in just over three weeks seriously undermined No. 3 Squadron's morale. When Lawrence Wackett arrived in the middle of June to replace Simpson as B Flight's leader he found the airmen's spirits at rock bottom. 'The Fokker Triplane seemed principally responsible for this,' he surmised, 'together with the fact that owing to the big retreat in March we were now on new ground and pilots were required to take more risks in order to get it photographed as soon as possible.' Another problem, he noted, was that no one was getting much sleep on account of the nightly shelling and bombing of neighbouring towns.[65]

Wackett, as mentioned previously, flew with No. 1 Squadron in the Middle East in 1916 and 1917. A Duntroon graduate and talented engineer, he was responsible for several in-house inventions, including his 'homemade' Lewis gun turret. In early 1917, Wackett's ingenuity secured him an invitation to work for the Air Ministry's Technical Development Department in Britain. He spent the following year at Orfordness Experimental Station in Suffolk, which tested the RFC's new equipment prior to entering service. 'It was a great opportunity for a newcomer from Australia,' thought Wackett. 'Every day I was mixing with men on the highest technical qualifications, including the leading designers of aircraft.'[66]

Shortly after arriving at No. 3 Squadron, Wackett received orders to report to Bertangles to meet with the Australian Corps' commanding officer, Lieutenant General John Monash:

> General Monash had heard of me from Duntrooners on his staff and sent for me to say that he was planning offensive operations and wished to reduce casualties by having ammunition conveyed by air to troops in the front line during battle. He asked if I could carry out such a task and I replied that I could and would be ready within a few days to give a demonstration.[67]

Within a few days, Wackett had a solution. He intended the RE8 to carry two 40 lb boxes of machine-gun ammunition (1000 rounds each) on a modified version of the standard RAF bomb rack. Cloth parachutes were rolled and stored in half oil drums attached to the aircraft's underside. They were fixed to the crates by rope; when the pilot pulled the bomb release toggle, the crates fell away, pulling the parachutes with them. It was, thought Air Mechanic Frank Rawlinson, 'a very clever improvisation'.[68] Monash brought his superior, General Sir Henry Rawlinson (Fourth Army's commanding officer), to No. 3 Squadron's aerodrome at Villers-Bocage to watch a demonstration. 'They stood on the flying field,' Wackett recalled, 'while I deposited two large cases of ammunition close beside them, from 500 feet.' It was clear to Wackett that he had won the generals' favour as soon as he landed. They walked out to meet him as he climbed from the cockpit. 'Can you do that on a large scale in a month's time?' Rawlinson asked. Wackett replied that he could, if given the authority, staff and equipment. 'Go ahead,' replied Rawlinson. 'You can have everything necessary to do the job.'[69]

Wackett took command of a section in No. 3 Squadron to manufacture the parachutes and modified bomb racks. Trucks delivered six sewing machines, rolls of aeroplane fabric, cordage, steel strip and hoop iron, bomb racks and hundreds of boxes of Vickers machine-gun belts. He set up a 'factory' in one of the hangars and put a flight sergeant in charge to supervise day and night shifts.[70]

At this stage, no one in the squadron, including Wackett, knew specifically what the parachutes were for. What they did know, though, was that since early May the Australian Corps had enjoyed some stunning successes on the Somme. Adopting an informal tactic known as 'peaceful penetration', small parties of Australian infantry had been creeping out through the long crops separating the lines and capturing German outposts. Sometimes the work was done by souvenir-famished individuals, sometimes by groups of mates without the sanction of their officers. Although the gains were small—an enemy outpost here and there—by the end of June the Australian line had advanced considerably and the morale of the Germans opposite them was crumbling. One nervous German soldier described the Australians as 'very quick and cunning' in a letter to his mother: 'They creep up in the night like cats to our trenches so that we don't notice them. Last night they were in our trench and killed two men and dragged one away with them.'[71]

The tactic was particularly effective north of the Somme, where the undulating ground and high crops allowed the diggers to move about in no man's land undetected. South of the Somme, though, where the Australian line ran across a high, bare plateau in front of Villers-Bretonneux, the terrain was less conducive to peaceful penetration. By the middle of June, the Australian line had a bend in it, the line north of the Somme being some 2 kilometres further east than it was south of the river. Monash's intention was to straighten his corps' line by capturing the village of Hamel, immediately south of the river. The job could be done, he reckoned, with just the equivalent of one under-strength division of infantry, heavily supported by the 'mechanical' arms: 639 guns, 60 tanks and five squadrons of aircraft. The objectives were strictly limited, just 2 kilometres deep on a 7 kilometre frontage and, as at Cambrai, there would be no preliminary bombardment to alert the enemy.

Monash held a large conference on 30 June at his headquarters to brief the officers and staff of the various formations involved in the operation. It was a huge affair—a reflection on Monash's insistence on meticulous planning and belief that everyone involved should know the plan thoroughly. There were over 250 officers present and it took four and a half hours to cover the 133 agenda items.[72] Major Blake was on leave, so Wackett (acting as squadron commander) represented No. 3 Squadron. 'It was a remarkable experience for me,' he later recalled, being a 22-year-old captain in a room of colonels and generals. 'In amazement I heard each of the commanders recite his part of the battle to the corps commander.'[73]

When it was Wackett's turn, he explained how No. 3 Squadron would support the infantry during the battle. A and B Flights would fly 'contact patrols', to report on the progress of the battle. C Flight would meanwhile fly 'counter-attack patrols' to watch for enemy reinforcements and send zone calls or drop bombs on any, which should attempt to join the battle. The most interesting aspect of Wackett's briefing concerned his new invention. A dozen RE8s and crews from No. 9 Squadron RAF would be attached to No. 3 Squadron to drop crates of ammunition to Australian troops on the battlefield. Monash was pleased to hear that Wackett's improvised factory had 200 000 rounds ready to drop. Keeping his troops' Vickers guns supplied with ammunition was crucial to fend off German counter-attacks. In past battles, it had taken two men a dangerous journey across 4 or 5 kilometres of open ground to deliver a single box of 1000 rounds—a quantity one Vickers could fire in less than five minutes.[74] From No. 3 Squadron's aerodrome, an aircraft could drop two boxes at the battlefront and land again inside 30 minutes.

Orders arrived at Villers-Bocage on the evening of 3 July indicating the attack would commence at 3.10 a.m. the following morning. Francis Lock and Bob Barrett were first to take off, leaving the ground on a counter-attack patrol ten minutes before zero hour. They were over Hamel ten minutes later when the artillery barrage started. Twenty-three-year-old Barrett had only joined the squadron in mid-May, and this was the first 'real bit of war' he had seen.

For kilometres to the north and south, Barrett saw the gun flashes. 'They lit up our machine,' he explained, 'and when we flew over the guns it was almost like day, although the first glimmers of dawn hadn't appeared.' Within moments, the dust and smoke from the 550 metre-deep barrage joined up with the clouds and blotted out the lines of infantry rising up from their trenches and advancing steadily behind the tanks.

Lock and Barrett were 9 kilometres into 'Hunland' before they could see anything on the ground. This was, Barrett later explained to his mother, 'an almost unheard of distance for the machines we fly'. He admitted feeling 'very lonely', being the only crew over that far and completely hidden from their line by the barrage smoke. They got on with their job, though, turning their guns and bombs on to 'everything they saw'. They strafed a train first, stopping it on its tracks, and then silenced some machine gun nests with bombs. Next, they spotted a pair of German field guns being pulled towards the battlefront: 'We shot the horses of one and it was overturned and the other seemed in difficulties.' German machine guns stitched the dark sky around them with tracers. At one point, Barrett counted fourteen streams arcing up towards them. 'They leave a smoke trail behind them, and if I had not been so personally involved, I should have been more appreciative of the display.' Crossing back across the battlefield, Lock flew so low their eyes began running from tear gas. 'I have not heard of anyone being gassed in the air before,' wrote Barrett.[75]

By the time Lock and Barrett landed at Villers-Bocage, another eight crews from No. 3 Squadron had taken off. Three from A and B Flights flew low over the battlefield at 4.45 a.m. sounding klaxons, the signal for the infantry to mark their position with flares. The response was a line of twinkling lights on the dark ridge beyond Hamel and Vaire Wood indicating the diggers had captured all their objectives in just under 95 minutes. The pilots of these machines then dropped reports in message bags at divisional headquarters. Frank Rawlinson was nearby with a salvage team to retrieve crashed aircraft. He watched the RE8s circle about, signalling with the 'deep "ur ur" blurting' of their klaxons. It made him think of 'a particularly large masculine bird in great pain from indigestion'. They were doing a 'marvellous job', he thought.[76]

The battle wasn't over yet, though, and now the critical consolidation phase began. At 5.45 a.m., British crews started dropping ammunition on predetermined locations behind the Australian objectives, marked with a canvas 'N'. Individual machine gun crews in the front line could also signal for ammunition by laying out a 'V'. Wackett's invention worked, and during the day the eight crews dropped 93 crates of ammunition on to the battlefield.[77] Accuracy varied, of course, with one box landing within 10 feet of a machine gun post while another couple drifted across no man's land and into the enemy's lines. Nevertheless, Australian infantry commanders reported the aerial resupply to be 'of great assistance' and Monash wrote of its 'obvious economy in lives and wounds'.[78]

Two British carrier planes were shot down during the morning, one by German scouts that appeared over Hamel in large numbers at 9.30 a.m. and the other in more remarkable circumstances. When its pilot released his crates, one of the parachutes tangled on the wing. Australian infantry then saw him climb out of his cockpit on to the wing (presumably while the observer took the control stick) and free the entanglement. Moments later, the aircraft plunged into the ground from 100 feet, apparently hit by an artillery shell in mid-flight. Both men were killed. One Australian soldier managed to take a photo of the RE8 diving headlong into the ground, moments before it crashed (see Plate 26).[79]

No. 3 Squadron kept three crews over Hamel all day on counter-attack patrol. They signalled the Australian Corps' artillery with zone calls whenever enemy reinforcements or guns approached the battlefront. Seventeen enemy batteries were 'neutralised' in this way, and the Australian airmen bombed and strafed others. 'Altogether,' noted the squadron's war diarist, 'things were made most unpleasant for the enemy' and there were no counter-attacks.[80]

In the evening, No. 3 Squadron photographed the new front line. The Australian infantry now occupied the high ridge east of Hamel, giving them a commanding view of the German positions beyond. Australian casualties numbered about 1400, and while enemy casualties are not known precisely, they almost certainly exceeded 2000. In any case, 1600 were captured, along with 200 of their machine guns and mortars.[81] Like the rest of the plan, No. 3 Squadron's part in the 4 July battle went more or less like clockwork. It was, noted Knox in the squadron's record book, 'a truly glorious fourth'.[82]

Hamel was a small battle, but it has significance in the history of 1918 that far outweighs its size. In addition to being a milestone in the history of battlefield resupply from the air, it drew together infantry, tanks, aircraft and artillery in a stunningly successful combination. British commanders studied Monash's Hamel plan in the following weeks, and features of it would crop up in tactical pamphlets and offensive schemes in the future. As the distinguished First World War scholar John Terraine described it, Hamel was 'a little master piece, casting a long shadow before it'.[83] But Hamel was something else too. It was the first offensive the British Expeditionary Force had mounted since the Battle of Cambrai the previous November. With its emphasis on limited objectives and consolidation of gains over sweeping breakthrough, it corrected the mistakes of that operation and indicated a way forward to defeating the German Army on the Western Front. It was also the culmination of the peaceful penetration operations, which made it clear that the Germans were scraping the bottom of the barrel in terms of manpower and morale.

Monash congratulated Wackett for his part in the Battle of Hamel. He devoted two pages to it in his widely read memoir, *The Australian Victories in France, 1918*, and secured Wackett a £300 'reward' for his invention. Wackett, who after the war would be hugely influential in the Australian aviation industry, was proud of his achievement and lived to see it cement a closer operational relationship between pilots and soldiers: 'I was the first to put the simple idea into practice, though in World War II such schemes were used most extensively.'[84]

12

'DOWN WHERE THE WAR IS BEING WON'
The British offensive, July and August 1918

80th Wing's raid on Haubourdin aerodrome on 16 August 1918. The aircraft is a Bristol Fighter from No. 88 Squadron, which stayed above to cover the AFC squadrons and take photographs. *AWM P02163.003*

> The war, after all, might finish within a reasonable time.
>
> —Captain Arthur 'Harry' Cobby, No. 4 Squadron, Australian Flying Corps

'To the rest of the world they are most jealously united': The Australian scout squadrons at Reclinghem, July–August 1918

At the end of June 1918, the two Australian scout squadrons came together at Reclinghem aerodrome, in the Pas-de-Calais region of northern France. No. 4 Squadron's pilots landed there at noon on 30 June after a fifteen-minute flight from Clairmarais. No. 2 Squadron's SE5as had just arrived and the pilots greeted each other warmly. 'There was great hand shaking between the two Australian squadrons,' recorded Vern Knuckey. 'Everyone was very pleased to think that in future we were to work in conjunction instead of having an English squadron on the same aerodrome as ourselves.'

Reclinghem was not an established aerodrome. It was just a conveniently flat, bare field on a rise between the tiny villages of Reclinghem and Bomy. 'Everything was as we expected,' recalled Edgar McCloughry, 'just the hangar standing and nothing else.' The men of both squadrons had to pitch tents among some fruit trees on the edge of the aerodrome and make do with a few scratch-built huts for messing arrangements.

The villages didn't offer much in the way of hospitality, either. At the foot of the hill to the north was Reclinghem. 'Dirty and small is the best way to describe it and not worth walking down to visit,' is what Knuckey had to say about it. In the other direction, the larger village of Bomy appeared to offer better prospects until the Australians learned they weren't welcome there. A British military police unit was billeted there, and its commanding officer declared the village off limits to the Australians as soon as he learned of their arrival. 'When asked the reason for such an action,' explained Knuckey, 'his only excuse was that he did not want his men knocked about.'[1]

The two Australian squadrons had come together on Reclinghem's bare hilltop to join the newly established 80th Wing. Under the command of Lieutenant Colonel Louis Strange, a British pilot who had gone to France with the RFC in August 1914, the wing also included two British units—No. 46 (flying Camels) and No. 103 (DH9 bombers). The wing was, in turn, part of the RAF's 10th Brigade, which was attached to the British Fifth Army. The Australians' sector ranged from the Nieppe Forest to La Bassée; a familiar hunting ground for No. 4 Squadron's pilots, who had been in the area since April.

The standard work of both squadrons continued to be 'o-pips'—two- to three-hour offensive patrols on the enemy's side of the lines at least twice a day. No. 2 Squadron worked at high altitudes (above 17 000 feet) to take advantage of the SE5a's high compression engine and diving performance, while No. 4 Squadron patrolled below 8000 feet, where the Camel was more manoeuvrable than anything else in the sky. German squadrons continued to be finicky, though. The Australians typically put this down to cowardice on the German pilots' behalf, but the truth is that, since June, fuel and airframe shortages had curbed the work of all German flying units. Their high command set a monthly consumption of 7000 gallons for each squadron and ordered them 'to avoid all flights that were not urgent and to make a great limitation on photographic reconnaissance'.[2]

The Australian pilots quickly earned the respect of their new wing commander. Lieutenant Colonel Strange saw them in a romantic light, believing they possessed a resilience and resourcefulness from having to 'fend for themselves against known and unknown dangers in the wide, open, lonely spaces of their continent'. He considered the Australian pilot's 'sense of initiative' his most outstanding characteristic, and endeavoured to give them latitude to pursue their own operational style. Strange visited Reclinghem regularly to find out what they were doing, and learned to 'adapt Wing Routine Orders to suit their methods and at the same time satisfy the demands made from higher up'.[3]

Edgar McCloughry was one flight commander who relished the flexibility of Strange and 80th Wing's staff. 'They allowed our squadron to do much as we pleased at first,' he recalled. 'This was my great opportunity, and I did not delay in getting my idea of small formation into practice.'

McCloughry's flight began experimenting with a more flexible approach to the standard 'o-pip'. He would take a small formation across the lines at height, surprise any enemy patrols or reconnaissance machines from above and the east, then return back across the lines under 500 feet to bomb and shoot up enemy troops in their camps and billets along the River Lys. After some successful experiments with his deputy, Gordon Jones-Evans, McCloughry found 'it was quite safe to come down to these low altitudes and that it only wanted a first trial and one gained wonderful confidence, besides getting real sport out of it'.[4] No. 4 Squadron's other flights and No. 2 Squadron also adopted the tactic, dubbing it the 'destroyer patrol'.

One of McCloughry's new pilots, Jack Wilkinson, had his first taste of ground strafing on a destroyer patrol in early July. They were still dangerous, despite the dose of confidence his flight commander intended it to imbue in him:

> I saw a white Verey light fall away from McCloughry's machine in front. Well, I thought, this is where we see what shooting up trenches is like. Down we went in a steep dive, still in formation, until I could clearly see the shell pocked ground in front of Merville. As we came lower, Archie sent up innumerable shells but they exploded in a long line above. We were moving too quickly for him. At about 1000 feet the formation broke up and indulged in individual firing into the Hun trenches. Now and then a heap of earth would rise lazily from the ground as a shell burst, but, now that we were too low for the anti aircraft guns to fire at us, we became running targets for their machine guns on the ground which were clacking away, full bore.

Wilkinson made 'two quick dives with guns hammering' but, while wheeling around for a third, collected a burst of machine gun fire which all but severed the control wires in one of his wings. He nursed his Camel back to Reclinghem, working the ailerons with just three strands of wire.[5]

The lack of observation points in the pan-flat terrain around the River Lys meant the German Air Service devoted its limited resources to artillery observation and photography. No. 4 Squadron's 'destroyer patrols' encountered numerous German two-seaters at low altitudes, as well as plenty of balloons. Balloon busting remained a popular pursuit among the Camel pilots, although they found that since May, the Germans had brought additional anti-aircraft units into the sector, making a risky job even more dangerous. An early attempt at bringing down a Lys balloon nearly killed Cobby on 9 July. 'My machine got shot to pieces for my trouble and I had my work cut out in getting home safely.' He landed with most of the control wires shot away and 'forty odd bullet holes in different parts of the old bus'.[6] Five days later, Reg Nelson was shot down and taken prisoner trying the same thing, at nearby Estaires.[7]

It was McCloughry who once again devised a solution. Building on Cobby's tactic of surprising balloons by diving on them, he thought of reconnoitring the balloon lines just before sunset, to note their position on the ground. Before dawn the following morning, he would then take a couple of pilots back to the locations and, just as it grew light, dive on them as they were being inflated. One of McCloughry's pilots, Roy Youdale, described the process in a letter.

> Just as a faint light appears, we shut off engines and glide right down nearly to earth without being detected. A few well placed shots and two balloons, tethered to the ground, burst into flames. We are attacked by all sorts of guns, machine and otherwise, but we head for home with all taps turned on, landing at the 'drome at 4.30 am, turning straight into bed and having another four hours sleep before breakfast, which is at 9.00 am.[8]

Again, the pilots discussed the tactic in the mess, and other flights started using and adapting it. The absence of German Jastas in the first few weeks of July imbued the Australians with confidence, and they began opting to patrol in pairs or singly to get the best results. Described in the squadron record book as 'Special Missions', these soon began to occupy a larger proportion of the squadron's flying hours (and successful combats) than the traditional 'Offensive Patrol'. Official historian Charles Bean described No. 4 Squadron's fluid tactics when he visited Reclinghem in mid-August: 'They found when they went out with five that they found no Germans. Then they began to go out with 4; still no Germans. They then reduced to 3 and lastly to 2. They said that they began to find a few Germans then.'[9] A 'few Germans' indeed. No. 4 Squadron's first month at Reclinghem was its most successful yet—the squadron claimed 38 enemy aircraft. The lion's share went to McCloughry, who had a remarkable streak in July, bringing down ten enemy aircraft and a pair of balloons. He was awarded a Distinguished Flying Cross, and no doubt would have kept scoring in August, but was shot in the leg in a dogfight on the final day of the month and spent the next few weeks recovering.

No. 2 Squadron's month was, by contrast, nowhere near as exciting. There were few German aircraft to be found at 17 000 feet, and a combination of mechanical problems and thunderstorms kept them from getting up as often as their colleagues in No. 4 Squadron. The SE5a pilots made only eleven claims on their high-altitude patrols—one for every four the Camel pilots made at lower altitudes. The SE5a pilots were frustrated at being outdone by No. 4 Squadron. During his visit to Reclinghem in August, Bean detected 'a considerable rivalry' between the two squadrons to get victories. He thought them 'a strange pair', likening them to twins who, although fiercely competitive, appeared 'to the rest of the world most jealously united'.[10]

Unseasonably wild weather in the late summer gave some of the Australians their first experience of flying through thunderstorms in an open cockpit. Thomas Edols, a newly posted Camel pilot, found himself in one in mid-July—'a thing which I hope never to have to do again,' he told his sweetheart in a letter:

> It looked like a solid wall of water. I offered a prayer to the effect that it was a thunderstorm and not a tidal wave or some other monstrosity. But when we entered it I was still undecided as it was mostly water. And oh the lightning, it made one see pink. However we eventually arrived through it and I nearly fouled one of the steeples on a neighbouring church. When we landed we found a great deal of paint had been knocked off the planes by the rain, and all the propellers had the binding fabric torn off them.

Edols' flight all made it back physically safe, but the experience had clearly distressed at least one of his comrades. 'One chap was most amusing,' explained Edols. 'When he tried to go to sleep after it, he would start kicking and thinking that he was back in it again.'[11]

Thomas Edols was among a number of fresh faces in the Australian scout squadrons in the mid-summer of 1918. The RAF's policy was to keep pilots at the front for between nine months and a year (depending on their health) before sending them on 'home establishment' leave, to work as instructors for a few months' 'rest'. The new faces replaced tired ones as the few remaining 'originals' went back to Britain. No. 2 Squadron lost its two top scorers, Henry Forrest and Roy Phillipps, to home establishment, and No. 4 Squadron lost an experienced flight leader in Garnet Malley.

A shortage of Australian cadets to replace them meant British pilots (known to the Australians as 'leppers') stood in as temporary replacements.

Jack Wilkinson was one, a twenty-year-old from Yorkshire. The 'crude' language the colonial pilots used initially took him aback:

> The word 'bastard' was continually on their lips, but they thought no more of it than we would of 'blighter'. 'Had a good scrap this morning?' Waddy would say as he climbed out of his Camel, loosening the chinstrap of his helmet. 'Get a Hun?' 'You bet!' was the reply. 'Fried the bastard' . . . Or there would be a group listening to Taplin, who specialised in stalking enemy two seaters. 'And how did it finish, Tap?' 'Well,' he drawled, 'I went into the cloud again and when I came out the bastard was just above me. So I pulled up the bus and blew the observer's bum through the back of his neck!'

The exit of some of the veterans also opened the way for a new crop of talent to emerge. Notable in No. 2 Squadron was Roby Manuel, a 22-year-old farmer from Kerang in Victoria. He had joined the squadron in February, the German spring offensives providing him with a demanding but effective apprenticeship. By the end of July he had claimed eight enemy machines, earned a Distinguished Flying Cross and replaced Forrest as C Flight's commander. His equivalent in No. 4 Squadron was Roy 'Bo' King. One year older than Manuel, and originally from Bathurst, he was in charge of a motoring business when the war began. He had also arrived just before Operation Michael, scored slowly at first but then got into his stride at the end of June. By the end of July, he had six victories, and within another month, thirteen. Cobby liked Bo King immensely, and recalled how his impressive career almost ended before it had begun. King was a large man and had trouble fitting in the cockpit. He couldn't pull the stick all the way back to get his tail down when landing. 'The CO cursed him every time he landed,' remembered Cobby, 'and there was some speculation that he might go home—but he proved himself an impressive pilot.'[12]

Despite being another 'original', Harry Cobby soldiered on throughout the summer, only taking a fortnight leave in Scotland in July. Before going, though, he claimed another six enemy aircraft, bringing his personal tally to 24. Returning from Scotland at the beginning of August, Cobby learned through an official RAF communiqué that he had been approved for the award of not one, but two bars to his Distinguished Flying Cross.[13] It was an unprecedented honour. Not only was Cobby the first pilot in the RAF's history to be awarded the medal three times, but he would also be one of just four pilots during the war to do so (Ross Smith from No. 1 Squadron being another).

Of course, there was a boisterous celebration in the officers' mess. The Australian pilots had, according to McCloughry, 'a reputation for skylarking and enjoying themselves', and their mess at Reclinghem was known to units throughout the region for throwing wild 'binges'. On this occasion, guests included the staff from 80th Wing Headquarters and a senior RAF chaplain. 'This guest,' recalled Jack Wright, 'was very stiff and unbending, very stuffy in fact.' Cobby saw it as something of a personal mission to show the lemonade-sipping padre how to have a good time: 'Leave him to me boys,' he told the other pilots, 'I'll get him in the right mood.' Cobby had the barman mix a 'Widows Kiss'—a squadron specialty 'of deceptive appearance and delayed reaction' containing milk and absinthe. As Wright recalled, the old man accepted it 'very tentatively', smelling it and then sipping it carefully. He finished the cocktail and accepted another, and then some more after that. The night culminated with behaviour most unbecoming of an Anglican clergyman:

> Well, he certainly got in the mood of the party ... in a most hilarious and uninhibited act. Our Group Captain padre was up on the table in the Mess conducting an auction of an article he held in his hand for which he was soliciting bids. The article was a well-known and universally accepted contraceptive device!

The night finished with the pilots of No. 4 Squadron carting the unconscious padre and some of his high-ranking colleagues to their car. 'They came to other parties again,' explained Wright, 'but we never saw the group captain padre again.'[14]

'The black day of the German Army': The Battle of Amiens, 8–11 August 1918

As far as British Fourth Army's commander, General Henry Rawlinson, was concerned, the Battle of Hamel was irrefutable proof that the German Army's morale and defensive capabilities were deteriorating rapidly. Moreover, it was evidence that his army now had the resources and tactics to shatter the enemy's front and force them back to their pre-spring offensive line. On the very day after Hamel, Rawlinson secured permission from General Headquarters to draft plans for another offensive in the Somme sector along the lines of the Hamel plan. This would be a substantially bigger affair, though.

After a series of revisions involving political wrangling between the British, French and supreme allied high commands, Rawlinson's scheme turned out to be a coalition effort, involving the British Fourth and French First Armies along a 30 kilometre front, extending from the Ancre, across the Somme and south to Moreuil. The British would advance in the north, parallel to the Somme, with three corps in the line: the Australian Corps between the Somme River and the Villers-Chaulnes railway; the British III Corps to their north (on the other side of the Somme); and the Canadian Corps immediately to their south.

Rawlinson's objectives were ambitious: a single-day advance of 11 kilometres in three stages. In the Australian sector, the 3rd and 2nd Divisions would advance side by side, 3.5 kilometres to the 'Green Line'. They would pause for two hours and dig in, while the field artillery moved forward to get in range of the next objective. Fresh troops (the 4th and 5th Divisions) would then 'leap frog' through the first wave and advance 5.5 kilometres to the second objective—the 'Red Line'. If enemy resistance broke down completely, these troops would then push forward another 1800 metres to occupy the 'Blue Line', the day's 'ultimate' objective.

Rawlinson's plan for what became known as the Battle of Amiens was based explicitly on the Hamel plan. To surprise the enemy, there would be neither pre-registration of artillery on to enemy targets, nor a preliminary bombardment. Fourth Army's 2070 guns would remain silent until 'zero hour'. The infantry would, as at Hamel, be preceded by tanks (537 of them) and would have ample air support. The RAF and Aéronautique Militaire had an overwhelming superiority in numbers on the Amiens front—1904 aircraft to oppose the German Air Service's 365 machines.[15] On 29 July, as the multitudes of men, machines and materiel quietly deployed behind the battlefront, Rawlinson's headquarters finalised the scheme and set 'zero hour' for 4.20 a.m. on 8 August.

In the fortnight prior to the offensive, No. 3 Squadron shouldered a heavy workload to help the Australian Corps prepare for battle. First, there was a concern with secrecy. Special flights patrolled 'continuously by day over the whole Australian Corps area in order to detect and report any activity which might disclose to the enemy our preparation for the attack'.[16] Then there were artillery patrols (255 of them in July) to identify the location of as many enemy guns as possible prior to the attack. By the eve of the battle, the British gunners knew the precise location of 504 of the 530 enemy guns facing them.[17] Finally, there were photography patrols. The squadron photographed the Australian Corps front and, with the wing's photographic section, produced 90 000 prints.[18] These were overlaid with topographic lines and each Australian infantry platoon received one, depicting the section of terrain they were required to advance across. It is no wonder Air Mechanic Frank Rawlinson recalled seeing 'his' pilot 'off with the first rays of daylight and back after the setting sun, for a good while' prior to the Battle of Amiens.[19]

On the afternoon of 7 August, Major Blake briefed the airmen on the plans for the following day. A Flight was responsible for artillery observation and B Flight for counter-attack patrols. Both would also drop smoke along the south bank of the Somme to protect the Australians' left flank from German guns on the high ground across the river. C Flight would do the contact patrols. Using klaxon horns fitted to their RE8s, the pilots would signal the infantry to light flares and then drop reports of their progress to corps headquarters. In this, the airmen of C Flight would play a critical role in the direction of the battle. If the infantry advanced as far as Rawlinon planned, they would be well beyond the range of telephone cables for several days.

A heavy mist blanketed the battlefield at dawn on 8 August 1918. Fourth Army's 2070 guns thundered to life at 4.20 a.m., shaking the earth and lighting up the sky. A British bomber pilot was above the sea of grey mist when it began:

> The landscape was a mass of flame, the stabs of fire from the guns and shells only lighting up a haze of smoke. It was an inspiring sight and many were the shells that swept unseen past our planes. The greatest day of the war in the air had begun.[20]

Eight No. 3 Squadron crews took off on smoke dropping sorties between 4.00 a.m. and 6.00 a.m., but ironically couldn't even find their targets because of the mist already covering the landscape. Half the crews couldn't find their way back to the aerodrome and landed around the countryside. 'One of ours flew nearly to the coast, before he could get out of it,' recalled Frank Rawlinson. 'They were down on roads and on cottages, and one chap who had spotted our Verey lights made a marvellous landing.' In spite of the fog, the rest of the RAF got on with its job too. Rawlinson and his fellow mechanics were 'heartened' to count 400 British aircraft passing over their aerodrome on their way to the battlefield that morning.[21]

The sun started burning the mist off at 9.00 a.m., and half an hour later James Smith and Oscar Witcomb took off on a contact patrol to check on 4th Division's progress on the left. Their report was promising. The first objective was secure, and the Australian infantry and tanks were well on their way to the second objective. 'Apparently not much opposition,' they recorded, 'very little shelling' and the enemy in front of the advancing Australian line was limited to 'isolated groups'. The German defenders, it appeared, had been completely overwhelmed by the artillery barrage and rapid advance. Smith saw a group of 200 enemy prisoners and 'several groups of 50' heading west in the wake of the advancing Australians. He dropped copies of his report at divisional, corps and then army headquarters before landing.[22]

Meanwhile, Lock and Barrett were on their way to see how the 5th Division was getting along, on the right side of the advance:

> We got nearly to the place the infantry were thought to have reached when one of our magnetos failed, and the engine did not have sufficient power to fly us home. We had to land in a field, just near Villers Bretonneux, and although it looked all right from the air, we found it was full of shell holes, one of which we struck when we landed. The machine hopelessly crashed, but my pilot and I got off with a few bruises, although my right arm is still sore owing to the knock it got.[23]

A mobile 'breakdown gang' of squadron mechanics was on the scene shortly afterwards to retrieve Lock, Barrett and the bits and pieces of their RE8.

The next contact patrols went up an hour later, and just before 11.00 a.m. reported Australian troops digging in along their second objective. They faced 'not much opposition' and 'only light shelling' from the enemy, suggesting the advance would continue to the final objective.[24]

As the morning wore on, enemy Jastas arrived from neighbouring sectors and made their presence felt. Hugh Foale and Frank Sewell, both ex-infantry and both 20 years old, successfully identified the 5th Division digging in on its final objective at noon. Just as they were about to leave and drop their reports at divisional headquarters, Foale spotted a pair of Fokker DVIIs strafing the diggers. Perhaps because of an affinity he felt with his old comrades, he turned the lumbering RE8 around and circled above them. Sewell opened fire with his Lewis gun and 'one enemy aircraft dived steeply and burst into flames'.[25]

The other noon contact patrol crew, Edward Bice and John Chapman, were further north checking on 4th Division's progress when nine Fokker biplanes bounced them. Later in the day, advancing Australian troops found their bodies beside their wrecked RE8. A chaplain buried them on the battlefield, and fortunately (and this wasn't always the case) recorded the location. After the war, exhumation units moved them into Heath Cemetery at Harbonniéres. Apparently, their remains couldn't be distinguished, as today they lie together in the same plot. Ted Bice's death was especially tragic, and not just because he was an only son. He had enlisted in the infantry in early 1915 and survived a string of military blunders at Gallipoli, Poziéres and Bullecourt, only to die on his nation's most triumphant day in the war. Bice had also recently married a girl in London. She was five and a half months pregnant with his daughter when he was killed.

When Bice and Chapman failed to return, another C Flight crew set out to determine 4th Division's progress. They flew over the battlefield at 200 feet and used their klaxon to call for flares. A line of them, along with waved hankies and flashed tin plates, indicated that the majority of the 4th Division was digging in on its final objective too. During the afternoon, another crew photographed the Australian Corps' new front line, 11 kilometres beyond where it had been that morning and with little enemy opposition before it. The Canadians had likewise secured all of their objectives, although north of the Somme, III Corps had a tough time and had not kept up with the Australians south of the river.

A and B Flights worked hard throughout the day but found their services of limited value. The Australian infantry had surprised the German artillery lines in the dawn mist, capturing 173 guns.[26] There were few targets, therefore, for A Flight to direct fire onto. Likewise, B Flight didn't see any counter-attacks develop, so instead dropped their bombs on retreating troops and motor transport.

The impressions recorded by observer Tom Prince capture a sense of the tidal wave of men and machinery the Germans faced at Amiens on 8 August 1918:

> As we flew to the forward area, we saw all of it spread out below us, a panorama denied to the limited view of the men on the ground. First there was the motor transport crowding the long straight roads and bringing up the stores and ammunition to the dumps. Then there were the tractors hauling the heavy guns forward after each engagement. The field artillery, however, had still to gallop their horse drawn batteries into action. The infantry continued to advance in artillery formation or extended order. But the fighting men had learned at last to trust the new deadly machines that had come to their aid. These were the tanks, crawling like beetles over the terrain. No longer were barbed wire and trenches great obstacles to the attackers. These armoured vehicles made light work of such defences. They crushed wire and crossed the trenches, with the infantry following in their wakes, to storm the former impregnable barriers of the German lines.

Reflecting on it in 1970, Prince considered the battle to be 'the end of an era'. It 'marked a stage in the transition from the pace of a man and a horse to the swifter progress of mechanised war'.[27]

The German commander Erich Ludendorff famously wrote in his memoirs that 8 August 1918 was 'a black day for the German Army in the history of the war'. Likewise, the official German history of the battle (*Die Katastrophe des 8 August 1918*) acknowledged ruefully that 'the heaviest defeat suffered by the German army since the beginning of the war had become an accomplished fact'. What was perhaps most disturbing to German commentators was the number of their soldiers who surrendered readily. 'Men had sought safety in flight,' is how the German official historian summed it up, an interpretation the Allied statistics certainly support.[28] Fourth Army and the French First Army had taken about 18 500 prisoners during the day and, according to German sources, had killed or seriously wounded another 9000. The advance had cost Fourth Army, by comparison, fewer than 9000 casualties in total.[29]

'Down to where the war is being won': Advance to the Somme bend, August–September 1918

The extent of German losses on 8 August convinced Rawlinson to continue the advance over the following three days. These follow-up actions were to be of a vastly different character to the initial advance, though. Fourth Army's troops were exhausted and only had a handful of tanks functioning properly after the first day. What's more, the Germans poured reserves on to their broken front much faster than Rawlinson had anticipated. This all amounted to a much more strenuous few days for No. 3 Squadron, as it struggled to support a corps that was already far in advance of its command centres, artillery and supply dumps.

C Flight's contact patrols continued to do their crucial work, although by the second day of the advance, the infantry had run out of flares. The pilots therefore needed to fly below 50 feet and watch for waved handkerchiefs, rifles laid across the top of trenches or the glint of the tin discs the infantry wore on their backs. After recovering from their crash landing near Villers-Bretonneux on the first day, Lock and Barrett were out looking for the Australian line at dawn on 10 August:

> The only way we could find it was by flying low until we were fired on by the Hun, and then looking for our infantry a little further back. I had some funny experiences doing this, and on more than one occasion I have seen Huns in trenches waving with one hand and firing at us with the other and I have often waved to Huns and had them wave back; on this particular job you haven't time to use your gun so you miss a lot of beautiful targets.[30]

Later that morning, Smith and Witcomb were marking 1st Division's line on a map for its headquarters when a bullet fired from the ground went through Smith's foot, forcing them to land on the battlefield. The following morning, Lock and Barrett were trying to determine the position of the front line when a bullet hit their petrol tank. 'The pilot switched off the engine and glided down,' wrote Barrett. 'Where we landed there was a bit of fog and we couldn't see the ground at all. But our luck was in and we got down quite OK, about 1500 yards from the front line.' They managed to get a lift back to an infantry headquarters, where they ate breakfast with the staff, before 'lorry hopping' back to the aerodrome in time for lunch. They were on another contact patrol later in the afternoon, and had to fly at 50 feet to distinguish the German uniforms from the Australian ones. While at that very low—and vulnerable—altitude, nine Fokker biplanes set on them. 'Neither my pilot nor I knew they were there,' wrote Barrett to his mother. 'However they got the wind up and cleared out, or otherwise we would have had another forced landing to say the least.'

C Flight's airmen were acknowledged for their crucial but very dangerous work by the award of four Distinguished Flying Crosses. Frank Sewell earned his for a daring contact patrol on 11 August: 'He flew for two hours under two hundred feet, amidst heavy machine gun fire, on the front Bray-Corbie Road to the Somme and established the position of the line by actual recognition of troops, bringing back a most useful report.'[31]

By nightfall on 11 August, Fourth Army had advanced another 7 kilometres or so, but for more casualties than the initial 11 kilometre advance on the first day. It was evident that Fourth Army's offensive had run its course, and Rawlinson subsequently ordered his corps to consolidate their gains.

Rawlinson's order meant a return to routine work for the corps squadrons. 'We are back to the old programme today ie two early morning patrols and the dusk,' recorded Max Shelley.[32] That day, No. 3 Squadron photographed the new Australian front and then returned to drop prints to troops in the forward positions. Barrett, who had survived two crashes on the battlefield in four days, was glad to be back on these routine jobs, which he considered 'tame' compared to contact patrols during a battle: 'We did quite a lot of flying at 50–800 feet and it plays up with your nerves rather.'[33]

The infantry, in their new forward positions, meanwhile returned to their routine of peaceful penetration. Shelley was over the battlefield on 13 August, and noted: 'The Australians and Canadians are still nibbling at the

Bosche line and quite successfully.'[34] The trench raiding yielded a constant stream of prisoners, who along with those captured in the initial advance marched past the aerodrome. Everyone in the squadron was eager to see the enemy up close. 'They all seemed to be happy,' observed Air Mechanic James Barnes. 'No doubt they are quite pleased to get away from the fighting.' He also noticed the enemy was scraping the bottom of the barrel for its fighting men, a 'good many' of them being 'boys' and 'aged men'.[35] Charles Bean noted the same when he inspected the enemy in a prison cage near Amiens and also learned it wasn't the British artillery, tanks or cavalry that had been most demoralising for them during the Battle of Amiens. Bean asked one particularly fierce-looking German sergeant what had caused him to run away. He replied, 'with a sort of a laugh "die flieger—the flying men" with their machine guns'.[36]

Starting on 10 August, the RAF began shifting additional fighter squadrons to the Amiens sector to meet the numerous enemy air units (including JG I) that had deployed as reinforcements. Within a few days, there were 480 additional British fighters, or 70 per cent of the RAF's scout strength, concentrated on the battlefront. The two Australian scout squadrons contributed a dozen aircraft each. On 12 August, they flew, as Thomas Edols told his sweetheart, 'down to where the war is being won' and landed at Horseshoe Wood, just outside of Amiens.[37]

Each morning, for three days, the Australian scout pilots flew down to Horseshoe Wood, patrolled over the Australian Corps during the day and returned to Reclinghem in the evening. 'This meant a scratch breakfast at 3am,' explained Cobby. 'On arrival we would fill up with petrol and oil, put the bombs on and fit ammunition belts and go straight off on a squadron patrol.' Horseshoe Wood had no workshops, accommodation or mess at all, so the pilots had to take a packed lunch and refuel and rearm their own 'buses'. 'It seemed to us a poor way to win the war,' thought Cobby.[38]

Nevertheless, being on the Somme gave the Australian scout pilots a boost of morale. The roads were filled with British troops, tanks and guns and the skies dominated by squadron-sized flights of the RAF. 'Take it from me,' Edols wrote to his sweetheart, 'Australia has good reason to be proud of her troops, as the work they have done in this last week has been absolutely wonderful.'[39] To Cobby, the infantry 'seemed literally to leap across country almost without interference'. It all gave him the encouraging impression that 'the war, after all, might finish within a reasonable time'.[40]

Germany's military and political leaders had reached the same conclusions. On 11 August, on hearing reports of German losses at Amiens, the Kaiser concluded that 'we have reached the limit of our power of resistance. The war must be ended.' Two days later, at a high-level military conference in Spa, Ludendorff acknowledged the German Army was spent—'the termination of the war would have to be brought about by diplomacy'. His superior, the Chief of the General Staff Paul von Hindenburg, was slightly more optimistic. The Allies' decision to pause their offensive after just three days gave him 'hope that we should overcome further crisis'.[41]

This was fanciful, though. Just ten days after shutting down the Amiens offensive, the British Third Army attacked between the Somme and Arras. The left-hand side of Fourth Army (including the Australian Corps, astride the Somme) joined in the following day, and the Germans were again pushed back across a wide front. Progress was nowhere near what it had been on 8 August, but it was enough to convince Ludendorff that his armies' current position (the trenches of the old 1916 Somme battlefield) was untenable. On 26 August, he ordered his forces to withdraw to a 'winter line', which on the Australian Corps front lay 12 kilometres back, where the Somme bends sharply to the south (see Map 4).

No. 3 Squadron detected the enemy withdrawal first. Patrols on 25 and 26 August found the countryside between the Australian front line and the Somme bend 'practically deserted', and spotted fires burning in villages and dumps.[42] At dawn on 27 August, Australian infantry patrols confirmed what the aerial patrols suggested when they found the enemy's outposts abandoned. Monash ordered 'an immediate general advance' along the Australian Corps' entire front.

As Monash put it, 'there followed a merry and exciting three days of pursuit; the enemy was really on the run'.[43] The infantry moved forward in companies and platoons, in true open warfare-style conditions that can now be seen as a precursor to Second World War combat. Monash's divisional and brigade commanders had to rely entirely on No. 3 Squadron's contact patrols to keep track of what was happening at the front. 'It was under just these circumstances,' he wrote, 'that rapid and reliable information as to the progress of the various elements of our front line troops was more important than ever, and no means of obtaining such information was so expeditious as the contact aeroplane.'[44]

To enable the quick dissemination of No. 3 Squadron's reports, the Australian Corps established a 'Central Intelligence Bureau' to receive wireless reports from airmen and then transmit them to units on the battlefield. In the official history, Cutlack analogised the system as 'the army's eyes registering to the army's brain'.[45]

At sunset on 29 August, a No. 3 Squadron crew reported Australian troops lined up along the Somme, south of the bend. The Germans had retreated across the river, destroying the bridges behind them and were establishing 'very strong posts' across the river at Péronne and on the commanding heights of Mont St Quentin. The German Army, the report seemed to suggest, had reached its 'winter line' and was preparing to make a stand.[46]

'To catch old Jerry eating his meal of sauerkraut': The Lille Raids, 16–17 August 1918

Since the formation of 80th Wing at the beginning of July, its commander Lieutenant Colonel Louis Strange had envisaged a massed raid against a German aerodrome. Endorsed by his superior, Brigadier General Ludlow Hewitt of 10th Brigade RAF, Strange held a series of conferences with his squadron and flight commanders during July. They planned to strike an enemy aerodrome with four squadrons of the wing in a single raid. To have the most impact, the squadrons would form up over Reclinghem, cross the lines together and hit their target from the lowest possible altitude.

Strange emphasised the need for the 'utmost precision' and discipline on the raid. To prevent aircraft colliding and hitting each other with bombs, he drew up a strict timetable and allocation of targets. He made it clear that the strike had to be quick and directed 'solely on the objectives of the raid'. Strange was experienced enough to know 'how tempting some targets look' to young scout pilots with 'eager eyes' and 'itching fingers'.[47]

The raid would mark the pinnacle of Harry Cobby's remarkably successful career. He would lead the whole show at the head of No. 4 Squadron. Behind and 1000 feet above would follow Murray Jones and No. 2 Squadron. The SE5as and Bristol Fighters of Nos 92 and 88 Squadrons would follow, 1000 and 2000 feet higher respectively to cover the Australians while they attacked the aerodrome. Each flight would fly in a 'V' formation, echeloned upwards between 7000 and 10 000 feet. Over the target, they would shake out into single file and head in at one-minute intervals while the rest of the formation flew circuits.

The plans were set and the pilots briefed, but bad weather postponed the raid day after day for several weeks, leading most pilots to conclude that it would never happen.[48] Then, on the afternoon of 15 August, orders arrived at Reclinghem that the raid was set for the following morning. The pilots were excited—this was going to be the largest daylight raid by a scout unit to date—but Cobby was apprehensive. Such a large formation, he thought, was sure to invite casualties from 'even the most indifferent shooting by enemy anti-aircraft gunners'. So that evening, he made some 'private arrangements', and organised for British corps squadrons to direct fire on to German Archie batteries while the wing crossed the lines.[49]

The morning of 16 August dawned with a drizzly anti-climax. The raid was postponed yet again and the pilots waited around, irritated and anxious. The sun appeared late in the morning, though, and at 11.30 a.m. wing headquarters phoned through a message that the 'show' was on. The target was Haubourdin, an aerodrome on the outskirts of Lille with ideally crowded hangars and barracks. Fifteen minutes later, No. 92 Squadron arrived over Reclinghem at 9000 feet. It was followed by No. 88 Squadron's Bristols, which stacked themselves above. Murray Jones and Cobby led their squadrons up and joined the formation while it circuited the aerodrome. Unusually for a wing commander, Strange accompanied the raid, taking up position next to Cobby at the front.

It took 40 minutes for the 65 aircraft to assemble in formation and just another five minutes to cross the line. Cobby peered down at the trenches and quietly hoped the armada behind him would inspire the Tommies below and terrorise their adversaries on the other side of no man's land. His 'private arrangements' were obviously working—the response from German anti-aircraft gunners was negligible. Over the front, Lille came into view, 25 kilometres away. Cobby couldn't see the aerodrome yet, but aimed for its position on the southern edge of the city and pitched his nose down, intending to cross the aerodrome's boundary fence at top speed and about

200 feet. 'Looking back,' he recalled, 'I got a tremendous thrill from the sight of everyone keeping perfect formation.'

Not surprisingly, German pilots didn't interfere with the wing on its long shallow dive into Lille. In fact, the Australian pilots saw just a single enemy two-seater about halfway there. It was flying in the same direction, and when its pilot saw the formation he went into a frantic dive towards Lille. 'If he had turned away he would have been perfectly safe,' explained Cobby. But instead he went down, 'with one foot on the stick and the other on the throttle, with his head nearly screwed off, as he watched us follow him down'. He continued towards the aerodrome, and crashed into a tree on its edge.[50]

As Haubourdin emerged in detail, Strange recalled the sky above it was 'a perfect mass of Archie bursts'. They were inaccurately ranged, though, and within moments the German gunners were fleeing into the surrounding fields. 'Then,' wrote Strange, 'came the Verey signal fired by Captain Cobby and the inspiring spectacle of that squadron driving straight down to its mark.' Strange stayed above and watched them streak down and become 'mere specks that spat streams of tracer bullets and left bursts of bombs here, there and everywhere about the hangars.'[51]

Cobby released his first two bombs at 50 feet. They slammed into a hangar, making it erupt in clouds of dust and debris. Then, in his words:

> I circled out round the drome to come back along the tarmac to shoot up several Fokkers in front of the hangars. Bo King suddenly appeared on my left, obviously with the same intentions. He tried to jockey me out of position, but I wouldn't give way, so he dropped in closer still and a little behind, and we sprayed the Fokkers with incendiary ammunition and they went up in flames.

By this time, bombs from the next wave were raining down and exploding around A Flight's Camels. It was obviously someone else's turn to be over the target area so they sheared off to get out of the way. On their way across the field, Cobby and King gave the aircraft sitting in their open hangars one last blast of Vickers .303: 'Some of them caught fire and it looked as though the whole thing was going up in smoke.'[52]

At this point, claimed Cobby, instead of returning to its place in the wing, A Flight broke formation (and orders) and went for anything moving in the surrounding countryside. Bo King machine-gunned a column of cavalry heading out of Lille. Norm Trescowthick hit a car and later quipped that 'the owner would find it hard to start'.[53] Thomas Edols, thrilled at the prospect of catching 'old Jerry eating his meal of sauerkraut', laid his 'eggs' on the officer's quarters and then, with the others, flew around shooting up everything he could find. 'One chap got a Hun on a motor bike, another got a staff car and I got a pair of lorries in a supply wagon and a search light.' Edols got as low as 10 feet—'a very funny thing to do', he thought, so deep in 'Hunland'.[54] One of the German pilots ran out of the officers' mess to find that 'flames were everywhere'. More than half the machines in his flight were burning and two of its mechanics lay injured.[55]

Gillies Watson's B Flight was next on to the aerodrome. The whole scene was already wreathed in smoke and flame, with German mechanics, aerodrome staff and horses bolting in all directions. Watson dropped a phosphorus bomb and a pair of high explosives on to the officers' mess and started a fire among the huts. Coming down to 50 feet, he fired 200 rounds into a group of mechanics making for the cover of a railway embankment. He left several sprawled on the ground and turned his guns on to a mob of panicking horses and men at a transport dump. Coming in behind him, Thomas Baker loosed his bombs into a brick building by the hangars and then machine-gunned a train in the nearby railway station. Before pulling out, he flew along the main road and ripped into a touring car, sending it crashing into a ditch. 'No one left the car,' he recorded.[56]

Jack Wright led the last flight of Camels across the aerodrome. All the hangars and a couple of aircraft appeared to be 'well alight'. From 100 feet he dropped two bombs into the blazing hangars, 'just to make sure of their destruction', and the rest on to a group of barracks and workshops. 'Still at about 100 feet,' he wrote, 'I turned my attention to the aerodrome personnel fleeing in all directions around the surrounding countryside.' After five minutes of this 'sport', Wright spotted a locomotive full of troops in the railway siding and 'went up and down each side raking it' with fire: 'The whole area around the airfield was almost blotted out with flames and smoke, and as there was a danger of collision I turned for home.'[57]

No. 2 Squadron had meanwhile done three left-hand circuits of Haubourdin at 2000 feet. When Wright's Camels were clear, Murray Jones led the first flight in. He passed over the western hangars, lashing them with fire as he went, before releasing his bombs into the billowing smoke above the southern hangars. Francis Smith saw that some enemy aircraft had been wheeled out of the burning hangar and fired 200 rounds into them. Eric Cummings and Roby Manuel followed in with their flights and slung more bombs and bullets into the target area. Precise aiming was out of the question for the SE5a pilots. The whole aerodrome was completely obscured by smoke. From above, Strange watched the 'fearsome spectacle': 'Clouds of dust flew up, mingled with pieces of machines, huts and hangars.'[58]

Charles Copp recalled that after releasing their bombs, No. 2 Squadron's pilots flew around the aerodrome perimeter 'shooting up anything that they could see'. For him, this included some sheds in a nearby wood and a machine gun post on its northwestern perimeter. He then flew low over the village of Haubourdin and, to his surprise, saw a Camel 'flying along the main road, straight through the middle of the village, about level with the windows of the houses'. Copp recognised it as Bo King and could see him waving to the houses as he swept by. When Copp later asked 'what on earth' he was doing, King replied: 'I thought the girls in that village must have had a heck of a time with all that bombing and must have been terribly scared so I thought I'd cheer them up a bit.' This, according to Copp, 'was typical of "Bo" King'.[59]

Cobby and the other flight leaders found it impossible to regroup their pilots in the face of so many targets and so little opposition. The five-minute precision strike stretched out into a 45-minute shooting gallery.[60] The enemy had barely fired a shot once the raid began, and 80th Wing returned home without a single loss.

That night, the pilots held 'an impromptu inter-squadron binge'. Each mess threw a party and pilots drifted between them, drinking and enthusiastically swapping stories about the raid. The revelry was only just dying down at 4.30 a.m. when Strange phoned through orders that another wing-sized raid was planned for 7.00 a.m. With, as Cobby put it, 'most of 80th Wing scattered around Flanders and "exhilarated" to one extent or another', it was a tall order. But nevertheless, everyone found their way back on to the tarmac by 7.00 a.m. 'You could almost feel the air vibrating from the number of throbbing heads,' claimed Cobby as the ashen-faced pilots quietly gathered to watch their machines wheeled out of the hangars. With flight suits pulled over their pyjamas, a couple of aspirins and a quick 'bracer', they climbed aboard and ran up their engines.[61]

Seven o'clock came and the British units arrived over Reclinghem and began their circuits. But no one knew the target yet. No. 4 Squadron took off and left Cobby sitting on the tarmac, 'twiddling his thumbs'. Finally, Strange pulled up in a car and handed Cobby a photograph and map. The target was Lomme, an aerodrome on the other side of Lille—and a good target, too, considering its timber and canvas hangars and the hot wind, which was blowing right along them to fan the flames.

The wing crossed the line without incident and approached Lille. Over Lomme, Cobby fired a light and pushed his stick forward into an almost vertical dive. Strange was right behind him:

Down we went with every wire screaming in protest. I pressed the triggers of my Constantinesco gear as I saw tracer bullets stream out in front of the bull-like nose of his Camel, and a second later thought I was bound to crash vertically into the roof of the hangar below us, which was one in a row of six. As we flattened out and streaked over those hangars, I tugged hard at the release thongs of my bomb gear and then heard the most awful din of crashes when the whole of the flight sent down their total of twenty-four 20 lb bombs.[62]

Cobby wheeled around and led his flight across another row of five hangars on the other side of the aerodrome:

Down along the second row, letting my bombs go without sighting, as I couldn't miss, being only about twenty feet above the roof tops, and at least one hangar started to burn immediately after the bombs had burst. Then back to the first row again, across the centre of the aerodrome and firing as I went, with my wheels almost touching the ground, and Strange doing his utmost to keep alongside. Skidding over the hangars which were burning furiously, with bombs going off all around us, I raced round the outside of the aerodrome firing bursts at odd groups of officers and mechanics that were making for the 'tall timbers'.[63]

The German pilots and their mechanics were helpless. Carl Degelow, commanding officer of one of the Jastas stationed there, recalled that they couldn't even attempt to extinguish the fires: 'As soon as one of us dared to come out of the trenches, a Tommy would come down and spray us, his hammering machine gun making it necessary to take cover as quickly as possible.'[64]

Climbing away, Strange saw the six hangars on the northern side 'enveloped in black smoke clouds, edged with reddish yellow flames that poured out the windward side'. Shrapnel bursts and tracer criss-crossed the sky above the aerodrome and rocked the Camels as they climbed back into formation. Edgar McCleery, a 25-year-old coach builder from Moss Vale in the New South Wales southern highlands, was hit in the back and his Camel rolled and dived on to the tarmac. The Germans afterwards found him 'dead from many chest wounds, amidst the wreckage of his machine'.[65]

Adrian Cole led No. 2 Squadron in from the east. They swept in across the workshops and released their bombs. Cole saw his tracers knock over a German soldier behind a machine gun. There was a series of explosions among the buildings and Cole then led the SE5as in left-hand circuits while the British machines dropped their bombs. Within ten minutes, smoke and flames fanned by a hot summer's wind obscured the whole aerodrome. In the face of heavy fire from the town, the pilots joined formation and flew home.

With the exception of McCleery, the entire wing was safely back at its aerodromes before 9.00 a.m. According to 80th Wing's files the Australian squadrons had fired nearly 32 000 rounds and dropped 2.8 tonnes of bombs on the two aerodromes.[66] Both were practically wiped out and three squadrons of enemy machines—perhaps as many as 54—were destroyed.

The pilots again celebrated wildly. Each received an aerial photograph of Lomme wreathed in smoke and flame as a keepsake. News travelled throughout the AIF and the official war correspondent, Charles Bean, came to Reclinghem the following day to meet the pilots and interview some of them.

There was a different mood in the mechanics' mess, though. While the pilots had their raucous binge, Vern Knuckey and his mates waited anxiously. He noted in his diary how the neighbouring squadrons 'have the wind up and feel like swearing at us for starting this new scheme as Fritz is sure to retaliate'.[67] Brigade headquarters was concerned too. It issued special aerodrome defence schemes to all aerodromes and assigned each a platoon of machine gunners. It proved unnecessary, though. The days following the Lille raids were conspicuously quiet, the German Air Service apparently incapable of any kind of riposte. In fact, it would be three weeks before Jasta 43 at Haubourdin received replacement aircraft and, with the German armies falling back down south, the enemy pilots' priorities were shifting from the offensive to the defensive.

13
'GOOD SPORT TO THE MAN IN THE AIR'
Fighting to the finish, September to November 1918

Mechanics of No. 3 Squadron with an RE8 at Premont in October 1918. For the last three months of the war, No. 3 Squadron followed the Australian Corps and operated from makeshift aerodromes just behind the front. *Author's collection*

> Strafing a retreating army is good sport to the man
> in the air, though probably far from agreeable to the Hun
> plodding back to Hunland.
>
> —Lieutenant Bill Palstra, No. 3 Squadron, Australian Flying Corps

'The push (or rather chase) is going well and St Quentin is not far off': No. 3 Squadron and the breaking of the Hindenburg Line, September–October 1918

The German Army's stand in its 'winter line' behind the Somme was supposed to see it through the winter of 1918 and into 1919 while Germany's military and political leaders negotiated a peace with favourable terms. In the event, it lasted barely 48 hours. Arriving at the north–south stretch of the Somme on 29 August, the Australian Corps sent its 2nd Division across the river to the north, where it broke into the German line at Mont St Quentin. Like at Villers-Bretonneux back in April, poor weather once again prevented No. 3 Squadron from supporting the diggers in another of their finest achievements of the war.

With their winter position ruptured, the German command had little option but to order a retreat to the Hindenburg Line, a 145 kilometre-long system of defensive positions they had been building since late 1916. In a sense, the name 'Hindenburg Line' (as the British dubbed it) is misleading. It was, in fact, a series of trenches and fortified positions some 15 kilometres deep. Immense belts of barbed wire hemmed the system together and hundreds of concrete pillboxes and dugouts, as well as canals and even entire fortified villages, made it seemingly impregnable. Indeed, as far as the German command was concerned, it had to be. The Hindenburg Line's trenches, concrete and wire were the last prepared fortifications between the Allied armies and Germany's border.

The retreat to the Hindenburg Line began on 4 September. The Australian Corps pursued vigorously, supported overhead by No. 3 Squadron. Lawrence Wackett and Max Shelley 'saw plenty of large explosions' while they were over the corps front that afternoon: 'The Bosche seem to be clearing out fast.' They strafed some retreating German troops, with Shelley managing to 'Stonker a Bosche officer on horseback'. Wackett was impressed with the way the Australian infantry and artillery used the air reports to overcome stubborn German rearguards: 'It was fine to see how the 18 pounders were following up and helping the infantry by placing small barrages on troublesome places.'[1] In four days, this impressive collaboration between airman, digger and gunner won the Australian Corps an advance of almost 8 kilometres.

To keep up with the rapidly shifting front, No. 3 Squadron moved to Proyart. Stan Tuck found the new aerodrome, which had recently been a battlefield, 'a most unsavoury site'. The ground was torn up and the area stank of 'dead horses and Huns'.[2] Despite some hasty land filling, five pilots had accidents in the first 24 hours.[3]

Nevertheless, the Australian Corps' demand for air support left the airmen with little option but to risk the bumpy landings. Wackett recalled that during the chase to the Hindenburg Line, 'there were always two machines on the line continuously, and in the evenings, three or four'. The German reconnaissance squadrons, flying their Hanoveranners, were active too, as they tried to keep touch with the rapidly retreating German line. 'We made great efforts to stop these machines doing their contact patrols,' explained Wackett. 'It was a common thing to see an old RE8 diving for all its worth after a Hanoveranner which had managed to sneak onto the lines for a few minutes, frantically firing Verey lights to the infantry below.'[4] Each day, the Australian crews found the front line further east. 'The push (or rather chase),' noted Shelley on 9 September, 'is going well and St Quentin is not far off.'[5]

Over the following two days, the Germans fell back into the old, 1917-era British trench lines which, conveniently for them, screened the Hindenburg system. The Australian Corps, and the other British formations in Fourth Army, captured the first of these (the old British reserve line) by peaceful penetration, but found the Germans intending to make a stand in the next two (the old British main and outpost lines). General Rawlinson and Fourth Army's staff planned a formal offensive operation to capture the old British lines and, if possible, gain a foothold in the Hindenburg outpost line, which lay just beyond them on a ridge (somewhat inconveniently for the Germans), overlooking the main system.

The battle commenced at dawn on 18 September in what was by now the now characteristic weather of British offensives: dense fog and pouring rain. The first contact patrol crew to see anything was Dave Dimsey and Roland Machin, just after 10.00 a.m. They spotted Australian troops on their second objective (the old British outpost line) but were hit by 'heavy' machine gun fire from German positions on the ridge. A bullet struck Machin, knocking him down into his cockpit. Dimsey returned to Proyart where the usual difficult landing conditions were augmented by the fact that Machin's unconscious body was jamming up the exposed control wires in the back of the aircraft. Frank Rawlinson and his fellow mechanics watched as Dimsey made an impressive, but hair-raising landing: 'He may have had his wheels on the ground in the finish, but he flew straight into the open tent hangar, which pulled him up as neatly as could be.' They rushed in, lifted Machin on to a stretcher and rushed him to the nearest dressing station. He was dead by the time they got there. 'We carried him into the tent,' recalled Rawlinson, 'and my friend gave his name to the Padre, and he was laid out with the rest of the many men who had died that day.'[6]

The Australian infantry meanwhile fought their way up into the Hindenburg outpost line on the ridge. No. 3 Squadron covered their advance with smoke bombs. Tom Prince described the assistance they provided:

> The bombs were dropped and we could see from the air that as they exploded, they made an almost continuous line in front of the battalion that was attacking, and they made a very effective screen to hide our troops from the enemy. Although it was hard to pick them out, we could see the small figures that were our infantry advancing right up to that wall of smoke, and some were plunging into it to go through and surprise the enemy by the quickness of their recovery from the setback they had suffered.[7]

A 'bright spell' in the afternoon allowed contact patrols to confirm that Australian troops were in the Hindenburg outpost line, overlooking the main system in the valley below.[8] After some consolidation during the night, early morning patrols the next day confirmed that the Australians had captured all their objectives. 'As far as we can hear,' recorded Max Shelley, 'everything has gone like clockwork.'[9]

From where the diggers now stood, they could clearly see what the airmen had seen looming in the distance for weeks. The Siegfried Stellung ('Siegfried Position') that barred the Australian Corps' path was the strongest part of the Hindenburg system. Its main line, which faced the Australian Corps and the neighbouring British corps on either side of it, was shielded by belts of barbed wire and the 10 metre-wide St Quentin Canal. Tanks could probably deal with the former, but the canal, at 20 metres deep and filled with water and mud, made the German trenches effectively tank proof—or at least, as one pilot described it laconically, represented 'a significant snag'.[10] The only exception was directly in front of the Australians, where the canal ran underground, through the 5.5 kilometre Bellicourt tunnel. To make up for the shortfall, the Germans had reinforced this section of line with six wide belts of barbed wire and a series of trenches and concrete pillboxes a thousand metres deep.

Nevertheless, it was precisely here, where tanks could operate, that Monash proposed to breach the system. Rawlinson, his superior at Fourth Army Headquarters agreed, and delegated planning responsibilities to the Australian staff. 'Z-day' for the attack on the Hindenburg Line was to be 29 September 1918. Supreme Allied headquarters determined that it would be the third in a coordinated series of four major offensives spread across the Western Front, to commence over a period of four consecutive days.

No. 3 Squadron's aerial photographs played a crucial role in the planning and preparation for the assault on the Hindenburg Line. Especially important was a special reconnaissance conducted by Wackett and Shelley on 24 September over the Beaurevoir Line—a reserve position 4 kilometres beyond the main Hindenburg system. To attract minimal attention, they did it alone in a Bristol Fighter recently acquired by the squadron.

Wackett and Shelley got to the Beaurevoir Line without attracting unwanted attention. 'I now had before me,' recalled Wackett, 'about twenty miles of zigzag flying, taking approximately ten minutes, with a photograph every twenty seconds'. Within half a minute, the sky was full of Archie bursts and tracers, arcing up from the ground: 'The noise of the bursting shells was terrific and some were very close indeed.' After five minutes, Wackett glanced over his shoulder and saw 'the smoke of hundreds of bursts extending back for five miles or so'. He zigzagged violently to throw the enemy gunners' aim, assisted partly by the irregularity of the line he was photographing.

After ten minutes, they reached the end of their run and climbed away:

> I could see streams of tracer bullets passing under me, and others were passing over me ... The huge cloud of anti-aircraft bursts over ten miles long had alerted every anti-aircraft battery on the whole front, and I was speeding home and climbing fast. Although I changed course erratically every twenty

seconds I was surrounded by shell bursts for several minutes. Then there was calm, I had crossed our lines.

At this point, Wackett and Shelley noted the state of their machine. Sections of torn fabric flapped in the wind all over the wings and fuselage. A bullet had gone through the altimeter on the instrument panel, and oil and water from the engine had drenched both airmen. 'Soon the temperature was up to boiling point and the engine began to make unusual noises,' recalled Wackett. Remarkably, the engine kept up, seizing up only as the Bristol Fighter crossed the aerodrome boundary. They touched down with a stopped propeller.

Astonished riggers counted 80 bullet holes in the aircraft. It was a wonder the wings had stayed on the aircraft at all—the eight spars in the wings were all shot through, as were two of the struts. Miraculously, neither pilot had collected a bullet—although, as they walked from their machine congratulating each other, Shelley found a hole through the fabric of his trouser leg.[11] The army's staff officers found the photographs useful and congratulated the airmen. Wackett also received a Distinguished Flying Cross and a pass to England, for a well-earned rest.

In the three days before zero hour, No. 3 Squadron's airmen revived their old trench warfare duty of pre-arranged artillery shoots to engage and destroy as many enemy batteries as possible before the infantry 'hopped the bags'. Tom Prince was one of the squadron's old hands, not only in the sense he had done almost twelve weeks with the squadron, or that he was 27 years old. Prince had enlisted in the war's first month and gone ashore at Gallipoli at dawn on 25 April 1915. He had done three and a half years of trench warfare before volunteering for the AFC—a fact which, he learned in mid-September, would get him home to Australia on a special leave rotation for original Anzacs in the AIF. He was due to leave the squadron on 26 September, but due to an administrative mix-up was delayed. While he waited for it to be cleared up, Major Blake put him back on the flying roster for the afternoon artillery shoot. 'This took me back a little,' admitted Prince, 'but orders were orders, and I was in no position to argue with him.'

He went up with pilot Geoff Deans that afternoon. 'It was a clear autumn day with good visibility,' he remembered. 'We could see plenty of movement on the roads towards St Quentin. We had to dodge a lot of fire from the German Archies but that was always part of the day's work ... High up above, at ten to fifteen thousand feet, many formations of scouts were cruising around on their own mysterious missions.'

For three hours, Deans and Prince transmitted shot corrections without seeing any enemy machines. They had just finished over Belleglise and were turning for home when five Pfalz dived from high above. What happened next was still indelibly imprinted in Prince's memory when he recalled it, 43 years later:

> Their leader opened fire, but missed us altogether, as his dive passed us by. The bursts from the second one were going into the port wing and ripping the fabric from the frame. The bullets from the next one tore into our fuselage, knocking splinters from the longeron near my arm. All the bursts were going into the port side, the tracers flashing as they hit the wing.

Prince returned fire as each Pfalz dived by. In about 10 seconds the drum on top of his Lewis gun rattled empty and he replaced it with another. In the next instant, one of the German pilots had done a climbing turn and was below them, firing:

> Suddenly I felt a hard blow on my thigh. I reached down to touch the wound and my hand was covered with blood. I could clearly see the face of the Hun as his Pfalz went by. I touched my head to indicate to Geoff that I had been hit, but in doing so I left some of the blood on my face. He looked grim, as he thought I had been shot in the head. The Huns' bursts seemed to be tearing us to pieces. I huddled down in the cockpit, feeling very tired and alone, but it was not yet time for despair, as the two most vital parts of the machine, the pilot and the petrol tank, were still intact. Some of the Pfalz Scouts were wheeling to come back at us again. Then there was a flick like the lash of a whip across the calf of my leg, and this, strange to say, aroused me to anger. I thought a man may as well die fighting, so I stood up and swung the gun. The drum was empty, so I plucked it from the gun and flung it at a Hun flying alongside of us. I clamped on a full drum and fired at him as he wheeled away.

Prince fixed his ring sight on another machine and was about to fire when he noticed the roundels on its wings. It was another RE8 from the squadron, come to assist them. 'I looked around me and the sky was full of aircraft, in a scene of whirling dogfights. Then my sight blurred and I faded away.'

When Prince woke up he was on a stretcher, being tended to by the squadron medical orderly. Other pilots and observers crowded around anxiously. Major Blake was there and Prince said to him, 'I'll get to Blighty now, Major.' 'I'm sure you will Tom,' he replied. Prince fell unconscious again. When he next woke, he was in a field hospital receiving a blood transfusion. From there, he finally made it back to 'Blighty'—although he didn't get to Australia until January 1919.[12]

The preliminary barrage for the assault on the Hindenburg Line started at 10.30 p.m. on 26 September. For two full days, 1637 guns deluged the German positions with a quarter of a million gas and high-explosive shells.[13] The barrage's bark was worse than its bite, though. Bad weather and active enemy fighter units severely disrupted the work of artillery observation aircraft, meaning that the flying corps couldn't verify whether enemy batteries would be neutralised when the infantry attacked—or, for that matter, whether the wire in front of them was cut.

The battle plan required the Australian Corps (with American reinforcements) to attack across the tunnel with infantry and tanks, while the British IX Corps attempted to cross the canal immediately to the south. The ambitious plan required them to fight their way through the Hindenburg Main and Support Lines (the first and second objectives) and then advance another 4 kilometres to breach the Beaurevoir Line. 'It is going to be some day,' predicted observer Bill Pomroy in his diary, after the squadron's briefing on the evening of 28 September. 'It will decide the war if it comes off.'[14]

The attack began at 5.55 a.m. the following day. The Australian Corps' first assault wave consisted of two American divisions, who were supposed to capture the first two objectives before two Australian divisions leap-frogged through them to attack the Beaurevoir Line. George Pickering and Max Shelley were scheduled for the dawn contact patrol, but thick fog prevented them leaving the ground until 8.30 a.m. According to Shelley: 'Even at that time, the line was practically completely covered and we could hardly do any useful work.' They flew as low as possible to try to capture a glimpse

FIRE IN THE SKY

through the fog but saw very little, except 'about 12 tanks on fire'. For his trouble, Shelley had another close shave. 'A bullet came up through the bottom of the bus, cutting a couple of large holes in my trench coat between my legs.'[15]

As the morning wore on, the situation on the battlefield remained, both literally and figuratively, foggy. At midday, a contact patrol over the southern sector reported American troops east of Bellicourt—that is, across the Main Line and close to their second objective. Bill Palstra's mid-afternoon patrol to check progress in the northern sector was less promising. He sounded his klaxon over the Americans' second objective but saw no flares in response. Ominously, he saw 'many Huns' still in the Hindenburg Main Line—the first objective—and 'a good number' of tanks burning in front of it. 'No advance appears to be made on this flank,' Palstra concluded. 'Whole situation very obscure and dangerous.'[16]

By evening, the Australian Corps was a long way short of its intended objectives in the Beaurevoir Line. In the northern sector, as Palstra's report indicated, the Americans had been pinned down well before reaching their first objective and the Australians following them couldn't make headway either. To the south, things had gone better. The Americans captured the southern tunnel entrance at Bellicourt and managed to reach Nauroy, just beyond the Hindenburg Support Line where they linked up with British troops who had successfully crossed the canal further south.

Attacks resumed at 6.00 a.m. the following morning. Heavy rain and wind restricted No. 3 Squadron's efforts, although several machines got airborne to report the situation and direct fire on to German batteries that were pummelling the infantry as they tried to advance. Palstra was on the early afternoon contact patrol. He and his pilot braved strong winds (blowing them towards 'Hunland') and machine gun fire, which severed their elevator control wires. They reported the line practically unchanged from the day before. 'Our Diggers OK,' he noted in his diary that night. 'Yanks appear to have suffered pretty heavily. The dead lie in patches.'[17]

Prospects brightened on 1 October. 'Splendid weather', as the squadron record book recorded it, allowed the squadron to have aircraft over the battlefront all day.[18] Their reports were encouraging—first that the enemy had abandoned Bony and its strong points in the Australian Corps' troublesome northern sector and then, in the afternoon, that the Australian divisions were through the Support Line and advancing through open country towards the Beaurevoir Line. Shelley, on a contact patrol in the middle of the day, noted further encouraging news: 'The Hun appears to be clearing out a good deal along the front judging by several explosions and transports moving east.' The afternoon patrols transmitted the location of retreating enemy transport to the Central Intelligence Bureau, which passed the information on to special RAF ground attack units that went out to strafe them. The mood in No. 3 Squadron's mess that night was upbeat, with Shelley recording in his diary: 'Good news comes from practically the whole of the Western Front tonight.'[19]

The good news, along with the good weather, continued the following morning. At 6.30 a.m., Palstra and Ernest Hamilton reconnoitred the southern sector, noting that British troops had a foothold in the Beaurevoir Line, east of Joncourt. They had captured the village of Seqehart and Palstra was pleased to see 'some hundreds of Hun prisoners being marched back west'. Swooping down to pinpoint the location of the most advanced British troops, he spotted a line of enemy soldiers 'about a mile long' suddenly stand up and start advancing. Suspecting a counter-attack, he dropped a parachute flare over them and sent a wireless 'SOS' call to the artillery. Within seconds, the German line was being pummelled by artillery and three British fighters attracted by Palstra's flare:

> Swooped down on flank of advancing line with engine full out. Ham fired 400 rounds, one burst catching a party of six and killing five ... Streams of Buckingham [incendiary bullets] were soon spurting towards us. 'Collected' one ... which smashed the wireless reel and klaxon horn.[20]

The German counter-attack was cut to pieces and stopped before it had advanced a thousand metres. In this way, as the British historian Peter Hart has pointed out, the humble RE8 crew could cause more damage with a wireless radio and flare than a fighter ace could in an entire career.[21]

At dawn on 3 October, the Australian Corps launched an attack to capture the Beaurevoir Line, its original objective for the battle's first day. In bright, clear weather, No. 3 Squadron supported the diggers by bombing

German strong points and dropping smoke screens. Bill Pomroy, a new observer in the unit, was 'badly Archied' but still managed to appreciate the corps' awesome firepower: 'It was a very pretty sight to see thousands of guns firing and shells bursting in one sector where the stunt took place.'[22] Unfortunately, one of the shells hit the aircraft flown by squadron veterans, 22-year-old John Gould-Taylor and his observer, 24-year-old Bruce Thomson. Their smashed RE8 was later discovered on the battlefield, with two graves beside it.[23]

Although ejected from the Beaurevoir Line, the Germans stubbornly held on to two towns, Beaurevoir and Montbrehain, just to the east of it. The 2nd Australian Division attacked the latter on 5 October. The fog returned, as did the German Jastas, which made a dangerous nuisance of themselves. Max Shelley had yet another eventful day. It started over Montbrehain in the middle of the morning when eight Fokkers attacked him and his pilot, George Pickering. 'After firing 70 rounds from my gun,' explained Shelley, 'it jammed badly and all I could do was to hold a magazine in front of my head and trust to Pickering's capabilities and God.' Both did their job, with Pickering managing to spiral down to 300 feet and escape back across the lines. They landed, replaced Shelley's Lewis gun and took off to complete the patrol. The engine coughed as they left the ground and then stopped dead. Pickering had few options at such a low altitude, and they smashed into A Flight's mess, destroying both it and the RE8. 'Luckily neither of us were hurt, but we had rather a shaking up,' recorded Shelley in his diary.[24]

By nightfall on 5 October, despite facing fresh German troops and weathering a savage counter-attack, the exhausted Australian infantry had secured Montbrehain. When Beaurevoir fell to British troops on the following night, all that stood between the British Fourth Army and the German border were exhausted and dispirited enemy troops with no more prepared defensive positions. Montbrehain's capture marked the end of the war for the diggers. The Australian Corps was removed from the line on 5 October and granted a rest period that, as it would turn out, would last until the armistice. It is here, therefore, that most narratives of the AIF's war end. But No. 3 Squadron's war wasn't over yet. While their corps marched away from the front to rest, they were attached to II American Corps, which replaced the Australians on the line but lacked a flying unit. 'We have been told tonight that we will probably move in a day or two and to expect to move at an average rate of 7 or 8 miles a day,' wrote a weary Max Shelley in his diary. 'The Hun army appears to be breaking.'[25]

'Perhaps a man can see the end coming at last': Massed dogfights, September 1918

The skies around Lille remained conspicuously empty in the fortnight following the raids on Harbourdin and Lomme. The damage 80th Wing caused these two major enemy aerodromes had coincided with the widening of the offensive down south, astride the Somme, and stretched the German army's limited air resources paper thin in sectors not immediately threatened by an Allied offensive. Day after day, both squadrons' offensive patrols recorded 'No EA seen' in the war diaries. 'To see Fritz over our side is a remarkable thing now-a-days,' noted Vern Knuckey. 'Prospects are bright at present,' he continued, 'and perhaps a man can see the end coming at last.'[26]

'Fritz' wasn't finished yet, though. The situation on the Lille front changed dramatically on 1 September when two Jagdgeschwaden arrived in the sector to cover the German Army's withdrawal from the salient it had won during the April 1918 offensive. Between them, these enemy wings (JG III and IV) had some of Germany's most experienced fighter pilots and were equipped with the superb second generation of Fokker DVII biplanes.

JG III made its presence known by going on a killing spree in the skies between Douai and Lille over the following few days. Twenty-six British machines were, as the Geschwader commander put it, 'netted' in a series of big dogfights on 2 September.[27] Two days later, a flight of twelve British Camels were ambushing some enemy scouts when they, themselves, were set upon by fifteen Fokkers from above. In the fury that followed, the British squadron suffered the most grievous losses experienced by any RAF unit in a single action of the war—four British pilots killed, another four crashed and taken prisoner and another wounded. JG III didn't report a single loss.[28]

With this deadly menace in its sector, it wasn't a good time for No. 4 Squadron to be losing its most experienced flight commanders. Nevertheless, at the beginning of September, Harry Cobby received orders to go on 'home establishment' leave. He was to meet a shortage of experienced Camel instructors at the No. 8 (Training) Squadron in Cirencester. Cobby appealed to be allowed to stay in France, but the 1st Australian Wing's CO, Lieutenant-Colonel Oswald Watt, insisted that his expertise was desperately needed to teach air combat tactics. 'The prospect of being chased around the sky by enthusiastic, but partly trained pilots was not pleasing,' noted Cobby, wryly. 'France was dangerous enough, but England seemed more so.' He had a point—the training squadron's previous two air fighting instructors had both been killed in accidents. 'The prospect of passing out in that manner was not inspiring.'[29]

On the afternoon of 5 September, Cobby did the rounds of neighbouring units to farewell comrades he might never see again. He left A Flight's evening patrol in charge of 23-year-old Norm Trescowthick—a very capable pilot with as much active service experience as Cobby, and six victories to his credit. Trescowthick's flight of five missed a rendezvous with two other flights from the wing but continued the patrol anyway. They were over Douai when 30 Fokkers from JG III appeared overhead. Discerning their precarious situation, Trescowthick gave the signal to dive back towards the lines and made to do so, but the other four were all cut off and shot down. The fight, as related by the only survivor, Len Taplin (who crashed and was captured), formed the basis for the prologue of this book.

Cobby was back at Reclinghem in time to welcome his flight home. 'A tension always gripped everyone on the tarmac on the return of patrols from the line,' he explained. One could usually sense how a patrol had gone by the way pilots approached the aerodrome. If they stunted about and did aerobatics, it was a sure sign there had been no combat or losses. 'In Trescowthick's case,' wrote Cobby, 'he was early and flew in low, made a half circuit of the 'drome and came straight in and landed.' It wasn't a good sign: 'We were all immediately seized with a cold apprehension.'[30]

Trescowthick's report justified Cobby's anxiety. He was A Flight's only survivor of what would be recorded as No. 4 Squadron's 'blackest day'.[31] Trescowthick didn't leave any clues as to how he felt about this but, interestingly, he reported at the time to have left the fight because of 'pressure trouble'.[32] Perhaps this was a more acceptable explanation among the other pilots than a botched attempt at retreat in which a flight commander escaped while the rest of his flight was destroyed. Trescowthick's mistake hadn't been the retreat, however. As the official historian acknowledged, it was the only sensible option open to him given JG III's overwhelming strength. His mistake had been to proceed with the sweep in the first place, when the rendezvous failed. As No. 2 Squadron pilot James Ross acknowledged in a letter home a few days later, the incident was 'caused by people becoming over confident owing to the previous inactivity of the Bosche'. Yet he maintained that, 'by playing a shrewd game, we can easily beat him'.[33]

The two Australian squadrons sought revenge the next day with just such a 'shrewd game'. Jack Wright got together with his fellow flight leader in No. 2 Squadron, Frank Smith, and developed a plan. Wright, leading a lower formation of Camels, would act as 'the bait' while Smith kept his SE5as overhead to spring the trap. Six British Bristol Fighters above them would provide reinforcements if necessary. They set out in the late afternoon for Douai, where they suspected the perpetrators of A Flight's destruction would be. Sure enough, southeast of Douai, Wright spotted a formation of seven Fokkers, above his flight of Camels but below the SEs. He led his pilots underneath the enemy formation while Smith manoeuvred his flight in between them and the sun. The German pilots, apparently thinking they had the upper hand, dived on to Wright's Camels. Smith timed his attack from above perfectly and the Fokkers were trapped in between the two Australian flights. In moments, five of them were spinning down out of control, while the British Bristol Fighters higher up kept another formation of Fokkers from intervening.

James Ross was piloting one of the SE5as in Smith's flight. His account of the action highlighted that, even with a 'shrewd game', the Fokker DVII's outstanding climbing performance made it a dangerous adversary:

> I picked out a Hun and dived vertically at a great speed on him firing with both my machine guns. When about a hundred yards from him I noticed another Hun on my left climbing for all he was worth. As it doesn't do to let a Hun get height on you, I pulled out into a zooming turn. As I went over the top of him he pulled up and fired a burst at a fairly long range. He was either a wonderful shot or a fluker as I stopped one in the leg. I immediately started to throw things around and he didn't get another hit. My flight commander coming from behind fixed him up.[34]

Ross was the only Australian casualty. He made it back to Reclinghem and was sent off to a casualty clearing station. The Australian pilots had avenged A Flight's losses and claimed five of JG III's machines.

The 6 September ambush was a model for how the scout squadrons would do things for the rest of the war. Offensive patrols became highly organised affairs, usually involving three or four squadrons rendezvousing over a given point at various heights and working their way up to 40 kilometres behind the enemy lines to 'sweep' the skies clear. Large enemy formations were met sporadically throughout September, a reflection of the fact that the German Air Service lacked the resources to contest the skies all along the front. Instead, the Jagdgeschwaden shifted back and forth along the line to support the beleaguered German Army.

Whenever they did appear, though, there were some titanic air battles involving dozens of aircraft. Camel pilot Jack Wilkinson captured the chaos of large, late-war fights:

> The air was full of machines flying around each other at every possible and impossible angle ... It was a case of each man for himself while it lasted, and I put my machine into a tight turn, climbing to get behind a Tripe-hound flying in the opposite direction. Before I could get him in my ring sight there was a 'clack-clack-clack-clack-clack' and the white streaks of tracer bullets appeared between my wings on either side. Hun on my tail! Over with the stick and rudder, and, as my assailant zoomed to dive again, I got off a short burst at a Hun diving in front of me, only to take my thumbs off the triggers to avoid hitting one of our own Camels that was on the tail of the Hun. And so it went on—a short burst from the guns, and a wriggle to dodge a Hun on my tail—round and round, up and down, until the sky and the earth seemed to reel around each other in sympathy.

In less than a minute, during which time Wilkinson caught glimpses of one enemy machine going down trailing smoke and 'another in evident difficulties', the air was suddenly empty: 'I looked about me, and was scarcely able to believe my eyes—not a machine was in sight!'[35]

As Wilkinson's account suggests, these big dogfights didn't typically involve lots of casualties. As Cobby explained, 'the air was too crowded and everyone so mixed up that there was little opportunity to settle down and have a steady shot at anything'.[36]

This is not to say that the Australian scout squadrons stopped making claims—or sustaining casualties; on the contrary, the final weeks of the war were among the costliest for both units. It is just that they usually didn't happen when wing and Jagdgeschwader clashed head on. As had been the case throughout the war, the killing usually happened when one surprised the other from above.

One flight leader who well understood this was Roby Manuel of No. 2 Squadron. Since joining the unit in February, he had learned his craft from the Cambrai veterans like Dick Howard, Roy Phillipps and Henry Forrest. By September 1918, he was one of the veterans who new pilots like Frank Roberts looked up to. Four decades after the war, Roberts recalled that Manuel was 'quite an amazing man':

> We had no radio contact or communications once we were in the air, except by signals. Roby had good eyes but strangely turned out to be a bit colour blind but he would scout us around the line, we wondering what the hell he was at but we'd dive around a cloud and then underneath would be a bunch of Huns. We'd attack through, diving towards the line. If we could win out we stayed—if they were too much for us we shot right through. But we were never caught—and that was Roby Manuel, an outstanding pilot, technically completely sound.[37]

It was just the right approach for the autumn skies of 1918. On 16 September, having not seen a large German formation for a week, Manuel led eleven SE5as on a high-altitude sweep over Lille while pairs of No. 4 Squadron Camels shot up enemy billets below.

Manuel spotted a flight of ten Fokker biplanes 17 000 feet over Lille, heading for the line. He led his flight around to the south while the leader of the other flight, Frank Smith, circled his pilots around behind them to attack from the east. The two flights of SEs fell on to the Fokkers together like a flock of hawks. Each pilot picked his man and fired. Within moments, six enemy machines were tumbling to the ground out of control—a pair going to Smith and another to Manuel. Of course, at such a high altitude there was no confirming their destruction by seeing a crash and there is a good chance some of the enemy pilots were using the 'out of control spin' as an evasive manoeuvre. Frank Alberry could be quite sure that he got his man, though. 'I singled out one and dived on it firing 50 rounds at close range,' he wrote. It did a sudden, clumsy turn and then fell wing over into a spin: 'Flames and smoke were observed to be coming from its cockpit.' This was Alberry's first of seven victories—a feat all the more remarkable considering he only had one leg. The other was amputated in 1916 after he was wounded in the trenches. Alberry was allowed to join the flying corps after petitioning King George V personally.

On the way home half an hour later, Manuel noticed some Archie bursts near La Basée. Despite being low on ammunition, he went down to investigate and spotted the very unusual sight of a lone Fokker flying at low altitude, well over the British side. He followed it north to St Omer, where he came into range. 'I followed him down to within a hundred feet of the ground, at last firing a burst of ten rounds at 20 yards range.' His gun actions clacked; they were empty. Nevertheless, his mark was good and the Fokker plunged into the ground. Downing an enemy machine in friendly territory was a rare experience for an Australian pilot and Manuel took the opportunity to inspect his quarry. He landed beside the wreck and stayed with its badly wounded pilot as he died. Manuel helped bury him before returning to Reclinghem.

Eric Dibbs saw Manuel land at the aerodrome that morning. 'He climbed down from his SE with a load in his arms.' When Major Murray Jones asked him what it was, Manuel explained he had 'got a German machine on our side of the lines' and had removed its black crosses and magnetos to confirm his claim, as no one else was around to see it. 'That was conclusive enough for me,' recalled Dibbs. It must have been for the Major too, as he credited Manuel with the kill (making it two for the day) and recommended him for the immediate award of a bar to his Distinguished Flying Cross. Although six of his colleagues in No. 2 Squadron received DFCs, Roby Manuel was the only pilot to receive the honour twice.[38]

'Objectives that simply asked to be bombed': Following the German retreat, October–November 1918

The attack on the Hindenburg Line on 29 September 1918, which No. 3 Squadron supported, was one in a series of hammer blows against the enemy.

It was preceded, on the day before, by a combined British and Belgian offensive in Flanders, just to the north of the two Australian scout squadrons.

The pilots supported the Flanders offensive (known as the Fifth Battle of Ypres) with low-flying attacks and, by nightfall, news from the battlefront was exciting. The Belgians and British had captured some 10 kilometres of ground—more than they had gained in three months of bloody fighting there the year before—and they continued to advance despite terrible weather on the following two days. On 29 September, the heads of the German military advised the Kaiser to seek an immediate Armistice.[39]

Allied progress in Flanders made the German positions immediately to the south around Lille untenable, and on 2 October the enemy began retreating. Of course, both squadrons were there to chase them all the way back with bombs and machine guns. 'Our combined squadron destroyer patrols harassed and worried anything they saw,' recalled Jack Wright. 'Trains, motor lorries, airfields, camps and here and there a battery in action or a barge on a canal. In a few days the whole countryside around Lille began burning as the Germans set fire to their abandoned dumps and camps.'[40]

Railway stations, packed with retreating enemy troops and equipment, were especially important targets. They 'resounded with the clatter of bomb explosions' as the scout squadrons worked back and forth along the enemy's withdrawing front.[41] On 6 October, the Australian squadrons received orders to 'carry out a special mission at dawn'.[42] All machines were to carry bombs. No. 4 Squadron's Camels would prowl along the railway routes leading from the front back to Lille, while eighteen SE5as from No. 2 Squadron, escorted by ten Bristol Fighters from No. 88 Squadron, attacked the main railway hubs around Lille.

Adrian Cole led the SE5as in low, across the lines. According to Eric Dibbs, they were 'immediately subjected to a warm welcome by the German anti-aircraft gunners'. Just over the lines, the formation began a shallow descent to Lille. As it came into view, they were 'greeted by more bursts of "frightfulness" in the shape of machine gun fire and "flaming onions" in large quantities'.

Above the outskirts of the city, Cole fired a Verey light to signal the flights to break up and attack railway stations filled with German troops waiting to be evacuated east. No. 88 Squadron's Bristols meanwhile provided a protective umbrella above. Dibbs' flight hit the large railway yard at Fives, on the eastern side of Lille. They paired off and went in at high speed, 'flying along the station at roof level, one after the other'.

> As we passed by we could hear the rattle of machine gun fire, but we were down only about 30 feet from the ground and were pretty hard to hit... We would leave the fire of one gun behind and immediately pick up the fire of another, and so on for the whole length of the platform. We dropped our four 25 lb bombs on the trains, or the station itself, or any other military objective we could see.

For 20 minutes, the SE5as buzzed around Lille, wreaking havoc. They bombed six trains and wrecked numerous station buildings. Troops and horses waiting to embark were pelted with bombs and bullets, as were the anti-aircraft batteries there to guard them. Cole fired another Verey light to signal 'regroup and head home'. 'Coming back was something too,' recalled Dibbs.

> It was terribly exhilarating; over 6 or 7 miles of Hunland, till we reached home. Skimming over the fields, over a row of trees or a house and down again, we were too low for the anti-aircraft gunners to bear their sights onto us. They really had no hope of hitting us at that height. Sometimes a field battery would open up, but their luck was no better. If you saw a line of flashes, say on a hedge line, you simply flew into it and put a burst of fire down, and they would shut up.

All of the SE5as arrived home in time for breakfast, with the exception of a rookie, Arthur Long. Fragments from a bomb he dropped punctured his petrol tank. He just managed to clear no man's land before his engine stopped and he came down in the British wire. 'A few hours afterwards,' said Dibbs, 'he reported back to the squadron, little worse for wear.'[43]

The squadrons joined in on more wing-sized raids on enemy railway lines and aerodromes over the following week. On 18 October, Frank Roberts' flight noticed a conspicuous absence of Archie over Lille. 'We went down lower and lower and finally we were right down, and up and down the streets of Lille. People were out waving—the Hun had gone.'[44]

For the pursuit into Belgium, No. 4 Squadron swapped its Camels for Sopwith's newer scout, the Snipe. The pilots were impressed: Wright described them as 'the last word on the British side in fighter design'. The Snipes performed better than the Camels at high altitudes, and were faster and more robust, although they lacked some of the Camel's whippy manoeuvrability. Some of the squadron's veterans were, nevertheless, reluctant to part with the machines that had faithfully seen them through so much fighting. 'I personally, was sorry to part with my Camel,' explained Wright. 'I found them lovely machines to fly, in spite of their "quirks".'[45]

The re-equip forced a reversal of roles on the Australian scout units. For the remainder of the war, No. 4 Squadron flew high-altitude patrols while No. 2 Squadron used its SE5as to bomb and shoot up the enemy retreat. Despite chronic shortages of fuel and equipment, the enemy Jastas tenaciously covered their army's retreat, giving the Snipe pilots the opportunity to test their new machines in a series of titanic air battles in the war's final fortnight.

On 29 October, George Jones was leading three flights of Snipes above the retreating German Army, northeast of Tournai, when he spotted 40 enemy Fokkers, strung out between 6000 and 15 000 feet. Not wanting to get underneath the highest enemy machines, he led his flight away, gaining height:

> Just then a formation of British two-seaters came onto the scene, and the Fokkers dived down onto them. This gave me the chance I needed, and we dived right down onto the Germans. I took my flight in on top of them, and in the tremendous mix-up there we bagged about 11 German machines. In the same fight, however, I lost one of my most valued men, [Percy] Sims, a man who knew nothing of fear. He went off on his own right into the thick of it, and before we could give him a hand, he was sent down in flames. It was a terrible sight to watch his aircraft spiralling down, till finally he crashed on the bank of a canal.[46]

The skies above the German retreat were full of Fokkers the following day too. Bo King (Cobby's replacement to lead A Flight) led eleven Snipes down on a similar-sized formation of Fokkers attacking some British bombers. In the first pass, the Australians hit four of the enemy machines, sending three down out of control and another in flames. Finding himself in the midst of the remaining Germans, being fired at 'from every direction', King zoomed up through their formation and into the path of a Fokker he hadn't seen. Its pilot threw his machine into a violent spin to avoid collision with King, but collided with another Fokker. Both machines went to pieces and fell to the ground, allowing the exceptionally fortunate King to claim three victories for the day. The fight had cost A Flight another one of its new pilots shot down and captured.[47]

Five days of rain extinguished the aerial action and brought the retreating Germans some respite. Bright sunshine on 4 November saw the pilots on both sides back out in force, though, in a pitched battle to control the air over the retreating German armies. Early patrols by both squadrons tangled with Fokkers northeast of Tournai. Seventeen of No. 2 Squadron's pilots tore an enemy formation of seven to pieces and claimed four of them. Four Snipes from No. 4 Squadron crossed the lines alone later in the morning (a risky venture at this stage of the war) and attacked a larger formation of Fokkers. The Australians claimed one out of control but lost two of their number, shot down and taken prisoner. One of them, 23-year-old Charles Rhodes, was on his first patrol and had probably not even had time to get to know all his fellow pilots' names yet.

The action intensified at noon when the entire wing crossed the lines together to harass enemy troops retreating towards Ath and hit the aerodrome at Chapelle-à-Wattines. No. 2 Squadron dived on the aerodrome while the Snipes circled above to protect them. Five Fokkers came up underneath and got among the SE5as forcing them to release their bombs early. In a furious, low-level clash, the Australians shot all of them down.

Bo King, in charge of the Snipes, was escorting the wing back across the lines when he noticed a dozen Fokkers climbing to pursue them. He wheeled No. 4 Squadron around and dived among them. He quickly shot two down, and his fellow flight commander George Jones got another in flames, but it was obvious the Australians were in above their heads. Their opponents were in fact the elite 'Jasta Boelcke', part of their old adversaries, JG III. In what he described as the 'wild, mixed up melee' that followed, the German commander Karl Bolle shot down two of the Australian machines, killing their pilots and raising his personal score to 37. Another Australian fell to the guns of Ernst Bormann, his sixteenth victory. Nevertheless, Bolle dubbed the dogfight Jasta Boelcke's toughest ever on account of the Snipes—'a new English fighter aeroplane much better in climb and manoeuvrability than the Fokker DVII'.[48]

Somewhat paradoxically, Jasta Boelcke's victims were among No. 4 Squadron's most experienced pilots. One, Thomas Baker, was a veteran flight commander with a dozen victories to his credit. The other two, Arthur Palliser and Parker Symons, had been at the front since August and Palliser had claimed five Fokkers in the week before his death. His was a particularly cruel fate, having survived four years of war, not only to be killed a week before the Armistice but also a day before he was scheduled for leave to Australia. Jones recalled speaking to Palliser before taking off that morning. 'I am due to return to Australia tomorrow,' he said. 'If I was only lucky enough to break my finger in the hangar door I would not be able to fly today.'[49] Palliser, along with Baker and Symons, were probably the last three Australians to die in action during the First World War.

After the climactic air battles of 4 November, the Germans faded from the skies and their army's hasty retreat degenerated into a rout. 80th Wing pursued them relentlessly through Belgium, finding 'almost daily', in the wing commander's words, 'objectives that simply asked to be bombed'. On 9 November, the wing hit an aerodrome and enemy camp at Enghien. Strange recalled coming down with engines full on to find a landscape of 'targets, which offered themselves in all directions'. They burnt five hangars and ten aircraft on the ground at one aerodrome and then flew along the roads. 'Two miles of motor and horse transport, guns, etc. were mercilessly shot up and bombed by No. 4 AFC, causing the utmost confusion and destruction,' wrote Strange.[50] The British pilot who led the raid reported that he had never seen 'such an opportunity' as far as targets were concerned. 'Horse transport was seen stampeding in all directions and in numerous cases troops endeavouring to get into houses were shot and many casualties caused.' The destruction was, in his assessment, 'almost indescribable and impossible to give in detail'.[51]

The AFC suffered its final battle casualty during this raid, when Frank Smith, one of No. 2 Squadron's flight commanders, crashed on the outskirts of Enghien. As if to prove the point one last time that ground fire was the great leveller among pilots of the First World War, Smith—the squadron's highest scoring pilot—had been felled by a rifle bullet. Before he could even think about burning his machine, some of the soldiers he had been strafing were running towards the crash site. Smith bolted and, despite his bulky flying kit, managed to outpace them and hide in a haystack until they passed. He then found a farmhouse, where a frightened Belgian farmer gave him some filthy old clothes but refused to shelter him. Smith walked back into Enghien, posing as a Belgian peasant, and spent the day in an estaminet while German soldiers swarmed through the city on their way east. His broken French helped maintain his disguise over the following days until the Armistice was signed. To the great surprise of his squadron mates, he turned up at the mess a few days later, 'looking like a scarecrow and making a most dramatic entrance just as everyone was in the middle of a more than usually hilarious celebration'.[52]

'What the hell—what'll we do now?' the Armistice, 11 November 1918

The Armistice of 11 November 1918 was probably all that saved the German Army from complete annihilation from the skies. Nevertheless, it was not expected by the Australian pilots—or, as we might assume, greeted with unfettered elation.

At 8.00 a.m. that morning, Jack Wright was sitting in his Snipe on No. 4 Squadron's aerodrome warming his engine to lead yet another bombing raid on the retreating enemy. He was just about to push the throttle forward, when he noticed a commotion over near the hangars. A car had pulled up, people were gathering and a man in uniform was sprinting across the aerodrome towards the line of aircraft. He arrived beside Wright's cockpit, breathless. 'Flight's been washed out, sir. Cancelled—peace has been signed.' When he managed to catch his breath, he explained that an armistice had been signed and fighting was to stop at 11.00 a.m. In the meantime, no airmen were to fly any further east than the British observation balloon line.

Wright sat there while the news sank in, 'trying to grasp all the implications'. Finally, he fired a flare to signal that the sortie was cancelled and switched off his engine.

The Australian pilots spent the rest of the morning wandering listlessly about their aerodromes. Most recorded feelings of scepticism. 'There must have been some mistake,' thought Wright, who described feeling 'like a fish out of water'.[53] The doubt persisted at higher levels of command too, with Lieutenant Colonel Strange admitting he expected to hear from brigade that it was only a rumour.[54]

Meanwhile, down south at No. 3 Squadron's forward landing ground at Flaumont, pilots were preparing to take off when news arrived that fighting would stop at 11.00 a.m. Bill Palstra recorded how the airmen 'reluctantly' switched off their engines and climbed down. 'Strafing a retreating army is good sport to the man in the air,' he explained, 'though probably far from agreeable to the Hun plodding back to Hunland.'[55] It seems some of the airmen in the scout squadrons felt the same. They took off anyway, afterwards professing 'most innocently' to have been out looking for the missing Frank Smith, but landing, as the wing commander noted, with conspicuously empty bomb racks.[56]

At 11.00 a.m., Palstra and some of the other airmen were sitting around, debating whether the news was true or not, when a great racket sprang up all around the countryside. Cheers and the sound of bagpipes filled the air, along with hundreds of Verey lights. 'We stood still and listened,' wrote Palstra in his diary, 'and the realisation dawned on us that this was the end of the war.'[57]

At first, some of the men didn't really know what to do. Frank Roberts later recalled:

We looked at each other and thought 'what the hell—what'll we do now?' Well we slunk away to the mess. We had been away for three or four years and were not trained for anything at home—we were only flying people. Where do we go?[58]

It wasn't just the pilots who felt like this. Frank Rawlinson sat in his workshop, with a 'deep feeling of anti-climax in this cold and quiet and empty land that had rumbled with incessant gunfire since August 1914.'[59]

In spite of their anxiety (or perhaps, because of it), everyone soon did what the occasion demanded. Roberts and his mates were snapped out of their melancholy by a carload of RAF officers careering past their aerodrome in a car, firing off Verey lights. 'Right—well here's something to do,' he thought. 'So we turned on a binge and that went on until the small hours of the following morning.'[60] Both scout squadrons went into Lille that night where, in Wright's words, 'the different branches of the services were in competition with one another to put on the noisiest and most uninhibited party that could be contrived'.[61]

'Deutschland unter alles': Occupation and homecoming, December 1918–June 1919

Although the fighting was finished, the three Australian squadrons remained in Europe over the winter of 1918–19 to help administer the terms of the Armistice and ensure the defeated enemy abided by them. The document Germany signed on 11 November was in effect an offer of ceasefire in exchange for the unconditional surrender of its army, along with much of its equipment and territory in the industrial Rhineland.

Under the Armistice terms, German pilots had to surrender their machines in airworthy condition. At enemy aerodromes around Belgium, Australian mechanics and flying officers helped inspect and impound German aircraft. The resentment of their old foes was obvious. JG III's pilots, for example, defiantly painted their names and victory tallies on their Fokkers before relinquishing them. Others deliberately sabotaged their machines.[62] Fergus Cox of No. 2 Squadron recalled how 'some petrol tanks had sugar in them, which meant a complete removal and wash. Loosened nuts on petrol pipes were plentiful. Once a machine was declared ready, it was isolated and guarded by Aussies.'[63] Australian pilots helped ferry surrendered machines back across the Channel, an opportunity many of them relished.

Nos 2 and 3 Squadrons remained in Belgium over the winter but No. 4 Squadron went to Germany with the army of occupation. Just before Christmas 1918, it arrived at Bickendorf aerodrome, just a few kilometres outside of Cologne. In contrast to the cratered fields and tents the squadron had been making do with in recent months, Bickendorf was a permanent establishment previously occupied by several German squadrons. In Wright's assessment, it was 'by far the finest aerodrome 4th Squadron had ever been stationed on'. The men made the aerodrome's spacious barracks their home while the officers moved into the Kaiser Wilhelm Hotel—a 'veritable home away from home', according to Wright—near the city's famous cathedral: 'The complete hotel building was taken over for our use, a number of German civilians being disposed for that purpose and most of the German staff being retained to look after us.' It was a good way to end a war.

The job of occupation was not an onerous one. The pilots each did two or three flights per week to make a show of strength to the Rhinelanders. Otherwise they relaxed, went sightseeing or competed at inter-squadron sports meetings. Most of the Germans were very accommodating, and after four years of being maliciously caricatured in British propaganda, seemed surprisingly ordinary to the Australians. Wright was surprised to note that he could see little difference between them (also 'Anglo-Saxons') and the British. He became friendly with two young fräuleins—a 'typical German blonde' and 'a beautiful brunette, volatile and vivacious'—and 'spent some very pleasant evenings being entertained by these lasses'. The distorting influence of propaganda cut both ways, though. George Jones was intrigued to note the German civilians 'did not seem to fully understand that they had lost the war'.[64] Four years of living under what was practically a military dictatorship left them with doubts Germany had in fact lost the war on the battlefield. Wright noticed this too, describing the German civilians as 'unrepentant' and leaving him in no doubt whatsoever that another war with Germany was inevitable.[65]

Despite having a free run of the bar in their hotel, the Australian pilots managed to behave themselves, although one notable exception involved the vandalism of a statue of Frederick the Great in the square outside the Kaiser Wilhelm Hotel. One evening, the pilots changed its inscription, *Deutschland uber alles*, to *Deutschland unter alles* and crowned the monarch with a chamber pot. Upset locals called the fire brigade to remove the 'crown', which they did, to the cheers and catcalls of the gathered Australians.

On Christmas Day, all ranks enjoyed a feast, with the aircraft mechanics and privates even having the likes of salmon croquets, roast beef, chicken, duck, goose and pudding with brandy sauce. The men were enjoying their banquet in the aerodrome mess, when a young boy appeared at the door. They invited him to join in and learned that his name was Henri Hemene, and that he had been orphaned in the opening weeks of the war. Since then, he had lived with British units and had come to Cologne with an RAF squadron. At the end of the meal, Henri declared, 'the diggers will do me' and asked if he could stay. The men accepted him and included him in their group photograph that afternoon. They took up a collection and paid a local tailor to make him a child-size Australian uniform. Over the following weeks, Henri—soon known as 'Digger'—stayed with the mechanics, doing odd jobs around the sheds. He became particularly close to one of them, Tim Tovell, a 40-year-old builder from Brisbane. Tovell wrote to his wife with news that he intended to bring Henri back to Australia and adopt him. 'One more in the family will not matter,' he told her, unaware that his eldest son had recently died in Brisbane.

At the end of February 1919, all three Australian squadrons handed their aircraft over to the RAF and made their way back to Britain. To smuggle Henri across the Channel at Le Havre, Tovell hid him in a large sack labelled 'oats' (see Plate 30). 'Tied up in the sack, he lay on the wharf for hours, but never moved,' explained the mechanic. Henri made the crossing undetected and travelled with No. 4 Squadron to Hurdcott at Salisbury Plain where the entire AFC was camped, waiting for repatriation to Australia.[66] Throughout March and April, leave passes were almost freely available. Those with money travelled around the British Isles. Others applied for leave to work in civilian trades or participated in vocational courses the AIF was running to help men prepare for their return to civilian life.

On 25 April 1919, the AFC participated in an Anzac Day parade through London to receive the salute of the Prince of Wales and Field Marshal Sir Douglas Haig. Roby Manuel was invited to lead twenty Australian pilots overhead in a flypast. Low flying and 'stunting' were not allowed, and they had to keep to the right side of the Strand. 'I told the lads we would fly up and down the Strand as instructed,' recalled Manuel. 'I will loop the loop and then you can do what you like.'[67] The pilots arrived above London just as the march was beginning. Manuel did his loop and everyone else broke formation and began stunting. Cobby recalled the spectacle of aircraft buzzing about over Australia House, 'looping and rolling and spinning everywhere'. As the column of troops neared the saluting base, occupied by the Prince and Haig, the aircraft went down and flew along the Strand to pass him first. 'It was probably the most foolish thing I have ever done,' remembered Cobby. The aircraft zoomed between the Strand's buildings, passing under the wires stretching across the street. 'Having got down, I had to stay down for about three quarters of a mile before I could get out.'[68]

Cobby's account seems exaggerated, but there is no doubt the AFC stole the show. As *The Argus* of 29 April 1919 reported:

> The most striking feature of the Anzac celebrations in London were the hair raising feats performed in the air by the Australian pilots, particularly a pilot in a red Sopwith machine, which was promptly named the 'Red Devil'. It travelled at terrible speed and looped and nose dived almost along the chimney pots. At times the machine seemed in imminent danger of becoming entangled in the telephone wires or of crashing into the steeple of St Mary le Strand, which caused women to scream.

Apparently, there were no disciplinary measures for the pilots. Manuel was 'up before the Beak' to explain himself, and he was probably told to expect punishment. But the matter was forgotten when the AFC received orders to prepare for embarkation to Australia just a few days later.[69]

On 6 May 1918, the AFC's 800 or so men travelled to Southampton to board the SS *Kaisar-i-Hind* for the month-long journey home. 'It was a damp, but striking send off,' recalled Cobby. The men of the three Australian fighting squadrons and the four training units hauled their duffle bags past a brass band and up the gangplank in drizzling rain. Two hours of English pomp and ceremony followed as Southampton's Lord Mayor and all the councillors delivered speeches from a dais on the dockside. Some Australians entertained themselves by trying to throw oranges down the ends of the band's larger brass instruments. Tim Tovell and his mates meanwhile smuggled the eleven-year-old French orphan Henri Hemene aboard in a hamper marked 'sporting materials'. The boy would remain in there for the next three days until the boat was well and truly out of port.

When the *Kaisar-i-Hind* finally weighed anchor and pulled away from the wharf, everyone on board cheered and sang Australian songs. Yet there were many, remembered Cobby, who couldn't conceal the sadness on their faces. 'We had had such a wonderful time and been so hospitably treated that there was no pleasure at that moment in leaving England. And we all left staunch and close friends behind.'[70]

14

'IT WILL SURPRISE MOST PEOPLE TO FIND THAT THE AUSTRALIANS DID SO MUCH FLYING'

Legacy of the Australian Flying Corps

'The Wizard of the Air', Captain Arthur 'Harry' Cobby, DSO and DFC with two bars. With 29 confirmed victories, he was the AFC's highest scoring pilot. This portrait was taken in late 1918, after Cobby had spent nine months at the front with No. 4 Squadron. The strain is evident on his 24-year-old face. *AWM A03697*

They were pioneers and heroes . . . they were wonderful and they did it without parachutes too.

—Brian Wright, son of Jack Wright, No. 4 Squadron, Australian Flying Corps

'Great fun to have played some little part': Homecoming and the years beyond

There were some 800 passengers on board the *Kaisar-i-Hind* when it docked in Port Melbourne on 16 June 1919. Besides the hundreds of air mechanics and pilots, there was a small party of esteemed guests, including two of Australia's divisional commanders and the Premier of Queensland.

Nonetheless, as the passengers disembarked there was one man in particular the press sought out for an interview. It was the 25-year-old ex-bank clerk they had dubbed 'the wizard of the air': the AFC's highest scoring pilot, Captain Arthur Cobby DSO and DFC with two bars. A journalist from *The Argus* bailed up Cobby on the wharf. He was surprised—the 'fresh complexioned and lightly built' Cobby didn't quite resemble 'the hawklike pursuer who downed no fewer than 29 Hun planes and five enemy balloons' of his imagination.

The journalist, pencil poised above a notebook, pressed Cobby for stories of his exploits but, like many in his profession who had sought to interview pilots, was disappointed. Cobby 'declined to discuss his own exploits', leaving the journalist with a declaration of his respect for his German adversaries (although he never doubted they'd lose the war) and his conviction that Australians made ideal pilots: 'They seemed to be temperamentally cut out for the work.' Before making off to a waiting car which would take him to the demobilisation depot—the last stop before a welcome home dinner with his family—Cobby told the journalist he intended 'sticking to the game' of flying in Australia 'if the opportunity offered.'[1]

The interest the press showed in Cobby reflected a fascination the Australian public had with 'their' airmen. Indeed, as Hudson Fysh discovered when he arrived home from Palestine with No. 1 Squadron in April 1919, public interest in pilots was tremendous. 'Even to walk up the street was an unbelievable experience,' he recalled:

> I can best describe the experience by comparing it to what would happen if two of our present day spacemen walked along the street in full space rig-out... To the world at large, airmen in 1919 wore haloes, which was both embarrassing and not good for our characters.[2]

The Department of Defence used the pilots' 'haloes' to promote a peace loan scheme in September and October 1919. To raise funds for the 'payment of war obligations' and repatriation, the government offered £25 million worth of bonds at 5 per cent interest. Pilots, especially those known to the Australian public, were chosen to fly between towns to promote the scheme with aerobatic displays, pamphlet drops, speeches and even autograph signings. The pilots who covered Victoria included some of the AFC's most esteemed—Harry Cobby, Adrian Cole, Frank McNamara, Fred Huxley, Bill Herbert and Charlie Matheson.[3] Flying an Avro 504K (the chief trainer in the latter part of the war), McNamara covered 1100 kilometres in nine days and called in at all the centres along the Murray as far as Mildura and then back through the towns on the Mallee.[4]

The airmen were a huge drawcard for the scheme. Large crowds turned out in towns all around Australia and within three weeks purchased over £20 million in subscriptions. Charlie Matheson's efforts at Traralgon on 6 September illustrate the influence airmen had on the public. According to *The Argus* of 8 September 1919, he was giving an aerobatics display when his engine failed, forcing him to crash in a paddock outside of town. The townspeople rushed to the site to find him coolly standing back from the wrecked aircraft snapping a photograph of it. He then climbed up on it and gave an appeal, after which the locals subscribed to £2000 worth of subscriptions.

The 1919 Peace Loan flights did more than raise money, though—they stimulated the Australian public's imagination and expectations of what aviation might have in store for peace time. When Captain Eric Cummings (ex-No. 2 Squadron) visited Hobart in his Sopwith Pup in late August, a local newspaper commentator saw the event in symbolic terms, representing both what aviation had done for the Australian soldier at war, and what it might now do for the Australian nation in peace. He reported in *The Mercury* of 29 August:

> His flight yesterday was reminiscent of the way the war was won, because without the airmen the other branches of the army would eventually have been helpless victims of the Germans. But the flight was equally suggestive of the days of peace which are beginning, and of the uses which may be

made of the lessons of the war. It is not conceivable that after the wonderful advances which have been made in five years in the mechanism and in the handling of aeroplanes there will be a sudden stop, and they will still be reserved only for the purpose of war. The question which is even now under consideration... is how far these machines may be used for commercial purposes.

A resounding answer, which only served to heighten the aviator's public standing, came at the end of the year when Ross Smith, the AFC's most successful pilot in the Middle East, made a remarkable record-breaking flight. Accompanied by his brother Keith (a pilot in the RAF) and a pair of mechanics from No. 1 Squadron, he flew a Vickers Vimy bomber from London to Darwin in just under 28 days. The four men shared a prize of £10 000 sponsored by the Australian government and became national heroes. In 1922, Ross Smith and one of the mechanics, Jim Bennett, were killed in an accident while preparing to circumnavigate the globe by air. Had Ross Smith lived to achieve what he certainly seemed capable of, he would undoubtedly feature as prominently in the public's consciousness as his successor, ex-RAF pilot Charles Kingsford-Smith, now does.

The sheen of service in the flying corps faded, though. By the end of 1919, the wartime squadrons were disbanded and the returned men found themselves, as Fysh put it, 'amongst tens of thousands of young men who had not been securely launched into life before leaving for the war' and who needed to find work in a deflated labour market. Even an ex-flight commander with a service record like George Jones' faced an uncertain future:

I think most servicemen find it a curious experience when they return to civil life. They have to fend for themselves again, and make their own decisions about their futures. After holding the rank of captain in the AIF I found it particularly difficult, for apart from the six hundred pounds I had saved from my deferred pay, my financial prospects seemed dim.[5]

The natural solution, for many, was to return to their old vocations and try to pick up where they had left off. According to Richard Williams, the mechanics were generally successful in this, representing as they did in

1919, the nation's most experienced tradesmen and engineers.[6] Pilots had more difficulty, though—if for no other reason than that it was hard to settle down again after such an exciting and dangerous war. And while some airmen inevitably did, and never touched the controls of an aircraft again, the majority of AFC pilots found their way back into the cockpit sooner or later. It was this group of men who would ensure that the AFC's legacy was a profound one for Australia's transportation and defence history.

In 1919 and 1920, there was vigorous debate among the upper echelons of Australia's military and government about forming a permanent, independent (from the army or navy) air force. In the meantime, a temporary 'Australian Air Corps' (AAC) was established to preserve a nucleus of flying and technical skills and maintain equipment. However, with only nine officers and 70 other ranks appointed, there were—at least for the time being—strictly limited prospects for ex-AFC men keen to fly again.[7]

Some took matters into their own hands and sought work in the infant commercial aviation industry. Bored in his pre-war job as a mechanic, George Jones was lucky to find work as a pilot with a newspaper company, which delivered papers by air to towns along the Murray River.[8] Pard Mustard likewise tried farming but found it dull and purchased an old BE2e—a machine that 'would have given him the shudders if he had been asked to fly it in Palestine in 1918'. With an old comrade, he did a 'joyous but rickety grand tour of the country towns of Victoria, South Australia and NSW'. Using showgrounds and racetracks as aerodromes, they offered people joy flights for 30 shillings. The people of rural Australia responded enthusiastically to what became known as 'Gipsy-flying' or 'barnstorming', many having never seen a 'flying machine' let alone ridden in one.[9] Roby Manuel was another rural barnstormer. He supplemented his farming income with a Boulton P9 two-seater biplane. He advertised with a flyer, calling himself *The Flying Farmer* and offering punters: 'In the air clear 10 minutes or roughly 15 miles ride for one pound. Longer flights can be arranged.' Although he stuck with his farming, Manuel kept flying for pleasure too. In 1967, he celebrated the fiftieth anniversary of earning his wings by giving the locals of Kerang an exciting aerial display in his Tiger Moth. He was, by then, the only AFC pilot still flying in Australia.[10]

The opportunity a number of ex-AFC men were waiting for came finally in March 1921, with the formation of the Royal Australian Air Force (RAAF). From the outset, the AFC's pilots dominated its ranks, filling fifteen of the 21 officer positions initially appointed. Naturally, the AFC's most experienced and decorated were heavily represented on the founding staff: Richard Williams, Alan Murray Jones, Lawrence Wackett, Adrian Cole, Frank McNamara and of course Harry Cobby. The RAAF doubled in size within six months, but still 80 per cent of personnel had served in the war— the majority with the AFC but some with the RFC/RAF and Royal Naval Air Service. The RAAF was shaped during its formative years by Richard Williams, its founding Chief of Air Staff. Williams, who held the position for thirteen years between the wars, had just the intelligence, administrative skill and political aptitude to build up the RAAF while fending off attacks on its independence. Williams' influence in the RAAF's history is immense. He was personally involved with most aspects of its early development, spanning the design of its ensign and uniform to writing an air defence strategy for Australia, which is still the cornerstone of the nation's defence strategy today.[11]

In 1925, the RAAF was expanded to include a citizen force component, which was likewise dominated by AFC personalities. This, along with the fact that a tight defence budget kept the RAAF small prior to the Second World War, made Australia's air force feel, in the words of George Jones (who enlisted as a flying officer in 1921), like an 'intimate club'.[12] The Second World War, and in particular the perceived threat of Japanese invasion, provided impetus for the 'club' to grow into the fourth largest air force in the world, with over 200 000 Australians serving in the RAAF by 1945. Although too old to fly, AFC veterans made considerable contributions to leadership and training in the RAAF during that conflict too. The outstanding example is Sir George Jones, who was Australia's Chief of the Air Staff for ten consecutive years, between 1942 and 1952.

Other ex-AFC pilots sought opportunities in Australia's burgeoning civil aviation industry. The most enduring example is provided by one of No. 1 Squadron's formidable Bristol Fighter teams, Paul McGinness and Hudson Fysh. In 1920 they teamed up with a pair of west Queensland graziers and established the Queensland and Northern Territory Aerial Services

Ltd—what we know today as Qantas, Australia's national airline. Initially based in Longreach and using old war surplus biplanes, the company serviced farmers and occasionally acted as an air ambulance. In 1922 it began domestic passenger services and by 1935 was conducting overseas flights, and was well on the way to being the major international carrier it is today. That its beginnings lay with the crew of a Bristol Fighter in the skies above Palestine in 1918 is far from common knowledge today.

Australia's amnesia concerning its First World War airmen is perhaps due to the fact that, over the last 90 years, the AFC has received scant attention from historians. The only substantial study of the corps throughout the war (prior to this one) was published in 1923 as Volume Eight of the twelve-volume series, *The Official History of Australia in the War, 1914–1918*. The series' general editor, Charles Bean, appointed a fellow journalist and his wartime assistant, Frederic Morley Cutlack, to write the volume. It was a difficult job from the outset, as Cutlack needed to balance his research with his day job as a journalist for the *Sydney Morning Herald* (which included an assignment to New Guinea in the middle of the project). The AFC's records were substantially incomplete in places, and there was practically no secondary literature for him to consult (relevant volumes of the British official history of the air war weren't published until the following decade). Nonetheless, Cutlack produced a very readable and very detailed account of the AFC —if at times dry and marred by some inaccuracies—that pleased Bean and told a story that had previously only appeared in snippets via sensationalised news reports. One reviewer predicted in *The Argus* on 11 August 1923: 'It will surprise most people to find that the Australians did so much flying.'

Australians had indeed done some flying, a fact that is often missed given the AFC's relatively small size, compared with the rest of the AIF. Just 880 officers and 2840 men had served with it during the war. Those who had done the fighting represented an even more exclusive group—410 pilots and 153 observers.[13]

Nevertheless, the breadth and diversity of the AFC's service was tremendous, spanning three continents and nearly every type of aerial operation in the First World War. Australian airmen and mechanics were contributors to the pioneering days of aerial warfare in Mesopotamia and Egypt, when aeroplanes were still widely perceived as a reconnaissance arm only. They were there too in 1918, keen participants in the evolution of air power as a tool for gaining air superiority, bombing strategic targets and directly supporting ground operations.

The cost, however, might also surprise Australians. A total of 179 airmen, or about a third of all active service pilots, were killed, wounded or taken prisoner during the war, and Australian squadrons lost 60 aircraft over enemy lines. Although all units suffered significant casualties, No. 4 Squadron was the most dangerous unit to serve in, sustaining 25 killed, nineteen wounded and fourteen captured during eleven months at the front. Without counting men sent home on the verge of nervous breakdown with 'aero-neurosis', this represented a casualty rate of 44 per cent. As a point of comparison, the diggers of the AIF's 1st Battalion faced only marginally steeper odds—a casualty rate of just over 50 per cent, which is ironic considering the common view that service in the flying corps was safer than the trenches.[14] If the casualties of training squadrons are included in the reckoning, flying in the AFC emerges as clearly one of the most dangerous jobs an Australian man could do in service of the nation and empire between 1914 and 1918.

Between them, the four squadrons claimed 527 enemy machines—just under half of them 'destroyed' and the rest 'driven down'. These figures certainly need to be viewed with some scepticism, given the difficulty in precisely verifying claims when so much combat took place over the German side of the lines (not to mention the enthusiasm of pilots to augment their scores). But even with an over-claim factor as high as 60 per cent—suggested as plausible by one historian who has spent over two decades evaluating claim and loss data—the AFC still shot down many, many more enemy aircraft than it lost itself.[15]

It is not surprising, therefore, to discover that the sons of AFC men were proud of what their fathers had achieved. Jack Wright's son Brian recalls how having a 'fighter pilot father' was a mark of distinction in the schoolyard in the 1930s, and something he remains immensely proud of today. 'They were pioneers and heroes,' he told me at his home in November 2009. 'They were wonderful and they did it without parachutes too.' Brian followed in his father's footsteps, joining the RAAF in 1942 as a fighter pilot.

He recalls that his father, who also volunteered to fight in the Second World War but spent most of it as a prisoner of the Japanese in Changi, was 'very pleased' that he chose the air force.[16] Lawrence Wackett was likewise proud when his 17-year-old son, Wilbur, who had 'been close to aviation' his whole life, enlisted as a pilot in the RAAF in 1939. Understandably, though, Wackett was also quietly concerned about the dangers his boy would face at war. Sadly, his concerns were justified when Wilbur's Beaufighter went missing over the Timor Sea in 1944. 'They were presumed dead,' he recalled sadly, 'and no trace was ever found.'[17]

Another son to follow in the footsteps of his ex-AFC 'father' was Henri Hemene, the French orphan No. 4 Squadron's mechanics adopted at Cologne in December 1918. Three days into the voyage home, Tim Tovell (the mechanic who intended adopting him) brought Henri out of hiding. The Premier of Queensland, who was aboard the *Kaisar-i-Hind*, kindly made arrangements to allow Henri to land in Australia. Arriving in Melbourne, Henri told a journalist that he didn't know exactly how old he was or where he was born and that he didn't have any brothers or sisters. 'But the Aussies have been very kind to me all through,' he said, 'and I never want to leave their country.'[18]

Tovell and his wife adopted Henri and raised him in Brisbane. He attended St Mary's Church of England School at Kangaroo Point and afterwards apprenticed as a fitter and turner. In 1925, Henri moved to Point Cook to join the RAAF as a mechanic. Three years later, just before he would turn 21 and become eligible for Australian citizenship, Henri was killed in a motorcycle accident in Melbourne. Henri's story was reasonably well known in Australia and the major metropolitan newspapers covered his death. He was buried in Fawkner Cemetery and an elaborate tombstone paid for by public subscription marked his grave. Over the years, Henri's story faded from the nation's consciousness, though, and was all but forgotten until the release of author Anthony Hill's book *Young Digger* in 2002. As well as restoring interest in the story of 'Digger', Hill's book prompted the RAAF Association in Victoria to replace Henri's grave, which had been vandalised in the 1950s.

The experiences of ex-AFC men's sons who joined the RAAF bore little resemblance to those of their fathers in the Great War. The remarkably swift development of aviation technology in the 1920s and 1930s antiquated First World War aircraft to the point of novelty by the time the Second World War began. As one reviewer of Cobby's memoir, *High Adventure*, remarked in 1942: 'In the First War the pilots fought in crates that would now be regarded as museum pieces.' He emphasised the gap between the machines of the two World Wars by estimating that the aircraft of 1942 were 'about 400%' quicker than those used in 1917 and had much more reliable engines. 'The pilot of a Hurricane would scarcely take into the air in the best machine' of 1918, he considered.[19]

By the mid-1960s, in the era of supersonic jets and space exploration, the first air war had well and truly become the stuff of movies, novels and toys. In his late sixties, Frank Rawlinson was intrigued by the way his real-life experiences had transformed into history. 'Adults and children alike still make those scale models of our machines,' he observed, 'and read all about those "aces" that flew them too.'[20]

One enthusiastic young hobbyist named Larry Seyferth wrote to Rawlinson in the late 1960s. He wanted to know whether he could have some of the elderly veteran's Richthofen souvenirs. By this time, Rawlinson had donated his collection—which included a section of the 'Red Baron's' machine gun belt, a buckle and strap from his overalls and sections of the aircraft, including a step and pieces of fabric—to the Australian War Memorial. Larry enthusiastically chased them there, writing to the Memorial's director in June 1970:

> I was wondering (begging) if you were in no further need of these I should dearly like to have them for my collection. I am young (15) and have studied the life and death of the Baron for nearly 4 years and would really like to have something from his plane. If this is at all possible, please, please contact me.

Unfortunately, the Memorial's director informed him, the Richthofen relics were not available for 'disposal' at that time—and indeed, they remain in its collection to this day.[21]

Despite the attention from enthusiastic youngsters, Rawlinson remained modest about what he and his comrades in the AFC had achieved. He simply acknowledged that he 'may have possibly contributed, in some small way, to the progress of aviation'. As far as this elderly gentleman, whose life spanned the dawn of aviation and the lunar landing, was concerned: 'Ours was a fascinating era though, like that of the Clipper ships, and it was great fun to have played some little part in it.'[22]

NOTES

Abbreviations of sources

NAA	National Archives of Australia
NLA	National Library of Australia
SLV	State Library of Victoria
SLNSW	State Library NSW
AWM	Australian War Memorial
NAUK	National Archives, UK
RAAF	RAAF Museum, Point Cook
RAF	RAF Museum, London
CitAR	'Combats in the Air Report–Army Form 3348'. A standard report filed by pilots following a sortie involving air combat recording details such as location of the action, height, types of machines involved and a short narrative of the engagement.

Prologue

1. The 5 September 1918 dogfight involved No. 4 Squadron's A Flight. The reconstruction here is based on 'Account of No. 4 Squadron AFC, Trescowthick's patrol September 1918, by Lieut. L.T.E. Taplin', AWM44 8/1, Part 3 and 'Billy-Montigny, statement made by prisoner of war. Lieut. L.T.E. Taplin, AWM30, B3.15. The pilot quoted in regards to usage of the term 'ace' is Eric Dibbs, interviewed by *The 14–18 Journal* in 1967.

Chapter 1

1. *The Argus*, 16 and 19 March 1910.
2. 'The Air Age and Its Military Significance', delivered at the United Service Institution of New South Wales, 22 July 1910 by Lieutenant George A. Taylor,

Australian Intelligence Corps. 'Aerial League of Australia, NSW Section', NAA, A289 1849/8/222.

3. George Taylor, letter, 19 August 1912, NAA, 1849/8/222.
4. Lindsay-Campbell, letter, 9 January 1911, NAA 1849/8/221.
5. Military Board Minute Paper, 17 January 1911, NAA 1849/8/221.
6. Buckley, letter, 6 January 1911, NAA, A38/3/221.
7. Pearce, *Carpenter to cabinet*, pp. 81–3.
8. Papers relating to Eric Harrison's application for position at Central Flying School, NAA A38/3/221.
9. High Commissioner's office, letter, 24 July 1912, NAA A38/3/221.
10. Military Board meeting minutes, 11 September 1912, reproduced in Williams, *These are facts*, p. 380.
11. Williams, *These are facts*, p. 21.
12. Brenchley, *White's Flight*, p. 15.
13. Stephens, *The Royal Australian Air Force*, p. 6.
14. Williams, interview, NLA TRC 121/50.
15. White, *Guests of the unspeakable*, p. 13.
16. Williams, *These are facts*, p. 25.
17. ibid., p. 26.
18. ibid.
19. ibid.
20. ibid.
21. Williams, interview, NLA TRC121/50.
22. Brenchley, *White's flight*, p. 22.
23. This version of the story is Williams', from his autobiography, *These are Facts* (1977), White contested it, stating that he didn't fail, but rather simply made his attempt after Williams (see Brenchley, *White's Flight*, pp. 22–3). In any case, there is no question that Williams was the first to qualify.
24. 'Central flying school first course of instruction report on the course', NAA A38/7/339.
25. Williams, *These are facts*, p. 31.
26. White, *Guests of the unspeakable*, p. 14.
27. Sheffield and Bourne (eds), *Douglas Haig: War diaries and letters, 1914–1918*, p. 71.
28. Steel and Hart, *Tumult in the clouds*, pp. 30–1.
29. Cutlack, *The official history of Australia in the war of 1914–1918*, vol. 8, p. 422.

NOTES

30. 'First and second half flights—AFC establishment formation and organization recruitment and selecting of personnel', NAA A38/8/188.
31. 'Australian Flying Corps: Miscellaneous, No 67 Squadron and in India', AWM224 MSS513.
32. Cutlack, *The official history*, vol. 8, p. 3.
33. White, *Guests of the unspeakable*, p. 19.
34. Summary of reconnaissance flights, 31 May–10 June 1915, NAA A38/8/202.
35. White, *Guests of the unspeakable*, p. 21.
36. Brenchley, *White's Flight*, p. 30.
37. Petre, report to the Chief of General Staff in Melbourne, 14 June 1915, NAA A38/8/202.
38. White, *Guests of the unspeakable*, p. 38.
39. Wheeler, 'Formation of first Half Flight', unpublished manuscript, RAAF Museum.
40. White, *Guests of the unspeakable*, pp. 28–9.
41. Petre, report to the Chief of General Staff in Melbourne, 8 September 1915, NAA A38/8/202.
42. ibid.
43. White, *Guests of the unspeakable*, p. 29.
44. ibid.
45. Bean, *The official history of Australia in the war of 1914–1918*, vol. 5, p. 708.
46. 'Australian Flying Corps: Miscellaneous, No 67 Squadron and in India', AWM224 MSS513.
47. Treloar, handwritten account, AWM PR84/224.
48. White, *Guests of the unspeakable*, p. 84.
49. ibid., pp. 35–6.
50. Hodges, 'The Mesopotamian Half Flight', *Wartime*, no. 27, 2004, p. 29.
51. White, *Guests of the unspeakable*, p. 44.
52. ibid., p. 47.
53. ibid., pp. 47–53
54. Lax, 'The skies over Mesopotamia: Part 1 to Kut', *The 14–18 Journal*, 2005, p. 38.
55. Petre also commanded one of the AFC's training squadrons in Britain before transferring to the RFC in early 1918. He applied to take command of No. 1 Squadron in Palestine in mid-1917, but was passed over in favour of Richard Williams. Years later, Petre claimed that Williams had 'done him out of the Command' (Williams, *These are facts*, p. 69). A report on his poor performance as commander of a British unit in 1917 by the RFC's home defence

group suggests otherwise. It noted that, despite being an experienced and gallant flyer, Petre had 'shown very little power of initiative in commanding his squadron, he has not any great powers of command over officers and men and has very little military experience'. The report is in Petre's AIF service dossier, NAA B2455.
56. For a full list of their particulars, see Lax, 'The skies over Mesopotamia: Part 1 to Kut', *The 14–18 Journal*, 2005, pp. 49–50.
57. Cutlack, *The official history*, vol. 8, p. 423.
58. Williams, interview, NLA TRC 121/50.
59. Williams, 'Experience in connection with the war of 1914/1918', unpublished manuscript, RAAF Museum.
60. Williams, *These are facts*, p. 42.

Chapter 2

1. Wrigley, Air Board report for Charles Bean, 21 March 1924, AWM 3DRL 8042/64.
2. Wrigley, Air Board report for Charles Bean, 28 April 1924, AWM 3DRL 8042/64.
3. Richards, *Australian airmen*, p. 52.
4. Sutherland, *Aces and kings*, p. 12.
5. ibid., pp. 9–11.
6. Howard, letter, 17 October 1917, *The 14–18 Journal*, 1998.
7. Knuckey, diary no. 6, AWM PR03193, p. 12.
8. Lockley, letter, 17 July 1918, private collection.
9. Edols, letter, 27 July 1918, AWM PR86/385.
10. Edgar Percival, interview, NLA TRC 391/36–38.
11. The following material is based on a statistical sample of 129 Australian pilots and observers from the AFC's embarkation rolls (AWM8). A more substantial analysis of these statistics is in Molkentin, 'Unconscious of any distinction'.
12. Knibbs, *Census of the Commonwealth of Australia taken for the night between the 2nd and 3rd April, 1911*, vol. 3, table 16, p. 1306.
13. Deduced from evidence in the Australian War Memorial Roll of Honour circulars (AWM131) of 202 AFC airmen.
14. 'Medical Requirements for Australian Flying Corps', 1918, AWM25 481/115.
15. 'Selection of candidates for appointment as flying officers. AFC 1st Anzac Circular (Aug 1917)', AWM10 4343/29/17.

NOTES

16. Knuckey, diary no. 7, AWM PR03193, p. 8.
17. Smith, interview, AWM S04307.
18. Cornish, letter, 10 September 1918, AWM 1DRL/0214.
19. Conrick, diary, 27 July 1918 and 11 August 1918 (Conrick, *The flying carpet men*).
20. McCloughry, unpublished manuscript, NAUK AIR1 2389/228/11/121.
21. Hurley, diary, 15 February 1918, NLA MS883.
22. Harris, letter, 12 June 1918, AWM PR84/003.
23. Richards, *Australian airmen*, p. 55.
24. Lewis, diary, 5 and 6 February 1918, AWM PR00709.
25. Sutherland, *Aces and kings*, p. 26.
26. Richards, *Australian airmen*, p. 57.
27. The AFC constituted approximately 1 per cent of the AIF overseas. Yet it only accounted for 0.2 per cent of the force's court martials. Ashley Ekins of the Australian War Memorial kindly provided me with these statistics from his forthcoming study on discipline in the First AIF.
28. Strange, *Recollections of an airman*, pp. 176–7.
29. Richards, *Australian Airmen*, p. 58.
30. Strange, *Recollections of an airman*, p. 176.
31. The splitpin mechanic of AFC Association, 'Sophie: The sad story of a stray Sop 1a', *Slipstream*, vol. 2, no. 8, 1931, p. 29.
32. Sutherland, *Aces and kings*, pp. 58–9.
33. Fysh, *Qantas rising*, p. 49.
34. Harris, letter, 23 December 1917, AWM PR84/003.
35. Sutherland, *Aces and kings*, pp. 53–4.
36. Winter, *The first of the few*, p. 178.
37. Sutherland, *Aces and kings*, pp. 135–6.
38. Winter, *The First of the few*, p. 82.
39. Conrick, diary, 8 August 1918 (Conrick, *The flying carpet men*).
40. Billings, 'The story of my life, 1917–1918' unpublished manuscript, AWM 3DRL/6060, pp. 111–12.
41. Fysh, *Qantas rising*, p. 49.
42. Lewis, *Sagittarius rising*, p. 116.
43. Winter, *The first of the few*, p. 82.
44. Williams, *These are facts*, p. 92.
45. Sutherland, *Aces and kings*, p. 3.
46. Lockley papers, private collection.

47. Lewis, diary, 31 March 1918, AWM PR00709.
48. Cobby, *High adventure*, p. 61.
49. Winter, *The first of the few*, p. 175.
50. Harris, diary, 30 October 1917, AWM PR84/003.
51. Winter, *The first of the few*, p. 79.
52. Lockley, flying log book, private collection.
53. ibid.
54. Richards, *Australian airmen*, p. 67.
55. Lockley, letter, 17 July 1918, private collection.
56. Sutherland, *Aces and kings*, pp. 211–12.
57. Lewis, *Sagittarius rising*, p. 141.
58. ibid., p. 140.
59. Winter, *The first of the few*, p. 134.
60. HMSO, *Textbook for aerial gunnery*, 1917, p. 2.
61. Pentland, interview, NLA TRC 425/6.
62. Sutherland, *Aces and kings*, p. 4.
63. Cobby, *High adventure*, p. 90.
64. Tabulated from data in 'No 2 Squadron, Australian Flying Corps: Huns brought down', AWM224 MSS517 PART 3.
65. Conrick, 31 July 1918 (Conrick, *The flying carpet men*).
66. Winter, *The Great War and the British people*, pp. 90–1.
67. Dibbs, interview, NLA TRC 425/5.
68. Henshaw, *The sky their battlefield*, p. 575.
69. Hart and Steel, *Tumult in the clouds*, p. 255; Morrow, *The great war in the air*, p. 239.
70. Henshaw, *The sky their battlefield*, p. 574.
71. Calculated from casualty figures for killed, wounded, missing and prisoners in *The Official History of Australia in the War of 1914–1918*.
72. Winter, *The first of the few*, p. 159.
73. Lewis, diary, 16 March 1918, AWM PR00709.
74. Lewis, diary, 5 February 1918, AWM PR00709.
75. Barrett, letter, 9 December 1917, AWM 2DRL/0053.
76. Richards, *Australian airmen*, p. 66.
77. Dibbs, interview, NLA TRC 425/5.
78. Harris, diary, 12 January 1918, AWM PR84/003.
79. ibid., 16 November 1917.
80. Hoddinott, unpublished manuscript, AWM MSS0791, p. 101.

NOTES

81. 'No. 2 Squadron, Australian Flying Corps: Huns brought down', AWM 224, MSS517, Part 3.
82. 'No. 1 Squadron, Australian Flying Corps: Reports and statistics', AWM 224, MSS515, Part 2.
83. Tabulated from biographical data in Richards, *Australian airmen*.
84. 'Medical Requirements for the Australian Flying Corps, 1918', AWM 25 481/115.
85. Garrett, letter, 10 February 1918, SLV MS10762
86. Garrett, letter, 30 March 1918.
87. Rawlinson, 'Story of No. 3 Squadron AFC', unpublished manuscript, RAAF.
88. Winter, *The first of the few*, p. 115.
89. Rawlinson, 'Story of No. 3 Squadron AFC', unpublished manuscript, RAAF.
90. Nunan, letter, July 1917, AWM 3DRL/6511.
91. Williams, interview, NLA TRC 121/50.
92. The rank of Flight Sergeant was equivalent to the Army rank of Sergeant and would have put Nunan in charge of several aircraft mechanics.
93. 'Routine Orders No 1 Squadron, Australian Flying Corps, September–December 1916', AWM25 707/13, Part 41.
94. Sutherland, *Aces and kings*, p. 11.
95. Bull, diary, 8 May 1917 (Lax, *One airman's war*).
96. Billings, 'The story of my life, 1917–1918', unpublished manuscript, p. 108 AWM 3DRL/6060.
97. ibid., p. 107.
98. ibid., p. 111.
99. Sutherland, *Aces and kings*, pp. 1–2.
100. Winter, *The first of the few*, p. 119.
101. ibid.
102. Edols, letter, 7 August 1918, AWM PR86/385.
103. Winter, *The first of the few*, p. 119.
104. Bull, 18 March 1917 (Lax, *One airman's war*).
105. Bull, diary, 25 December 1916, 18 March 1917 and 17 October 1917 (Lax, *One airman's war*); Roberts, diary, 9 November 1916 AWM 3DRL/7866.
106. Winter, *The first of the few*, p. 119.
107. Hoddinott, unpublished manuscript, p. 96, AWM MSS0791.
108. Nunan, letter, 20 March 1918, AWM 3DRL/6511.
109. Bull, diary, 30 April 1917 (Lax, *One airman's war*).
110. Roberts, diary, 25 December 1916, AWM 3DRL/7866.

Chapter 3

1. Gullett, *The official history of Australia in the war of 1914–1918*, vol. 7, p. 22.
2. ibid., p. 26.
3. Williams, interview, NLA TRC 121/50.
4. Roberts, *Box kites and beyond*, p. 9.
5. Roberts, diary, 15 and 16 April 1916, AWM 3DRL/7866.
6. Morley, 'Earning their wings: pilot training 1912–1918', p. 111.
7. Roberts, *Box kites and beyond*, pp. 10–11.
8. Mott, diary, 8 July 1916, AWM 2DRL/0011.
9. Williams, *These are facts*, p. 43.
10. Cutlack, *The official history*, vol. 8, p. 42.
11. Richard Williams, interview, NLA TRC 425/1.
12. 'General Notes on the Co-operation of the Royal Flying Corps with a mobile force', AWM25 81/31.
13. Richard Williams, interview, NLA TRC 425/1.
14. Roberts, *Box kites and beyond*, p. 15
15. Williams, *These are facts*, p. 43.
16. Roberts, *Box kites and beyond*, p. 15.
17. Bennett, *Highest traditions*, pp. 4, 12.
18. Smith, *Oswald Watt: A tribute to his memory by a few of his friends*, p. 17.
19. Leckie, unpublished manuscript, pp. 4–5, AWM 3RDL/4180.
20. Sutherland, *Aces and kings*, p. 34.
21. 'No. 1 Squadron Australian Flying Corps, Report 1917–1919', AWM224 MSS515.
22. ibid.
23. Gullett, *The official history*, p. 116.
24. Williams, *These are facts*, p. 45.
25. Richard Williams, interview, NLA TRC 121/50.
26. Jones, *The war in the air*, vol. 5, p. 192.
27. Williams, interview, NLA TRC 425/1.
28. 'No. 1 Squadron Australian Flying Corps, Report 1917–1919', AWM224 MSS515, Part 1.
29. Williams, 'Experience in connection with the war of 1914/18', unpublished manuscript, RAAF.
30. Jones, *The war in the air*, vol. 5, p. 195.
31. Gröschel and Ladek, 'Wings over Sinai and Palestine', p. 19.
32. Billings, diary, 4 August 1916, AWM 3DRL/6060.

NOTES

33. Gullett, *The official history*, vol. 7, p. 159.
34. Bean, *Anzac to Amiens*, p. 282.
35. Williams, interview, NLA TRC 121/50.
36. Mills interview (*The 14–18 Journal*, 1968).
37. Forsyth, letter, 29 October 1916, AWM MSS1276.
38. Forsyth, letter, 4 November 1916.
39. Sutherland, *Aces and kings*, p. 115.
40. Williams, *These are facts*, pp. 52–3.
41. '67 Squadron Reconnaissance Reports Sept–Oct 1916', NAUK AIR1 209/75/54.
42. Roberts, *Box kites and beyond*, p. 18.
43. Gullett, *The official history*, p. 200.
44. '67 Squadron Reconnaissance Reports Sept–Oct 1916', NAUK AIR1 209/75/54.
45. Roberts, *Box kites and beyond*, p. 21.
46. '67 Squadron Reconnaissance Reports Sept–Oct 1916', NAUK AIR1 209/75/54.
47. 'Australian Flying Corps [Royal Flying Corps]. General notes on the co-operation of the Royal Flying Corps with a mobile force', AWM25 81/31.
48. Roberts, interview, NLA TRC 536.
49. Williams, *These are facts*, pp. 54–5.
50. Wackett, *Aircraft pioneer*, p. 52.
51. Williams, *These are facts*, pp. 55–6.
52. 'Correspondence with reference to training of observers', AWM25 81/20.
53. Roberts, *Box kites and beyond*, p. 22.
54. Wackett, *Aircraft pioneer*, p. 52.
55. CitAR, Guilfoyle, 11 November 1917, 5 Wing RFC war diary, NAUK AIR 1/1756/204/141/20–21.
56. Cutlack, *The official history*, vol. 8, p. 46.
57. Gröschel and Ladek, 'Wings over Sinai and Palestine', pp. 7, 23, 25.
58. Erich Jan Zürcher, 'Between death and desertion: The experience of the Ottoman soldier in World War I', *Turcica*, vol. 28, 1996, p. 250.
59. CitAR, Muir, 17 December 1916, 5 Wing RFC war diary, NAUK AIR 1/1756/204/141/22. The standard Lewis gun drum magazine contained 47 rounds. The RFC began issuing a specially modified version to its squadrons in mid-1916 that held 97 rounds. Photographic evidence seems to suggest No. 1 Squadron didn't start using these 'double drums' until early 1918.
60. Cole, 'Courageous companions', unpublished manuscript, folder 9, p. 13, AWM PR88/154.
61. Bull, 20 December 1916 (Lax, *One airman's war*).

62. Cole, 'Courageous companions', unpublished manuscript, folder 9, p. 13, AWM PR88/154.
63. Bull, diary, 20 and 21 December 1916 (Lax, *One airman's war*).
64. Benham, letter, 16 January 1917, AWM PR04011.
65. CitAR, Muir, 22 December 1916, 5 Wing RFC war diary, NAUK AIR 1/1756/204/141/22. The available German records do not record the fate of this machine and the RFC didn't claim it as a confirmed kill, which suggests FA 300 probably retrieved it.
66. Bull, diary, 23 December 1916 (Lax, *One airman's war*).
67. Roberts, *Box kites and beyond*, p. 25.
68. Pedersen, *The Anzacs: Gallipoli to the Western Front*, p. 292.
69. Joe Bull, diary, 28 December 1916 (Lax, *One airman's war*).

Chapter 4

1. Roberts, *Box kites and beyond*, p. 26.
2. Gröschel and Ladek, 'Wings over Sinai and Palestine', p. 29.
3. Roberts, *Box kites and beyond*, p. 26.
4. Bull, diary, 10 and 14 January 1917 (Lax, *One airman's war*).
5. Roberts, interview, NLA TRC 536.
6. 'History of the RFC in Sinai Palestine during 1917', Williams papers, RAAF.
7. Williams, 'Experience in connection with the war of 1914/18', unpublished manuscript, RAAF.
8. Sutherland, *Aces and kings*, pp. 142–3.
9. Wright, 'From horses to horsepower', unpublished manuscript, RAAF.
10. Mills, interview, *The 14–18 Journal*, 1968.
11. Roberts, *Box kites and beyond*, p. 29.
12. ibid., p. 30.
13. Roberts, diary, 30 January and 1 February 1917, AWM 3DRL/7866.
14. Roberts, service dossier, NAA B2455.
15. All quotes from Williams in this section from Williams, interview, NLA TRC 121/50.
16. Williams, *These are facts*, p. 60.
17. 'RFC reconnaissance and bombing reports with sketches, EEF', NAUK AIR 1/209/75/58.
18. Williams, 'Experience in connection with the war of 1914/18', unpublished manuscript, RAAF.
19. Jones, *The war in the air*, vol. 5, p. 206.

NOTES

20. Williams, *These are facts*, p. 61.
21. *Australian Dictionary of Biography*, vol. 10, p. 349.
22. Coulthard-Clark, *McNamara, VC*, p. 37.
23. *Daily Telegraph*, 22 June 1917.
24. Statement by Ellis, McNamara's recommendation for the Victoria Cross, AWM28.
25. McNamara's log book, *Cross & Cockade*, 2(3), 1971.
26. Coulthard-Clark, *McNamara, VC*, p. 42.
27. McNamara's log book, *Cross & Cockade*, 2(3), 1971
28. Coulthard-Clark, *McNamara, VC*, p. 43.
29. *Daily Telegraph*, 22 June 1917.
30. Statement by Rutherford, McNamara's recommendation for the Victoria Cross, AWM28.
31. Adrian Cole, 'Courageous companions', unpublished manuscript, folder 9, p. 19, AWM PR88/154.
32. Coulthard-Clark, *McNamara, VC*, pp. 66–7.
33. Jones, *The war in the air*, vol. 5, p. 209. Dobell shared a headquarters with his corps commander, Chetwode, at El Braji.
34. Wavell, quoted in Gröschel and Ladek, 'Wings over Sinai and Palestine', p. 35.
35. CitAR, Snell, 25 March 1917, 5 Wing RFC war diary, NAUK AIR 1/1757/204/141/26.
36. Bull, diary, 25 March 1917 (Lax, *One airman's war*).
37. Williams, 'Experience in connection with the war of 1914/18', unpublished manuscript, RAAF.
38. Williams, interview, NLA TRC 121/50. The remaining quotes from Williams in this section are from this interview.
39. Gröschel and Ladek, 'Wings over Sinai and Palestine', p. 36.
40. Bull, diary, 27 March 1917 (Lax, *One airman's war*).
41. Gröschel and Ladek, 'Wings over Sinai and Palestine', p. 36.
42. Williams, 'Experience in connection with the war of 1914/18', unpublished manuscript, RAAF.
43. Williams, interview, NLA TRC 121/50.
44. Williams, *These are facts*, p. 64.
45. Hyam, Australian Red Cross wounded and missing enquiry bureau files, AWM 1DRL/0428.
46. Gullett, *The official history*, pp. 297–8.
47. ibid., p. 300.

48. Bull, diary, 12 April 1917 (Lax, *One airman's war*).
49. Williams, *These are facts*, p. 64.
50. Gröschel and Ladek, 'Wings over Sinai and Palestine', p. 37.
51. Williams, interview, NLA TRC 121/50.
52. Williams, 'Experience in connection with the war of 1914/18', unpublished manuscript, RAAF.
53. Gröschel and Ladek, 'Wings over Sinai and Palestine', pp. 38–40.
54. Williams, interview, NLA TRC 121/50.
55. Steele, Australian Red Cross wounded and missing enquiry bureau files, AWM 1DRL/0428.
56. Williams, *These are facts*, pp. 65–6.
57. Cole, 'Courageous companions', unpublished manuscript, folder 9, p. 16, AWM PR88/154.
58. Haig, *Airman oilman*, p. 17.
59. Roberts, *Box kites and beyond*, p. 17.
60. Sutherland, *Aces and kings*, pp. 54–5; Fysh, *Qantas rising*, p. 45.
61. Gullett, *The official history*, pp. 341–2.
62. Cutlack, *The official history*, vol. 8, pp. 64–5.
63. Bull, diary, 7 June 1917 (Lax, *One airman's war*).
64. Leckie, unpublished manuscript, p. 8, AWM 3DRL/4180.
65. Joubert, *The forgotten ones*, p. 103.
66. CitAR, Cole, 16 May 1917, 5 Wing war diary, May 1917, NAUK AIR 1/1759/204/141/40.
67. Henshaw, *The sky their battlefield*, pp. 575–6.
68. Fysh, *Qantas Rising*, p. 48.
69. Bull, diary, 26 June 1917 (Lax, *One airman's war*).
70. Brasell, Australian Red Cross wounded and missing enquiry bureau files, AWM 1DRL/0428.
71. Lax, *One airman's war*, p. 56.
72. Williams, interview, NLA TRC 425.
73. Hughes, *Allenby and the British Strategy in the Middle East*, p. 15.
74. Fysh, *Qantas rising*, p. 47.
75. Bull, diary, 2 July 1917 (Lax, *One airman's war*).
76. Sutherland, *Aces and kings*, p. 31.
77. ibid., pp. 140–1.
78. Cutlack, *The official history*, pp. 64–5.
79. Vautin, repatriated prisoner of war statement, AWM30 B3.3.

80. Sutherland, *Aces and kings*, pp. 144–5.
81. Cutlack, *The official history*, pp. 72–3.
82. ibid., p. 65.
83. Vautin, letter to Cutlack, 2 October 1941, AWM38 3DRL 7953/9, Part 2.
84. Cutlack, *The official history*, p. 72.
85. Harris, diary, 21 January 1918, AWM PR84/003.
86. Interview with Frank McNamara concerning the fate of Norman Steele, 28 September 1917, Australian Red Cross wounded and missing enquiry bureau files, AWM 1DRL/0428.
87. 'History of the RFC in Sinai Palestine during 1917', Williams papers, RAAF. This number includes Eric Roberts, sent home with 'aero-neurosis'.
88. Williams, 'Experience in connection with the war 1914/18', unpublished manuscript, RAAF.

Chapter 5

1. Prentice, letter, 3 April 1918, AWM PR85/022.
2. Williams, interview, NLA TRC 121/50.
3. Sutherland, *Aces and kings*, pp. 34–5.
4. Hudson Fysh, *Qantas rising*, p. 47.
5. Smith afterwards told Joe Bull that he thought it was Felmy's aircraft. Bull, diary, 4 August 1917 (Lax, *One airman's war*).
6. CitAR, Smith, 4 August 1917, 5 Wing war diary, NAUK AIR 1/1758/204/141/35.
7. CitAR, Smith, 1 September 1917, 5 Wing war diary, NAUK AIR 1/1759/204/141/38.
8. Bull diary, 8 September and 8 October 1917 (Lax, *One airman's war*).
9. Hudson Fysh, *Qantas rising*, p. 51.
10. Williams, interview, NLA TRC 425/1.
11. Williams, 'Experience in connection with the war of 1914/18', unpublished manuscript, RAAF.
12. Williams, interview, NLA TRC 425/1.
13. Translated report by Von Kressenstein, 29 September 1917 in GHQ intelligence summary, 30 October 1918, No. 1 Squadron war diary, AWM4 8/4/10, Part 2.
14. Williams, 'Experience in connection with the war of 1914/18', unpublished manuscript, RAAF.
15. Hughes, *Allenby and British strategy in the Middle East*, p. 46.
16. Bull, diary, 18–20 October 1918 (Lax, *One airman's war*).
17. Hughes, *Allenby and British strategy in the Middle East*, p. 49.

18. Jones, *The war in the air*, vol. 5, p. 238.
19. 40th Wing report, November 1917, AWM45 44/5.
20. 'Bavarian Flying Squadron 304: Extracts from report on the evacuation of the aerodrome at Arak el Manshije', RAAF.
21. ibid.
22. Jones, *The war in the air*, vol. 5, pp. 243–4.
23. Major von Papen to von Falkenhayn, 21 November 1917, translated in GHQ Intelligence Summary, 1 November 1918, No. 1 Squadron war diary, AWM4 8/4/11.
24. CitAR, Austin, 29 November 1917, 40 Wing war diary, NAUK AIR 1/2212/209/28/3.
25. Jones, *The war in the air*, vol. 5, p. 249.
26. Gröschel and Ladek, 'Wings over Sinai and Palestine', p. 52.
27. Bull, diary, 16 November 1917 (Lax, *One airman's war*).
28. Harris, diary, 12 November 1917, AWM PR84/003.
29. Harris, letter, 6 April 1918, AWM PR84/003.
30. Williams, *These are facts*, pp. 84–5.
31. Harris, diary, 15 December 1917, AWM PR84/003.
32. Williams, interview, NLA TRC 121/50.
33. Bull, diary, 29 December 1917 and 2 January 1918 (Lax, *One airman's war*).
34. CitARs, Brown and Austin, 3 January 1918, No. 1 Squadron war diary, AWM4 8/4/1, Part 1.
35. 'Account of operations of the 1st Squadron, AFC, 40th Wing, RFC, 1917–1919', p. 5, SLNSW MLMSS1046.
36. Harris diary, 4 and 12 January 1918, AWM PR84/003.
37. CitAR, Potts, 17 January 1918, No. 1 Squadron war diary, AWM4 8/4/1, Part 1.
38. Bull, diary, 17 January 1917 (Lax, *One airman's war*).
39. CitAR, Taplin, 17 January 1917, No. 1 Squadron war diary, AWM4 8/4/1, Part 1.
40. No. 1 Squadron war diary, January 1918, AWM4 8/4/1, Part 1.
41. Cutlack, *The official history*, vol. 8, p. 95.
42. Hurley, diary, 13 February 1917, NLA MS883.
43. Hurley, diary, 16 February 1917, NLA MS883.
44. Bull, diary, 16 February 1917 (Lax, *One airman's war*).
45. Cutlack, *The official history*, vol. 8, p. 103.
46. Sutherland, *Aces and kings*, p. 93.
47. No. 1 Squadron war diary, March 1918, AWM4 8/4/3, Part 1.

NOTES

48. Reconnaissance report, Addison and Fysh, 22 March 1918, No. 1 Squadron war diary, AWM4 8/4/3, Part 1.
49. Reconnaissance report, Brown and Kirk, 24 March 1918, No. 1 Squadron war diary, AWM4 8/4/3, Part 1.
50. CitAR, Rutherford, 27 March 1918, No. 1 Squadron war diary, AWM4 8/4/3, Part 1.
51. Cutlack, *The official history*, p. 110.
52. Haig, *Airman oilman*, p. 20.
53. ibid., p. 21
54. ibid., p. 21. Magpie was Haig's nickname for his machine on account of its black and white paint scheme.
55. Curwen-Walker, Australian Red Cross wounded and missing enquiry bureau files, AWM 1DRL/0428.
56. GHQ Intelligence Summary, 1 April 1918; No. 1 Squadron war diary, AWM4 8/4/4, Part 3.
57. German officer's diary, 12 March 1918, GHQ Intelligence Summary, 26 April 1918, No. 1 Squadron war diary, AWM4 8/4/4, Part 3.

Chapter 6

1. Sutherland, *Aces and kings*, p. 130.
2. Williams, interview, NLA TRC 121/50.
3. Sutherland, *Aces and kings*, pp. 130–1.
4. Fysh, *Qantas rising*, p. 51.
5. No. 1 Squadron war diary, May 1918, AWM4 8/4/5, Part 1.
6. CitAR, Tonkin, 4 June 1918, No. 1 Squadron war diary, AWM4 8/4/6, Part 1; Bull, diary, 4 June 1918 (Lax, *One airman's war*).
7. No. 1 Squadron war diary, June 1918, AWM4 8/4/6, Part 1.
8. Sutherland, *Aces and kings*, pp. 138–9.
9. According to John Harris, 'these Huns were probably the ones who shot down Tonkin & Camm'. Harris, diary, p. 172, AWM PR84/003.
10. Cutlack incorrectly describes this action as occurring on 9 June. The squadron war diary as well as Joe Bull's diary indicate it occurred on 19 June 1918.
11. CitAR, Smith, 19 June 1918, No. 1 Squadron war diary, AWM4 8/4/6, Part 1.
12. Fysh, *Qantas rising*, p. 51.
13. CitAR, Addison, 23 June 1918, No. 1 Squadron war diary, AWM4 8/4/6, Part 1.
14. CitAR, Brown, 27 June 1918, No. 1 Squadron war diary, AWM4 8/4/6, Part 1.
15. Smith, unpublished manuscript, AWM PR83/100.

16. Smith, assorted correspondence, AWM PR83/100.
17. Smith, interview, AWM S04307.
18. Guttman, *Bristol F2 fighter aces of World War I*, p. 82.
19. Smith, unpublished manuscript, AWM PR83/100.
20. Conrick, diary, 9 July 1918 (Conrick, *The flying carpet men*).
21. Nunan, letter, 19 December 1916, AWM 3DRL/6511.
22. Sutherland, *Aces and kings*, p. 63.
23. Nunan, letter, 28 June 1918, AWM 3DRL/6511.
24. '1st Squadron Australian Flying Corps Review of Operations: From 1st January 1918 till Return to Australia March 1919', SLNSW MLMSS1046.
25. Williams, interview, NLA TRC 121/50.
26. Cutlack, *The official history*, vol. 8, pp. 128–9.
27. Report on attack on troops by aircraft, Smith, 21 June 1918, No. 1 Squadron war diary, AWM 4 8/4/6, Part 1.
28. Cutlack, *The official history*, p. 130.
29. Bull diary, 9 July 1918 (Lax, *One airman's war*).
30. Haig, *Airman oilman*, p. 20.
31. Sutherland, *Aces and kings*, pp. 24–5.
32. Fysh, *Qantas rising*, p. 59.
33. ibid., p. 53.
34. CitAR, Tonkin, 16 July 1918, No. 1 Squadron war diary, 8/4/7, Part 1.
35. Sutherland, *Aces and kings*, pp. 2–3.
36. ibid., p. 13.
37. Conrick, diary, 19 August 1918 (Conrick, *The flying carpet men*).
38. Harris, diary, 25 June 1918, AWM PR84/003.
39. Williams, *These are facts*, p. 90; Bull, diary, 22 August 1918 (Lax, *One airman's war*).
40. '1st Squadron Australian Flying Corps Review of Operations: From 1st January 1918 till Return to Australia March 1919', SLNSW MLMSS1046.
41. Conrick, diary, 22 August 1918 (Conrick, *The flying carpet men*).
42. Harris, diary, 24 August 1918, AWM PR84/003.
43. Bull, diary, 22 August 1918 (Lax, *One airman's war*).
44. Conrick, diary, 26 August 1918 (Conrick, *The flying carpet men*).
45. Harris, diary, 23 May 1918, AWM PR84/003.
46. Cutlack, *The official history*, p. 145.
47. CitARs, Peters and McGinness, 24 August 1918, No. 1 Squadron war diary, AWM4 8/4/8, Part 1.

NOTES

48. Gröschel and Ladek, 'Wings over Sinai and Palestine', p. 53.
49. Captured documents quoted by No. 1 Squadron's commanding officer, Major Addison in his unpublished history of the unit. See SLNSW MLMSS1046.
50. Conrick, diary, 27 August 1918 (Conrick, *The flying carpet men*).
51. Fysh, *Qantas rising*, p. 56.
52. Hall, *Flying high*, pp. 16–17.
53. Allenby is reported to have given these statistics in an unpublished squadron history, SLNSW MLMSS1046.
54. Jones, *The war in the air*, vol. 6, p. 207.

Chapter 7

1. Mühlmann, *Das Deutsch-Türkische waffenbündnis im weltkrieg*, p. 228.
2. Gullett, *The official history*, vol. 7, p. 687.
3. Nunan, letter, 26 September 1918, AWM 3DRL/6511.
4. Bull, diary, 18 September 1918 (Lax, *One airman's war*).
5. Conrick, diary, 19 September 1918 (Conrick, *The flying carpet men*).
6. Sutherland, *Aces and kings*, p. 246.
7. Jones, *The war in the air*, vol. 6, p. 215.
8. Sutherland, *Aces and kings*, p. 247.
9. ibid., pp. 150–4.
10. Reconnaissance reports, 19 September 1918, No. 1 Squadron war diary, AWM4 8/4/9, Part 1.
11. Sutherland, *Aces and kings*, p. 249.
12. Conrick, diary, 19 September 1918 (Conrick, *The flying carpet men*).
13. Jones, *The war in the air*, vol. 6, p. 219.
14. Harris, diary, 19 September 1918, AWM PR84/003.
15. Sutherland, *Aces and kings*, p. 250.
16. ibid., p. 252.
17. ibid., pp. 228–9.
18. Jones, *The war in the air*, vol. 6, p. 222.
19. Mustard, letter to official historian F.M. Cutlack, 23 April 1922, AWM44 8/1, Part 11.
20. ibid. and Peters, letter to official historian F.M. Cutlack, 22 March 1922, AWM44 8/1, Part 11.
21. Conrick, diary, 20 September 1918 (Conrick, *The flying carpet men*).
22. Sutherland, *Aces and kings*, p. 252.
23. Conrick, diary, 21 September 1918 (Conrick, *The flying carpet men*).

24. ibid.
25. Sutherland, *Aces and kings*, pp. 255–6.
26. Conrick, diary, 21 September 1918 (Conrick, *The flying carpet men*).
27. Sutherland, *Aces and kings*, p. 259.
28. ibid., p. 256.
29. Jones, *The war in the air*, vol. 6, p. 225.
30. Williams, *These are facts*, p. 96.
31. Bull, diary, 16 May 1918 (Lax, *One airman's war*); Sutherland, *Aces and kings*, p. 74.
32. Williams, interview, NLA TRC 121/50.
33. Bull, diary, 16 September 1918 (Lax, *One airman's war*).
34. Conrick, diary, 16 September 1918 (Conrick, *The flying carpet men*).
35. CitAR, Smith, 21 September 1918, No. 1 Squadron war diary, AWM4 8/4/9, Part 2.
36. Clune, *D'air devil*, p. 94
37. CitAR, Smith, 21 September 1918, No. 1 Squadron war diary, AWM4 8/4/9, Part 2.
38. Clune, *D'air devil*, p. 97.
39. Conrick, diary, 27 September 1918 (Conrick, *The flying carpet men*).
40. Nunan, flying log book, AWM 3DRL/6511.
41. Sutherland, *Aces and kings*, p. 260.
42. ibid., pp. 180–1.
43. Conrick, diary, 30 September 1918 (Conrick, *The flying carpet men*).
44. Cutlack, *The official history*, vol. 8, p. 168.
45. Conrick, diary, 30 September 1918 (Conrick, *The flying carpet men*).
46. Bull, diary, 26 and 27 September 1918 (Lax, *One airman's war*). Bull had made the journey a few days earlier with C Flight, but his experiences provide an impression of what the rest of the squadron saw as it moved north on 3 October 1918.
47. Conrick, diary, 4 October 1918 (Conrick, *The flying carpet men*).
48. Nunan, letter, 7 October 1918, AWM 3DRL/6511.
49. Conrick, diary, 7 October 1918 (Conrick, *The flying carpet men*).
50. Fysh, *Qantas rising*, p. 57.
51. Nunan, letter, 26 September 1918, AWM 3DRL/6511.
52. Sutherland, *Aces and kings*, pp. 36–47. Not surprisingly, there is no evidence of this story in the squadron's official records, although Williams verified that there was indeed a 'cave full of wine' at Jenin in his 1973 interview with Mel Pratt (NLA TRC 121/50).

NOTES

53. Sutherland, *Aces and kings*, p. 266.
54. Nunan, letter, 11 December 1918, AWM 3DRL/6511.
55. ibid., 18 December 1918.
56. Sutherland, *Aces and kings*, p. 67.
57. Conrick, diary, 13 December 1918 (Conrick, *The flying carpet men*).
58. Bull, diary, 3 January 1919 (Lax, *One airman's war*).
59. Williams, interview, NLA TRC 121/50.
60. 'Statistics of 1st Squadron, Australian Flying Corps, AIF', February 1919, No. 1 Squadron war diary, AWM4 8/4/14.
61. Williams, *These are facts*, p. 102.
62. Fysh, *Qantas rising*, p. 60.

Chapter 8

1. Knuckey, diary no. 5a, p. 10, AWM PR03193.
2. Ross, letter, 31 July 1917, AWM 3DRL/4111.
3. McCloughry, 'Some war experiences', p. 1, NAUK AIR 1/2389/228/11/121.
4. Day, unpublished manuscript, p. 107, AWM PR85/344.
5. ibid.
6. Howard, letter, 29 December 1916 (*The 14–18 Journal*, 1997).
7. Nunan, letter, 12 July 1917, AWM 3DRL/6511.
8. Howard, letter, 10 January 1917 (*The 14–18 Journal*, 1997).
9. Cornell, lecture notebook, AWM 1DRL/0212.
10. Penny, 'Memories of flying', unpublished manuscript, RAAF.
11. At different times of the year this schedule varied slightly. Based on notes in Day, unpublished manuscript, p. 106, AWM PR85/344; Ferguson, letter, 12 January 1918, AWM PR00005.
12. Ferguson, letter, 12 January 1918, AWM PR00005.
13. Day, unpublished manuscript, pp. 106–7, AWM PR85/344.
14. Nunan, letter, 12 July 1917, AWM 3DRL/6511.
15. Joubert, *The forgotten ones*, p. 93.
16. Ross, letter, 9 August 1917, AWM 3DRL/1298.
17. Day, unpublished manuscript, p. 113, AWM PR85/344.
18. Nunan, letter, 12 August 1917, AWM 3DRL/6511.
19. Forsyth, diary, 7 and 12 July 1917, AWM MSS1276.
20. Howard, letter, 20 February 1917 (*The 14–18 Journal*, 1997).
21. 'War experiences of Squadron Leader R.S. Brown of Australian Flying Corps', NAUK AIR 1/228/11/54.

22. Cadet Leigh (surname unknown), letter, 2 May 1917, RAAF.
23. Day, diary, pp. 110–11, AWM PR85/344.
24. Ross, letter, September 1917, AWM 3DRL/1298.
25. Winter, *The first of the few*, p. 36.
26. Gareth Morgan, 'Australian Flying Corps Roll of Honour', *The 14–18 Journal*, 2008, 2009.
27. Morley, Earning their wings, p. 111.
28. Wright, 'From horses to horsepower'.
29. Ross, letter, August or September 1917, AWM 3DRL/4111.
30. Penny, 'Memories of flying', unpublished manuscript, RAAF.
31. Hart, *Aces falling*, p. 35.
32. Weingarth, letter, 26 January 1918 (*The 14–18 Journal*, 1993).
33. Weingarth, letter, 3 February 1918 (*The 14–18 Journal*, 1993).
34. McDougall, diary, 29 August 1918, AWM PR01381.
35. McCloughry, 'Some war experiences', p. 3, NAUK AIR 1/2389/228/11/121.
36. Cobby, *High adventure*, pp. 31, 36.
37. Hoddinott, unpublished manuscript, p. 107, AWM MSS0791.
38. Nunan, letter, 12 July 1917, AWM 3DRL/6511.
39. Reports by squadron commanders on pilots recommended for further training, AWM25 81/51.
40. Sharples, diary, 8 August 1917, private collection.
41. ibid.
42. ibid., 9 August 1917.
43. ibid., 12 August 1918.
44. ibid., 14 August 1918.
45. ibid., 17 August 1918.
46. Henshaw, *The sky their battlefield*, p. 575
47. Bean, diary, 24 August 1917, AWM 3DRL 8042/64.

Chapter 9

1. Garrett, letter, 27 August 1917, SLV MS10762.
2. ibid.
3. Tuck, diary, 5 September 1917 (Kirby, *The war diaries of Stanley Thomas Tuck*).
4. Wrigley, *The battle below*, p. 31.
5. Tuck, diary, 10 September 1917 (Kirby, *The war diaries of Stanley Thomas Tuck*).
6. ibid.

NOTES

7. Garrett, letter, 22 September 1917, SLV MS10762.
8. 'War experiences of Squadron Leader R.S. Brown of Australian Flying Corps', NAUK AIR 1/228/11/54.
9. Treacy, interview, *The 14–18 Journal*, 1972–73.
10. Dibbs, interview, *The 14–18 Journal*, 1967.
11. Garrett, letter, 22 September 1917, SLV MS10792.
12. 'War experiences of Squadron Leader W.H. Anderson, No. 3 Squadron Australian Flying Corps', NAUK AIR 1/228/11/101.
13. Dibbs, interview, *The 14–18 Journal*, 1967.
14. Tuck, diary, 12 October 1917 (Kirby, *The war diaries of Stanley Thomas Tuck*).
15. Garrett, letter, 6 November 1917, SLV MS10762.
16. Howard, letter, 31 July 1917 (*The 14–18 Journal*, 1998)
17. Knuckey, diary no. 6, p. 19, AWM PR03193.
18. Knuckey, diary no. 5, p. 15, AWM PR03193.
19. Ure Smith et al, *Oswald Watt*, p. 23.
20. ibid., p. 27.
21. Knuckey, diary no. 6, pp. 4–5, AWM PR03193.
22. Howard, diary, 26 September 1917 (*The 14–18 Journal*, 1998).
23. ibid., letter, 1 October 1917.
24. ibid., letter, 3 August 1917.
25. Report on Morrison's death, AWM25 171/8.
26. CitAR, McCloughry, 16 October 1917, No. 2 Squadron war diary, AWM4 8/5/3.
27. Howard, letter, 17 October 1917 (*The 14–18 Journal*, 1998).
28. Knuckey, diary no. 6, p. 19, AWM PR03193.
29. Wilson, account in *The School Sportsman*, 8 June 1920, AWM44 8/1, Part 12.
30. Lee, *No parachute*, pp. 162–3.
31. ibid., p. 183.
32. Wilson, account in *The School Sportsman*, 8 June 1920, AWM44 8/1, Part 12.
33. Ward, Australian Red Cross wounded and missing enquiry bureau files, AWM 1DRL/0428.
34. Bean, diary, November–December 1917, AWM38 3DRL 606/94/1.
35. Bennett, *Highest traditions*, p. 37.
36. Knuckey, diary no. 6, p. 21, AWM PR03193.
37. Report of attack on enemy infantry, Huxley, 23 November 1917, No. 2 Squadron war diary, AWM4 8/5/4.
38. Sheldon, *The German army at Cambrai*, p. 165
39. Jones, *The war in the air*, vol. 4, p. 246.

40. Knuckey, diary no. 6, p. 21, AWM PR03193.
41. Lee, *No parachute*, p. 177.
42. CitAR, Howard, 29 November 1917, No. 2 Squadron war diary, AWM4 8/5/4.
43. Lee, *No parachute*, p. 186.
44. Cornell, diary, 30 November 1917, AWM 1DRL/0212.
45. CitAR, Huxley, 1 December 1917, No. 2 Squadron war diary, AWM4 8/5/5.
46. Service dossiers, NAA B2455.
47. 'Medical Requirements for the Australian Flying Corps, 1918', AWM 25 481/115.
48. Lee, *No parachute*, p. 198.
49. Cornell, diary, 10 December 1917, AWM 1DRL/0212.
50. No. 2 Squadron war diary, December 1917, AWM4 8/5/5.

Chapter 10

1. Garrett, letter, 24 November 1917, SLV MS10762.
2. Rawlinson, 'Story of No. 3 Squadron AFC', unpublished manuscript, p. 28, RAAF.
3. ibid., p. 33.
4. Billings, interview, *The 14–18 Journal*, 1991.
5. Garrett, letter, 3 December 1917, SLV MS10762.
6. Garrett, letter, 1 December 1917, SLV MS10762.
7. No. 3 Squadron war diary, December 1917, AWM4 8/6/12, Part 1.
8. Rawlinson, 'Story of No. 3 Squadron AFC', unpublished manuscript, p. 29, RAAF.
9. CitAR, Sandy, 17 December 1917, No. 3 Squadron war diary, AWM4 8/6/12, Part 1.
10. *Sydney Morning Herald*, 26 December 1917.
11. Garrett, letter, 29 December 1917, SLV MS10762.
12. 'War experiences of Squadron Leader W.H. Anderson', NAUK AIR 1/228/11/101.
13. Lewis, diary, 4 and 6 February 1918, AWM PR00709.
14. Lewis, diary, 23 February 1918, AWM PR00709.
15. Cobby, *High adventure*, pp. 37, 44.
16. ibid., p. 34.
17. Hart and Steel, *Tumult in the clouds*, p. 221.
18. Wright, 'From horses to horsepower', unpublished manuscript, RAAF.
19. Wright, ibid.
20. Cobby, *High adventure*, p. 59.

NOTES

21. ibid., p. 52.
22. ibid., pp. 53–8. Cobby and Pflaum's victories are not recorded in the squadron's war diary or the RFC's communiqués. They are, however, awarded in the unit's manuscript history (AWM224 MSS520).
23. Bean, diary, 9 December 1917, AWM38 3DRL 606/94/2.
24. Jones, *The war in the air*, vol. 4, p. 265.
25. ibid., p. 444.
26. Jones, *From private to Air Marshal*, p. 18.
27. Rackett, diary, 6 March 1918, private collection.
28. No. 2 Squadron war diary, February 1918, AWM4 8/5/7.
29. CitAR, Huxley, 18 February 1918, No. 2 Squadron war diary, AWM4 8/5/7.
30. Howard, letter, 19 February 1918 (*The 14–18 Journal*, 1999).
31. George Jones, interview, *The 14–18 Journal*, 1968.
32. Jones, interview, AWM S04722.
33. Howard, letter, 12 and 25 February 1918 (*The 14–18 Journal*, 1999).
34. Cobby, *High adventure*, pp. 72–3.
35. Randell, repatriated prisoner of war statement, AWM30 B3.12.
36. Cobby, *High adventure*, p. 73
37. Howard, letter, 12 January 1918 (*The 14–18 Journal*, 1999).
38. Howard, letter, 11 March 1918 (*The 14–18 Journal*, 1999).
39. Jones, *From private to Air Marshal*, p. 20.
40. Jones, interview, NLA TRC 452/2.
41. Cobby *High adventure*, p. 72.
42. Jones, *The war in the air*, vol. 4, p. 273.
43. Cobby, letter to FM Cutlack, no date, AWM44 8/1, Part 8.
44. Wright, 'From horses to horsepower'.
45. Cutlack, *The official history*, vol. 8, pp. 226–7.
46. Franks et al., *The Jasta war chronology*, and Jasta 35's war diary (*Cross & Cockade*, vol. 24, 1983) strongly suggests that it was Jasta 35 (and not Jastas 4, 6, 10 and/or 11, that made up Richthofen's JG I) in the combat, and that they suffered no casualties.
47. MacKenzie, 'My most thrilling flight', *Popular flight*, June 1934, p. 134.
48. Documents from the court of inquiry into Howard's death (4 October 1918) are in his service dossier, NAA B2455.
49. Rackett, diary, 22 March 1918, private collection.
50. Cobby, *High adventure*, p. 86.
51. Wright, 'From horses to horsepower'.

52. Cobby, *High adventure*, pp. 83–4.
53. Weingarth, letter, 25 March 1918 (*The 14–18 Journal*, 1993).
54. Wright, 'From horses to horsepower'.
55. No. 2 Squadron war diary, April 1918, AWM4 8/5/9.
56. Jones, *The war in the air*, vol. 4, p. 320.
57. Rackett, diary, 25 March 1918, private collection.
58. Jones, *The war in the air*, vol. 4, p. 336.
59. Hart, *Aces falling*, p. 127.
60. Hosking, Australian Red Cross wounded and missing enquiry bureau files, AWM 1DRL/0428.
61. Flight, repatriated prisoner or war statement, AWM30 B3.6.
62. Cobby, *High adventure*, p. 88.
63. Love and Woolhouse, Australian Red Cross wounded and missing enquiry bureau files, AWM 1DRL/0428.
64. Jones, *The war in the air*, vol. 4, p. 382.
65. Cobby, *High adventure*, p. 91.
66. Jones, *The war in the air*, vol. 4, p. 382.
67. Weingarth, letter, 15 April 1918 (*The 14–18 Journal*, 1993).
68. Knuckey, diary no. 7, AWM PR03193, pp. 22–3.
69. Stone, diary, 20–21 April 1918, SLV MS12245.
70. Knuckey, diary no. 7, AWM PR03193, p. 31.
71. Cobby, *High adventure*, p. 87.

Chapter 11

1. Lewis, diary, 11 April 1918, AWM PR00709.
2. Treacy, interview, *The 14–18 Journal*, 1970. It should be noted that Treacy's explanation for the accident is not corroborated by any official squadron records.
3. Athol Lewis, diary, 13 April 1918, AWM PR00897, item 21.
4. Lewis, *Our war*, pp. 334–5
5. Garrett, letter, 25 April 1918, SLV MS10762.
6. Franks and Bennett, *The Red Baron's last flight*, pp. 134–5.
7. Garrett, letter, 25 April 1918, SLV MS10762.
8. Paterson, private papers, AWM 3DRL/3389.
9. Garrett, letter, 25 April 1918, SLV MS10762.
10. Van Wyngarden, *Richthofen's circus*, p. 80.
11. Quotations from Brown's CitAR, 21 April 1918, in Jones, *The war in the air*, vol. 4, p. 392.

NOTES

12. Nicolson, diary, 21 April 1918, AWM 3DRL/2715.
13. Bean, *The official history*, vol. 5, p. 699.
14. Love, interview, *The 14–19 Journal*, 1970.
15. Alexander, diary, 21 April 1918, AWM PR86/133.
16. Love, interview, *The 14–18 Journal*, 1970.
17. Paterson, private papers, AWM3DRL/3389.
18. Garrett, letter, 25 April 1918, SLV MS10762.
19. Rawlinson, 'Story of No. 3 Squadron AFC', unpublished manuscript, p. 49, RAAF.
20. Titler, *The day the Red Baron died*, p. 198.
21. Barber, letter, 23 October 1935, AWM38 3DRL 7953/6, Part 1. The original report Barber submitted to Birdwood, commander of the Australian Corps, has apparently been lost.
22. Wrigley, *The battle below*, pp. 66–7.
23. Bean, *The official history*, vol. 5, p. 699.
24. ibid., p. 698.
25. Titler, *The day the Red Baron died*, pp. 122–4.
26. Miller, 'The death of Manfred von Richthofen'.
27. Franks and Bennett, *The Red Baron's last flight*, pp. 37–46.
28. For example, Peter Hart who, while acknowledging Popkin as the likely victor, 'sentimentally' prefers to believe Brown was the victor. Hart, *Aces falling*, p. 174.
29. Titler, *The day the Red Baron died*, p. 220.
30. Barnes, letter, 27 April 1918, RAAF.
31. Alexander, diary, 21 April 1918, AWM PR86/133.
32. Morrow, *The Great War in the air*, p. 300.
33. Report by Major Murray Jones, No. 2 Squadron war diary, May 1918, AWM4 8/5/10, Part 1.
34. Primrose, letter, 9 May 1918, AWM25 81/51.
35. Fraser, 'Ours or theirs?', p. 30.
36. Report by Mills, 10 May 1918, AWM25 81/51.
37. Shores et al., in *Above the trenches*, p. 79, suggest Sheldon was posted because of the Blaxland incident. Fraser, in 'Ours or theirs?', p. 30, claims Sheldon's recall to Australia was 'to assist in the organisation of an air corps'. Sheldon's service dossier (NAA B2455) confirms his appointment to command the Point Cook school.
38. Forrest, recommendation for DFC, 6 June 1918, AWM28.
39. CitAR, Hammond, 11 June 1918, No. 2 Squadron war diary, AWM4 8/5/11.

40. James Hammond, Australian Red Cross wounded and missing enquiry bureau files, AWM 1DRL/0428.
41. CitAR, Phillipps, 12 June 1918, No. 2 Squadron war diary, AWM4 8/5/11.
42. Franks et al., *The Jasta war chronology*, p. 188.
43. Cole, 'Courageous companions', unpublished manuscript, p. 31, AWM PR88/154.
44. Knuckey, diary no. 7, p. 31, AWM PR03193.
45. Richards, *Australian airmen*, p. 63.
46. McCloughry, letter, 21 February 1921, AWM 1DRL/0426.
47. Wright, 'From horses to horsepower'.
48. Cobby, *High adventure*, p. 106.
49. ibid., p. 111.
50. McCloughry, letter, 21 February 1921, AWM 1DRL/0426.
51. William Martin, Australian Red Cross wounded and missing enquiry bureau files, AWM 1DRL/0428.
52. Cobby, *High adventure*, pp. 111–12.
53. Edgar McCloughry, letter, 21 February 1921, AWM 1DRL/0426.
54. Cobby, letter, c. 1921, AWM44 8/1, Part 8.
55. Cobby, *High adventure*, p. 108.
56. ibid., p. 123.
57. ibid., pp. 129–31.
58. Royal Air Force communiqué No. 12, 26 June 1918, AWM4 8/14/2.
59. Cobby, *High adventure*, p. 106.
60. Stephens, *The Royal Australian Air Force*, p. 124.
61. Tuck, diary, 24 May 1918 (Kirby, *The war diaries of Stanley Thomas Tuck*).
62. Franks et al., *The Jasta war chronology*, pp. 167–8.
63. Treacy, interview, *The 14–18 Journal*, 1970.
64. Garrett, letter, 11 May 1918, SLV MS10762.
65. Wackett, letter, 15 February 1919, AWM 1DRL/589.
66. Wackett, *Aircraft pioneer*, p. 63.
67. ibid., p. 72.
68. Rawlinson, 'Story of No. 3 Squadron AFC', unpublished manuscript, p. 62, RAAF.
69. Wackett, *Aircraft pioneer*, p. 72.
70. ibid.
71. 7th Infantry Brigade AIF, captured enemy letter dated 5 May 1918, AWM EXDOC039.

NOTES

72. Bean, *The official history*, vol. 6, p. 268.
73. Wackett, *Aircraft pioneer*, p. 73.
74. Monash, *The Australian victories in France, 1918*, p. 41.
75. Barrett, letter, 30 August 1918, AWM 2DRL/0053.
76. Rawlinson, 'Story of No. 3 Squadron AFC', unpublished manuscript, p. 62, RAAF.
77. This figure differs substantially in various sources. The squadron war diarist, who presumably was closest to the original data, claims it was 93 crates.
78. Bean, *The official history*, vol. 6, p. 309; Monash, *The Australian victories in France 1918*, p. 42.
79. Bean, *The official history*, vol. 6, p. 309.
80. No. 3 Squadron war diary, July 1918, AWM4 8/6/19, Part 1.
81. Bean, *The official history*, vol. 6, p. 326.
82. No. 3 Squadron war diary, July 1918, AWM4 8/6/19, Part 1.
83. Terraine, *To win a war*, p. 85.
84. Wackett, *Pioneer airman*, p. 74.

Chapter 12

1. Knuckey, diary no. 8, pp. 9–10, AWM PR03193.
2. Hoeppner, *Germany's war in the air*, p. 154.
3. Strange, *Recollections of an airman*, pp. 176–7, 180.
4. McCloughry, letter, 21 February 1919, AWM 1DRL/0426.
5. J.C.F. Wilkinson, unpublished manuscript, pp. 249–51, RAF.
6. Cobby, *High adventure*, p. 138.
7. Nelson, repatriated prisoner of war statement, AWM B30 B3.8.
8. Youdale, letter, 18 July 1918 (*The 14–18 Journal*, 1996).
9. Bean, diary, 15 August 1918, 3DRL 606/116/2.
10. Bean, diary, 18 August 1918.
11. Edols, letter, 21 July 1918, AWM PR86/385.
12. Cobby, *High adventure*, p. 82.
13. RAF Communiqué No. 17, 31 July 1918, AWM4 8/14/2.
14. Wright, 'From horses to horsepower', unpublished manuscript, RAAF.
15. Jones, *The war in the air*, vol. 6, p. 436.
16. Wrigley, *The battle below*, p. 87.
17. Harris, *Amiens to the armistice*, p. 106.
18. Wrigley, *The battle below*, p. 87.
19. Rawlinson, 'Story of No. 3 Squadron AFC', unpublished manuscript, p. 64, RAAF.

20. Hart, *Aces falling*, p. 213.
21. Rawlinson, 'Story of No. 3 Squadron AFC', p. 65.
22. No. 3 Squadron war diary, AWM4 8/6/20, Part 1.
23. Barrett, letter, 30 August 1918, AWM 2DRL/0053.
24. No. 3 Squadron war diary, August 1918, AWM4 8/6/20, Part 1.
25. CitAR, Foale, 8 August 1918, No. 3 Squadron war diary, AWM4 8/6/20, Part 3.
26. Harris, *Amiens to the armistice*, p. 104.
27. Prince, interview (*The 14–18 Journal*, 1970).
28. Jones, *The war in the air*, vol. 6, p. 437.
29. Harris, *Amiens to the armistice*, pp. 103–4.
30. Barrett, letter, 30 August 1918, AWM 2DRL/0053.
31. Sewell, recommendation for DFC, 17 August 1918, AWM28.
32. Shelley, diary, 12 August 1918, AWM 2DRL/0290.
33. Barrett, letter, 30 August 1918, AWM 2DRL/0053.
34. Shelley, diary, 13 August 1918, AWM 2DRL/0290.
35. Barnes, letter, 17 August 1918, RAAF.
36. Bean, diary, 16 August 1918, AWM38 3DRL 606/116/2.
37. Edols, letter, 13 August 1918, AWM PR86/385.
38. Cobby, *High adventure*, p. 153.
39. Edols, letter, 13 August 1918, AWM PR86/385.
40. Cobby, *High adventure*, pp. 152–3.
41. Messenger, *The day we won the war*, p. 221.
42. Brearley, reconnaissance report, 25 August 5.10 p.m., No. 3 Squadron war diary, AWM4 8/6/20, Part 2.
43. Monash, *The Australian victories in France, 1918*, p. 146.
44. ibid., p. 149.
45. Cutlack, *The official history*, vol. 8, p. 314.
46. Reconnaissance reports, 29 August 1918, No. 3 Squadron war diary, AWM4 8/6/20, Part 2.
47. Strange, *Recollections of an airman*, pp. 188–9.
48. Richards, *Australian airmen*, pp. 25–6.
49. Cobby, *High adventure*, pp. 160, 162
50. ibid., p. 164.
51. Strange, *Recollections of an airman*, p. 189.
52. Cobby, *High adventure*, p. 165.
53. ibid., p. 166.
54. Edols, letter, 19 August 1918, AWM PR86/385.

NOTES

55. Raesch, diary, 16 August 1918 (*Cross & Cockade*, 4, 1967).
56. Baker, flying log book, AWM 1DRL/0084.
57. Wright, 'From horses to horsepower', p. 29.
58. Strange, *Recollections of an airman*, p. 189.
59. Copp, interview, *The 14–18 Journal*, 1965, Part 2.
60. Bean, diary, 18 August 1918, AWM38 3DRL 606/116/2.
61. Cobby, *High adventure*, p. 167.
62. Strange, *Recollections of an airman*, pp. 190–1.
63. Cobby, *High adventure*, p. 169.
64. Degelow, *Germany's last knight of the air*, p. 145.
65. ibid., p. 147.
66. Reports on Lomme and Haubourdin raids, NAUK AIR1 204/254/9.
67. Knuckey, diary no. 8, p. 13, AWM PR03193.

Chapter 13

1. Wackett, letter, 15 February 1919, AWM 1DRL589.
2. Tuck, diary, 3 September 1918 (Kirby, *The war diaries of Stanley Thomas Tuck*).
3. Shelley, diary, 8 September 1918, AWM 2DRL/0290.
4. Wackett, 15 February 1919, AWM 1DRL589.
5. Shelley, diary, 9 September 1918, AWM 2DRL/0290.
6. Rawlinson, 'Story of No. 3 Squadron AFC', unpublished manuscript, p. 72, RAAF.
7. Prince, interview (*The 14–18 Journal*, 1970).
8. No. 3 Squadron war diary, September 1918, AWM4 6/6/21, Part 1.
9. Shelley, diary, 18 September 1918, AWM 2DRL/0290.
10. Palstra, diary, 2 October 1918, 1DRL/0538.
11. Wackett, *Aircraft pioneer*, pp. 75–8.
12. Prince, interview (*The 14–18 Journal*, 1970).
13. Harris, *Amiens to the armistice*, p. 216.
14. Pomroy, diary, 28 September 1918, private collection.
15. Shelley, diary, 29 September 1918, AWM 2DRL/0290; No. 3 Squadron, war diary, September 1918, AWM4 8/6/21, Part 2.
16. Palstra, diary, 29 September 1918, AWM 1DRL/0538.
17. Palstra, diary, 30 September 1918.
18. No. 3 Squadron war diary, October 1918, AWM4 8/6/22, Part 1.
19. Shelley, diary, 1 October 1918, AWM 2DRL/0290.

20. Palstra, diary, 2 October 1918, AWM 1DRL/0538.
21. Hart, *Bloody April*, p. 204.
22. Pomroy, diary, 3 October 1918, private collection.
23. Bruce Garie Thomson, Australian Red Cross Society Wounded and Missing Enquiry files, AWM 1DRL/0428.
24. Shelley, diary, 5 October 1918, AWM 2DRL/0290.
25. Shelley, diary, 4 October 1918.
26. Knuckey, diary no. 8, pp. 14, 17, AWM PR03193.
27. H.J. Nowarra, 'Jagdgeschwader 3', *The 14–18 Journal*, 1965, no. 2.
28. Franks and Van Wyngaren, *Fokker DVII aces of World War 1: Part 2*, p. 80.
29. Cobby, *High adventure*, p. 172.
30. ibid., p. 174.
31. No. 4 Squadron manuscript history, AWM MSS520.
32. CitAR, Trescowthick, 5 September 1918, No. 4 Squadron war diary, 8/7/19, Part 1.
33. Ross, letter, 9 September 1918, AWM 3DRL/1298.
34. ibid.
35. Wilkinson, unpublished manuscript, pp. 270–1, RAF.
36. Cobby, *High adventure*, p. 171.
37. Roberts, interview, NLA TRC 536.
38. This is with the exception of the squadron's commanding officer, Major Allan Murray Jones, who received a bar to his DFC shortly after the war finished.
39. Harris, *Amiens to the armistice*, p. 202.
40. Wright, 'From horses to horsepower', unpublished manuscript, RAAF.
41. ibid.
42. Operation Orders No. 21, 6 October 1918, No. 2 Squadron war diary, AWM4 8/5/15, Part 3.
43. Dibbs quotations on the raid on Fives from letter to F.M. Cutlack, AWM44 8/1, Part 4, and interview (*The 14–18 Journal*, 1967).
44. Roberts, interview, 1977, NLA TRC 536.
45. Wright, 'From horses to horsepower'.
46. Jones, interview, AWM S04722.
47. CitAR, King, 30 October 1918, No. 4 Squadron war diary, AWM4 8/7/20, Part 3.
48. Van Wyngarden, *Jagdstaffel 2 Jasta 'Boelcke'*, pp. 116–18.
49. Jones, *From private to air marshal*, p. 23.
50. Strange, *Recollections of an airman*, pp. 201–2.

51. Jones, *The war in the air*, vol. 6, pp. 551–2.
52. Strange, *Recollections of an airman*, pp. 205–6.
53. Wright, 'From horses to horsepower'.
54. Strange, *Recollections of an airman*, p. 204.
55. Palstra, diary, no date, AWM 1DRL/0538.
56. Strange, *Recollections of an airman*, pp. 204–5.
57. Palstra, diary, no date, AWM 1DRL/0538.
58. Roberts, interview, NLA TRC 536.
59. Rawlinson, 'Story of No. 3 Squadron AFC', RAAF.
60. Roberts, interview, NLA TRC 536.
61. Wright, 'From horses to horsepower'.
62. Van Wyngarden, *Jasta 'Boelcke'*, p. 119.
63. Bennett, *Highest traditions*, p. 87.
64. Jones, *From private to air marshal*, p. 24.
65. Author's interview with Brian Wright, 29 November 2009.
66. *The Daily Mail*, 26 May, 1928.
67. *Mid Murray Flying Club Newsletter*, November 1975.
68. Cobby, *High adventure*, p. 192.
69. Quoted in Mexted, 'The life and legacy of Roby Lewis Manuel DFC', p. 66.
70. Cobby, *High adventure*, p. 191.

Chapter 14

1. *The Argus*, 17 June 1919.
2. Fysh, *Qantas rising*, p. 69.
3. *The Argus*, 3 September 1919.
4. Coulthard-Clark, *McNamara, VC*, p. 61.
5. Jones, *From private to air marshal*, p. 27.
6. Williams, interview, NLA TRC 121/50.
7. Coulthard-Clark, *The third brother*, p. 79.
8. Jones, *From private to air marshal*, p. 29.
9. Clune, *D'air devil*, p. 110.
10. Mexted, 'The life and legacy of Roby Lewis Manuel DFC'.
11. Stephens, *The Royal Australian Air Force*, p. 43.
12. Coulthard-Clark, *The third brother*, pp. 36–7.
13. Wrigley, Air Board report for Charles Bean, 21 March 1924 and 28 April 1924, AWM 3DRL 8042/64.
14. Blair, *Dinkum diggers*, p. 168.

FIRE IN THE SKY

15. Wrigley, letter, 21 March 1924, 'Historical notes Australian Flying Corps, 1916–1918', AWM38 3DRL 8042/64; these notes appear to correlate with the statistics provided by the squadrons themselves in their unit manuscript histories, held by the AWM in the MSS series. These figures do not include the Mesopotamian Half Flight's losses. The historian referred to is Russ Gannon (email correspondence, 9 February 2009).
16. Interview with Brian Wright by author, 29 November 2009.
17. Wackett, *Aircraft pioneer*, p. 209. Actually, the wreckage of Wackett's Beaufighter was discovered in 1945 in what is now the Kakadu National Park.
18. *The Daily Mail*, 26 May 1928.
19. *The Argus*, 31 October 1942.
20. Rawlinson, 'History of No. 3 Squadron AFC', unpublished manuscript, p. 77, RAAF.
21. Correspondence relating to F.R. Rawlinson's donation of relics to the AWM, 749/084/005.
22. Rawlinson, 'History of No. 3 Squadron AFC', unpublished manuscript, p. 77, RAAF.

NOTE ON SOURCES AND FURTHER READING

As a glance at the endnotes or bibliography will indicate, this book is based on extensive archival research. This is partly because of my belief that an experience of contemporary source material (the more contemporary the better) leads to good historical interpretation and narrative. But it is also partly the result of necessity, for there is very limited published material on the AFC.

Books devoted to the AFC that have been published over the 92 years since the First World War finished can be reviewed fairly succinctly. In 1923, Frederic Cutlack published his volume of the official history. He provides a detailed, chronological, event-driven narrative. His main sources were the squadron war diaries, and the reminiscences of some veterans (though fewer than I would have expected). Cutlack was perhaps disadvantaged by a lack of contextual sources—his book appeared before the relevant volumes of the British or Australian official histories and at a time when there was strictly limited literature on the air war. Although certainly adequate (and pleasing to his boss, Charles Bean), the AFC's official history is marked by some inaccuracies and a fairly narrow focus. It also might seem dry and repetitive to modern readers, moving from one dogfight to the next without much quoted directly from the airmen themselves. Cutlack's book also neglects to address the AFC's social and cultural dimensions, and does not cover aspects like recruitment, training and tactics (although, of course, to have done so would have put him well ahead of his time).

In the inter-war years, ex-members of No. 3 and No. 4 Squadrons wrote and published unit histories. Again, both stuck to a straightforward narrative of events as given in the squadron war diaries. No. 3 Squadron's history

(*The Battle Below*) is notable for its surprisingly lucid grasp of events in the wider context (battles, developments in the RFC, etc.) and the No. 4 Squadron book (*Australian Airmen*) contains some interesting essays by squadron members Wilfred McCloughry, Bo King and Harry Cobby. McCloughry's essay on squadron organisation is particularly important and goes a long way (in my view) to absolving him of Cobby's allegation that he was a negligent and ineffective squadron leader.

A few pilots published memoirs in the inter-war years. Notable are Les Sutherland's (*Aces and Kings*) and Arthur Cobby's (*High Adventure*). Both make for exciting reading, but almost certainly contain exaggerations and personal prejudices. Others wrote more prosaic accounts in retirement, during the 1960s and 1970s. Lawrence Wackett's *Aircraft Pioneer* is excellent—detailed, modest and very insightful—as is Richard Williams' *These are Facts* and Hudson Fysh's *Qantas Rising*.

The AFC has been neglected in most general histories of Australia and the First World War. Les Carlyon's *The Great War*, for example, doesn't contain a single mention of it in over 700 pages. Air force-focused histories usually feature a chapter or two on the AFC, with Alan Stephen's *The Royal Australian Air Force* and John Bennett's *Highest Traditions* providing two of the best examples. A few private diaries have been edited and published. Mark Lax's *One Airman's War* (Joe Bull's diaries) is an incredibly important contribution given the paucity of No. 1 Squadron records, as is Pat Conrick's *The Flying Carpet Men* (Clive Conrick's diaries). In 1972 Chas Schaedel published a brief, well-illustrated narrative of the AFC, *Men and Machines of the Australian Flying Corps, 1914–1919*. David Goodland and Alexander Vaughn did a curious book called *Anzacs Over England* in 1992 to accompany a television documentary of the same name. It is a kind of cultural history of the mark made by AFC training units on Gloucestershire in 1918. It contains some interesting insights about the men and their interactions with British communities there but doesn't examine AFC training in detail.

British history of the first air war has been much better serviced. There are literally dozens of published memoirs and diaries from pilots and mechanics. The best (and perhaps most relevant to the AFC's experiences) are Louis Strange's *Recollections of an Airman*, in which he describes his time as commanding officer of 80th Wing (containing Nos 2 and 4 Squadrons),

Arthur Lee's *No Parachute* (for his description of ground strafing at Cambrai) and Cecil Lewis's *Sagittarius Rising*, for its eloquent description of the lifestyle pilots led on service aerodromes. V.M. Yeats' semi-autobiographical novel *Winged Victory* is also mandatory, if depressing, reading. His vivid descriptions of ground strafing and air combat during the German offensives in 1918 are second to none. His portrayal of the protagonist's descent into nervous breakdown is bleak but riveting stuff, and useful in highlighting an issue often glossed over in other sources.

Modern British authors have also been prolific. The best concise overview of the air war is currently *Tumult in the Clouds* by Peter Hart and Nigel Steel. Peter has also written a trilogy of engaging, readable and well-researched books (*Somme Success*, *Bloody April* and *Aces Falling*) that focus on the air war over the Western Front in 1916, 1917 and 1918 respectively. Denis Winter's *The First of the Few* is beautifully written and vividly captures a sense of what it was like to be a First World War pilot, from enlistment and training through battle and into the post-war years. It was Winter's book that fired my interest in the topic when I read it as a teenager. Many of the other books devoted to First World War aviation give, in my opinion, undue (and indeed, anachronistic) attention to 'ace' pilots and the colour schemes and mechanical intricacies of the aircraft they flew.

The paucity of books on the AFC is all the more surprising when one considers the volume of relevant and publicly available archival records. Most are held in Canberra (at the Australian War Memorial) and Melbourne (RAAF Museum, Point Cook). Broadly, the records fall into two categories: official and private.

Official records include those the AFC generated for administrative and operational purposes during the war. The most practical for constructing a narrative are the squadron war diaries (digitally available on the Australian War Memorial's website), which record day-to-day events in the unit, including sorties flown, reconnaissance and combat reports from the airmen and returns on casualties. Sometimes they also contain orders (from higher formations such as wing and brigade) and intelligence reports. The AFC's war diaries are quite detailed, but are neither perfectly accurate nor complete. No. 1 Squadron's diaries from 1916 and 1917, for example, are missing despite searches by the staff of the Australian War Memorial and the UK National

Archives. Contemporary records chastising the squadrons' commanding officers also point to slack record-keeping in some of the units (especially No. 4 Squadron early in 1918), and suggest that war diaries were sometimes hurriedly prepared in retrospect to meet the demands of higher commands.

Gaps in the Australian squadron records are partially covered by British records. The UK National Archives holds war diaries for the British formations (wing and brigade) in which Australian squadrons served. These contain copies of Australian reconnaissance, bombing and aerial combat reports. I consulted these records in Britain and found much useful material that Cutlack apparently never saw. One combat report in particular led me to challenge the notion that Ross Smith scored the AFC's first aerial victory on 1 September 1917. A combat report by Stan Muir (from 5th Wing's war diary in the British National Archives) suggests he was in fact the first, on 20 December 1916, although further records don't confirm this. In any case, the documents in Britain significantly modified my initial view that No. 1 Squadron's airmen were practically helpless in 1916.

Beyond the squadron war diaries, there is a mass of other documents generated as part of the AFC's day-to-day administration. These were not intended to be historical records; rather, they were the necessary by-product of a large, complex organisation in a pre-digital age. This only increases their historical value, though. Records filed in the Australian War Memorial's AWM25 series in particular inadvertently provide an insight into the internal mechanics of the AFC, its members, training regime and culture. Especially interesting are documents relating to combat strain in pilots and the selection of cadets for flight training. The latter unintentionally reveal what a socially exclusive bunch the AFC's pilots in fact were.

Private records are those created by members of the AFC (or their families) for non-official purposes. They are diverse, including letters and diaries written during the war, memoirs or essays penned after it and interviews recorded in later years. The largest collections of private material are at the Australian War Memorial (donated by families) and the RAAF Museum at Point Cook. I was surprised to discover that the descendants of AFC men also hold a large amount of evidence-rich private documents. Many enthusiastically answered my advertisements and letters, and generously shared their material with me.

NOTES ON SOURCES AND FURTHER READING

I consulted well over 100 different private records while preparing this book. While I didn't always quote directly from them in the text, each shaped my interpretations and helped verify the veracity of other sources. Of course, letters and diaries need to be evaluated carefully in terms of their purpose, audience and context. Thomas Edol's letters to his sweetheart, for example, are full of dashing tales of derring-do and narrow escapes from swarms of Huns. Edmund Cornish's letters to his mother, on the other hand, are much more restrained, and tend to focus on the comforts and safety he enjoys as a pilot in the AFC. Both are potentially very useful sources, but each needs to be understood in terms of the context in which it was created, and corroborated with official records.

Although no AFC veterans were still alive by the time I started my research, I was able to draw on the National Library of Australia's substantial collection of recorded interviews with AFC veterans. Most were carried out by aviation historian Fred Morton during the 1970s, and are useful, if general and anecdotal in nature. They also need to be checked carefully, given the fallibility of human memory over time. The other shortcoming of oral history is the memory's tendency to compress multiple events and ideas into a few memorised anecdotes. As an example, George Jones, who was interviewed a few times in the 1970s and 1980s and wrote his memoirs, provides almost identically worded accounts of the same few events in each, despite the different questions of interviewers. An exception is Richard Williams' interview with Mel Pratt for the National Library in 1973. Williams' sharp, detail-driven mind is fully evident in this extremely lucid and thorough account of No. 1 Squadron's operations and the formation of the RAAF.

If it does nothing else, though, oral history is important evidence for understanding how the men perceived their wartime service later in life, in the light of the Depression, another world war (in which some of their sons—and indeed some of them—fought), families, work and the development of a collective national legend. One of the things I found most fascinating was how some of the veterans were perplexed by certain aspects of first air war historiography—in particular, the modern obsession with 'the aces'.

During the four years I have spent researching and writing this book, it has been the private records which I have enjoyed working with most. They offer not only an insight into the daily routine of life in the AFC but also into relationships within the squadron and the mentalities and outlook of the men who wrote them. It is the private records that allow us to see these men in human terms and get to know them on a more personal level. I was touched by Stan Nunan's uncharacteristically vulnerable letter to his father, in which he revealed his anxiety about coming home to Australia after the war. I felt ill when, after nearly a day spent reading Owen Lewis's diary in the War Memorial's research centre, it ended abruptly the evening before he was killed. The blank pages that followed prompted me to consider the opportunities this dux of Wesley College and talented engineering student missed (and indeed, what his community missed too). I laughed at Vern Knuckey's description of No. 4 Squadron's 'parson hunt' at Bruay in April 1918 and I had just a glimpse of the turbulent mixture of grief, pride and anger Mrs Hammond must have felt when she received Captain Forrest's description of her son's death. 'The trouble is he was too brave ...'

It has been thoroughly rewarding, if at times emotionally and personally draining, to work with the material their rich lives have left behind.

ACKNOWLEDGEMENTS

The origins of this book lie back in late 2003. I was 21 years old—about the average age of an Australian scout pilot in 1918—and looking for a topic on which to write an Honours thesis in the University of Wollongong's School of History and Politics. Associate Professor John McQuilton encouraged my ideas about an 'AFC thesis' from the outset and provided me with dedicated supervision over the following twelve months. Shortly after finishing my thesis, I met Dr Peter Stanley—then head of the Australian War Memorial's Military History Section. Dr Stanley took me into his section over the summer on a research scholarship and enthusiastically encouraged my interest in the AFC. During the following year or so, he convinced me 'somebody' needed to write a book about Australian airmen in the First World War—and it should be me.

During the four years it has taken to research and write this book, Dr Stanley and Associate Professor McQuilton have provided me with an incredible amount of support and encouragement. They are without doubt among the nation's finest scholars and teachers of Australian history. I consider myself immensely fortunate to have had their guidance and friendship. I dedicate this book them, with appreciation.

I have also benefited from the wisdom, knowledge and friendship of a number of other professional historians. Dr Craig Wilcox, Dr Karl James, Rhys Crawley, Aaron Pegram, Jen Hawksley and Mat McLachlan all provided helpful comments on draft chapters. Karl, Rhys and Aaron also put me up in Canberra at various times and ensured I didn't go hungry—or for that matter thirsty—after long days in the archives.

Others have been generous in their knowledge of aerial warfare and the First World War in general. Peter Hart and Dr Nigel Steel helped with British sources, advice about writing and tips on travelling to the battlefields. Ashley Ekins kindly shared some material on court martials from a yet to be published work. Fellow Allen & Unwin authors Peter Brune and Peter Rees have both shared their wisdom and experience. Kathy Mexted and Vin Ryan put me in contact with family members of AFC veterans and generously shared private records.

Over the course of my research, I got to know (sometimes, only by email) a handful of aviation history experts. Russ Gannon, who has spent over two decades comparing claim and loss data, was incredibly generous with statistical evidence and other sources. I regularly drew on his immense knowledge and tried out my interpretations on him before committing them to paper. He read and commented on a draft of the manuscript too. Mike O'Connor, whose 'Battlefield Europe' books on aerodromes are excellent, kindly sent me a large collection of documents from the United Kingdom that never made it to Australia after the war. Roger Harris, the editor of www.popularflying.com, scanned articles from his collection of vintage aviation magazines. Gareth Morgan shared his exhaustive work on the AFC's honour roll before it was published and read the draft manuscript. The Australian Society of World War One Aero Historians, formed in 1962, has collected an impressive amount of material on the AFC. Its annual publication, *The 14–18 Journal*, provided a number of important sources. People interested in the AFC can find out more at the society's website, www.ww1aero.org.au. Society members Colin Owers, Andrew Smith and David Perkins provided insightful comments on the draft manuscript.

I have also been fortunate to draw on the expertise of Royal Australian Air Force personnel. Dr Chris Clark, the air force historian, and Wing Commander Mark Hinchcliffe offered expert advice on the draft manuscript. Air Commodore Mark Lax (Retd) helped me with sources relating to the Mesopotamian and Palestine campaigns. I thank Chief of Air Force, Air Marshal Mark Binskin for his generous foreword and for his ongoing support of Australian aviation history projects.

I worked in and with a number of public institutions to prepare this book. It is with gratitude that I acknowledge the friendly and efficient service of the staff at the National Library of Australia, the National Archives of Australia, the Australian War Memorial (especially Jeremy Richter, Margaret Lewis and

Eric Carpenter), the Mitchell Library (Sydney), the State Library of Victoria, the RAAF Museum (Point Cook, Victoria), the RAF Museum (London) and the National Archives (London). I am especially grateful to the RAAF Museum's senior curator, Monica Walsh, for copying a large number of records and giving me permission to use some of the museum's photographs.

Although public collections form the backbone of this work, it was my intention from the beginning to involve families of AFC veterans as much as possible. To my pleasant surprise, they hold an incredible amount of material privately. I thank the following for their generosity and hospitality: Peter Vyner, Margaret and Lachlan Lewis, Phil Rackett, Charles Betteridge, Andrew Smith, Brian Wright, Paul Watson, Les Parsons, the Pomroy family, the Crawford family and the Lockley family. Space constraints haven't always allowed me to quote directly from the material they provided, but it helped me to develop new interpretations and determine the veracity of other accounts.

This book was mostly written in the evening during the four years I taught history at the Shellharbour Anglican College near Wollongong. My colleagues encouraged me along the way and, most importantly, reminded me that although not 'curriculum related', researching and writing were important things for a teacher to be modelling to his young students. In particular, I would like to acknowledge the support and encouragement of Head of College Tony Cummings, the Deputy Head, Mark Whitelock, and the head teachers I worked for, Dan Nichols and Jodie Liddiard. My friend and colleague Gemma Bartlett generously translated some French documents and has my gratitude.

Thanks to Allen & Unwin for supporting young Australian authors. Ian Bowring has been an enthusiastic advocate of this project and offered much helpful advice and encouragement. I also appreciate the efforts of his colleagues, Andrea Rejante, Aziza Kuypers, Jaclyn Richardson and Christa Munns, as well as the outstanding work of my editor, Sue Jarvis.

I gladly acknowledge the absolutely crucial support of my family. My parents fostered my keen interest in history when I was young, and raised me to value reading and writing.

Finally, my enormous gratitude goes to my extraordinarily patient, gracious and affectionate wife, Melissa. I was just starting the preliminary research when we were married in 2006. In a sense, 'the book' has been a third wheel in our relationship ever since. I realise it has been expensive for us—costing far too many hours together—but thank you for giving me your full support and pushing me when it all seemed 'too hard'. I hope it justifies the time we've lost.

Michael Molkentin
December 2009
(27 now—too old to be a scout pilot in the AFC)
www.michaelmolkentin.com

Since the first edition of *Fire in the Sky* was published several people have suggested minor but important revisions and provided me with wonderfully generous support and encouragement. I'd like to acknowledge, in particular, the keen eyes of James Oglethorpe and his colleagues in the 3 Squadron association (RAAF3Squadron@yahoo.com.au); Mark Lax and the members of the Australian Society of World War 1 Aero Historians, Chas Schaedel and Alan Pearson. The first edition included a photograph (Plate 9) of Lawrence Smith after he had been shot down and captured in June 1918. Behind him was the wreckage of his Bristol Fighter in which his pilot, Gordon Oxenham had died. A few weeks after the book was published, Oxenham's great nephew Alan Oxenham contacted me with evidence that the man in the photograph I had included was, in fact, not Lawrence Smith. He quickly convinced me that the RAAF Museum, the Australian War Memorial and another publication had incorrectly captioned the photograph. Alan generously put me in contact with Dr Dieter Groschel, an authority on German aviation in the Middle East during the Great War, who in turn, obtained a genuine photograph of Smith from Mr Horst W. Laumanns. Mr Laumanns, a collector, had found the photograph in the pocket of a First World War German officer's uniform and has generously permitted me to include it in this revised edition.

Michael Molkentin
March 2012

BIBLIOGRAPHY

Archival sources
Australian War Memorial, Canberra
Official Records
AWM4 Australian Imperial Force unit war diaries, 1914–18 War:
    8/3 15th Wing Headquarters, Royal Flying Corps
    8/4 No. 1 Squadron, Australian Flying Corps
    8/5 No. 2 Squadron, Australian Flying Corps
    8/6 No. 3 Squadron, Australian Flying Corps
    8/7 No. 4 Squadron, Australian Flying Corps
    8/14 Royal Flying Corps Communiqués and Press Reviews
AWM8 Unit embarkation nominal rolls, 1914–18 War
AWM10 Australian Imperial Force Administrative Headquarters registry, 'A'
    4343/4/2 'Administration of the Australian Flying Corps in France'
    4343/29/17 'Selection of candidates for appointment as flying officers, AFC, 1st Anzac circular (Aug 1917)'
AWM25 Written records, 1914–18 War
    81/3 'Australian Flying Corps [Royal Flying Corps] Historical Records of Australian Imperial Force, Aviation Section'
    81/20 'Correspondence with reference to training of observers'
    81/47 'No 67 Australian Flying Squadron—Summary of Work. Reports of Bomb Attacks on Enemy Camps, November 1916'
    81/51 '[Australian Flying Corps—Royal Flying Corps] Officers—Regarding Postings—Transfers etc 1918'
    81/54 'Notes on AFC for General Birdwood' and draft article 'Air Supremacy' by 'Penguin' (J.L. Treloar)

FIRE IN THE SKY

    171/8 'Australian Flying Corps, Battle Casualties. Daily report rendered to Australian Section, 3rd Echelon and Administrative Headquarters, AIF, October 1917–November 1918'

    481/115 'Medical requirements for Australian Flying Corps, 1918'

    943/3 'Training. United Kingdom—Egypt Australian Flying Corps, 1917'

AWM27 Records arranged according to AWM Library subject classification

    174/5 'Copy of official report of the death of Baron von Richthofen, compiled from evidence that was taken at the enquiry immediately following the event (21 Apr 1918)'

    174/6 'Baron von Richthofen—Statement to C.E.W. Bean by Gunner G. Ridgway 29 Battery Australian Field Artillery (Apr–May 1934)'

AWM28 'Recommendation files for honours and awards, AIF, 1914–18 War'

AWM30 'Prisoner of war statements, 1914–18 War'

    B3.2 'Prisoner of war statements—Palestine'

    B3.4-3.17 Prisoner of War Statements, AFC Squadrons on the Western Front

AWM38 'Official History, 1914–18 War: Records of C.E.W. Bean, Official Historian'

    3DRL 7953/6 Part 1 Correspondence 1920–1939

    3DRL 7953/9 Correspondence relating to the official history of the AFC

    3DRL 606/94/2 Diary, November–December 1917

    3DRL 606/101/2 Diary, February–March 1918

    3DRL 606/116/2 Diary, June–September 1918

    3DRL 8042/64 'Papers, 1916–24; contain copies of Bean's diary no 87 and correspondence of the Australian Flying Corps, 1916–18'

AWM 44 Official History, 1914–18 War, manuscripts

    8/1 F M Cutlack's research papers for the AFC's official history

AWM45 Copies of British war diaries and other records, 1914–18 War

    44/1 40 Wing, RFC despatches and reports

AWM131 Roll of Honour circulars, 1914–18 War

AWM224 Unit manuscript histories

    MSS511 1st Half Flight, Australian Flying Corps: Brief record

    MSS510 Australian Flying Corps: History, by Lt Col R Williams

    MSS512 Australian Flying Corps Training Depot: Brief record

    MSS513 Australian Flying Corps: Miscellaneous, No 67 Squadron and in India

    MSS515 No 1 Squadron reports and statistics

    MSS517 No. 2 Squadron reports and statistics

MSS518 No. 3 Squadron reports and statistics
MSS520 No. 4 Squadron reports and statistics
EXDOC039 7th Infantry Brigade AIF papers

Private Records
PR86/133 2nd Class Air Mechanic John Alexander, No. 3 Squadron
1DRL/0084 Captain Thomas Baker, No. 4 Squadron
2DRL/0053 Lieutenant Arthur Barrett, No. 3 Squadron
PR04011 Private Jenkyn Benham, No. 1 Squadron
3DRL/6060 Corporal Herbert Billings, No. 3 Squadron
PR01547 Air Mechanic Joseph Bull, No. 1 Squadron
PR88/154 Lieutenant Adrian Cole, No. 1 and No. 2 Squadrons
3DRL/6113 Private Richard Cooper, No. 1 Squadron
1DRL/0212 Lieutenant Harold Cornell, No. 2 Squadron
1DRL/0214 Lieutenant Edmund Cornish, No. 2 Squadron
PR83/187 Captain Eric Cummings, No. 2 Squadron
PR04018 Private Fergus Cox, No. 1 Squadron
PR85/344 Lieutenant Donald Day, No. 6 Training Squadron
PR86/385 Lieutenant Thomas Edols, No. 4 Squadron
3DRL/4103 Mrs J.E. Faukes papers
PR00005 Lieutenant Douglas Ferguson, AFC Training Wing
MSS1276 2nd Lieutenant Robert Forsyth, No. 2 Squadron
PR83/078 Lieutenant Hudson Fysh, No. 1 Squadron
2DRL/0530 Lieutenant Frederick Hancock, No. 1 Squadron
PR84/003 Captain John Harris, No. 1 Squadron
MSS0791 Lieutenant Uriah Hoddinott, RFC
PR03193 Private Verner Knuckey, No. 2 and No. 4 Squadrons
3DRL/4180 Private Harry Leckie, No. 1 Squadron
P02771.001 Lieutenant Athol Lewis, 8th Australian Field Artillery
PR00709 Lieutenant Owen Lewis, No. 3 Squadron
1DRL/0426 Captain Edgar McCloughry, No. 4 Squadron
PR01381 Lieutenant Wallace McDougall, No. 3 Squadron
2DRL/0011 Lieutenant Arthur Mott, No. 1 Squadron
3DRL/2715 Captain Norman Nicolson, 14th Field Artillery Brigade
3DRL/6511 Lieutenant Stanislaus Nunan, X Flight RAF and No. 1 Squadron
1DRL/0538 Lieutenant William Palstra, No. 3 Squadron
3DRL/3389 Lieutenant Alec Paterson, No. 3 Squadron

PR85/022 Private Tom Prentice, No. 1 Squadron
MSS0770 Private Frank Rawlinson, No. 3 Squadron
3DRL/7866 Lieutenant Eric Roberts, No. 1 Squadron
3DRL/1298 Lieutenant James Ross, No. 2 Squadron
2DRL/0290 Lieutenant Max Shelley, No. 3 Squadron
PR83/100 Lieutenant Lawrence Smith, No. 1 Squadron
PR90/087 and 1DRL/0655 Captain Ross Smith, No. 1 Squadron
2DRL/0988 Lieutenant Leslie Sutherland, No. 1 Squadron
PR01760 Lieutenant William Thompson, No. 1 Squadron
PR87/199 Henri Hemene Tovell
PR84/244 Lieutenant William Treloar, Mesopotamian Half Flight
PR83/230 Lieutenant Leslie Ward, No. 2 Squadron
3DRL/6113 Lieutenant Colonel Oswald Watt, No. 1 and No. 2 Squadrons
1DRL/0589 Major Lawrence Wackett, No. 1 and No. 3 Squadrons
1DRL/0428 Australian Red Cross Wounded and Missing Enquiry Bureau files

Oral History
S03420 2nd Class Air Mechanic Harold Edwards, No. 3 Squadron (1996)
S01644 2nd Class Air Mechanic Hugh Griffiths, No. 2 Squadron (1993)
S04722 Captain George Jones, No. 4 Squadron (1981)
S04307 Lieutenant Lawrence Smith, No. 1 Squadron (no date)

National Archives, London
Air Historical Branch Records: Series I (AIR1)
- 1754/204/141/9-1/1759/204/141/44 '5 Wing RFC war diary' April 1916–December 1917
- 2286/209/75/21 'No 67 Australian Squadron RFC Reconnaissance Reports 27–31/10/1916'
- 2287/209/75/54 '67 Squadron Reconnaissance Reports Sept–Oct 1916'
- 2288/209/75/58 'Reconnaissance and bombing reports', March–April 1917
- 2212/209/28/1-11 '40 Wing RFC war diary', October–December 1917
- 2389/228/11/121 'An account by course students of war experiences: F/Lt. E.J. McCloughry'
- 2387/228/11/54 'War experiences of Squadron Leader R.S. Brown of Australian Flying Corps'
- 2388/228/11/78 'War experiences of Flight Lieutenant J.R. Bell, No. 3 Squadron, Australian Flying Corps ...'

2389/228/11/101 'War experiences of Squadron Leader W.H. Anderson, No. 3 Squadron, Australian Flying Corps...'
2390/228/11/131 'War experiences of Squadron Leader G. Jones, No. 4 Squadron, Australian Flying Corps'
2392/228/11/177 'War experiences of Squadron Leader F.W.F. Lukis, No. 1 Squadron, Australian Flying Corps'
2424/305/20 'War effort of the Dominions'

National Archives of Australia, Canberra

A289 1849/8/222 'Aerial League of Australia—NSW Section'
A289 1849/8/221 'Early suggestions for the establishment of a Commonwealth School of Aviation and an Australian Flying Corps'
A289 1907/2/356 'Aircraft—Department of Defence competition for the design of a flying machine for military purposes. Entry by Mr W. Paris Myers of London'
A2023 A38/3/221 'Aviation 1910–1914. Correspondence with High Commissioner'
A2023 A38/3/61 'Parliamentary Question re Purchase of additional aeroplanes for use at Point Cook'
A2023 A38/7/339 'Reports on the Instructional Courses C.F.S.'
A2023 38/8/188 'First and second half flights, establishment, recruitment, organisation and selecting personnel, 21 July 1915'
A2023 A38/8/202 'First Half Flight (AFC) in Mesopotamia—Reports by Commanding Officer Captain Petre, H.A., AFC'
B2455 AIF personnel dossiers
MP84/1 1849/8/287, 'Formation of Flying Corps'

National Library of Australia, Canberra

MS883 Frank Hurley, diary, 1917–1918
TRC 121/50 Richard Williams interviewed by Mel Pratt, 1973–74
TRC 391/36–38 Edgar Percival interviewed by Neil Bennetts, 1980
TRC 425/1 Richard Williams interviewed by Fred Morton, 1976
TRC 425/2–3 Henry Wrigley interviewed by Fred Morton, 1976
TRC 425/2 George Jones interviewed by Fred Morton, 1976
TRC 425/4 C.S. Sutherland interviewed by Fred Morton, 1976
TRC 425/5 Eric Dibbs interviewed by Fred Morton, 1976
TRC 425/6 Jerry Pentland interviewed by Fred Morton, 1976
TRC 653/2 Frederic Haig interviewed by Fred Morton, 1979
TRC 536 Frank Roberts interviewed by Fred Morton, 1977

TRC 900 Joel Treacy interviewed by Fred Morton, 1980
TRC 536 Eric Roberts, interviewed by Fred Morton, 1977

Mitchell Library, Sydney
MLMSS 1046, Leslie Sutherland, No. 1 Squadron

State Library of Victoria, Melbourne
MS10762 Lieutenant Stanley Garrett, No. 3 Squadron
MS10752 Lieutenant Owen Lewis, No. 3 Squadron
MS12245 Air Mechanic Harold Stone, No. 4 Squadron

RAF Museum, London
J F C Wilkinson, unpublished manuscript

RAAF Museum, Point Cook
Anon (filed with Richard Williams' papers), 'History of the RFC in Sinai and Palestine during 1917'
Anon, 'Bavarian Flying Squadron 304: extracts from report on the evacuation of the aerodrome at Arak El Manshije'
Cadet Leigh [no surname], letter to mother from No. 8 Reserve Squadron, 2 May 1916
2nd Class Air Mechanic James Francis Barnes, letters, 1917–18
Lieutenant Francis Cooper Penny, 'Memories of flying', unpublished manuscript
2nd Class Air Mechanic F R Rawlinson, 'Story of No. 3 Squadron AFC', unpublished manuscript
Sergeant William Wheeler, 'Formation of First Half Flight', unpublished manuscript
Lieutenant-Colonel Richard Williams, 'Experience in connection with the war of 1914/1918', unpublished manuscript
Captain John Wright, 'From horses to horsepower', unpublished manuscript

Private Collections
Captain John Wright, No. 4 Squadron, unpublished manuscript (also held at the RAAF Museum), private papers and photographs
Lieutenant Alex Lockley, No. 4 Squadron, private papers
Private William Lord, Mesopotamian Half Flight, letters
Lieutenant William Pomroy, No. 3 Squadron, diary and unpublished manuscript
Lieutenant Norman Sharples, No. 7 Squadron (RFC), diary and letters

Lieutenant Charles Vyner, No. 1 Squadron, photographs and private papers

Lieutenant Archie Rackett, No. 2 Squadron, manuscript diary/memoir

Published Sources
Books

The Australian Dictionary of Biography, available from http://adbonline.anu.edu.au/adbonline.htm

Text book on aerial gunnery, HMSO, London, June 1917

Ralph Baker, *A brief history of the Royal Flying Corps in World War I*, Robinson Publishing, London, 2002

C.E.W. Bean, *Anzac to Amiens: A shorter history of the Australian fighting services in the First World War*, Australian War Memorial, Canberra, 1946

—— *The official history of Australia in the war of 1914–1918*, volume 5, 'The Australian Imperial Force in France during the main German offensive, 1918', Angus & Robertson, Sydney, 1938

—— *The official history of Australia in the war of 1914–1918*, volume 5, 'The Australian Imperial Force in France during the Allied offensive, 1918', Angus & Robertson, Sydney, 1942

John Bennett, *Highest traditions: The history of No. 2 Squadron RAAF*, AGPS, Canberra, 1995

Dale Blair, *Dinkum diggers: An Australian battalion at war*, Melbourne University Press, Melbourne, 2001

Fred and Elizabeth Brenchley, *White's flight: An Australian pilot's epic escape from Turkish prison camp to Russia's revolution*, John Wiley & Sons, Brisbane, 2004

Stanley Brogden, *The history of Australian aviation*, Hawthorn Press, Melbourne, 1960

A.H. Cobby, *High adventure*, Robertson & Mullens, Melbourne, 1942

Pat Conrick, *The flying carpet men*, self published, 1993

Chris Coulthard-Clark, *McNamara, VC: A hero's dilemma*, Air Power Studies Centre, RAF, London, 1997

Frank Clune, *D'air devil: The story of 'Pard' Mustar, Australian air ace*, Allied Authors and Artists, London, 1941

F.M. Cutlack, *Official history of Australia in the war of 1914–1918*, volume VIII, 'The Australian Flying Corps in the eastern and western theatres of war 1914–1918', Angus & Robertson, Sydney, 1923

Carl Degelow, *Germany's last knight: The memoirs of Major Carl Degelow*, William Kimber, London, 1979

H.G. Edwards, *The trusty one*, Assembly Press, Brisbane, 1985

Norman Eustis, *The greatest race: England–Australia, 1919*, McPherson's Printing Group, Brisbane, 1994

Norman Franks, Frank Bailey and Rick Duiven, *Casualties of the German Air Service 1914–1920*, Grub Street, London, 1999

Norman Franks, Frank Bailey and Rick Duiven, *The Jasta war chronology: A complete listing of claims and losses, August 1916–November 1918*, Grub Street, London, 1998

Norman Franks and Alan Bennett, *The Red Baron's last flight*, Grub Street, London, 2006

Norman Franks and Greg Van Wyngarden, *Fokker DVII Aces of World War I, Part 2*, Osprey Publishing, Colchester, 2004

Ernest von Hoeppner, *Germany's war in the air: The development and operations of German military aviation in the First World War*, The Battery Press, Nashville, TN, 1994

Wilmot Hudson Fysh, *Qantas rising*, Qantas Association, Sydney, 1965

H.S. Gullett, *Official history of Australia in the war of 1914–1918*, volume VII, 'The Australian Imperial Force in the Sinai and Palestine', Angus & Robertson, Sydney, 1923

J.E. Gurdon, *The German Air Force in the First World War*, Hodder & Stoughton, London, 1921

Jon Guttman and Harry Dempsey, *Bristol F2 fighter aces of World War I*, Osprey Publishing, Colchester, 2007

Frederick William Haig, *Airman oilman: Frederic William Haig autobiography*, Frederick Publishing, Los Angeles, 1996

Timothy Hall, *Flying high: The story of Hudson Fysh, Qantas and the trailblazing days of aviation*, Methuen, Sydney, 1979

Peter Hart, *Bloody April: Slaughter in the skies over Arras, 1917*, Cassell, Melbourne, 2006

—— *Aces falling: The war above the trenches, 1918*, Weidenfeld and Nicolson, London, 2007

Bryn Hammond, *Cambrai 1917: The myth of the first great tank battle*, Weidenfeld and Nicolson, London, 2008

J.P. Harris and Niall Barr, *Amiens to the armistice: The BEF in the Hundred Days campaign, 8 August–11 November 1918*, Brassey's, London, 1999

Trevor Henshaw, *The sky their battlefield: Air fighting and the complete list of allied air casualties from enemy action in the first war*, Grub Street, London, 1995

BIBLIOGRAPHY

Matthew Hughes, *Allenby and the British strategy in the Middle East 1917–1919*, Frank Cass, London, 1999

C.J. Jefford, *Observers and navigators and other non-pilot aircrew in the RFC, RNAS and RAF*, Airlife, Shrewsbury, 2002

Sir George Jones KBE CB DFC, *From private to Air Marshal*, Greenhouse Publications, Santa Clarita, CA, 1988

H.A. Jones and Walter Raleigh, *The war in the air: Being the story of the part played in the Great War by the Royal Air Force*, volumes 1–6, Oxford University Press, Oxford, 1922–37

Philip Joubert, *The forgotten ones: The story of the ground crews*, Hutchinson, London, 1961

Gertrude Kirby (ed.), *The war diaries of Stanley Thomas Tuck, 1917 and 1918, transcribed and compiled, with prelude, epilogue & postscript*, self published, 1989

G.H. Knibbs, *Census of the Commonwealth of Australia taken for the night between the 2nd and 3rd April, 1911*, 3 volumes, 1914–17

Mark Lax (ed.), *One airman's war: Aircraft mechanic Joe Bull's personal diaries 1916–1919*, Banner Books, Maryborough, Qld, 1997

Arthur Gould Lee, *No parachute*, Time Life Books, New York, 1991

Brian Lewis, *Our war: Australia during World War I*, Melbourne University Press, Melbourne, 1980

Cecil Lewis, *Sagittarius rising*, Penguin, Ringwood, 1977

Charles Messenger, *The day we won the war: Turning point at Amiens 8th August 1918*, Weidenfeld and Nicolson, London, 2009

John Monash, *The Australian victories in France in 1918*, Angus & Robertson, Sydney, 1936

John H. Morrow Jr, *The Great War in the air: Military aviation from 1909 to 1921*, Smithsonian Institution Press, New York, 1993

Carl Mühlmann, *Das Deutsch-Türkische waffenbündnis im Weltkrieg*, publisher unknown, 1940

Michael O'Connor, *Airfields and airmen: Ypres*, Pen & Sword, London, 2001

Ian Passingham, *Pillars of fire: The Battle of Messines Ridge June 1917*, Sutton, Stroud, UK, 1998

Sir George Foster Pearce, *Carpenter to cabinet: Thirty years of parliament*, Hutchinson, London, 1951

Peter Pedersen, *The Anzacs: Gallipoli to the Western Front*, Viking, Ringwood, 2007

E.J. Richards et al. *Australian airmen: History of the 4th Squadron Australian Flying Corps*, Bruce & Co., London, 1922

E.G. Roberts, *Box kites and beyond*, Hawthorne Press, Melbourne, 1976

Charles Schaedel, *Men and Machines of the Australian Flying Corps, 1914–1919*, Kookaburra Technical Publications, Dandenong, 1972

Gary Sheffield, *Forgotten victory: Myths and realities of the First World War*, Headline Review, London, 2002

Gary Sheffield and John Bourne (eds), *Douglas Haig war diaries and letters 1914–1918*, Weidenfeld & Nicolson, London, 2005

Jack Sheldon, *The German Army at Cambrai*, Pen & Sword, London, 2009

Christopher Shores, Norman Franks and Russell Guest, *Above the trenches: A complete record of the fighter aces and units of the British Empire air forces, 1915–1920*, Grub Street, London, 1990

Sydney Ure Smith, Bertram Stevens and Ernest Watt (eds), *Oswald Watt, Lieut.-Colonel A.F.C., O.B.E., Legion of Honour, Croix de Guerre: A tribute to his memory by a few of his friends*, Art in Australia, Sydney, 1921

Nigel Steel and Peter Hart, *Tumult in the clouds: The British experience of the war in the air 1914–1918*, Hodder & Stoughton, Melbourne, 1997

Alan Stephens and Brendan O'Loghlin (eds), *The decisive factor: Air power doctrine by Air Vice-Marshal HN Wrigley*, AGPS, Canberra, 1990

Alan Stephens, *The Royal Australian Air Force*, Oxford University Press, Melbourne, 2001

L.A. Strange, *Recollections of an airman*, The Aviation Book Club, London, 1940

L.W. Sutherland, *Aces and kings*, John Hamilton, London, 1935

John Terraine, *To win a war: 1918 the year of victory*, Cassell, Melbourne, 2001

Dale Titler, *The day the Red Baron died*, Walker and Company, New York, 1970

Tim Travers, *How the war was won: Command and technology in the British army on the Western Front, 1917–1918*, Pen & Sword, London, 2005

Greg Van Wyngarden, *Jagdstaffel 2 'Jasta Boelcke'*, Osprey Publishing, Colchester, 2007

——— *Pfalz scout aces of World War 1*, Osprey Publishing, Colchester, 2006

——— *Richthofen's circus: Jagdgeschwader Nr 1*, Osprey Publishing, Colchester, 2004

Lawrence Wackett, *Aircraft pioneer: An autobiography*, Angus & Robertson, Sydney, 1972

T.W. White, *Guests of the unspeakable*, Angus & Robertson, Sydney, 1932

Richard Williams, *These are facts: The autobiography of Air Marshal Sir Richard Williams, KBE, CB, DSO*, Australian War Memorial, Canberra, 1977

Denis Winter, *The first of the few: Fighter pilots of the First World War*, Allen Lane, London, 1982

J.M. Winter, *The Great War & the British people*, Macmillan, 1987

Wrigley, H.N., *The battle below: Being the history of No. 3 Squadron Australian Flying Corps*, H. Gorton & Co., Sydney, 1935

Articles and conference papers

Anon, 'The War Diary of Royal Bavarian Jasta 35', *Cross & Cockade (US)*, 24, 1983

F. Clark, 'Harry Tate pilot: an interview with Mr Nigel Love', *The 14–18 Journal*, 1970

C.H. Copp, 'The experiences of Captain C.H. Copp formerly of No. 2 Squadron AFC', *The 14–18 Journal*, 1965

Eric Dibbs, 'Interview with Captain Eric Rupert Dibbs formerly of the AFC', *The 14–18 Journal*, 1967

Walter Eastman, 'Twenty-Three Brave Young Men', *Tasmanian Historical Research Association Papers and Proceedings*, 30(2), 1983

Brian P. Flanagan, 'Palestine Jagdstaffel: The puzzling history of Jasta 55', *Cross & Cockade*, 13(1), 1972

Alan Fraser, 'Ours or theirs?', *Journal of the Australian War Memorial*, 6, 1986

Dieter H.M. Gröschel and Jürgen Ladek, 'Wings over Sinai and Palestine: The Adventures of Flieger Abteilung 300 "Pascha" in their fight against the Egyptian Expeditionary Force', *Over the Front*, 23(1), 1998

Ian Hodges, 'The Mesopotamian Half Flight', *Wartime*, 27, 2004

George Jones, 'An interview with Sir George Jones, KBE, CB, DFC. Formerly Capt., AFC, later Air Marshal, RAAF', *The 14–18 Journal*, 1968

Mark Lax, 'A hint of things to come: Leadership in the AFC', *The 14–18 Journal*, 2000

—— 'The skies over Mesopotamia: Part 1 to Kut', *The 14–18 Journal*, 2005

Paul Leaman, 'Frank McNamara, VC', *Cross & Cockade (UK)*, 2 (3), 1971

Captain R.W. MacKenzie, 'My most thrilling flight', *Popular Flying*, June 1934

J. P. McCoy and G. A. Ruddock, 'Interview with G.N. Mills former Observer with the Australian Flying Corps', *The 14–18 Journal*, 1968

—— 'Air war in the desert: Some experiences of Lt M.D. Lees, No. 1 Squadron AFC, *The 14–18 Journal*, 1969

Kathy Mexted, 'The life and legacy of Captain Roby Lewis Manuel DFC', *Flightpath*, November 2008

Geoffrey Miller, 'The death of Manfred von Richthofen: Who fired the fatal shot?' *Sabretache*, 39(2), 1998

Michael Molkentin, 'Fire-eater', *Wartime*, 34, 2006

—— 'That dreadful Flying Corps: Responses to life and death in the Australian Flying Corps, 1914–1918', *Cross & Cockade*, 35(4), 2005

—— 'Unconscious of any distinction? Social and vocational quality in the Australian Flying Corps, 1914–1918', *The Journal of the Australian War Memorial*, 40, 2006

Gareth Morgan, 'Australian Flying Corps Roll of Honour', *The 14–18 Journal*, 2008, 2009

H.J. Nowarra, 'Jagdgeschwader 3' *The 14–18 Journal*, 1965, no. 2

Colin A. Owers, 'Memories of No. 3 Squadron: An interview with Jack Treacy by Colin A. Owers', *The 14–18 Journal*, 1972–73

'Raesch of Jasta 43 (diary of a fighter pilot)', *Cross & Cockade*, 8(4), 1967

Eric Watson, 'Letter from a flying officer [Roy Youdale, No. 4 AFC], *The 14–18 Journal*, 1996

Eric Watson and Alan Fraser, 'The personal letters of Captain R.W. Howard MC, Australian Flying Corps', Parts 1–3, *The 14–18 Journal*, 1997–99

Gerald Weingarth, 'Camel pilot: Lieutenant Jack Henry Weingarth Australian Flying Corps', *The 14–18 Journal*, 1993

Richard White, 'Motives for joining up: Self-sacrifice, self-interest and social class 1914–1918', *Journal of the Australian War Memorial*, 9, October 1986

Erich Jan Zürcher, 'Between death and desertion: The experience of the Ottoman soldier in World War I', *Turcica*, 28, 1996

Theses

Peter Helson, Ten years at the top: Air Marshal Sir George Jones, University of New South Wales, Sydney, 1996

Mark Lax, Impact of technology and command on No 1 Squadron operations 1916–1958, University of New South Wales, Sydney, 1995

Michael Molkentin, Culture, Class and Experience in the Australian Flying Corps, University of Wollongong, Wollongong, 2004

Robert M. Morley, Earning their wings: British pilot training 1912–1918, University of Saskatchewan, Saskatoon, Canada, 2006

Adam Garth Pye, Evolution in action: The Royal Flying Corps/Royal Air Force and the development of ground attack in World War I, University of Calgary, Calgary, 2003

Newspapers and magazines

The Age (Melbourne)
The Argus (Melbourne)
The Brisbane Courier

The Daily Mail
Flightpath
The Mercury (Hobart)
Slipstream
The Sydney Morning Herald
The Windsor and Richmond Gazette

INDEX

accommodation 28–9
Adair, Ronald 134–5, 138
Addison, Sydney 117, 123, 135–6, 140, 146, 174–5
Aerial League of Australia 2–3
aerodromes
  Ali Gharbi 17
  Amara 15–16
  Arak el Menshiye 112
  Aziziyeh 18
  Bailleul 223
  Baizeux 28, 205–6
  Basra 13
  Bertangles 35
  Bickendorf 326
  Bruay 228, 231
  Clairmarais North 263
  Deir el Belah 100–1
  El Afule 160
  Foquorolles 261
  Haifa 169–73
  Haubourdin 295–8, 313
  Homs 172
  Horseshoe Wood 292
  Huj 99
  Kantara 72
  Kilo 80, 143
  Kut 18
  La Bellevue 243, 258
  Lomme 299–300, 313
  Mejdel 116, 121
  Mustabig 72, 75
  Poulainville 250
  Proyart 304
  Ramleh 80, 93, 132
  Rayak, 173–4
  Reclinghem 28, 278
  Savy 197–8, 231
  Villers–Bocage 269
Agnew, Ivo 207
aircraft
  Albatros DIII 99
  BE2a 10–11
  BE2c 59–60, 63, 71
  BE2e 80, 99
  BE12a 78, 98
  Bristol Boxkite 1, 8–9
  Bristol F2b 109, 116
  Caudron G III 16
  DH5 204, 206
  Fokker Dr I Triplane 269, 270
  Fokker DVII 262, 313, 315, 323
  Handley Page 0/400 155
  Martinsyde G100 71, 78
  Martinsyde S1 17
  Maurice Farman Longhorn 13
  RE8 78, 109, 197, 302
  Rumpler CI 62
  SE5a 231
  Sopwith Camel 222, 228, 231
  Sopwith Snipe 321, 323
Alberry, Frank 318
alcohol 36, 119, 170, 194, 284, 298–9
Aldis sight 43
Alexander, John 255, 258
Allenby, Edmund 100, 110, 122–3, 125, 153, 168, 175
American Expeditionary Force
  II American Corps 309–10, 312
Anderson, William 201–2, 225–6
anti-aircraft fire 81–2, 229
Anzac Day 1919 328–9

INDEX

Armistice 324–6
armourers 49
artillery observation 64, 201, 224, 226
Ascroft, William 65, 66
Austin, Ron 112, 114, 117
Australian Air Corps 334
Australian Flying Corps
  No. 1 Squadron
    accidents in 1917 115
    aerodrome bombing 93–4
    air-ground communication 70–1
    bombing March 1917 83–5
    casualties 105, 175
    cooperation with light horse 59
    designation as an 'army squadron' 98
    discipline 174–5
    Distinguished Flying Cross 173
    formalities 33
    formation of 23–4, 56, 75
    hostile aircraft alarm 144–5
    initial campaign 1916 60–2
    light horsemen 67–8, 70–1
    medical arrangements 115
    messing arrangements 35–6
    observers 131
    obsolete aircraft 100, 105
    photography campaigns 119–20, 123, 132, 143
    receives Bristol Fighters 116–17
    time served by airmen 47
    Transjordan reconnaissance 123
  No. 2 Squadron
    accidents 204, 221
    Amiens patrols 292
    bombing 241, 319–20, 323
    casualties 44, 220
    circus patrols 258–60, 279, 281–2, 315–16
    claims 44
    Distinguished Flying Cross 318
    formation 72, 80, 178–9, 204–5
    looting 35
    mobility 27
    time served by airmen 47
  No. 3 Squadron
    accidents 197, 202, 224, 251, 312
    ammunition dropping 271, 273, 274–5
    artillery observation 201, 224, 226, 289
    battle preparations, Amiens 286
    bombing 203, 294–301
    contact patrols 273–4, 286–7, 290–1, 310
    corps squadron role 198–201, 226–7
    counter-attack patrols 273–5, 286, 289
    formation of 179, 196–7
    inexperience 199, 200
    long range reconnaissance 306–7
    morale 270
    open warfare 293–4, 303
    regimental history 374
    Richthofen's death 253–8
    shelled 236
    winter flying 223–6
  No. 4 Squadron
    accidents 228
    Amiens patrols 292
    army of occupation 326–8
    balloon busting 264–5, 268, 280
    'blackest day' 314
    bombing 233–4, 239–40, 243–5, 294–301, 319, 323
    casualties 337
    circus patrols 279, 315–16
    claims 44
    'destroyer patrols' 279–80, 319
    formation 179, 227–8
    inexperience 227–8
    Mannock's influence 263–4
    mess 34, 284
    regimental history 374
    shelled 246–7
    'special missions' 267, 281
    strain among airmen 47
  Half Flight
    arrival in Mesopotamia 13–14
    formation of 12–13
    reconnaissance 19–20
    statistics 23
  statistics 336–7
Australian Imperial Force
  Anzac Mounted Division 68, 75, 79–80, 89–90, 111, 122, 124, 168
  Australian Corps 223, 241, 243, 250, 272, 285, 288, 293, 303–4, 309–12
  1st Division 246, 290
  2nd Division 285, 303, 312
  3rd Division 285
  4th Division 285, 287, 288
  5th Division 285, 287, 288
  1st Light Horse Brigade 63, 124

Australian Imperial Force (*Cont.*)
  2nd Light Horse Brigade 56
  3rd Light Horse Brigade 76, 95
  4th Light Horse Brigade 125
  11th Light Horse Regiment 70
  12th Light Horse Regiment 70
Australian perceptions of the AFC 88, 226, 331–3
Australian Society of World War One Aero Historians 380
Australian War Memorial xvi–xvii, 88, 103, 226, 339, 375, 376
Ayers, Sydney 215

Baillieu, Reginald 103
Baker, Thomas 297, 323
balloon busting 264–5, 268, 280
Banks, Edmond 253
Barber, George 256
Barnes, James 292
barnstorming 334
Barrett, George ('Bob') 45, 273–4, 287–8, 290–1
Barrow, Alfred 253
battles
  Amiens 285–91
  Amman raid 123–5
  Bir el Mazar 68–9
  Cambrai 208–20
  Ctesiphon 19–20, 22
  Es Salt raid 125–8
  Gaza, First Battle of 88–91
  Gaza, Second Battle of 92, 94–5
  Gaza, Third Battle of 110–13
  'Georgette' offensive 244–7
  'Gneisenau' offensive 261–2
  Hamel 272–6
  Hindenburg Line 309–12
  Hindenburg outpost line 304–5
  Jericho 122
  Katia 55–6
  Kurna 14
  Kut 18, 22–3
  Magdhaba 75–7
  Maghara 69–71
  'Mars' offensive 241, 243
  Megiddo 153, 155–64
  'Michael' offensive 236–43
  Mont St Quentin 303
  Montbrehain 312–13
  Nasiriyeh 16
  Rafa 79–80
  Romani 63–7
  Villers-Bretonneux 252
  Ypres 189, 191, 223
Baxter, James 189–90
Bean, Charles 67, 192–3, 212–13, 226, 231, 256, 281–2, 292, 300, 336
Beersheba 72, 110–11
Bell, John 204, 210
Bell, John Rennison 201, 225
Benham, Jenkyn 75
Bennett, Jim 333
Bennett, John 374
bereavement 45–7, 119, 145, 251–2
Best, George 250–1
Bice, Edward 288
Billings, Hubert ('Bert') 37, 50–1, 66
Blair, John 202
Blake, David 199, 256, 273, 286, 307, 309
Blaxland, Gregory 239, 259–60
Blériot, Louis 2
Bolle, Karl 322–3
bombsights 69
Bormann, Ernst 323
Borton, Amyas 120, 166
Brasell, Jack 99
Brinsmead, Harold 205
British Army
  Indian Expeditionary Force D 13
  First Army 231
  Second Army 263
  Third Army 208–9, 212–13, 236, 239, 241, 293
  Fourth Army 271, 285–6, 290–1, 293, 304, 306
  Fifth Army 236–7, 239, 241, 278
  Imperial Camel Corps 75–6
  III Corps 285, 288
  IV Corps 214
  IX Corps 309
  XIII Corps 199
  60th Division 125
Brookes, Charles 102
Brown, Alan 124, 136–7, 142, 144, 146, 161
Brown, Rolf 184, 199
Brown, Roy 254, 256–7
Bull, Joseph 50–2, 75, 79, 80, 85, 91, 93–4, 98, 108, 111, 116, 122, 147, 170–1, 374

INDEX

Burn, William 13–14, 16–17
Busteed, Harry 5
Byng, Julian 208, 216

Cameron, Colin 157
Camm, Richard 133–4
Canadian Corps 199, 285, 288
Carlyon, Les 374
Carter, Duncan xiii–xvi
casualties
  accidents, No. 1 Squadron 115
  AFC, overall 337
  Amiens 290
  Cambrai 212, 215, 220
  Gaza, First Battle of 91
  Gaza, Third Battle of 114
  German offensives 1918 247
  Hamel 275
  Magdhaba 77
  No. 1 Squadron 1917 105
  No. 1 Squadron total 175
  rates and statistics 44–5
  Romani 66
  siege of Kut 22–3
  training 186–87
Central Intelligence Bureau 294
Challinor, Ronald (Dick) 126–7
Chapman, John 288
Chauvel, Harry 56, 79, 125, 127
Chaytor, Edward 64, 153, 168
Chetwode, Philip 75–6
chivalry 43–4, 93, 103–5, 147, 257–8
Clark, David 214
Clark, Robert 212, 214
Climie, Leslie 166
Coates, William 99
Cobby, Arthur ('Harry')
  aerial sorties 43, 229–30, 233–4, 236–7, 239, 243, 245, 264–5, 267–8, 294–301, 316–17
  Amiens, Battle of 292–3
  Anzac Day 1919 328–9
  balloon busting 264–8, 280
  biographical details 228
  conflict with McCloughrys 266–8
  Distinguished Flying Cross 268, 283–4
  fame 331
  home establishment leave 313–14
  Mannock's influence 263–4
  memoirs 339, 374
  post war 268–9, 332, 335
Cole, Adrian 75, 96–7, 99, 260, 262–3, 300, 319, 335
combat stress (see 'strain')
Conrick, Francis Clive 31, 37, 44, 137–8, 145–7, 149, 159, 161–3, 168–71, 374
Conrick, Pat 374
Copp, Charles 298
Cornell, Harold 181, 217–18, 220–1
Cornish, Edmund 31, 377
Courtney, John 243–4
Couston, Alec 234
Cox, Fergus 326
Cummings, Eric 298, 332
Curwen-Walker, Jack 127
Cutlack, Frederic 73, 104–5, 125, 170, 237, 266, 294, 315–16, 336, 373, 376

Damascus 168–70
Davies, Ernest 259
Day, Donald 180, 182, 184–5
Deans, Geoffrey 307–8
Degelow, Carl 300
Dibbs, Eric 44, 46, 200–2, 318–20
Dimsey, David 304–5
discipline 33–5, 39–40, 205
Dobell, Charles 89–91
dogfights
  No. 1 Squadron
    11 November 1916 72–3
    17 December 1916 74–5
    21 December 1916 76
    6 April 1917 93
    25 June 1917 99
    8 July 1917 102
    13 July 1917 103
    4 August 1917 108–9
    1 September 1917 108
    29 November 1917 114
    3 January 1918 117
    15 January 1918 119
    17 January 1918 120
    27 March 1918 124
    1 May 1918 126
    22 May 1918 133
    4 June 1918 133
    13 June 1918 134–5
    19 June 1918 135
    23 June 1918 135–6

dogfights
  No. 1 Squadron (*Cont.*)
    28 June 1918 138–9
    16 July 1918 144
    3 August 1918 143
    22 August 1918 146
    24 August 1918 147–8
    31 August 1918 149–50
    21 September 1918 166
    28 September 1918 169
    19 October 1918 172–3
    23 October 1918 173
  No. 2 Squadron
    2 October 1917 206–7
    13 October 1917 207
    16 October 1917 208
    21 November 1917 213
    29 November 1917 215–16
    1 December 1917 218
    18 February 1918 232
    8 March 1918 234–5
    22 March 1918 238, 239
    28 March 1918 242
    11 June 1918 261
    12 June 1918 261–2
    13 June 1918 262
    17 June 1918 265–6
    6 September 1918 315
    16 September 1918 317–18
    4 November 1918 322
  No. 3 Squadron
    21 October 1917 201
    31 October 1917 201–2
    21 April 1918 253
    9 May 1918 269–70
    8 August 1918 288
    27 September 1918 308–9
    5 October 1918 312
  No. 4 Squadron
    3 February 1918 229
    21 February 1918 233
    15 March 1918 235
    21 March 1918 237
    21 May 1918 264
    25 May 1918 265
    1 June 1918 265
    28 June 1918 267
    5 September 1918 xv–xvi, 314
    6 September 1918 315
    29 October 1918 321
    30 October 1918 321–2
    4 November 1918 322–3
Dowling, Dudley 157
Drummond, Peter 86
Duigan, John 253, 269–70

Eddie, Maxwell xiii–xvi
Edols, Thomas 51, 282, 292, 297, 377
El Arish 74
Ellis, Alfred 65–6, 86–7, 108
engines 48
England to Australia air race 333

Farquhar, Arthur ('Wally') 136
Feez, Cecil 242
Fell, William 128
Felmy, Gerhardt 95–6, 102–4, 108
Felmy, Helmuth 80
Ferguson, Douglas 182
Finlay, Garfield 114, 131–2, 136–9, 142, 144, 146, 161–2
fitters 48
Fletcher, Howard 147, 157
Flight, Oscar 242
Foale, Hugh 288
Foch, Ferdinand 241
Forrest, Henry 219, 238, 241–2, 260–2, 268, 282
Forsyth, Reginald 67, 107, 183
Fraser, Harold 120
friendly fire 259
Fysh, Hudson 36, 38, 99, 109, 123, 132, 135–6, 143, 149–50, 154, 156, 171, 176, 331, 333, 335

Garrett, Stanley 47, 199, 201, 203, 224, 226, 253–5
German Air Service
  FA 300 62–5, 69, 72–3, 80, 89, 91, 93–5, 108–9
  FA 301 148
  FA 304b 112–13
  Jagdgeschwader Nr I 189, 192, 215, 237, 252–3, 269–70, 292
  Jagdgeschwader III 313–16, 322, 326
  Jagdgeschwader IV 313
  Jasta 2 ('Boelcke') 322–3
  Jasta 5 215
  Jasta 26 262
  Jasta 35 237

INDEX

Jasta 43 301
supply problems 73–4, 108, 279, 301
Gould-Taylor, John 312
Griggs, Albert 214
Guilfoyle, James 72–3
Gullett, Henry 192–3

Haig, Douglas 12, 208–9, 213, 328
Haig, Frederick 25, 33, 126–7
Hainsworth, Roy 270
Hamilton, Ernest 311
Hammond, James 261–2, 378
Harper, Stanley 173
Harris, John 32, 36, 115–16, 119, 128, 145, 146, 158
Harrison, Eric 5–6, 10–11, 23–4
Hart, Peter 228, 311, 375
Harvey, Frederick 115
Hawley, Frederic 165
Headlam, Eustace 25, 124, 156, 166, 173
Heathcote, Leonard 54, 85
Hejaz railway 122, 165
Hemene, Henri 327–8, 329, 338
Henshaw, Trevor 44
Herbert, William 332
Hill, Anthony 338
Hindenburg Line 209, 303–6
Hindenburg, Paul von 236, 293
historiography of AFC 336, 373–8
Hoddinott, Rupert Uriah 46, 52
Hodgson, Keith 225
Holden, Leslie 206–7, 212, 215
Hosking, Thomas 242
Houdini, Harry 2
Howard, Richard ('Dick') 28, 180–1, 183–4, 205–8, 213, 215–16, 232–5, 239
Hughes, Henry 225–6
Hughes, Matthew 100
Hurley, Frank 120–2
Huxley, Frederick 213–14, 218–20, 232, 332
Hyam, William 91–2

Imperial Conference 4
inter-rank relationships 36, 50–3
interrupter gear 49, 69

jams, machine gun (see 'stoppages')
jealousy between airmen 36–7
Jones, Allan Murray 61, 66, 93, 99, 103, 260–3, 294–5, 298, 318, 335

Jones, Ernest 202, 225, 270
Jones, George 232–3, 235, 240, 321–3, 327, 333–5, 377
Jones-Evans, Gordon 279

Kaisar-i-Hind 329, 331
Kenny, Edward ('Ted') 159, 169
King, Roy ('Bo') 41, 45, 267–8, 283, 296–8, 321–2, 374
Kingsford-Smith, Charles 333
Kirk, Walter Alister 124, 132–5, 140–1
Knox, Errol 256
Knuckey, Vernon 28, 30, 209, 213–14, 244, 246–7, 263, 278–9, 300–1, 313, 378
Kressenstein Kress von 110, 113
Krieg, Paul 145

Lawrence H.A. 63–6
Lawrence T.E. 123, 153, 164–7
Lax, Mark 374
leave 282, 313–14
Leckie, Harry 98
Lee, Arthur 210, 215, 220, 374
Lee, Oliver 117
leisure activities 31–2
Letch, Walter ('Hal') 128, 146–7
Lewis, Cecil 38, 42, 375
Lewis, Owen 31, 33, 40, 45, 189–91, 227, 250–2, 378
Lilly, William 156, 166, 173
Lock, Francis 273–4, 287–8, 290–1
Lockley, Alexander xiii–xvi, 32, 39, 40–1
Loerzer, Fritz 262
Long, Arthur 320
looting 35, 160, 171–2, 198, 254–5
Love, Howard 245
Love, Nigel 255
Ludendorff, Erich 236, 243, 289, 293
Ludlow Hewitt, Edgar 294
Lyndsay Campbell, Charles 3

Machin, Roland 304–5
Malley, Garnet 244, 265, 267, 282
Mannock, Edward ('Mick') 263–4
Manuel, Roby 268, 283, 298, 317–18, 328–9, 334
Manwell, David, 8, 11
map making 20
Martin, Charles 229
Martin, William ('Jerry') 265–6

Matheson, Charles 332
Maughan, Harold 156–7, 169
May, Wilfred 254
McCann, Ashley 144, 172–3
McCleery, Edgar 300
McCloughry, Edgar 31, 180, 264–6, 268, 278–81, 284
McCloughry, Wilfred 27, 32–3, 49, 206–8, 228, 266–8, 374
McCudden, James 43
McCulloch Leigh 189
McDougal, Wallace 188
McElligott, Joseph 126
McGinness, Paul 143, 147–50, 154, 156, 171, 335
McKenzie, Robert 210, 237–8
McNamara, Frank 54, 86–8, 104, 332, 335
Merrett, Charles 58
Merz, George 8, 11, 13, 16–17
Mesopotamian campaign
  Basra 13
  climatic conditions 15, 17
  decision to capture Baghdad 19
  impact of aircraft 15
  origins 12–13
  siege of Kut 22–3
mess arrangements 34–6
Miller, Geoffrey M. 256
Mills, George 67, 82–3
Mills, R.P. 259–60
Monash, John 271–3, 276, 293–4, 306
Morrison, Douglas 207
Morton, Fred 377
Mott, Arthur 58
Muir, Stanley 54, 66, 68–9, 74–6, 80, 204, 375
Mulford, Edwin 141, 157
Murphy, Arthur 128, 136, 165
Murray, Archibald 55, 63, 65, 74, 88–9, 100
Mustard, Ernest 134, 154–5, 158, 160, 166, 334

National Archives, Kew 376
National Library of Australia 377
Nelson, Reginald 280
Nicholson, Norman 254
Nixon, John 13–14, 17, 19, 22
Nunan, Stanislaus 49–50, 52, 138–9, 141, 148–9, 154, 159, 161, 165, 168, 171–4, 181–3, 378

O'Hara-Wood, Arthur 229–30
oral history 377
Orsova 56
Oxenham, Gordan 136–8

Paget, Gerald 103
Palliser, Arthur 323
Palstra, William 310–11, 325
parachutes 44–5
patrols 199–200, 206
Paterson, Alec 253, 255, 269–70
Paul, Carrick 134–5, 140–2, 158, 160, 174
Paxton, Anthony 232
Peace Loan scheme 332–3
peaceful penetration 272
Pearce, Sir George Foster 3–4
Penny, Francis 181
Pentland, Augustus ('Jerry') 43
Percival, Edgar 29
Peters, George 144, 147–8, 160, 166
Petre, Henry 5–6, 13–15, 22–3, 343–4
Pflaum, Elliot ('Tab') 229–30, 237
Phillipps, Roy 213, 232, 238, 241, 262, 282
photography 61–2, 98, 200
Pickering, George 309–10, 312
Pippart, Hans 261
Point Cook Central Flying School 6, 8–11, 23, 179, 260
Pomroy, William 309, 312
Popkin, Cedric 256
Porter, John 255
Potts, Jack 101–2, 118–19
Potts, Leonard 119, 128
Pratt, Mel 377
Primrose, Leslie 259
Prince, Thomas 289, 305, 307–9
prisoners of war 22, 102, 137, 234, 242

Qantas 335–6

Rackett, Archie 232, 239, 241
Ralfe, Henry 269
Randell, Wentworth 234
Rawlinson, Frank 48–9, 223, 255, 271, 274, 286–7, 305, 325, 339–40
Rawlinson, Henry 271, 284–5, 290–1, 304, 306
recruitment for the AFC 6–7, 24, 67–8
Reynolds, Edgar 56
Rhodes, Charles 322

INDEX

Richthofen, Manfred von 189, 192, 215, 237, 252–8, 339
riggers 48
Roberts, Eric 56–8, 60, 69, 71, 76–7, 79–83
Roberts, Frank 317, 320, 325–6
Ross, James 179, 182–3, 315
Royal Australian Air Force 268–9, 335
Royal Australian Air Force Association 338
Royal Australian Air Force Museum 375–6
Royal Flying Corps/Royal Air Force
   10th Brigade 278
   Palestine Brigade 120, 175
   5th Wing 57, 65
   11th Wing 263
   40th Wing 109, 114, 140
   51st Wing 259
   80th Wing 278, 294–5, 300, 323, 374
   No. 7 Squadron 189–91
   No. 9 Squadron 273, 275
   No. 11 Squadron 44
   No. 14 Squadron 57, 62, 64, 66, 91, 98, 109
   No. 17 Squadron 57, 59
   No. 30 Squadron 17
   No. 32 Squadron 192–3
   No. 43 Squadron 258
   No. 46 Squadron 278
   No. 74 Squadron 263
   No. 80 Squadron 258
   No. 88 Squadron 294–5, 319
   No. 92 Squadron 294–5
   No. 103 Squadron 278
   No. 111 Squadron 109–11, 116, 162
   No. 113 Squadron 109
   No. 144 Squadron 162
   No. 145 Squadron 162
   No. 209 Squadron 254
   X–Flight 138, 165
   amalgamation 243
   operational role 38–9, 59, 206
Rutherford, Douglas 86–8, 91–2, 124, 126–7
Rutledge, Forster 59, 91, 97

Salmond, Geoffrey 58, 72, 77, 164
Sanders, Liman von 155, 158, 159
Sandy, James 225–6
Scott, William 224
Searle, Archibald 103
Sewell, Frank 288, 291
Seyferth, Larry 339
Shapira, Franics ('Frank') 197
Sharples, Norman 190–2
Sheldon, William 60, 231, 259–60
Shellal redoubts 81
Shelley, Max 291–2, 303–7, 309–10, 312, 313
Simpson, Thomas 253, 268, 270
Sims, Percy 321
Sloan, William 197
Smith, Francis 298, 315, 317, 323–4
Smith, James 287, 290
Smith, Keith 333
Smith, Lawrence 30–1, 134–7
Smith, Ross 76–7, 80–3, 107–8, 112, 115, 121, 133, 135, 140–1, 154–5, 158, 166–7, 171–2, 333, 375
Smith-Barry, Robert (see 'training')
Snell, Percy 89
social class 29–30
squadron organisation 26–8
Steel, Nigel 375
Steele Norman 83
Stephens, Alan 269, 374
Stone, Harold 247
Stooke, Ernest 145
stoppages 33, 134
Storrer, Henry 223–4
strain 37, 47, 82, 83, 193–4, 220, 227, 235, 239, 375
Strange, Louis 34–5, 278–9, 294–6, 298–300, 323, 325, 374
Suez Canal 55
Sutherland, Leslie
   aerial sorties 41, 101–2, 117, 123, 169
   biographical details 101
   champagne at Ramleh 171–2
   hostile aircraft alarm 144–5
   inter-rank relationships 27, 36–7
   light horse observers 68
   mechanics 50–1
   Megiddo, Battle of 155–7, 159, 161–4, 168
   memoirs 374
   observers 131–2
Symons, Parker 323

tactics, air combat 41–3, 45, 132, 206, 232, 234–5, 258–9, 279–81
Taplin, Leonard xiii–xvi, 115, 120
Taylor, Albert 270
Taylor, Harry 209, 211–2, 215, 220
Terraine, John 276

Thomson, Bruce 312
thunderstorms 282
Tonkin, Albert 133–4, 144, 166
Tovell, Timothy 328–9, 338
Townshend, Charles 17
Traill, James 144, 166
training
  accidents 57–8, 186–7, 314
  adequacy of 188–9
  British system reorganised 180
  discipline 182
  elementary flight training 182–5
  financial pressure 183
  higher instruction 185
  on the job 1917 189–92
  School of Aerial Fighting 187
  School of Aerial Gunnery 187
  School of Military Aeronautics 180–2
  Smith–Barry system 180, 184–5, 187
  solo flight 184–5
Treacy, John ('Jack') 39, 200, 251, 269
Treloar, William 13
Trescowthick, Norman xiii–xvi, 314
Tuck, Stanley 197–8, 269
Tunbridge, John 85, 99
Turkey 55
Turkish Army
  4th Army 122, 158–9, 167–8
  7th Army 153, 158–64
  8th Army 153, 157–60
Turner, Vivian Paul 72–3

Vautin, Claude 102–4
Vyner, Charles 138

Wackett, Lawrence 23, 54, 65–6, 71–3, 270–6, 303–4, 306–7, 335, 338, 374
Wackett, Wilbur 338
Wady El Arish 74
Wady Fara 162–4

Walker, John 146–7
Ward, Leslie 212
Watson, Gillies 265, 267
Watt, Oswald 61, 72, 204–5, 207, 212–13, 231, 314
Weingarth, Jack 181, 184, 186–8, 244–6
Weir, William (Billy) 134–5, 140–2, 158, 160, 171
Weiss, Hans 254
Wesley College 251
White, Thomas 7–8, 9–11, 14, 16–17, 19, 20–2
Wilkinson, Jack 280, 283, 316
Williams, Richard
  aerial sorties 65–7, 72, 69, 83–4, 95–7, 146
  Allenby and Murray, comparisons 100
  character 62, 97
  Gaza, First Battle of 89–91
  Gaza, Second Battle of 94–5
  memoirs 374, 377
  night flying 85
  obsolescent aircraft 100, 105, 109–10
  post-war 10, 335
  squadron commander 96
  training 7, 9–11
  wing commander 140
Wilson, Gordon 210–12, 220
Winter, Denis 36–7, 40, 47, 51–2, 186, 375
Witcomb, Oscar 287, 290
Woolhouse, Fred 245
Wright, Brian 337–8
Wright, John ('Jack') 81–2, 185–7, 229, 237, 239–40, 264, 284, 297, 315, 319, 321, 324–7, 337–8

Yeats, V.M. 375
Yeats-Brown, Francis 19–22
Youdale, Roy 281

zone call 227, 311